菲律宾刑法

杨家庆　译
谢望原　审校

外国刑法典译丛

译丛

图书在版编目(CIP)数据

菲律宾刑法/杨家庆译;谢望原审校.—北京:北京大学出版社,2006.12
(外国刑法典译丛)
ISBN 7-301-11315-3

Ⅰ.菲… Ⅱ.①杨… ②谢… Ⅲ.刑法-菲律宾-汉、英 Ⅳ.D934.14

中国版本图书馆 CIP 数据核字(2006)第140554号

书　　　名:菲律宾刑法
著作责任者:杨家庆　译　谢望原　审校
责 任 编 辑:竹莹莹　孙战营
标 准 书 号:ISBN 7-301-11315-3/D·1633
出 版 发 行:北京大学出版社
地　　　址:北京市海淀区成府路205号　100871
网　　　址:http://www.pup.cn　　电子邮箱:law@pup.pku.edu.cn
电　　　话:邮购部62752015　发行部62750672　编辑部62752027
出版部62754962
印　刷　者:河北三河新世纪印务有限公司
经　销　者:新华书店
650毫米×980毫米　16开本　22.25印张　376千字
2006年12月第1版　2006年12月第1次印刷
定　　　价:36.00元

未经许可,不得以任何方式复制或抄袭本书之部分或全部内容。
版权所有,侵权必究
举报电话:010-62752024　电子邮箱:fd@pup.pku.edu.cn

《外国刑法典译丛》编译委员会

编译委员会主任: 国家重点研究基地中国人民大学刑事法律科学研究中心名誉主任、中国人民大学法学院高铭暄教授

总　　编　　译: 中国人民大学法学院谢望原教授、法学博士,曾访学丹麦王国

编译委员会委员(排名不分先后):

中国人民大学法学院冯军教授、法学博士,曾访学德国、日本,负责德文方面审译

清华大学法学院张明楷教授,曾访学日本、德国,负责日文方面审译

清华大学法学院黎宏教授,日本法学博士,负责日文方面审译

北京大学法学院王世洲教授,曾留学美国、德国,负责德文方面审译

北京师范大学刑事法律科学研究院卢建平教授、法国法学博士,负责法文方面审译

武汉大学法学院莫洪宪教授、法学博士,曾访学俄罗斯、前南斯拉夫,负责俄文方面审译

武汉大学法学院刘艳红教授、法学博士,曾访学德国,负责英文方面审译

西南政法大学陈忠林教授,意大利法学博士,负责意大利文方面审译

吉林大学法学院张旭教授、法学博士,曾访学德国、比利时,负责英文方面审译

中南财经政法大学齐文远教授、法学博士,曾访学丹麦王国,负责英文方面审译

北京师范大学刑事法律科学研究院大学李希慧教授、法学博士,曾访学英国,负责英文方面审译

华东政法学院郑伟教授、德国法学博士,负责德文方面审译

《外国刑法典译丛》编译委员会

[illegible]

[illegible]

[illegible]

[illegible]

[illegible]

[illegible]

[illegible]

[illegible]

[illegible]

[illegible]

[illegible]

[illegible]

[illegible]

[illegible]

《外国刑法典译丛》总序

译介外国刑法典是一件极其有意义的学术活动。早在20世纪中后期，美国法学界就曾经以《美国外国刑法典丛书》(The American Series of Foreign Penal Codes)形式译介过世界上数十个国家的刑事法典(包括西欧国家和东欧社会主义国家以及亚洲一些国家的刑法典)，作为美国法学界比较研究或者立法借鉴用书出版。我国台湾地区也在20世纪70年代翻译出版过《各国刑法汇编》(包括欧洲和亚洲十余国家的刑法典和刑法草案)，作为台湾地区立法和法学教学研究的参考。我国虽然有一些译介外国刑事法典的著作零星出版，但并未形成规模。且20世纪80年代以后，世界范围内掀起了刑法改革的浪潮，两大法系很多国家进行了刑事法典或刑事制定法的修订。这些新的刑事立法只有极少数被介绍到中国来。考虑到我国刑事法学教学研究以及立法参考需要，并弥补译介外国刑事法典的不足，我们拟组织一批包括有海外访学经历且有较高外语水平和法律专业素养的中青年学者译介一批外国刑事法典。

由于世界上两大法系的刑事法各有特色，且我国亟须吸收其立法优点和那些值得借鉴的先进刑法理论，尽快完善我国刑事立法，建立有中国特色的刑法学理论体系，因此我们拟用若干年时间，译介一批外国刑事法典(将包括大陆法系国家的刑事法典和英美法系国家的刑事制定法)。为了便于高明的读者完整地理解外国刑事法典且弥补翻译的失误，我们拟将译介之外国刑事法典的外文附录在后。

应当说明的是，由于各国刑法典一般以自己本民族语言为官方文本，而目前我国刑法学界很难找到通晓各国文字的人才，因此，我们一方面力求从各国的本国语文文本翻译成中文，另一方面，我们在不能直接从其本民族语文译成中文的情况下，将以其英文本为根据译成中文。好在各国刑法典之译成英文，均为各国著名刑事法学家所为，其专业水平与英文水平均有保障，虽然可能存在因为语文的转换出现难以避免的误差，但是对我们学习研究来说仍然是极具参考价值的。本译丛将首先考虑译介那些我国尚无中文本且在世界上具有重要影响的刑法典,同时,对于那些虽然曾经出版过中文本但年代已经久远且新近又有重大修订补充的具有重要影响的刑法典,我们也考虑将其纳入本译丛。

本刑法典译丛由国家重点研究基地中国人民大学刑事法律科学研究中心组织编译,由部分有海外留(访)学经历的知名刑事法学者组成编译委员会,以确保翻译质量。

我们热忱欢迎那些具有深厚专业素养和良好外文功底的刑事法学者加入到这个翻译外国刑法典的行列中来,也欢迎收集有我们尚缺的外国刑法典的同仁为我们提供译本原件并参与翻译。让我们共同携手为完善中国的刑事法制度、推进中国的刑法学研究作出自己的贡献!

国家重点研究基地
中国人民大学刑事法律科学研究中心
2006年10月16日

目　录

菲律宾刑法简介(译者序)

一

菲律宾全名为菲律宾共和国(The Republic of Philippines),位于亚洲的东南部,东临太平洋,西濒南海,共有大小岛屿7107个。菲律宾是一个宗教国家,其中天主教占84%,基督教新教占9%,伊斯兰教占5%,佛教和其他宗教占3%。

最早生活在菲律宾岛上的居民是内格里托人。公元前3000年后,印度尼西亚人和马来人来到菲律宾。公元700年,日本和中国的商人也曾来过。1531年,西班牙远征队在比萨亚群岛,现在的宿务港处登陆,并宣布占领菲律宾。1565年,莱加斯皮率西班牙军队入侵菲律宾,1571年占领了马尼拉,并很快建立了殖民统治,长达三百多年。

凭西班牙战刀的威力和基督教十字架的劝说,菲律宾变成亚洲世界的西班牙第一处殖民地。西班牙把菲律宾殖民化有三个目的:即(1)传播基督教;(2)取得经济上的财富;(3)造成政治上的荣誉。总之,西班牙的殖民政策受三个“G”字的指导:上帝(God)、黄金(Gold)、荣誉(Glory)。①

1899年1月23日,菲律宾共和国宣告成立,阿奎那多任总统,马比尼任内阁主席。菲律宾共和国的成立,标志着西班牙在菲律宾300年的殖民统治的结束。菲律宾人民不仅通过民族起义推翻了西班牙的殖民统治,而且选择了自己的现代政治发展道路。1902年美国国会通过了《菲律宾法案》,宣布菲律宾对美国的依附地位,美国政府控制了菲律宾的行政、司法和立法大权。

1941年12月8日,日军入侵菲律宾。1943年,美军在菲律宾抗日军队的协助下,于1945年重新占领马尼拉,并恢复对菲律宾的殖民统治。战争结束后,菲律宾人民要求独立的呼声更加激烈,美国于1946年7月4日被

---

① 参见〔菲〕格雷戈里奥·F. 赛义德著:《菲律宾共和国:历史、政府与文明》,吴世昌、温锡增译,商务印书馆1979年版,第150页。

迫同意菲律宾独立。通过选举，菲律宾共和国正式成立。自此，菲律宾政治制度框架基本确立。根据 1973 年通过的《菲律宾宪法》，菲律宾在很长一段时期内实行独裁统治，该专政制度在 1986 年终于被推翻。

二

（一）菲律宾的政治制度

菲律宾实行共和制，并按行政、立法、司法三权分立的原则组织国家机构。议会民主制是菲律宾政治制度的主要形式。菲律宾的最高立法机构是国民议会。国会的主要职权有：国会代表选民制定法令，或否决与宪法不符的法律；选举议长、内阁总理；决定对外宣战或媾和；检举违宪事件和弹劾违法官员。

国会由参议院和众议院两部分组成。参议院有议员 24 人，由全国直接选举产生，任期 6 年，每 3 年改选 1/2，可连任两期。参议员必须是在菲律宾本土出生，年龄在 35 岁以上，在其选区已有登记的非文盲公民。众议院有议员 250 人，其中 200 人通过直接选举产生；25 人由总统从社会各界选定；25 人由各党派按得票比例分配，任期 3 年，可连任 3 届。众议员必须是在菲律宾本土出生，年龄在 25 岁以上，在其选区已有登记的非文盲公民。

内阁是菲律宾的最高行政机构。《菲律宾宪法》规定：行政权属于总统，总统拥有国家最高行政权力，是国家元首、政府首脑和武装部队最高统帅。总统由选民直接选举产生，任期 6 年，不得连任。副总统可以连任 2 届，每届 6 年。当选总统必须是原生菲律宾人，在菲律宾居住不少于 10 年的登记选民，年龄在 40 岁以上，有一定的文化程度。

总统提名委任各部部长组成内阁，总统、副总统和内阁组成菲律宾共和国中央政府。中央政府的主要职权是：负责国家的内政、外交、国防、经济、文化和社会生活等具体事务；制定和执行有关政策措施；领导政府各部门和各级地方政府的工作；向国会提出议案和立法建议；任免政府官员和工作人员；指挥和控制军队、警察，维护社会秩序和国家安全。

最高法院由 1 名首席法官和 14 名陪审法官组成，均由总统任命，任期 4 年，拥有最高司法权和颁布宪法没有规定的法律和法令权。最高法院下设上诉法院、地区法院和市镇法院，另外还有反贪污法院、税务法院等专业性法院。为了促进廉政和提高效率，菲律宾还设立了公务员犯罪特别法院和行政监察委员会。菲律宾没有与最高法院平衡的检察机构,检察工作由司法部检察长办公室负责。

国家宪法为根本大法。菲律宾独立后共颁布过三部宪法。现行宪法于1987年2月2日经由全民投票通过,同年2月11日由总统宣布正式生效。这部宪法共有18个条款。

(二)菲律宾法律发展简史

菲律宾法律体系是世界上独一无二的法律体系,主要是大陆法、英美法、穆斯林法和本地法的混合体。菲律宾在公元7世纪至12世纪曾经是印度的殖民地,不可避免地受到摩奴法典的影响。到了14世纪由于马来西亚的伊斯兰教徒大量移居菲律宾,因此在菲律宾南部穆斯林地区的棉兰老岛在实施伊斯兰法。[①] 日本曾于1942年1月3日占领了菲律宾,一直到1945年均处于日本的占领下,在此期间也曾受日本法律的影响,但是影响不大,可见,菲律宾的法律体系是一个相当复杂的体系,但也有它的独到之处。根据菲律宾的国家发展历程可以将菲律宾的法律发展史分为七个阶段[②]:即西班牙统治前阶段(1521年以前)、西班牙统治阶段(1521年—1898年)、美国统治阶段(1898年—1935年)、自治政府阶段(1935年—1945年)、共和国政府阶段(1946年—1972年)、军法统治阶段(1972年—1986年)和共和国政府复兴阶段(1987年—现在)。

1. 西班牙统治前阶段(1521年以前)

自从公元前300—200年马来人进入菲律宾境内以后就出现了奴隶制,但是没有文字记载,一直到第二批马来人于公元初到13世纪期间的相继到来,才开始有文字记载。菲律宾的成文法主要是以13世纪的《马拉塔斯法典》和15世纪的《卡兰莱雅奥法典》为代表。14世纪以后,随着伊斯兰教会的传入,穆斯林苏丹国封建政权建立以后,开始实行政教合一的政治制度,其根据是伊斯兰法。苏丹政权的统治者根据伊斯兰法,颁布了《卢瓦兰法典》,还实行一些习惯法。由于宗教的影响,认为天赋神权,判案都是用神判法。但是,他们的立法在当时是比较完善的,诺贝托·罗穆阿德斯法官这样写道:“即使在史前时期,菲律宾人民早已显示了高度的智力与道义品德;

---

① *Philippines Penal Law*, http://www.photius.com/countries/philippines/national_security/philippines_national_security_penal_law.html.

② 有的学者将菲律宾的法律制度分为四个阶段:即伊斯兰法时期、本地法时期、西班牙法律时期和美国法时期。参见王元霞、何戌中著:《东方法概述》,法律出版社1993年版,第133页。

品德与智力清楚地表现在他们的立法中;如果到制定立法的时代和当时的环境,那就很清楚,比起当时最文明国家的立法,菲律宾古代的立法同样的明智、审慎而合乎人道。”①

2. 西班牙统治阶段(1521 年—1898 年)

1521 年,麦哲伦率领西班牙远征队到达菲律宾群岛,1565 年西班牙入侵,在此创建殖民地。1530 年西班牙就通过了一项皇家勒令,宣称:卡斯提尔和托罗城现在以及将来都可以在菲律宾没有被殖民地的立法所调整的事项。16 世纪中期,西班牙取得了菲律宾的统治权,废除了菲律宾各地原有的习惯法和成文法,推行西班牙法。在西班牙统治的早年,除了原有的西班牙法以外,治理菲律宾的法律主要是包含在《印地亚群岛的法律》(las leyes de Indias),这部法典是历代西班牙国王在不同时期为治理西班牙的殖民地而颁布的王室诏谕的总集,它被法律学者赞为世界上殖民地法律的最伟大的法典之一。有些在西班牙本国施行的老法律也应用在菲律宾,例如,《七部律》(Las Siet Partids)、《牛城法律》(Las Leyes de Toro)以及《最新编法典总集》(La Novisima Recopilacion)②,还有 1805 年以后编纂的最新法令集以及相继制定的民法典、刑法典、商法典、典当法、矿业法和版权法等,菲律宾几乎适用所有的西班牙法。

菲律宾沦为西班牙的殖民地后,西班牙政府颁布一系列法令,大力加强菲律宾总督的权力。首先,他有广泛的行政权,他是首席执行长官,执行从西班牙来的王室诏渝和法律,任免殖民地官吏和驻外使节,监督财政收入,控制所有行政机关。其次,他有立法权,可以颁布行政法令,他还有否决权,有权暂停执行西班牙王室诏渝和法律。再次,他享有司法权。总督是最高法院院长(1861 年以前),最高法院审案时,他是主席,有权宣布大赦。最后,他还是军队总司令,并行使宗教上的最高权力,教区与大教区的创立、划分与取消,均需经总督批准。

尽管西班牙的许多法律在菲律宾实施,但其司法制度主要还是以菲律宾的习惯法为基础的,如果习惯法与西班牙法律和教会法严重冲突,则以后者为标准;如果习惯法不能解决问题,就适用西班牙—罗马法。西班牙法律在菲律宾实施过程中的一个最大特点是与当地实际脱节。虽然西班牙统治

---

① 参见〔菲〕格雷戈里奥·F. 赛义德著:《菲律宾共和国:历史、政府与文明》,吴世昌、温锡增译,商务印书馆 1979 年版,第 105 页。

② 同上书,第 159—160 页。

者认识到在殖民地实施法律的重要性,但忽略了古代东方伊斯兰法律文化对菲律宾社会和人民所产生的影响。因此,虽然制定了许多适用于殖民地的法律,但在当地却很难有理想的效果。最终起作用的还是当地的传统法律。①

3. 美国统治阶段(1898 年—1935 年)

从 1898 年开始,菲律宾掀起了资产阶级民族民主革命的新高潮,不少地区爆发了武装起义。受到美国支持的菲律宾地主、资产阶级保守派的代表人物阿奎纳多夺取了反西斗争的领导权。1898 年 6 月 12 日,阿奎纳多发表了《独立宣言》,98 名来自各阶层的代表在《独立宣言》上签了字。宣称菲律宾已取得"自由和独立";并且声言菲律宾的独立是"在强大而人道的北美合众国的保护下"宣布的。这样一来,实际上就把菲律宾宣布为美国的保护国了。

1898 年 9 月 15 日,议会在马洛洛市附近召开,资产阶级激进派和小资产阶级代表占了较大的比重。由菲利普·卡尔德隆为首的委员会起草了一个限制行政权力,建立立法机关,确保资产阶级民主权利的三权分立的宪法草案。讨论时,对"教会与国家"的关系有不同意见,以安东尼奥·卢纳为首的激进派坚决反对政教合一的主张取得了胜利。结果,在宪法上规定"国家承认宗教的自由与平等以及教会与国家的分离"。11 月 29 日,议会通过了宪法草案。但阿奎纳多因对政教分离和取消、限制总统权力的规定不满,而不签署和颁布此宪法。后在保守派的压力下,宪法中加上一个"临时协定",暂缓执行有关教会与国家分离和限制总统权力的条文。1899 年 1 月 21 日,阿奎纳多正式颁布宪法,史称《马洛洛宪法》。1 月 23 日,宣布菲律宾共和国正式成立。②

1902 年 7 月,美国国会通过《菲律宾法案》,赤裸裸地宣布菲律宾对美国的依附地位,菲律宾的行政、立法、司法大权均由美国政府掌握。法案规定,菲律宾最高法院的法官由美国总统任命,其成员美国人应占多数,美国最高法院有权审查、修正、补充和取消菲律宾各级法院的任何判决。法案还规定,民政总督、副总督、委员会委员及各部部长,均由美国总统任命。菲律宾还按美国法的模式制定了公司法、破产法、担保法、保险法、银行法等。③

---

① 参见王元霞、何戌中著:《东方法概述》,法律出版社 1993 年版,第 134—135 页。
② 林榕年主编:《外国法律制度史》,中国人民公安大学出版社 1992 年版,第 379 页。
③ 同上书,第 378—380 页。

随着美国对菲律宾统治的确立，那些具有政治性的西班牙法律被加以废止，但是，调整私权和规制地方机构的法律以及刑法仍然有效。由菲律宾委员会、菲律宾议会和菲律宾立法机关在1900年—1935年制定的法律被称为公法法令或法案(Public Acts英文缩写为PA)。

4. 自治政府阶段(1935年—1945年)

第一次世界大战后，美国采取各种措施加紧控制菲律宾经济，使它严重依赖美国市场。在资本主义世界的经济危机中，美企图将危机损失转嫁给菲律宾人民。美国的残酷剥夺，加剧了菲律宾的民族矛盾和阶级矛盾，激起菲律宾人民的强烈反抗。1933年1月，美国国会被迫通过了“菲律宾独立法”，即“黑尔一霍斯一卡廷法”。这个法案名义上允诺10年后给菲律宾“独立”，实质上是为了限制菲律宾移民，限制农产品输美，稳定美国的统治。因此，它一出笼就遭到菲律宾人民的强烈反对。1933年10月，菲律宾参议院否决了“菲律宾独立法”。美国对此法进行了修改，1934年3月24日，经罗斯福总统正式签署，颁布了“泰丁斯——麦克杜菲法”。该法规定，菲律宾成立自治政府，10年后独立。

1934年5月，菲律宾参、众议院联席会议通过这个法案。1935年2月根据“泰丁斯——麦克杜菲法”制定了新宪法。宪法规定：菲律宾建立自治政府，10年后宣布独立，成立菲律宾共和国。菲律宾的立法权属于一院制的议会，司法权属于最高法院和地方法院，行政权属于总统，总统由选民直接选举产生，任期6年。1935年5月14日全民投票通过新宪法①，一部与美国宪法极为相似的宪法草拟了出来，同年11月在马尼拉正式公布施行。至此，由美国精心扶持并托管的美国式的法制国家建成了。这是法制史、政治史上的特例。同时，与政治制度相配套的法律制度也在逐步建立起来。比如对刑法作了一些修改，并修订了一部刑法典，取代过去西班牙的刑事法律。对婚姻法也作了重要改革，废除了西班牙的《七部律》和天主教法律所规定的原则，建立了自由和世俗化了的婚姻制度。在诉讼程序方面和司法制度方面，也建立了新的原则和制度。② 但是，菲律宾仍受美国控制，推行美国的法律制度。在联邦时期(1935—1941年)由国民大会通过的法律被称为联邦法案(Commonwealth Acts英文缩写为CA)。

在这10年期间，前7年时间实际上是美国控制，后3年是日本统治。

---

① 林榕年主编：《外国法律制度史》，中国人民公安大学出版社1992年版，第381页。

② 参见王元霞、何戌中著：《东方法概述》，法律出版社1993年版，第136页。

自1941年12月8日日本军队的入侵,轰炸了美国军事空军基地帕番加(Pampanga),标记着持续3年的日本统治时代的开始。以劳雷尔(Jose P. Laurel)为总统的日本共和国建立,1943年,特别国民大会年批准宪法,建立了恐怖的军事独裁统治,所有工厂、银行、学校、教会等都置于法西斯军事管制之下。1944年,日本统治时期以日本军队战败而结束。日本占领菲律宾期间,由日本人组成的国民会议在1943—1945年通过的法律被称为法案。最高法院认为除了那些具有政治性的法律外①,这些法律在1945年恢复联邦政府后仍然完全有效。②

5. 共和国政府阶段(1946年—1972年)

二次大战结束后,美国重新占领菲律宾,向人民革命力量发动疯狂进攻,激起菲律宾人民更为强烈的反抗。汹涌澎湃的民族独立运动,迫使美国不得不改变策略,表示"愿意"让菲律宾"独立"。1946年7月4日,宣布菲律宾独立,成立菲律宾共和国。菲律宾大买办、大地主的政治代表罗哈斯就任第一任总统,美国驻菲最高专员公署改为美国驻菲大使馆。美国依然掌握着菲律宾的经济命脉,并享有种种特权。

出于菲律宾人民的强烈要求和统治者的需要,执政者于1947年3月设置了法典编纂委员会,以制定具有菲律宾特色的各项法律。1950年8月新民法诞生,接着又制定了关税法、农业改革法、国土建设法等。到20世纪60年代,要求修改具有殖民时代烙印的现行宪法的呼声高涨。1965年马科斯当选总统,提倡"新菲律宾主义"。1972年11月通过新宪法。菲律宾在很长一段时间内实行独裁统治,该专政制度一直到1986年才被推翻。从1946—1972年由菲律宾国会通过的法律被称为共和国法案(Republic Acts英文缩写为RA)。

6. 军法统治阶段(1972年—1986年)

1972年9月21日,制宪会议正在开会,马科斯总统宣布,"鉴于棉兰老岛和苏禄群岛的许多地方实际上处于战争状态",颁布"军管法"对全国实行军法管制,发布1081号总统令,宣布整个菲律宾戒严,在戒严令控制下制定了宪法。该法第17条第3款第三项的"过渡条款"规定,总统发布的所有公告、命令、条例、指示,都是国家法律的组成部分,都是合法有效的,即使在戒严令解除以后。除非……被现任总统……以后的法令所废除或者代替,

① Peraha v. Director of prison. 75 phil. 285(1945).
② Alcantara v. Director of prisons 75 phil. 494(1945).

或者,除非它被正常的国民议会所明文、明确修改或废除。马科斯总统把菲律宾置于军法统治下,按1973年宪法规定,它不仅享有总统权力,而且享有内阁总理的权力,在没有立法机关时还有立法者的权力,而立法机关已经被强令关闭了。这样,总统集立法、行政、司法权于一体了。在1978—1986年期间菲律宾的立法机构为"Batasang Pambansa"(国民大会),因而该时期的立法就称为"Batas Pambansa"(英文缩写为BP);1972年—1979年马科斯废除国会后签发的总统令称为"Presidential Decerees"(英文缩写为PD),是具有强制力和法律效力的总统法令;在现行共和国政体下,从1972年起由国会通过的法律又被称为"Republic Acts"(共和国法案英文缩写为RA)。[1]

7.共和国政府复兴阶段(1987年—现在)

菲律宾共和国是在不流血的革命以后再次成立的,1986年2月25日,阿奎诺(Corazon Aquino)和劳瑞尔(Salvador H. LAUREL)就职宣誓成为菲律宾共和国的总统和副总统,宣布成立了一个新政府和采用一部临时自由宪法。菲律宾根据1978年宪法再次成为共和国,共和国法案由国会再次发布,从公布的军法以前所使用的最后的编号开始编号,阿奎洛总统依据1986年临时自由宪法授予的权力签发执行令(Executive Orders 英文缩写为EO)(1986年3月26日第3号公告,第2条第1款)。[2]

前文已论及,菲律宾共和国由于历史原因,情况相当复杂,其法律制度明显是受到大陆法系和英美法系的影响,还保留某些原有的传统法律,所以才形成了一种复合体。它的法律渊源呈现多样化的特点,包括成文法、判例、习惯法、伊斯兰法、法令集、判令集等。一般认为,在婚姻法、家庭法、继承法、合同法、刑法这些部门法中,大陆法系的传统起主导作用;而在宪法、诉讼法、公司法、票据法、税法、保险法、劳动法、金融法方面,英美法系的原则有深远的影响。[3] 但菲律宾有许多法律又是模仿美国的,且菲律宾的法院是引用美国的判例法,到20世纪80年代中期已经有26个法典生效,其中包括1930年的修正刑法典(1932年1月1日生效)在内的许多法典取代了西班牙法,费迪南德·埃·马科斯总统时代签发了两千多个总统令。有一部分已被菲德尔·拉莫斯在最开始任总统的几年废除了,总统令统治结束

① 参见〔捷〕维克拉·纳普主编:《各国法律制度概况》,高绍先,夏登峻等译,法律出版社2004年版,第1138页。

② 同上注。

③ 齐树洁:《菲律宾继承法研究》,载梁慧星主编:《迎WTO——梁慧星先生主编之域外法律制度研究集》第三辑,国家行政学院出版社2000年版,第292页。

于 1987 年 2 月宪法的通过。①

三

(一) 菲律宾刑事法的发展历程

菲律宾在西班牙统治以前就有关于刑法的记载,但是他们那时的刑法与我国古代刑法差不多,都是刑民不分的。古代菲律宾的成文法主要体现在 13 世纪的《马拉塔斯法典》和 15 世纪的《卡兰莱雅奥法典》。

《马拉塔斯法典》是现在所知的菲律宾第一部成文法典,于 1250 年由马迪加亚斯国的大督萨马克韦尔颁布,所以也称《萨马克韦尔法典》。主要包括四个方面的内容:(1) 规定对消极怠工者处以重刑,应予逮捕或沦为奴隶;(2) 对任何种类的抢劫罪规定要予以严厉惩罚,犯者的手指应予斩去;(3) 规定只有能赡养一家孩子或几家孩子的人才能结婚一次以上,养育任意多的孩子;(4) 规定如有男人与一妇女生一子后,因不愿与此女结婚而逃跑,此女所生之子应即杀死。

《卡兰莱雅奥法典》是菲律宾第二部古老的成文法,它是阿克郎的大督卡兰莱亚奥于 1433 年 12 月 8 日颁布的。该法典共有 18 条,内容广泛,涉及保护贵族财产、宗教建筑、家庭婚姻和惩罚犯罪等。法典规定,必须逮捕那些在给奴隶主贵族服役时偷懒或消极怠工的人;不准破坏贵族坟墓和其他宗教建筑,违者轻则断指,重则处死;奴隶必须随时还清所欠酋长的一切债务,第一次不能归还时鞭打或断指,第二次不能归还者,则处死。刑罚十分残酷,18 条中有 10 条要处死刑(溺死、打死、烧死)。

苏丹政权的统治者根据伊斯兰法,颁布了《卢瓦兰法典》,还实行一些习惯法。南部的法律反映了苏丹国内部的阶级关系,也反映出南部社会发展水平,其商品经济水平比北部、中部高。法律规定"严惩盗窃者":初犯罚金,再犯则判为奴;盗窃黄金四两以上者,除归还原物外,还要判为奴隶;盗窃黄金超过一斤者,则要判处死刑或全家被判为奴。法律规定,两人合股经商,如一方带股本外出经商时被俘,另一方必须带着一半的赎款将他赎回。被俘者获释后,要赔偿股本的损失和承担另一半赎金;如外出经商的人私自挥霍掉股本,他必须如数偿还合股者的股本,否则,他和他的一半子女就要沦

---

① Sources: The Library of Congress Country Studies; CIA World Factbook 载 http://www.photius.com/countries/philippines/national_security/philippines_national_security_penal_law.html.

为合股者的奴隶。这些条款说明菲律宾虽已进入封建社会,但仍严重存在着奴隶制残余。另外,法律还规定了严厉镇压人民的条款:如对首领非礼、讲粗野语言者,要处死或缴纳罚金十五两;夜间进入首领的房屋或违抗首领的意志者,要判处死刑。①

刑法方面主要是规定刑事与惩罚,将罪行分为重罪与轻罪。对于侮辱、谋杀、盗劫、放火、强奸、渎圣和夜间入侵大督的房子等归为重罪,处罚是很严厉的,主要是死刑、奴役、浸入滚水中、斩去手指、鞭打致死。轻微的不法行为是小偷、奸淫、作伪证、商业上的欺诈、深夜别人睡时唱歌。② 这些罪行受的惩罚是怠刑、给蚂蚁咬、迫使游泳数小时或罚款。并且,古代菲律宾人的刑法还对累犯予以重视,累犯处以比初犯重的刑罚。③ 1837 年西班牙的宪法就已经规定:所有西班牙殖民地,包括菲律宾在内,皆依特定法律治理。在以后 1845 年、1869 年和 1876 年的《西班牙宪法》中,都有这条规定。但它并没有阻止用王室诏谕的方式把西班牙(本土的)法律扩展到菲律宾去。在西班牙统治的最后几十年,包括刑事法典在内的法律就扩展到菲律宾了。④

菲律宾现行刑法是 1930 年 12 月 8 日修正、1932 年 1 月 1 日实施的菲律宾《修正刑法典》,主要是基于 1870 年的《西班牙刑法典》(1887 年生效)修正的。从修正刑法典产生的时间背景可知,当时正处于美国殖民统治时期,按照常理应该是美国法的影响更大。但是,1930 年的《修正刑法典》是基于 1870 年的《西班牙刑法典》修改的,有部分条文是从《西班牙刑法典》的条文中一字不漏地照搬,只有少部分条文为了适应当时菲律宾的形势作了少量的修改。这点也是西班牙殖民统治与美国殖民统治理念不一样的原因,西班牙殖民统治是想完全统治,而美国是"软性"统治,一般不来硬的,美国占领菲律宾以后在法律问题上是宣布西班牙的法律传统基本不变,司法权主要靠美国在菲律宾成立的最高法院来控制。所以,现行的《修正刑法典》基本维持原来《西班牙刑法典》的风貌,同时也夹杂着美国的很多思想和观念,体现了美国的殖民统治。如危害国家罪的犯罪对象就明确规定了

① 参见林榕年主编:《外国法律制度史》,中国人民公安大学出版社 1992 年版,第 375—376 页。

② 菲律宾现行的刑法也有相类似的规定,如第 202 条第 1 款第四项规定:被发现无任何合法和正当目的而游荡在任何他人的住所或者非住宿地的,处以短期禁闭或者不超过 200 比索罚金。

③ 参见〔菲〕格雷戈里奥 · F. 赛义德著:《菲律宾共和国:历史、政府与文明》,吴世昌、温锡增译,商务印书馆 1979 年版,第 95 页。

④ 同上书,第 160 页。

包含美国政府,有很多法条含有“美国”的字眼,并且至今一直没有删除,这也许是菲美之间长期处于一种既依赖又排斥关系的原因所致吧!

菲律宾《修正刑法典》自从1930年作了修正以后就没有作较大的修改,主要是以公法案、总统令、共和国法案的形式进行部分修正和补充。据译者不完全统计,到目前为止,一共有近四十个刑法法案[①](含公法案、总统令、共和国法案和BP等形式的修正和补充),有很多法案是在原来已修改的法案的基础上再进行修改,如2002年《危险毒品综合治理法》就是对1972年的《毒品法》进行全面修改。修改和补充得最多的就是关于谋反罪和颠覆罪的法案了,一共修改了8次,这与菲律宾历年来动荡不安的国家局势有关,2005年5月又通过了《反恐怖法案》(草案)。目前,菲律宾的刑事法主要由1930年的《修正刑法典》和其他相关修正和补充法案组成。

(二)现行刑法典的基本结构和基本原则

菲律宾现行刑法典的体例主要是册(book)、编(title)、章(chapter)、节(section)、条(art)、款(paragraph)、项(rule或subsection)[②],共367条。分为两册,第一册是总则,第二册为犯罪与刑罚。(1)第一册:册下面设编,在第一编前面还有序言性的一编(preliminary titlc),译者把它译成“序编”,规定了本法典生效日期和适用范围,规定了本法典自1932年1月1日起生效,不仅适用于菲律宾群岛,包括其领空、内水、领海,也适用于其管辖权限以外的几种特殊情形。第一册除序编外还有四编,分别是犯罪和影响刑事责任之情形、刑事责任主体、刑罚、刑事责任之消灭和民事责任。(2)第二册:第二册共有十四编,前十三编每一编是一个类罪名,分别是危害国家安全罪与违反国家法律之犯罪、违反国家基本法之犯罪、危害公共秩序罪、危害公共利益罪、有关鸦片和其他禁止毒品罪、危害公共道德犯罪、渎职犯罪、侵犯人身罪、侵犯人身自由与安全罪、侵犯财产罪、侵犯贞节罪、侵犯个人公民身份罪和侵犯名誉罪,第十四编为“准犯罪”,即下面单独设一章为“过失犯罪”。最后的附则主要是规定修正的刑法典对以前刑法典的适用与废止问题。

在《菲律宾宪法》和《修正刑法典》中都有相关的条文对刑法的基本原则进行规定,《菲律宾宪法》第三章“人民的权利”第14条规定:“非经正当

---

① 大部分修正和补充法案都已经在所修改的法条后注明。

② 在本法律条文中区分不是很明显,并且混用,例如:“section”在有的法案中也是“条”的意思;“paragraph”有时是指“项”。所以,译者在翻译时,尽可能的符合汉语的法律语言习惯,很难做到“译名同一律”。

法律程序,不得迫使任何人负刑事责任。在任何刑事诉讼中,被告在最终定罪之前应推定为无罪,并享有由其本人和辩护人进行陈述、被告知其所受控告的性质和原因、要求迅速进行公正和公开的审判,同证人对质,要求以强制程序保证证人出庭并提供对其有利的证据等权利。但在传讯后,尽管被告缺席,审讯得以继续进行,但以已正式通知被告且缺席为无理者为限。”《修正刑法典》第 21 条规定:“犯罪前法律未规定的刑罚不适用于该犯罪。”可见,菲律宾刑法是实行无罪推定和罪刑法定的基本原则。

(三) 关于犯罪

1. 关于犯罪的定义及其分类

《修正刑法典》第 3 条就明确对犯罪下了定义,犯罪是指应受法律惩罚的作为和不作为。犯罪不仅包括欺诈也包括过失。欺诈是指具有故意意图的实行行为;过失是指由于轻率、疏忽、缺乏预见力或缺乏技能而引起的不法行为。《修正刑法典》第 4 条规定:任何人实施了与主观意志不一致的违法行为应当承担刑事责任;任何人实施侵犯人身或财产之犯罪,但如果行为本来不可能完成或因为采用了不充分或者无效的犯罪手段而使犯罪不得逞的除外。这一点相当于我国刑法理论中的不能犯未遂,在我国刑法中是要受处罚的,但在菲律宾刑法中,这种情形下的不得逞不予以处罚。

菲律宾刑法对犯罪的分类在刑法典中就可以直接找到几种分类的方法:(1) 按照犯罪完成与否分为犯罪既遂、犯罪受阻和犯罪未遂。不过菲律宾刑法中的受阻犯(frustrated felonies)和未遂犯(attempted felonies)与我国的未遂犯不同,分别类似于我国的实行完了的未遂犯和未实行完了的未遂犯,所以在理解未遂犯时不能望文生义,应该具体结合它的解释进行理解,对于受阻犯和未遂犯都具体规定了处罚的原则。(2) 按照刑罚的轻重分别分为重罪、次重罪、轻罪。重罪是指根据本法第 25 条之规定,应处以死刑或者任一量刑幅度属于重刑的犯罪;次重罪是指刑法规定最高刑为矫正刑的犯罪;轻罪是指应单处或并处短期禁闭或不超过 200 比索的罚金的违法行为。(3) 共谋犯和建议犯。共谋犯是指两人或两人以上共同协商并决定共同实施犯罪行为;建议犯是指建议他人实施犯罪行为。(4) 故意犯罪和过失犯罪,菲律宾刑法将过失犯罪称为准犯罪,在刑法的最后一章中单独作一章来规定,包括轻率和疏忽行为,对过失犯罪一般处罚较轻。

2. 免责、减轻和加重情形

《修正刑法典》规定正当行为不负刑事责任,具体包括六种情形。[①] 规定了对弱智者、精神病人,未满9周岁的未成年人等七种情形免责,对于年满9周岁而未满15周岁的未成年人,除非犯罪时具有识别能力才能根据第80条之规定被暂缓起诉。规定了10种减轻情形和20种加重情形。并且还单独列了一章规定了其他情形,是指依照犯罪的性质和结果以及其他在犯罪中出现的情形,必须作为加重或减轻刑事责任予以考虑的情节,具体根据亲属关系、酒后犯罪以及罪犯知识水平和受教育程度等来考虑加重或减轻刑罚的情形。

3. 刑事责任主体

《修正刑法典》专门规定了刑事责任主体,具体包括主犯、共犯和从犯。对于犯重罪和次重罪的主犯、共犯和从犯都要负刑事责任;对于轻罪,仅仅主犯和共犯负刑事责任。但是菲律宾刑法中的主犯、共犯和从犯与我国刑法的规定也是不一样的,如从犯是指明知该行为构成犯罪,但未作为主犯或共犯参与犯罪,而是在犯罪后参与包庇、窝藏、协助等行为的罪犯,类似于我国刑法中的包庇、窝藏罪。值得一提的是对于为亲属提供犯罪帮助的从犯免于刑事责任,这一点相当于我国古代刑法中的"亲亲得相首匿"的刑罚理论。

(四)关于刑罚

1. 适用刑罚的基本原则

菲律宾《修正刑法典》规定了犯罪前法律未规定的刑罚不适用于该犯罪,当罪犯不是惯犯时,刑法在对罪犯有利的范围内具有追溯效力,尽管该刑法颁布时已作出终审判决且罪犯正在服刑。可见菲律宾刑法是推行"法无明文规定不为罪"的原则,并且在刑法的追溯效力上奉行"有利于被告"的原则。对于通奸罪、姘居罪、诱奸罪、诱拐妇女罪、强奸罪和猥亵罪,只要被害人宽恕就可以免责,但其他犯罪即使被害人宽恕也不免责。

2. 刑罚的种类

刑罚分为主刑和附加刑,主刑包括极刑、重刑、矫正刑和轻刑。极刑就是死刑一种;重刑包括无期徒刑、有期徒刑、终身或有期剥夺全部权利、终身或有期剥夺特别权利和监禁;矫正刑包括监狱矫正、长期禁闭、停职和流放;

---

① 见《修正刑法典》第11条。

轻刑包括短期禁闭和谴责。其中罚金和守法保证可以与上述三类刑罚同时并用,并且对罚金既可以作为重刑也可以作为矫正刑或者轻刑。[①] 附加刑包括终身或有期剥夺所有权利、终身或有期剥夺特别权利、临时剥夺公职、选举权与被选举权或者从事某种职业或行业的权利、民事权利禁止、赔偿、追缴或者没收违法所得和支付诉讼费用。在菲律宾刑法中,被告人是要承担诉讼费用的,这一点与许多国家都不相同。在菲律宾刑法中还有一个比较特殊的规定——补充刑,就是如果罪犯财产不足以支付罚金时,则负有每天支付 8 比索的责任来补充个人责任。

3. 刑罚的适用及其分级

菲律宾刑罚部分规定得最具体的就是刑罚的适用了,对主犯的刑罚适用、不适用死刑的情形、对混合罪之处罚、所犯罪行与其预期犯罪不一致时对主犯的处罚、受阻犯罪之主犯的处罚、未遂犯之主犯的处罚、既遂犯之共犯的处罚、既遂犯之从犯的处罚、受阻犯之共犯的处罚、受阻犯之从犯的处罚、未遂犯之共犯的处罚、未遂犯之从犯的处罚、对某些从犯的附加刑、由于使用的工具或者追求的目标不可能致使犯罪不能的处罚以及上述处罚之例外都进行了很详细的规定,与后面所述的刑罚适用的表格相结合,菲律宾的法官就仅仅是适用刑法的"机器"了。

菲律宾刑法将刑罚分成可分割刑罚和不可分割刑罚。可分割刑罚就是法定刑有几个不同的刑种或者同种刑种有几个量刑幅度的情形;而不可分割刑罚就是单一刑罚。对于各种刑罚的幅度一般都分成三种幅度,即最高幅度、中间幅度和最低幅度。为了准确地适用刑罚,在法典中专门列出了表格,这样,在适用刑罚时就一目了然了。在刑法分则中不具体规定从几年到几年的有期徒刑,而是到下列表格中对照,然后确定刑期的长短(见表 1、表 2)。如判处最低幅度的有期徒刑就是指判处 12 年零 1 天到 14 年零 8 个月的有期徒刑,中间幅度的有期徒刑就是 14 年零 8 个月零 1 天到 17 年零 4 个月,可见法官的自由裁量权就只在这个刑期段之间。

---

① 根据《修正刑法典》第 26 条的规定,在重刑、矫正刑罚或轻刑中,罚金不管是作为单独刑罚或是可选择刑罚,如其金额在 6000 比索以上时视为重刑;如其金额在 200 比索以上 6000 比索以下时视为矫正刑;如其金额低于 200 比索时视为轻刑。

表 1

刑罚	刑罚所包括的全部刑期	最低幅度所包括的刑期	中间幅度所包括的刑期	最高幅度所包括的刑期
有期徒刑	12年零1天到20年	12年零1天到14年零8个月	14年零8个月零1天到17年零4个月	17年零4个月零1天到20年
监禁、剥夺全部权利和有期剥夺特别权利	6年零1天到12年	6年零1天到8年	8年零1天到10年	10年零1天到12年
监狱矫正、停职和流放	6个月零1天到6年	6个月零1天到2年零4个月	2年零4个月零1天到4年零2个月	4年零2个月零1天到6年
长期禁闭	1个月零1天到6个月	1个月到2个月	2个月零1天到4个月	4个月零1天到6个月
短期禁闭	1到30天	1到10天	11到20天	21到30天

表 2

	对犯罪规定的刑罚	对主犯的受阻犯和既遂犯的共犯适用的刑罚	未遂犯的主犯、既遂犯的从犯和受阻犯的共犯的刑罚	受阻犯的从犯和未遂犯的共犯适用的刑罚	未遂犯的从犯
第一种情形	死刑	无期徒刑	有期徒刑	监禁	监狱矫正
第二种情形	无期徒刑至死刑	有期徒刑	监禁	监狱矫正	长期禁闭
第三种情形	最高幅度的有期徒刑至死刑	最高幅度的监禁至中间幅度的有期徒刑	最高幅度的监狱矫正至中间幅度的监禁	最高幅度的长期禁闭至中间幅度的监狱矫正	罚金和最低幅度和中间幅度的长期禁闭
第四种情形	最高幅度的监禁至中间幅度的有期徒刑	最高幅度的监狱矫正至中间幅度的监禁	最高幅度的长期禁闭至中间幅度的监狱矫正	罚金和最低幅度和中间幅度的长期紧闭	罚金

4. 刑罚的执行

《修正刑法典》对各种具体刑罚的执行作了很具体的规定。对精神病人的刑罚规定了暂缓执行，如果精神病人恢复正常后应继续执行其未执行完毕的刑罚；对于未成年罪犯则规定更详细，只要是未成年人犯重罪或次重罪时未满16周岁的，不分性别，法院将以正当的程序审查证据后，不作出有罪判决，而是中止所有的下一步诉讼程序，将未成年人交托给依法成立的负责孤儿、无家可归者、身心有缺陷者及少年犯矫正或教育的私立或者公立慈善机构。这种留待观察的暂缓执行方式也是别具一格的，体现了菲律宾对青少年的特别保护。刑法典规定刑事责任的完全消灭和部分消灭，在下列情形下刑事责任完全消灭：罪犯已经死亡的（只有在终审判决前被告死亡的，有关的个人刑事责任和有关罚款、债务才因此消灭，否则，仅仅消灭刑事责任）；服刑完毕的；完全消灭刑罚及其影响的特赦的；完全赦免的；已过追诉时效的；已过行刑时效的；根据本法第344条之规定，与受害妇女结婚的（即犯通奸罪、姘居罪、诱奸罪、诱拐妇女罪、强奸罪和猥亵罪后与被害妇女结婚后则刑事责任消灭）。《修正刑法典》还对不同刑罚的罪犯之追诉时效和行刑时效都规定了不同的追诉年限，对减刑的权力主体及具体减短的刑期都进行了规定。总则最后用13个法条规定了犯罪人的民事责任，可见，菲律宾刑法对刑事附带民事部分是规定得相当详细，它对民事责任主体、连带民事责任、补充民事赔偿责任以及民事责任的内容和形式、偿还的顺序都做了很具体的规定，这一点，我国的刑法和民法都是无法与之比拟的。①

（五）关于具体罪名

前面已经提到，在《修正刑法典》第二册中共有十四编，前十三编每一编是一个类罪名，一共有13个类罪名，分别是危害国家安全罪与违反国家法律之犯罪、违反国家基本法之犯罪、危害公共秩序罪、危害公共利益罪、有关鸦片和其他禁止毒品罪、危害公共道德犯罪、渎职犯罪、侵犯人身罪、侵犯人身自由与安全罪、侵犯财产罪、侵犯贞节罪、侵犯个人公民身份罪和侵犯名誉罪。基本上是按照危害性的严重程度来排列的，这点与我国刑法类似。至于所包含的具体个罪在此就不一一阐述，归纳起来，菲律宾《修正刑法典》

① 我国民法界探讨补充民事赔偿责任的理论是近十年的事情，真正以法律形式规定补充民事赔偿责任是2003年颁布的《最高人民法院关于审理侵权人身损害赔偿案件适用法律若干问题的解释》。

的分则有几点是比较有特色的。一是宗教色彩特别浓厚,特别注意保护宗教利益,但是宗教和法律冲突时,稍偏向于法律[1];二是殖民化和本土化相结合,既要保护菲律宾的利益也要保护美国的国家利益,并且明确在具体的罪名中规定不得危害美国的利益;三是照搬西班牙刑法的条文,有很多条文与本土不很协调;四是很多条文不甚简练,有的条文显得特别的累赘。不过规定很具体全面,可以说是涉及了生活的方方面面。

(六)菲律宾死刑制度

菲律宾的死刑制度确实值得密切关注,因为菲律宾的死刑制度是一波三折、时起时落,很具有研究价值。写死刑专著的学者都喜欢引用菲律宾总统阿罗约的一句话:"当我是参议员的时候,我的确支持过终身监禁,但现在我是总统,有更多压力迫使我必须这样做(指适用死刑)。"

其实在古代的菲律宾就有死刑的记载,如重罪的侮辱、谋杀、盗劫、放火、强奸、渎圣和夜间人侵大督的房子,对于这类罪行的惩罚是死刑、奴役、浸入滚水中、斩去手指、鞭打至死。在西班牙统治时代以前的菲律宾现在所知最早的成文法典——《马拉塔斯法典》,就有死刑的记载,如,有男人与一妇女生一子后,因不愿与此女结婚而逃跑,此女所生之子应立即被杀死,因女子无夫,难于赡养其子。村的主管人应寻回此男人,如被抓回后他仍拒不结婚,他应在其所遗弃的妇女所生之子前被处死刑,父子应埋在同一坟中。第二部成文法典《卡郎提奥法典》中,也有很多死刑的规定,如杀人、盗窃处以淹死于河水或者沸水中;第二次不能还清首长债务鞭打致死;第二次犯过分结婚、过分淫荡的则荆棘鞭打死;还有烧死、喂鳄鱼等酷刑处死。[2]

菲律宾现行刑法判处死刑的罪名包括叛国、谋杀、绑架和强奸等7项。二战期间,间谍罪也被列入其中,适用死刑的罪名具体包括《修正刑法典》第114条叛国罪、第123条特别海盗罪、第246条杀亲罪、第248条谋杀罪、第267条绑架罪和严重非法拘禁罪、第294条对人实施暴力或胁迫之抢劫罪、第326-A条纵火致人死亡罪、第335条强奸罪,第1613号总统令《纵火罪的修正案》第5条纵火致人死亡罪和第1744号总统令《对〈修正刑法典〉第320条关于纵火罪的修改》中规定的纵火罪。

---

① 如《修正刑法典》第352条规定:"任何宗派、教派的牧师或教士或民间权威机构执行或批准非法婚姻之仪式的,依据《婚姻法》相关规定给予处罚。"

② 参见〔菲〕格雷戈里奥·F. 赛义德著:《菲律宾共和国:历史、政府与文明》,吴世昌、温锡增译,商务印书馆1979年版,第197—199页。

1993年颁布第7659号共和国法案(即《对几种罪行极为严重的犯罪适用死刑的法案》)的理由是:鉴于宪法第三章第19条第1款特别规定:“不得判处过重的罚款,也不得判处残酷的、侮辱性的或不人道的刑罚。除非国会对非处死不可的滔天罪行今后另行规定,不得判处死刑。任何已经判处的死刑一律改判无期徒刑。”但是,本法案规定的应处死刑的犯罪是极严重可恶的犯罪,因为其固有和明显的不道德、邪恶、残暴和反常与正义、文明、有序的社会的公共标准、行为准则和道德严重不符,且令人无可容忍。因此,国会为了正义、公共秩序和法律规则的利益以及为罪行极恶的犯罪的刑罚执行的合理和协调,对上述犯罪适用死刑是有充分的依据的;采用有效的措施促进维持和平有序的生活,保护生命、自由和财产,促进人民在一个正义仁慈的社会里享受民主国家的福祉。1996年第8177号共和国法案(即关于《指定用注射方法适用死刑法案》)又对第7659号共和国法案(即《对几种罪行极为严重的犯罪适用死刑的法案》)进行修改,这次修改主要是将死刑的执行方式由电刑改为注射刑。可见《修正刑法典》颁布以来,菲律宾有关死刑的法律也正如菲律宾总统对死刑的态度,在不断地修改。

二战后的近二十年内,菲律宾约有三十多人被处以死刑。而到了马科斯时期,为了应对反政府情绪而导致的政治和社会局势紧张,国会通过将走私、劫机和勒索等列入死刑罪名,将死刑罪名最终扩充至24条。通过如此严格立法和更多数量的死刑判决,政府意图显示其果断、强硬的一面。尽管如此,在这一时期,被处死的犯人也只有12人。

1987年,克拉松·阿基诺夫人领导的菲律宾政府作出历史性决定,成为当代史上第一个对所有罪行都免除死刑的亚洲国家,而之前被法庭、特别是军事法庭判处死刑的五百多名犯人都改判终身监禁,而菲律宾唯一的一把实施死刑的电椅也被烧毁。当时,政府和国会作出这项重大决定依据四个理由,即死刑是对犯人及其家属不人道的行为;没有足够证据说明死刑能够有效控制严重犯罪;生命是神赐予的,人类法庭无权决定;现代刑事体系倾向于改善而非报复性的惩罚措施。在某种程度上,这一措施也是对马科斯军政的“矫枉过正”。

而后,拉莫斯力排众议,终于在1993年促使国会通过恢复死刑法案。1994年1月,死刑再次在菲律宾生效。除了将执行死刑的工具从电椅变为药品注射外,菲律宾还严格划分了强制性死刑罪名和适用性死刑罪名。但实际上没有一名犯人被真正处决。直至1999年2月5日,一名强奸继女的犯人莱奥·埃彻盖雷伊成为死刑废除23年后第一个被送上黄泉路的罪犯。

此后两年内,又有6人步其后尘,罪名都是强奸谋杀或抢劫谋杀。但在2000年,菲律宾政府又冻结了死刑。

2001年,格洛丽亚·马卡帕加尔·阿罗约上台后,作为天主教领导人,她明确表态,拒绝采用死刑。她颁布总统令暂停执行死刑,并将18名死刑犯改判为终身监禁。因此,死刑一直形同虚设。依照刑法判决,死刑犯仍不断产生,但却都无法执行。据劳教局统计,截至2003年3月,菲律宾共有死刑犯994人,其中28名为女性,除了其中少部分经最高法院审核后被无罪释放或者减刑外,大多数犯人仍在鬼门关外等待发落。

2003年12月5日,总统阿罗约宣布,取消在菲律宾暂时中止执行死刑的决定,理由是,目前国内抢劫、绑架等犯罪行为日益泛滥。菲律宾的天主教会闻讯后,对此深表失望和痛心。与此同时,菲律宾政府司法机构,已安排在2004年1月底之前,采用注射法对2名犯人执行死刑。此外,还有25名犯有抢劫罪的犯人和4名被指控走私贩毒的人正面临着死刑。菲律宾南部和北部的中产阶级代表们纷纷表示支持,因为他们是犯罪的主要目标,遭受了最为惨重的人员和物质损失。

为了寻找是否应该恢复死刑这个答案,菲律宾的司法界、政界和宗教界掀起论战,数十年来曲折反复,胜负难分。是否应该恢复死刑,在这个大部分国民虔诚信奉天主教的国家,在这个绑架成风、犯罪率居高不下的国家,情与理激烈碰撞,牵动着整个社会的神经。目前,能否恢复死刑在菲律宾依然是悬而未决的问题。

拉腊和里卡延是菲律宾死囚监狱中成百上千个等待发落的犯人的代表,而且这支队伍还在不断壮大。他们无法获得死的解脱或者生的自由,拥有的只是等待。殊不知,他们自己的命运早已不只是法律能够决定。从历史上看,这一问题还受到政治和宗教的左右。①

诚然,死刑能够结束罪犯,但不能结束犯罪。自古以来,"杀人偿命"天经地义,但至今仍有亡命之徒层出不穷。的确,没有一个国家不曾错判误杀罪犯,"包青天"只是一种理想状态。然而,所谓"杀一儆百",死刑对恶性犯罪的威慑作用,已经成为世界上大多数国家法律体系中不可或缺的一部分。死刑无法解决的问题,终身监禁更束手无策。

因此,让死刑犯生存还是死亡,菲律宾最终还是要作出选择,尽管这个决定是艰难的。

---

① http://news.sina.com.cn/w/2004-06-01/18363376678.shtml.

第 3815 号法令

《修正刑法典》

（1930 年 12 月 8 日）

序条 ——本法称为“修正刑法典”。

第一册 总 则

关于本法典的实施日期和适用范围以及关于犯罪、刑事责任人和刑罚。

序编 本法典生效日期和适用范围

第 1 条 本法典生效时间——本法自 1932 年 1 月 1 日起生效。

第 2 条 适用范围——除了优先适用的条约和法律另有规定以外，本法典不仅适用于菲律宾群岛，包括其领空、内水、领海，也适用于其管辖权限以外的下列情形：

1. 在菲律宾的船只或航空器上犯罪的；

2. 伪造或仿造菲律宾群岛的硬币或纸币或由菲律宾政府发行的债券和证券的；

3. 负责联络将上述伪造或仿造债券和证券引入菲律宾群岛的；

4. 在职公职人员或雇员执行职务时犯罪的；或

5. 犯本法第二册第一编规定的危害国家安全和触犯国家法律的犯罪的。

第一编　犯罪和影响刑事责任之情形

第一章　犯　罪

第3条　定义——犯罪是指应受法律惩罚的作为和不作为。

犯罪不仅包括欺诈也包括过失。

欺诈是指具有故意意图的实行行为；过失是指由于轻率、疏忽、缺乏预见力或缺乏技能而引起的不法行为。

第4条　刑事责任——以下行为应承担刑事责任：

1. 任何人实施了与主观意志不一致的违法行为；

2. 任何人实施侵犯人身或财产之犯罪，但如果行为本来不可能完成或因为采用了不充分或者无效的犯罪手段而使犯罪不得逞的除外。

第5条　法院对于应该受约束的行为而法律未规定时以及刑罚过当时的职责——已知某种行为应给予适当地约束而法律并未规定其应受处罚时，由法院作出适当决定，并且通过司法部向总统报告法院认为此行为应该被纳入立法范畴的理由。

同样，考虑到犯罪人的主观恶性以及犯罪行为所造成的危害程度，法院对于没有被判处暂缓执行刑罚的罪犯，认为严格执行本法典的规定会造成刑罚明显过重时，可以通过司法部向总统递交其认为适当处罚的说明。

第6条　既遂犯、受阻犯、未遂犯[①]——犯罪既遂、犯罪受阻和犯罪未遂都应受处罚。

犯罪实行行为和完成行为的必需要件全部具备时称犯罪既遂；行为人完成了能导致犯罪既遂的所有实行行为，但由于意志以外的原因而未发生犯罪结果称犯罪受阻。

犯罪未遂是指犯罪人直接着手实施犯罪行为，非出于本人主动中止，而是由于外界原因或意外事件导致犯罪人没有完成所有能引起犯罪发生的行为。

第7条　轻罪应受处罚之情形——轻罪只有在犯罪既遂形态下应受处罚，但不包括侵犯人身或侵害财产之犯罪。

---

① 在菲律宾刑法中的受阻犯(frustrated felonies)和未遂犯(attempted felonies)与我国的犯罪未遂不同，分别类似于我国的实行完了的未遂和未实行完了的未遂——译者注。

第8条　共谋犯罪与建议犯罪——共谋犯罪与建议犯罪只有在法律特别规定的情形下才予以处罚。

共谋犯是指两人或两人以上共同协商并决定共同实施犯罪行为。

建议犯是指建议他人实施犯罪行为。

第9条　重罪、次重罪、轻罪——重罪是指根据本法第25条之规定,应处以死刑或者任一量刑幅度属于重刑的犯罪。

根据第25条之规定,次重罪是指刑法规定最高刑为矫正刑的犯罪。

轻罪是指应单处或并处短期禁闭或不超过200比索的罚金的违法行为。

第10条　不属于本法规定之犯罪——依照特别法律应受处罚或将受处罚的犯罪行为不适用本法典。本法典将作为特别法的补充,除非有相反的特别规定。

第二章　正当行为与免责情形

第11条　正当行为——下列情形不负任何刑事责任:

1. 行为人在下列情形出现时保护自身安全或权利的行为:

第一,不法侵害。

第二,采取合理必要的手段阻止或抵制侵害。

第三,自我防卫时无充分的挑拨。

2. 在上一项第一种和第二种情形下,行为人出于保护其配偶、血亲或者姻亲的直系尊亲、直系卑亲、婚生、私生或被收养的兄弟姐妹和其他四代以内有血亲关系的亲属之人身安全和权利;在上一项第三种情形之下,除非被侵袭者拒绝帮助,否则行为人的保护行为可不负刑事责任。

3. 在出现本条第一项第一种和第二种的情形下,行为人非处于报复、怨恨或其他恶意动机而保护陌生人的人身安全或权利不受侵犯之行为。

4. 具有下列情形的,行为人为避免灾难或伤害而不作为,造成第三人损害的:

第一,设法避免的灾难确实存在;

第二,如不避免,损失会更严重;

第三,没有其他更有效或让损害更少的避免方法。

5. 行为人是在履行其义务或合法行使行其权利和职权;

6. 行为人是在执行上级下达的具有合法目的的命令。

第 12 条　免除刑事责任的情形——下列情形对行为人免除刑事责任：

1．行为人为弱智者或精神病人，除非精神病人在精神正常时犯罪。

弱智者或精神病人触犯了法定犯罪的行为，法院指令将其限制在专门的医院或精神病院，未经法院许可不得擅自离开。

2．行为人未满 9 周岁的。

3．年满 9 周岁而未满 15 周岁的未成年人，除非犯罪时具有识别能力才能根据本法第 80 条之规定被起诉。

经审判该未成年人不应负刑事责任的，法院依照本项和前述规定，将其交托给负有监护、教育等职责的亲属，由亲属转交给本法第 80 条所规定的机构或者个人。

4．行为人审慎地行使合法行为，但由于无过失或者非蓄意的意外事件而造成伤害。

5．行为人在他人强迫或不可抗拒的暴力下作出的行为。

6．行为人在受到一种无法控制的恐惧的刺激下作出的行为，而这种恐惧是一种相当或更为严重的伤害。

7．行为人由于受到合法的不可克服的原因阻使其不能完成法律要求之行为。

第三章　减轻刑事责任之情形

第 13 条　减轻情节——以下为减轻情节：

1．前面章节中所提及的正当和免责之必需要件不完全具备时。

2．罪犯未满 18 周岁或年满 70 周岁的，但对于未成年犯罪，应按第 80 条之规定起诉。

3．罪犯主观上无犯如此严重的罪行的故意。

4．行为人在行为前受到受害者足够的挑衅或威胁。

5．在配偶、血亲或者姻亲的直系尊亲遭到对方严重侵害后直接作出的保护行为。

6．罪犯因受到强烈刺激而自然引起愤怒或思维混乱的情况下作出犯罪行为。

7．罪犯向有关当局负责人员或者其代理人员自首，或在证据出示之前向法院主动坦白其罪行。

8．罪犯因聋哑、失明或其他身体缺陷而使其犯罪、防卫手段或与同伙

交流的能力受到限制。

9. 有导致罪犯自制力下降的疾病,但不使其完全失去意识时作出的行为。

10. 任何其他与上述情形相同或相类似的行为。

第四章　加重刑事责任之情形

第14条　加重情节——以下为加重情节:

1. 利用其公职犯罪。

2. 蔑视或侮辱政府当局的犯罪。

3. 侮辱或者不尊重受害人的地位、年龄、性别,或者在受害人无任何挑衅行为情况下侵入对方住宅而犯罪的。

4. 滥用信任或明显属于忘恩负义的犯罪行为。

5. 犯罪行为发生在总统办公大楼、总统出席的场所、政府当局刑事职权的场所或者宗教场所。

6. 犯罪行为发生在晚上或无人居住地,或以团伙的方式,只要这些情形有利于实施犯罪。

只要三人以上被武装的犯罪分子共同犯罪就被认为是团伙犯罪。

7. 犯罪行为发生在火灾、海难、地震、流行病区以及其他灾难或灾祸时。

8. 犯罪行为是在武装人员或者确保或获得免罚人员的帮助下进行的。

9. 被告人是累犯的。

累犯是指在接受审判时已经被终审判决犯有本法同一编所包括的另一罪行的犯罪分子。

10. 罪犯处以刑罚之前已被处以一个相当或更严重的刑罚,或者已经因为两个或两个以上属于更轻刑罚的犯罪被处罚。

11. 为了报酬、赏金或许诺而犯罪。

12. 采用决水、放火、投毒、爆炸、使轮船搁浅、造成国际灾难、火车出轨或者任何其他包括大量损耗和毁灭的手段犯罪。

13. 明显预谋的犯罪。

14. 使用技能、欺诈、伪装方式实施犯罪。

15. 利用体力优势或采取削弱对方防卫力量的手段实施犯罪。

16. 背叛犯罪。

当罪犯对某人实施犯罪行为时,采取直接保证犯罪行为实施的特殊方法、手段或形式,且该犯罪行为避免了被害人反抗的风险。

17. 犯罪手段或犯罪情节使得行为影响更为恶劣。

18. 非法侵入犯罪。

罪犯通过破坏墙壁、屋顶、地板、门窗而进入的为非法侵入。

19. 借助于未满15周的未成年人或者依靠机动车辆、机动船只、航空器或其他类似工具实施犯罪的。(第5438号共和国法案已修正)

20. 为了犯罪通过造成其他不必要的不法行为使犯罪中的不法行为被蓄意扩大。

第五章　其他情形

第15条　概念——其他情形是指依照犯罪的性质和结果以及其他在犯罪中出现的情形,必须作为加重或减轻刑事责任予以考虑的情节。包括亲属关系、酒后犯罪以及罪犯知识水平和受教育程度,考虑加重或减轻刑罚的情形。

当被害人是犯罪人的配偶,血亲或者姻亲的直系尊亲、直系卑亲,婚生、私生或被收养的兄弟或姐妹的,作为亲属关系中的其他情形进行考虑。

罪犯犯罪时处于一种醉酒状态,如果这种醉态不是习惯性的或者随犯罪计划后的,应作为一个减轻情节考虑;如果醉态是习惯性的或是蓄意的,应作为加重处罚情节考虑。

第二编　刑事责任主体

第16条　刑事责任主体——以下为重罪和次重罪责任主体:

1. 主犯。
2. 共犯。
3. 从犯。

以下为轻罪责任主体:

1. 主犯。
2. 共犯。

第17条　主犯——实施下列行为之一者为主犯:

1. 直接实施犯罪行为;

2. 直接强迫或劝诱其他人犯罪；

3. 通过协作犯罪，且这种协作对完成犯罪是必不可少的行为。

第 18 条　共犯——共犯是指不属于第 17 条规定的主犯，通过事前或事中行为来协作完成犯罪的罪犯。

第 19 条　从犯——从犯是指明知该行为构成犯罪，但未作为主犯或共犯参与犯罪，而是在犯罪后参与下列任何情形的罪犯：

1. 通过犯罪结果为自己谋利或帮助罪犯谋利。

2. 通过隐藏或毁灭尸体、财产、犯罪工具而使犯罪行为不被发现。

3. 包庇、窝藏、协助主犯逃跑，或者滥用职权或只要是为叛国罪、叛逆罪、谋杀罪，或者企图谋杀总统罪的罪犯或其他惯犯提供帮助。

第 20 条　免除刑事责任的从犯——为保护其配偶、血亲或者姻亲的直系尊亲、直系卑亲、婚生、私生或被收养的兄弟姐妹而实施帮助行为的，可以免除从犯的刑事责任，但前条的第一项规定的情形除外。

第三编　刑　　罚

第一章　刑罚总则

第 21 条　可以适用的刑罚——犯罪前法律未规定的刑罚不适用于该犯罪。

第 22 条　刑法的追溯效力——当罪犯不是惯犯时（此术语在本法第 62 条第五项下了定义），刑法在对罪犯有利的范围内具有追溯效力，尽管该刑法颁布时已作出终审判决且罪犯正在服刑。

第 23 条　被害人的宽恕效力——除本法第 344 条规定的犯罪情形之外，被害人的宽恕不能取消刑事诉讼，但如果受害方明确弃权，则可免除行为人的民事责任。

第 24 条　预防措施和安全措施不属于刑罚——以下情形不认为是刑罚：

1. 对被告人的逮捕和临时拘留以及因精神错乱和弱智而被拘留，或者因疾病需要被限制在医院。

2. 出于规定的目的将未成年罪犯转交第 80 条所规定的任何组织机构。

3. 在职人员在审讯期间或是因为被起诉而被停职。

4. 上级在行使行政纪律管理权时对下级采取的罚款和其他经济调整措施。

5. 民法以刑事形式规定的剥夺权利和赔偿。

第二章　刑罚的分类

第 25 条　可以适用的刑罚——根据本法典之规定可以适用的刑罚及其种类包括如下：

等级　主刑

极刑： 死刑。

重刑： 无期徒刑，
有期徒刑，
终身或有期剥夺全部权利，
终身或有期剥夺特别权利，
监禁。

矫正刑： 监狱矫正，
长期禁闭，
停职，
流放，

轻刑： 短期禁闭，
谴责。

可以与上述三类刑罚同时并用的刑罚：
罚金，
守法保证。

附加刑
终身或有期剥夺所有权利，
终身或有期剥夺特别权利，
临时剥夺公职、选举权与被选举权或者从事某种职业或行业的权利，
民事权利禁止，
赔偿，
追缴或者没收违法所得，
支付诉讼费用。

第 26 条　罚金刑的重刑、矫正刑或轻刑——在重刑、矫正刑罚或轻刑中，罚金不管是作为单独刑罚或是可选择刑罚，如其金额在 6000 比索以上时视为重刑；如其金额在 200 比索以上 6000 比索以下时视为矫正刑；如其金额低于 200 比索时视为轻刑。

第三章　刑期和刑罚的效力

第一节　刑　　期

第 27 条　无期徒刑——任何被处以无期徒刑的罪犯在服刑 30 年后都被赦免，除非总统认为由于罪犯的行为或有其他严重的原因不应赦免。

有期徒刑——有期徒刑的刑期为 12 年零 1 天到 20 年。

监禁和有期剥夺权利——监禁和有期剥夺权利的刑期为 6 年零 1 天到 12 年，除剥夺权利为附加刑时，其附加刑期限与主刑期限相等。

监狱矫正、停职和流放——监狱矫正、停职和流放的期限为 6 个月零 1 天到 6 年，除非停职为附加刑时，其附加刑期限与主刑期限相等。

长期禁闭——长期禁闭的期限为 1 个月零 1 天到 6 个月。

短期禁闭——短期禁闭的期限为 1 天以上 30 天以下。

守法保证——守法保证的期限由法院决定。

第 28 条　刑罚的计算——如果罪犯应该在监狱服刑，则其有期徒刑刑期从终审宣判有罪之日起计算。

如果罪犯没有被羁押的，则其剥夺自由刑期从司法机关执行刑罚之日起计算。其他刑罚刑期从罪犯开始服刑之日起计算。

第 29 条　防止性羁押期折抵监禁期——被采取过防止性羁押措施的罪犯，如果主动书面同意遵守罪犯规章制度，则其防止性羁押期可以全部折抵刑罚中的自由刑，但下列情形除外：

1. 罪犯为惯犯或已经有两次或多次任何犯罪；而且
2. 罪犯在被传唤服刑时有抵抗行为。

如果被羁押的罪犯在执行防止性羁押时不同意遵守与囚犯惩戒一样的规定，则其 4/5 的防止性羁押期间可以折抵刑期。（1970 年 6 月 17 日第 6127 号共和国法案已修正）

重审案件，当被告被执行防止性羁押的时间等于或长于其可能被判处的最长监禁且案件尚未审结的，在不影响庭审或上诉继续进行的情况下应立即释放。

同样，当被告最高刑可能被判处流放刑时，应在执行 30 天防止性羁押后释放。（1988 年 7 月 10 日通过的第 214 号总统令已修正）

第二节　各类刑罚之效力

第 30 条　终身或有期完全剥夺权利之效力——终身或有期完全剥夺公职产生以下效力；

1. 剥夺罪犯的公共职务和公共职业，即使其由全民选举产生的。
2. 剥夺罪犯在公共职务中的选举权与被选举权。
3. 剥夺其从事公职和公务的资格以及剥夺其行使上述权利。

如果是有期剥夺权利属于本条第二项和第三项所述的剥夺权利将持续到刑满为止。

4. 将丧失领取退休金和一切政府养老金的权利。

第 31 条　终身或有期剥夺特别权利的效力——终身或有期剥夺公共职务、公共职业或者公共行业的特别权利具有以下效力：

1. 剥夺罪犯行使公共职务、公共职业或者公共行业的权利；
2. 依照规定的剥夺权利的范围，终身剥夺或在服刑期间剥夺其担任类似公职或者工作的权利。

第 32 条　终身或者有期剥夺行使选举权的效力——根据上述刑罚的性质，终身剥夺或在服刑期间剥夺罪犯在任何普选中的任何公职的选举权或被选举权。而且，在剥夺特别权利期间，罪犯不允许担任任何公职。

第 33 条　中止公共职务、公共职业或者公共行业或者行使选举权的效力——在服刑期间，罪犯丧失在公共职务、公共职业及公共行业任职的权利以及选举权。

在服刑期间，中止行使公职的罪犯不能行使其他类似的职权。

第 34 条　民事权利禁止——民事权利禁止是指在服刑期间剥夺罪犯基于监护权、婚姻权、财产管理权而享有的对人或财产的父母代理权、监护权以及基于法律或当事人生前合法转让的财产的处置权。

第 35 条　守法保证之效力——任何罪犯都有义务作出守法的保证，同时须有两位担保人担保，保证罪犯不再犯此罪，如果罪犯犯罪，担保人得支付法院在判决中所决定的罚金，或将担保书规定的保证金交至法院书记员办公室来担保上述保证。

法院将酌情决定保证期限。

如果罪犯未按要求作出保证时将被拘留，当其被起诉为重罪或次重罪时，拘留期不超过6个月；当其被起诉为轻罪时，拘留期不超过30天。

第36条　赦免及其效力——赦免不能恢复罪犯担任公共职务的权利和选举权，除非这些权利在赦免期间明确规定可以恢复。

赦免将不能免除罪犯在判决中的民事赔偿责任。

第37条　诉讼费用——无论是法律法规生效时规定的还是生效前不可变更的，或者是不可预计的，只要是司法诉讼程序中所包括的费用和赔偿金都是诉讼费用。

第38条　债务与支付顺序——当罪犯的财产不足以支付其所有债务时，则按下列顺序受偿：

1. 直接损害赔偿。
2. 间接损害赔偿。
3. 罚金。
4. 诉讼费。

第39条　辅助刑——如果罪犯财产不足以支付前条第三项所述的罚金，则负有每天支付8比索的补充个人责任，并遵从以下规定：

1. 如果主刑为监狱矫正或禁闭和罚金刑，罪犯须缴清上述罚金才能解除羁押，但其补充的羁押期限不得超过所判刑期的1/3，且累计羁押期限不得超过1年，不许不利于羁押犯而将一天分开计算。

2. 当主刑只有罚金时，如果罪犯被起诉为重罪或是次重罪时补充羁押期不得超过6个月，如果轻罪时不得超过15天。

3. 主刑比监狱矫正更严重时，不得对罪犯补充羁押。

4. 当有确定刑期的主刑是在刑罚机构以外执行时，罪犯在上述确定的服刑期间内，与主刑所包括的剥夺权利仍应继续执行。

5. 罪犯由于无力偿还而导致的附带个人责任未能执行时，当其经济状况改善后附带个人责任中的罚金不能免除。（1969年4月21日第5465号共和国法案修正）

第三节　其他附加刑

第40条　死刑的附加刑——由于减刑或赦免而未被执行死刑的，应在判决确定后30年内执行终身完全剥夺权利和剥夺民事权利的刑罚，除非这些附加刑罚在赦免中被明确取消。

第41条　无期徒刑和有期徒刑的附加刑——被判处无期徒刑和有期徒刑的罪犯，即使其主刑被赦免，仍将根据案情对其处以剥夺终身民事权利或根据情况在刑期内剥夺民事权利和终身剥夺资格权，除非这些附加刑罚在赦免中被明确免除。

第42条　监禁的附加刑——被判处监禁的罪犯，尽管其主刑被赦免，仍将被执行有期剥夺全部权利和终身剥夺特别权利的附加刑，除非这些附加刑在赦免中被明确免除。

第43条　监狱矫正刑的附加刑——被判处监狱矫正刑的罪犯，如其监禁期超过18个月的，则罪犯将同时被处以中止公职、中止从事某种职业或者行业的权利以及终身剥夺选举权。即使其主刑被赦免，罪犯仍将被处以本条规定的剥夺权利，除非这些剥夺权利的刑罚已在赦免中被明确取消。

第44条　禁闭的附加刑——被判处禁闭刑的罪犯在服刑期间将附加中止行使公职和选举权。

第45条　追缴或者没收违法所得或犯罪工具——任何犯罪者将被处以没收犯罪所得和没收犯罪器具或工具。

这些犯罪所得和犯罪工具将由政府追缴或者没收，除非是属于与犯罪无关的第三人的财产，但其中的违禁物品将予以销毁。

第四章　刑罚的适用

第一节　刑事责任主体的刑罚适用及其分等级的规定

第46条　主犯适用刑罚的一般规定——法律规定的重罪刑罚适用于该罪主犯。

法律规定的重罪刑罚为一般性规定时，适用于重罪既遂。

第47条　不适用死刑的情形——死刑应在现行法律规定必须要适用的情形下才适用，但下列情形除外：

1. 犯罪分子年龄超过70周岁的。

2. 有提出上诉或者最高法院重审案件之情形，法庭成员对该死刑的执行意见不一致的。最高法院判处死刑或维持下级法院的死刑判决时，应作出法庭的决定意见，该意见应由除无资格参加该案件之外的所有法官签名外，还应包括其他法官的不一致意见和签名。

第48条　对混合罪之处罚——某一行为构成两种或者两种以上的重罪或者次重罪或者一犯罪行为构成其他犯罪的必要手段时，对犯罪分子处以数罪中最严重犯罪的最高幅度的刑罚。

第 49 条　所犯罪行与其预期犯罪不一致时对主犯的处罚——所犯罪行与预期的犯罪不一致时,应遵循以下规定:

1. 如果所犯罪行所规定的刑罚重于被告预期犯罪的相应刑罚的,则相应地对其处以后者的最高幅度的刑罚。

2. 如果所犯罪行的规定的刑罚轻于被告预期的相应犯罪的刑罚的,对犯罪分子处以前者的最高幅度的刑罚。

3. 前项规定不适用于犯罪人的犯罪行为成为另一犯罪的未遂或者受阻,如果法律对任一后者规定更重的刑罚时,则应处以后者的最高幅度的法定刑罚。

第 50 条　受阻犯罪之主犯的处罚——对受阻犯罪之主犯处以比既遂犯的法定刑轻一等级的刑罚。

第 51 条　未遂犯之主犯的处罚——对未遂犯之主犯处以比既遂犯的法定刑轻两等级的刑罚。

第 52 条　对既遂犯之共犯的处罚——对既遂犯之共犯处以比既遂犯的法定刑轻一等级的刑罚。

第 53 条　对既遂犯之从犯的处罚——对既遂犯的从犯处以比既遂犯的法定刑轻两等级的刑罚。

第 54 条　对受阻犯之共犯的处罚——对受阻犯的共犯处以比受阻犯的法定刑轻一等级的刑罚。

第 55 条　对受阻犯之从犯的处罚——对受阻犯的从犯处以比受阻犯的法定刑轻两等级的刑罚。

第 56 条　对未遂犯之共犯的处罚——对未遂犯的共犯处以比未遂犯的法定刑轻一等级的处罚。

第 57 条　对未遂犯之从犯的处罚——对未遂犯的从犯处以比未遂犯的法定刑轻两等级的刑罚。

第 58 条　对某些从犯的附加刑——属于本法第 19 条 3 款所规定的从犯滥用公职,如主犯犯重罪的,对从犯处以终身完全剥夺权利的附加刑,如其主犯犯次重罪的,对从犯处以有期完全剥夺权利的附加刑。

第 59 条　由于使用的工具或者追求的目标不可能致使犯罪不能的处罚——行为人故意犯某一罪行且已经完成了该行为的实施,但由于行为性质本身不可能完成或者由于犯罪分子所使用的工具本来就不适当而导致行为人没有达到预期得到的结果,导致犯罪仍然没有发生,法院根据罪犯所表现的社会危险性和犯罪危害程度,对其处以长期禁闭或者 200 至 500 比索的罚金。

第60条　第50条至第57条规定之例外——本法第50条至第57条的规定不适用于法律明确对受阻犯、未遂犯、共犯或者从犯规定了刑罚的情形。

第61条　刑罚等级规则——根据本法第50条至第57条的规定，为将刑罚分成不同的等级，对犯罪受阻和犯罪未遂的主犯、共犯或者从犯，应根据以下规则处罚：

1. 规定的刑罚是单一且不可分割时，轻一等级的刑罚为本法第71条规定的各种不可分割刑罚的下一等级刑罚。

2. 刑罚是由两种不可分割的刑罚组成，或在一个总幅度内适用一种或多种可分的刑罚时，轻一等级的刑罚即在刑罚等级规定的较轻的刑罚之下一等级的刑罚。

3. 刑罚是由一种或两种不可分割刑罚和另一最高幅度的可分割刑罚组成时，轻一等级的刑罚即是由中间幅度和最低幅度的适当的可分割刑罚和最高幅度的适当的可分割刑罚以及上述刑罚低一等级的最高幅度的刑罚组成。

4. 刑罚是由不同的可分割刑罚的几种不同量刑幅度组成时，轻一等级的刑罚是在法定的最低幅度的刑罚低一个或者两个等级的刑罚组成，其他情形下是上述各种刑罚低一等级的刑罚。

5. 法律对某一犯罪的处罚不在前四项规定的范围内时，法院通过类推，对受阻犯罪、未遂犯罪的主犯和共犯以及从犯处以相应的刑罚。

本节之规定的表格

	对犯罪规定的刑罚	对主犯的受阻犯和既遂犯的共犯适用的刑罚	未遂犯的主犯、既遂犯的从犯和受阻犯的共犯的刑罚	受阻犯的从犯和未遂犯的共犯适用的刑罚	未遂犯的从犯
第一种情形	死刑	无期徒刑	有期徒刑	监禁	监狱矫正
第二种情形	无期徒刑至死刑	有期徒刑	监禁	监狱矫正	长期禁闭
第三种情形	最高幅度的有期徒刑至死刑	最高幅度的监禁至中间幅度的有期徒刑	最高幅度的监狱矫正至中间幅度的监禁	最高幅度的长期禁闭至中间幅度的监狱矫正	罚金和最低幅度和中间幅度的长期禁闭
第四种情形	最高幅度的监禁至中间幅度的有期徒刑	最高幅度的监狱矫正至中间幅度的监禁	最高幅度的长期禁闭至中间幅度的监狱矫正	罚金和最低幅度和中间幅度的长期紧闭	罚金

第二节　关于减轻和加重情节以及惯犯的刑罚适用规则

第62条　减轻和加重情节以及惯犯的影响——为了减轻或者加重刑罚应根据以下规定考虑减轻或加重情节和惯犯：

1. 加重情节本身是一个法律特别规定可处罚的犯罪或者被法定的犯罪所包括且规定了刑罚的，则不可作为加重刑罚进行考虑。

2. 前项的规定同样适用于关于在犯罪中固有的在一定程度上必然伴随犯罪发生的加重情节。

3. 加重或者减轻情节是基于犯罪分子的道德品质、其与被害人的私人关系或其他个人原因发生的，则只能加重或减轻具有这些情形的主犯、共犯和从犯的刑事责任。

4. 加重或者减轻情节存在于主要实行行为或使用的手段中时，只加重或减轻实行行为或协作行为时就已经知道这些情节的行为人的刑事责任。

5. 惯犯产生以下法律后果：

(a) 对已是第三次被定罪的犯罪分子，按其最后一次被判决有罪的罪行对其进行处罚，同时处以中间幅度和最高幅度的监狱矫正额外刑。

(b) 对已是第四次被定罪的犯罪分子，按其最后一次被判决有罪的罪行对其进行处罚，同时处以最低幅度和中间幅度监禁额外刑。

(c) 已是第五次或更多次数被定罪的犯罪分子，按其最后一次被判决有罪的罪行进行处罚，同时处以最高幅度监禁至最低幅度有期徒刑之额外刑。

根据本条的规定，对犯罪分子的两种刑罚的总刑期不得超过30年。

根据本条的立法目的，从被释放之日其10年内或对最后一次严重或较严重的身体伤害、抢劫、盗窃、诈骗或伪造行为被判决有罪之日起，三次或三次以上上述行为被判决有罪的行为人被认为是惯犯。

第63条　对不可分割刑罚之适用规定——对任何法定的单一不可分割刑罚，法院不考虑此犯罪行为是否存在有减轻或加重情节。

任何由两种不可分割刑罚组成的法定刑罚，适用时应遵循以下规定：

1. 犯罪行为只存在一个加重情节的，适用次重的刑罚。

2. 犯罪行为既无减轻情节也无加重情节的，适用较轻的刑罚。

3. 犯罪行为伴有一些减轻情节而无加重情节的，适用较轻的刑罚。

4. 犯罪行为同时伴有减轻情节和加重情节的，为了适用的刑罚与前面的规定一致，法院依照其损害结果、数量和重要性，适当地酌情对两者进行相互抵消。

第64条　包含三个量刑幅度的刑罚的适用规定——法定刑罚包含三个量刑幅度，不管是单一可分割的刑罚还是由三种不同的刑罚组成的刑罚，根据第76条和第77条之规定，每一刑罚都形成一个幅度，法院依照是否是具有减轻情节或加重情节，按照以下规定确定刑罚：

1. 犯罪行为既无减轻情节也无加重情节的，处以中间幅度的法定刑。

2. 犯罪行为只存在一个减轻情节的，处以最低幅度的法定刑。

3. 犯罪行为存在一个加重情节的，处以最高幅度的法定刑。

4. 犯罪行为既有减轻情节也有加重情节的，法院根据其相应的重要性合理抵消。

5. 犯罪行为有两种或更多的减轻情节而并无加重情节的，根据这些情节的数量和性质，在适当的幅度内处以比法定刑轻一等级的刑罚。

6. 无论加重情节之数量和性质如何，法院不能处以比法定最高刑更重的刑罚。

7. 在各刑罚等级范围之内，法院根据加重情节和减轻情节的数量及性质以及犯罪所造成的次重或较轻的后果的程度决定刑罚的幅度。

第65条　不包含三个量刑幅度之刑罚的规定——法定刑罚不是由三个量刑幅度组成时，法院则适用前述条款的规定，并将法定刑罚分成三个相等的刑期，使所分的每一刑期形成一个量刑幅度。

第66条　罚金的确定——法院在法定的范围内确定罚金数额；确定罚金数额时不仅要考虑减轻情节和加重情节，而且更应考虑犯罪分子的财产或收入。

第67条　第12条第四项规定的全部免责要件情形不存在时应适用之刑罚——不具备本法第12条第四项所要求的全部免除刑事责任的条件时，对犯重罪的犯罪分子，处以最高幅度的长期禁闭至最低幅度的监狱矫正刑，犯次重罪的犯罪分子处以最低幅度和中间幅度的长期禁闭。

第68条　对未满18周岁的犯罪分子的处罚——犯罪分子为未满18周岁的未成年人且属于本法第80条倒数第2款规定的情形的，应遵循以下规定：

1. 对年满9周岁未满15周岁的未成年人，法院宣告其犯罪时具有识别能力的，不免除刑事责任，但应对其处以至少比所犯罪行之法定刑低两等级的刑罚。

2. 对年满15周岁未满18周岁的未成年人,在比法定刑低一等级的适当幅度内处以刑罚。

第69条　不完全免责时之刑罚的适用——如果由于缺乏证明其行为是正当的一些条件,或缺乏第11条和第12条所述的几种免责情形,而使该行为不可完全免责的,则处以比法定刑轻一等级或轻两等级的刑罚,法院根据已存在或缺乏的免责条件的数量和性质,在适当的幅度内处以刑罚。

第70条　判决的连续执行——犯罪分子应受两种或两种以上的刑罚的,如果根据刑罚性质可以同时执行的,将同时执行,否则应遵循以下规定:

在刑罚执行过程中,如果首先执行的一种或几种刑罚被赦免或已经执行完毕,则应该按照它们各自严重程度的顺序执行,使刑罚执行连续或尽可能的连续。

为适用前款之规定,对刑罚的各自严重程度的确定应根据以下等级确定:

1. 死刑,
2. 无期徒刑,
3. 有期徒刑,
4. 监禁,
5. 监狱矫正,
6. 长期禁闭,
7. 短期禁闭,
8. 流放,
9. 终身完全剥夺权利,
10. 有期完全剥夺权利,
11. 中止公职、选举权和被选举权、从事某种职业或者行业,及
12. 谴责。

虽然有上述规则的规定,但是对罪犯判处的最长刑期不得超过其最严重的刑罚的3倍。其合计的刑罚与上述最高幅度刑罚相等后,犯罪分子不再执行其他刑罚。

这样合计的最高幅度不得超过40年。

适用本规则的规定时,终身性刑罚之刑期按30年计算(已修正)。

第71条　刑罚等级表——法律规定一种刑罚比另一刑罚轻或重一级或者多级的,应遵循第61条分级规则规定。

较轻或者较重的刑罚从特定刑罚所包括的等级标准中确定。

法院在适用情节较轻或者较重的刑罚时应遵循以下等级标准：

等级表1：

1. 死刑，
2. 无期徒刑，
3. 有期徒刑，
4. 监禁，
5. 监狱矫正，
6. 长期禁闭，
7. 流放，
8. 短期禁闭，
9. 责难，
10. 罚金。

等级表2：

1. 终身剥夺所有权利，
2. 有期剥夺所有权利，
3. 停止公职、选举权和被选举权、从事某种职业或者行业的权利，
4. 责难，
5. 罚金。

第72条　民事债务的优先偿还——犯两种或者更多罪行的犯罪人之民事责任，应根据其判决时间的先后顺序执行，首先偿还在先的判决。

第三节　前述两节的一般规定

第73条　施以附加刑的推定——根据法律规定，只要法院所判处的某种刑罚含有其他刑罚的，则应根据本法第40条、第41条、第42条、第43条和第44条之规定，推定对罪犯也适用附加刑。

第74条　在某些情形下比无期徒刑更重之刑罚——法律规定某种刑罚重于另一特定刑罚的，但并未特别指明更重刑罚之刑种的情形下，如更重的刑罚将是死刑，第40条规定的相同的刑罚及附加刑则被认为是重一级的刑罚。

第75条　罚金刑之等级的增加或者减少——需要对罚金进行增加或者减少时，对每个等级分别增加或者减少法定最高罚金额的1/4，但是不能少于法定的最低罚金额。

罚金不是由确定的数额构成，而是按比例处罚时也应当按此规定执行。

第76条　可分割刑罚的法定刑期幅度——可分割刑罚的法定刑期幅度将考虑分成三部分，由最低幅度、中间幅度和最高幅度三个幅度组成，以下列表格进行说明：

可分割刑罚的期限和每个幅度所包括的刑期说明表

刑罚	刑罚所包括的全部刑期	最低幅度所包括的期	中间幅度所包括的刑期	最高幅度所包括的刑期
有期徒刑	12年零1天到20年	12年零1天到14年零8个月	14年零8个月零1天到17年零4个月	17年零4个月零1天到20年
监禁、剥夺全部权利和有期剥夺特别权利	6年零1天到12年	6年零1天到8年	8年零1天到10年	10年零1天到12年
监狱矫正、停职和流放	6个月零1天到6年	6个月零1天到2年零4个月	2年零4个月零1天到4年零2个月	4年零2个月零1天到6年
长期禁闭	1个月零1天到6个月	1个月到2个月	2个月零1天月到4个月	4个月零1天到6个月
短期禁闭	1到30天	1到10天	11到20天	21到30天

第77条　由三种不同的刑罚构成的复合刑——规定某种刑罚由三种截然不同的刑罚构成时，每种刑罚就构成一个幅度；最轻的刑罚为最低幅度，其次的刑罚为中间幅度，最重的刑罚为最高的幅度。

只要规定的刑罚不具有本法典特别规定中任一形式时，用规定的规则来类推该刑罚幅度的划分。

第五章　刑罚之执行与服刑

第一节　总　　则

第78条　刑罚执行之时间与方式——没有终审判决就不能执行刑罚。

刑罚不以法律规定以外的其他任何形式执行，除经特别授权外，也不因其他情形或事件而执行。

除了法律明文规定以外，也要遵守刑罚执行机构政府关于其执行工作性质、执行的时间以及与其相关其他事件、罪犯之间以及与他人之间的关系、可得到的救济及饮食的专门规章。

规章应该规定对男女分不同服刑机构管理或至少是在同一机构内分开管理，也要考虑罪犯的矫正和改过自新。

第 79 条　精神病人刑罚的暂缓执行——在终审判决宣告之后罪犯成为精神病患者或弱智者的，仅精神病患者或弱智者的刑罚将暂缓执行，法院应按本法第 12 条第 2 款第一项的规定指令将其限制在专门的医院或精神病院。

在罪犯恢复正常时将继续执行其刑罚，除非根据本法的规定该刑罚已过了时效。

罪犯在服刑期间变得精神失常或弱智的，应遵守本节各条之规定。

第 80 条　未成年罪犯之延迟宣判——只要是未成年人犯重罪或次重罪时未满 16 周岁的，不分性别，法院将以正当的程序审查证据后，不作出有罪判决，而是中止所有的下一步诉讼程序，将未成年人交托给依法成立的负责孤儿、无家可归者、身心有缺陷者及少年犯矫正或教育的私立或者公立慈善机构；或者如果有属于公共福利院长或其代理人或代表监管的其他任一地方的任一负责的人，则交托给他们，否则交托给或公共地方教育官员或其代表监管的其他机构监护，使服从下文规定的条件直到成年或法院认为合适的更短的期间。

交付上述未成年犯时，法院应考虑其本人、父母或近亲属的宗教信仰，以免将其交给不属于他们所信仰的教派或者派别的管理和监督下的私人机构。

公共福利院长或其正式授权代表或代理人、公立学校的地方教育官员或其代表，或已接收委托的未成年犯的监护人，每 4 个月或者当特别情形需要时，向法院提交关于上述未成年犯的行为的好坏以及心理和智力发展情况的书面报告。

公共福利院长或其正式授权的代表或代理人，或者公立学校的地方教育官员或其代表，对未成年犯的品行好坏与否和是否遵守施加给其之条件作出介绍，法院根据此介绍决定延长或缩短未成年犯的程序延期时间。但是其介绍的内容不影响本条第 1 款的规定。

如未成年犯被交托给本条第 1 款所规定的任一机构照管的，经公共福利院长和符合这些官员依照法律给其施加的正当的条件，允许未成年犯暂住在其他地方由其他可靠的人管理。

未成年犯在被限制期间行为表现良好并遵守其被施加的条件的，根据本条之规定，可决定对其恢复庭审并决定释放。

如果未成年犯表现不当,或不遵守所交机构的规定,或将其交给可靠的人监护时不遵守其被施加的条件的,或被发现不改悔,或没有必要继续留在监护机构的,将恢复庭审,根据其所犯之罪作出判决。

未成年犯在所交托机构的生活费用,应由其父母或亲属,或有抚养义务的抚养人全部或者部分承当,上述人员是否有能力承当由法院裁决。假如其父母或亲属或有抚养义务的抚养人没有被要求支付上述费用或因贫困而无能力支付上述费用时,犯罪所在地的市应承当1/3的费用,其所属的省应承当1/3的费用,剩下的1/3则由国家承当。然而,假如财政部长能证明某市不能承当其所分担的上述费用时,其分担部分由国家负责。特别市应承当2/3的上述费用;如果特别市不能承当上述费用的,根据行政法第588节之规定,其应被分配的国内税收将被拒付且用于解决上述债务。

第二节　主刑之执行

第81条　死刑执行的时间与方式——死刑判决执行应有他人证明,统一用电刑执行死刑。死刑由监狱长授权执行,在电刑及电刑前的程序中,尽可能减轻被执行人的痛苦。

如被判处死刑之罪犯要求,在执行电刑时应对其进行麻醉。

第82条　死刑的布告和执行以及对罪犯的帮助——法院指定一个工作日来执行死刑,但不具体指定几点钟执行;执行当天日出之前不得告知罪犯其具体的执行日,发出布告后至少届满8小时才能执行,但必须在日落前执行。在发出布告与执行死刑之间隔期间,要尽可能为犯人的要求提供帮助,例如,他要求他所信仰的宗教的神父或者牧师参加他生命的最后一刻和咨询律师,又如立遗嘱或与其家庭成员或负责他的商业经营、财产管理或照顾其后代的人协商有关事宜。

第83条　死刑之缓期执行——妇女从宣判之日起3年以内或怀孕期间不得处以死刑,对于70周岁以上的老人也不处以死刑。此种情况下,将其死刑减为无期徒刑并附加第40条规定的附加刑。

第84条　死刑执行地和目击者——死刑在比利比汤监狱内的一封闭空地执行,如罪犯要求,只有提供帮助的牧师、他的律师和其亲戚可以目击,且不得超过6人,刑场的医生和刑场必需的工作人员和经监狱长批准的人员可以目击。

第85条　死刑犯的尸体处置及埋葬之规定——除非其家属有要求,否则执行程序完成之后,将罪犯尸体交给为学习研究而首先申请的学术或科研机构,由这些机构负责对尸体进行合宜埋葬。否则由监狱长安排用政府费用埋葬尸体,并允许罪犯家朋参加葬送。对任何死刑犯均不得举行隆重的葬仪。

第 86 条　无期徒刑、有期徒刑、监禁、监狱矫正和长期禁闭之执行——无期徒刑、有期徒刑、监禁、监狱矫正和长期禁闭刑在现行行政法或今后法律规定的场所和刑罚机构执行。

第 87 条　流放刑之执行——被判处流放刑的罪犯不得进入判决指定的地方,也不得进入从该指定的地方起算最多 250 千米和至少 25 千米之半径范围内的地方。

第 88 条　长期禁闭刑的执行——长期禁闭刑是在地方监狱或在一个司法警官的监视下的被告人住所服刑,法院在判决确定这些场所时,应考虑罪犯的健康状况和觉得适合的其他理由。

第四编　刑事责任之消灭

第一章　刑事责任之完全消灭

第 89 条　刑事责任完全消灭之方式——下列情形下刑事责任完全消灭:

1. 罪犯已经死亡的,只有在终审判决前被告死亡的,有关的个人刑事责任和有关罚款、债务因此消灭;
2. 服刑完毕的;
3. 完全消灭刑罚及其影响的特赦的;
4. 完全赦免的;
5. 已过追诉时效的;
6. 已过行刑时效的;
7. 根据本法第 344 条之规定,与受害妇女结婚的。

第 90 条　追诉时效——应处以死刑、无期徒刑或者有期徒刑之犯罪的追诉时效为 20 年。

应处以其他重刑之犯罪的追诉时效为 15 年。

除了应处以长期禁闭刑之犯罪的追诉时效为 5 年以外,其他应处以矫正刑之犯罪的追诉时效为 10 年。

侮辱或其他类似犯罪的追诉时效为 1 年。

通过口头行为诽谤之犯罪的追诉时效为6个月。

轻罪的追诉时效为2个月。

法定刑罚为混合刑罚的，最高刑罚为本条第1款、第2款、第3款所包括之规定的追诉时效的起算点。（1996年6月19号通过的第4661号共和国法案修正）

第91条　追诉时效之计算——追诉时效的期限从被害人、有关当局或其代理人发现犯罪之日起开始计算，因提出控告或起诉而中断，当没有证据证明被告有罪或宣告无罪，或因为任何不可归咎于罪犯的原因而不合理地停止上述程序的，追诉时效的期限再一次开始计算。

犯罪分子不在菲律宾群岛期间，不计算追诉期限。

第92条　行刑时效——终审判决的刑罚经过以下期限不执行就失效：

1. 死刑和无期徒刑经过20年；
2. 其他重刑经过15年；
3. 除长期禁闭刑为5年以外，矫正刑经过10年；
4. 轻刑经过1年。

第93条　行刑时效之计算——行刑时效的期限从犯罪分子逃避服刑之日起开始计算，如果被告自首、被抓获、逃到一些与本国无引渡条约的外国，或在时效期限届满之前犯新罪的，行刑时效中断。

第二章　刑事责任之部分消灭

第94条　刑事责任之部分消灭——刑事责任部分消灭之情形：

1. 有条件之赦免；
2. 减刑；及
3. 罪犯在服刑期间因表现好而获得奖励。

第95条　被批准有条件赦免的罪犯所承担的义务——被同意附条件赦免的罪犯应承担严格遵守另外附加的条件的义务，对任一不遵守特定条件的行为将撤回赦免，并对其按第159条的规定处罚。

第96条　减刑的效力——原判刑罚减为另外一种不同刑期和不同性质的刑罚就产生由后者取代前者之法律效力。

第97条　对表现良好之奖励——任何刑罚机构之服刑人员表现良好的，给予其下列减短刑期的奖励：

1. 罪犯被关押前两年期间表现良好的，则每月减少5天的刑罚；

2. 罪犯被关押的第 3 年至第 5 年(包括本数)期间表现良好的,则每月减少 8 天的刑罚;

3. 罪犯被关押的第 6 年直到第 10 年(包括本数)表现良好的,则每月减少 10 天的刑罚;

4. 罪犯被关押的第 11 年及第 11 年以后表现良好的,则每月减少 15 天的刑罚。

第 98 条　由于忠诚而特别减短刑期——在本法第 58 条所列的情形下逃避服刑的任何服刑人员,如能在灾难或者灾祸的消失公告发出后 48 小时之内向有关当局自首的,准予减少 1/5 的刑期。

第 99 条　有权给予奖励的人员——只要证明合法,监狱长有权给予表现良好的囚犯减短刑期的奖励,这些奖励一旦给予就不得撤回。

第五编　民事责任

第一章　犯罪的民事责任人

第 100 条　犯罪人之民事责任——犯罪人既要负刑事责任也负民事责任。

第 101 条　某些案件的民事责任之特别规定——本法第 12 条第一项、第二项、第三项、第五项和第六项及第 11 条第四项关于刑事责任之免除的规定,不包括对民事责任的免除,应按以下规定执行:

第一,如果符合第 12 条第一项、第二项、第三项规定之情形,犯罪行为是一个智弱者或精神病人,或者是未满 9 周岁之未成年人所为,或者是不具有识别能力的年满 9 周岁未满 15 周岁的未成年人所为时,由具有合法代理权人或监督权人承担民事责任,除非后者无过错或无疏忽。

如果精神病人、弱智者或未成年人没有合法的监护人或管理人,或是这些人无能力偿还债务,上述精神病人、弱智者或者未成年人根据民法规定用其所有的财产承担民事责任,除非其财产被豁免执行。

第二,属于第 11 条第四项规定之情形,为防止其损害发生的受益人,根据其受益的比例承担民事责任。

法院根据受益的比例作出合理的判决。

对各方应负的责任不能作出公平的决定时,或者当责任涉及政府或大部分居民、且其损失是由权力机关或者其官员同意而造成的,应根据特别法或规章所规定的方式作出赔偿。

第三，属于第12条第五项、第六项规定之情形，使用暴力或使他人恐惧的行为人应负主要责任，如果没有上述行为人，具体实施者用其被豁免以外的财产负次要民事责任。

第102条　旅馆主人、客栈老板和业主之补充民事责任——具体的刑事犯罪人不能抓获，则旅馆主人、客栈老板及其他个人或团体对发生在其营业场所的犯罪行为和所有他们或者他们的雇员违反城市法令或者一些普通或特别的治安条例的行为承担民事责任。

顾客在住宿时财物被抢或被盗，假如已预先告知了老板本人或其代理人其存放了物品在其旅馆，并且根据老板或其代理人所给予的关于对物品要注意和谨慎的说明告知的，由老板承担赔偿财产或按价值赔偿的补充民事责任。其雇员以外的犯罪分子通过暴力或威胁进行抢劫的，老板不负民事责任。

第103条　其他人之补充民事责任——前条所规定的补充民事责任同样适用于雇主、老师、个人和从事任一行业的团体，由于他们的仆人、学生、工人、学徒、雇员犯罪但免责的情形。

第二章　民事责任包括的内容

第104条　民事责任包括的内容——本法第100条至第103条规定的民事责任包括：

1. 归还原物；
2. 赔偿直接损失；
3. 赔偿间接损失。

第105条　原物归还及其方式——只要有可能归还原物的就必须要物归原主，允许有一定的损耗，由法院决定具体减少的价值。

即使第三人是通过合法手段获得所有物的，也应归还原主，而第三人的损害由交易方负责赔偿。

本条不适用于如果第三人是通过法定的方式和要求取得原物而不需返还的情形。

第106条　直接损害赔偿的确定——法院应尽可能地考虑其财物的价格、受害人的特别情感价值以及应作出的补偿来决定赔偿数额。

第107条　间接损害赔偿的确定——间接损害赔偿不仅包括遭到损害

的被害人，而且也包括因为犯罪原因而受损害的家属或第三人。

第108条　恢复原状、直接损害赔偿或间接损害赔偿和诉讼；责任主体的转移——恢复原状、直接损害赔偿或间接损害赔偿之责任由责任人的继承人承担。

请求恢复原状、直接损害赔偿或间接损害赔偿的诉讼同样转移给被害人的继承人。

第109条　民事责任的分担——如果有两人或两人以上对同一犯罪应负民事责任的，由法院决定每一个责任承担者应承担的数额。

第110条　主犯、共犯和从犯的个别民事责任和补充民事责任；受优先偿还的权利——虽然由上一条规定，但是，主犯、共犯和从犯，在各自的责任范围内承担他们各自的责任份额，并且对他们当中的其他人员承担补充赔偿责任。

补充赔偿责任首先执行主犯的财产，其次执行共犯的财产，最后执行从犯的财产。

个别或者补充的责任已被执行的，已经支付了赔偿金的罪犯有权起诉要求其他犯罪人支付所应分担之赔偿份额。

第111条　某些情形下的归还义务——任何无代价地分享了犯罪所得收益的人，有责任赔偿按其所分享的范围给予等价物的赔偿。

第三章　民事责任之消灭和存在

第112条　民事责任之消灭——依照民法的规定，本法第100条、第101条、第102条和第103条规定的民事责任以相同的民事责任方式消灭。

第113条　承担民事责任之义务——除按上一条规定消灭民事责任外，尽管罪犯已被剥夺人身自由权和其他权利的形式服刑，或者因特赦、宽恕、减刑或其他原因不需要服刑，但罪犯还得继续承担因其犯罪所产生的民事责任。

第二册　犯罪与刑罚

第一编　危害国家安全罪与违反国家法律之犯罪

第一章　危害国家安全罪

第一节　叛国罪与间谍罪

第114条　叛国罪——任何隶属于(美国或)菲律宾共和国之本国国民,在菲律宾群岛或其他地方发动战争或拥护敌人而为其提供资助或帮助的,处以无期徒刑至死刑并处不超过20000比索的罚金。

除非至少有两个证人公开一致证明其行为或被告在公开法庭供认其行为,否则不定叛国罪。

定居于菲律宾之外国人,犯本条第1款规定之叛国罪行的,也处以长期禁闭至死刑并处不超过20000比索的罚金(1945年5月31日通过的第44号总统令修正)。

第115条　共谋与建议叛国罪及其刑罚——共谋或建议犯叛国的,分别处以监禁并处不超过10000比索的罚金和处以监狱矫正并处不超过5000比索的罚金。

第116条　包庇叛国罪——任何隶属于(美国或)菲律宾共和国之本国国民明知任何阴谋叛国行为,但隐瞒或者不揭发和不尽快地告知省长或者省检查官或者所在城市的市长或检查官的,以叛国罪的从犯处罚。

第117条　间谍罪——对任何以下犯罪行为处以监狱矫正:

1. 未经许可擅自进入军舰、堡垒,或者海军或陆军军事基地或者禁区以获取菲律宾国防部有关的情报、计划、照片或其他机密性资料的;或

2. 利用公职便利将其所持有的文件、数据或前项所涉的情报内容透露给外国代表的。

犯罪分子是公职人员或雇员的处以情节重一等级之刑罚。

第二节　煽动战争和战时不忠罪

第118条　煽动战争罪或给予报复动因罪——非法或未经授权煽动或

者给予机会使菲律宾陷入或者很有可能陷入一场战争或使菲律宾国民的人身与财产面临报复,对公职人员或雇员处以有期徒刑,对普通个人处以监禁。

第119条　违反中立罪——任何在政府没有参与战争时期,违反主管当局有关坚持中立的规定,处以监狱矫正。

第120条　与敌国通讯罪——任何人在战时与敌国或敌军占领的领土进行通讯行为的,应追究刑事责任:

1. 通讯行为是政府禁止的,处以监狱矫正;
2. 用密码或常用符号进行通讯的,处以监禁;
3. 传递的通知或情报对敌人可能有用的,处以有期徒刑,如果罪犯通过此类通知或情报帮助敌人的,处以无期徒刑至死刑。

第121条　逃往敌国罪——任何隶属于菲律宾的国民在主管当局禁止出国时企图逃往或转往敌国的,处以长期禁闭。

第三节　海盗罪和公海上暴动罪

第122条　普通海盗罪和公海上暴动罪——任何在公海上袭击或夺取船只,或者既不是船上的船员也不是乘客,夺取上述船只全部或者部分货物、装设备、船员或者乘客的私人财物的,处以有期徒刑。

海上暴动行为处以同样的刑罚。

第123条　特别海盗罪——在以下情形下犯前条所述任一罪行的,处以有期徒刑至死刑:

1. 通过强行登船或放火夺取船只的;
2. 海盗者抛弃无法自救的被害人的;或
3. 犯罪时伴有谋杀、杀人、伤害或强奸行为的。

第二编　违反国家基本法之犯罪

第一章　擅自羁押罪、驱逐罪、侵犯住所罪、阻止、干扰和解散和平会议罪及侵犯宗教信仰罪

第一节　擅自羁押罪和驱逐罪

第124条　擅自羁押罪——任何公职人员或雇员无法定理由羁押公民

的，按以下规定处罚：

1. 羁押期不满 3 天的，处以最高幅度的长期禁闭至最低幅度的监狱矫正；

2. 连续羁押超过 3 天但不满 15 天的，处以中间幅度和最高幅度的监狱矫正；

3. 连续羁押超过 15 天但未满 6 个月的，处以监禁；

4. 连续羁押超过 6 个月的，处以有期徒刑。

因犯罪或严重精神错乱或者其他疾病需要强制住院的病人进行羁押视为羁押他人的合法依据。

第 125 条　延迟将被拘留者交至有权的司法机关罪——对已被实施合法拘留行为却未在以下规定期限内将被拘留者交至有关司法机关的公职人员或者雇员，按前条规定处罚：对因犯罪应处以轻刑或者与之相当的刑罚的被拘留者，延迟 12 小时的；对因犯罪应处以矫正刑或者与之相当的刑罚的被拘留者，延迟 18 小时的；对因犯罪应处以重刑或者死刑或与之相当的刑罚的被拘留者，延迟 36 小时的。

任何情形下，必须要告知被拘留者其被拘留的原因，且根据被拘留者的要求允许在任何时候与其律师通信或交换意见。（分别于 1986 年 11 月 7 日通过的第 59 号总统令和 1997 年 7 月 25 日通过的第 272 号总统令修正）

第 126 条　延迟释放罪——公职人员或雇员延迟履行释放囚犯或拘留犯之司法或行政命令指定的期限，或者不正当地推迟提供给上述囚犯的决议的通知或耽搁释放他们的上诉程序的，按第 124 条之规定进行处罚。

第 127 条　驱逐罪——对未经法律授权，将任何公民驱逐出菲律宾或者强迫这些公民改变住所的公职人员或雇员，处以监狱矫正。

第二节　侵犯住所罪

第 128 条　侵犯住所罪——对未经司法授权，违背主人意愿进入其住所、事先未经同意搜查其文件或其他财物，或者秘密进入他人住所或者经要求离开而拒绝离开的公职人员或雇员，处于最低幅度的监狱矫正。

如犯罪行为在夜间实施，或者罪犯搜查后没有将其所搜查到的不属于犯罪证据的文件或者财物立即归还的，处以中间幅度和最高幅度的监狱矫正。

第 129 条　恶意获取搜查令罪和滥用合法搜查令罪——任何公职人员或雇员无正当理由获取搜查令，或者合法获取搜查令而超越职权或在进行搜查时使用不必要的严厉行为的,除因其他犯罪应承担责任以外,还应处以最高幅度的长期禁闭和最低幅度的监狱矫正,并处不超过 1000 比索的罚金。

第 130 条　没有证人的搜查住所罪——公职人员或雇员合法实施搜查行为时,如本人和家庭成员不在场,或者因失职而没邀请两位邻居作为证人到场而搜查他人住所、文件或其他财产的,对其处以中间幅度和最高幅度的长期禁闭。

第三节　阻止、干扰和解散和平会议罪

第 131 条　阻止、干扰和解散和平会议罪——公职人员或雇员非法阻止或者干扰和平会议的举行,或者解散和平会议的,处以最低幅度的监狱矫正。

公职人员或雇员妨碍他人参加合法社团或者出席社团会议的,处以同样的刑罚。

公职人员或雇员阻止或者妨碍他人个人或者集体上访、请愿的,处以同样的刑罚。

第四节　侵犯宗教信仰罪

第 132 条　妨碍宗教信仰罪——任何公职人员或者雇员阻止或干扰宗教仪式或者信仰表明的,处以最低幅度的监狱矫正。

如使用暴力或威胁实施上述犯罪行为的,处以中间幅度或者最高幅度的监狱矫正。

第 133 条　侵犯宗教情感罪——任何公职人员或者雇员在专门举行宗教活动的场所或者在进行宗教仪式时实行亵渎性行为冒犯信徒的宗教情感的,处以最高幅度的长期禁闭至最低幅度的监狱矫正。

第三编　危害公共秩序罪

第一章　谋反罪、暴乱罪和不忠罪

第 134 条　谋反罪或叛乱罪及其犯罪方式——谋反罪或者叛乱罪是指公然起义和为不忠效本国政府、法律、菲律宾群岛或其任何部分领土、海军或者其他武装力量的目的而夺取军权反抗政府、剥夺总统或者议会的全部

或者部分权力或者特权的行为。(第6968号共和国法案修正)

第134-A条　政变罪及其犯罪方式——为夺取或者削弱国家权力,在菲律宾内任何地方,由部队人员或者警察,或任何有权行使公共权力的人员,单独或同时适时地对菲律宾共和国合法当局或者军事阵地或军事装备、通信网络、公用设施或者其他为行使和维持权力所必要的设备进行伴有暴力、威胁、恐吓、阴谋或者秘密行动的快速攻击,不管有无平民支持或者参加,均构成政变罪。(第6968号共和国法案修正)

第135条　对谋反罪、叛乱罪和政变罪的处罚——任何促进、拥护或领导谋反、叛乱行为的,处以无期徒刑。

在谋反犯罪中仅仅参加或实施他人命令的,处以有期徒刑。

任何领导或以任何方式指挥或者命令他人进行政变的,处以无期徒刑。

任何公职人员在政变时参加或者执行他人的指示或者命令的,处以最高幅度的监禁。

任何非公职人员参加政变或者在政变时以任何方式支持、资助、煽动或者帮助的,处以最高幅度的有期徒刑。

当不能确定谋反、叛乱或者政变的领导者时,代表叛乱者的利益、实际指导他人、向他们发表演讲、以自己的名字签署收据或者文件,或者实施类似行为者被视为谋反、叛乱或者政变之领导者。(1990年10月24日通过的第6968号共和国法案修正)

第136条　共谋和建议政变罪、谋反罪或者叛乱罪——共谋和建议犯政变罪的,处以最低幅度的监禁并处不超过8000比索之罚金。

共谋和建议犯谋反罪或者叛乱罪的,分别处以最高幅度的监狱矫正并处不超过5000比索之罚金和中间幅度的监狱矫正并处不超过2000比索之罚金。(1990年10月24日通过的第6968号共和国法案修正)

第137条　公职人员或者雇员不忠罪——公职人员或者雇员在权力范围内不利用各种方法阻止叛乱或者继续在叛乱者的控制下履行职责或者接受他们任命的官职的,处以最低幅度的监狱矫正。(第187号总统令恢复适用)

第138条　煽动谋反或者叛乱罪——未使用武力或者公开反对政府,通过演讲、宣言、著述、徽章、标语或者其他表示方法,煽动他人实施本法第134条规定之任何行为的,处以最低幅度的监禁。(第187号总统令恢复适用)

第139条　煽动罪及其犯罪方式——煽动罪是指为达到以下目的,通过武力、胁迫或者其他非法方式公开和喧嚣的反抗：

1. 为阻止法律之颁布或者执行，或者阻止公民选举的进行的；

2. 为阻止国家、省或者市政府或者其任何公职人员自由行使其职权，或者阻止任何行政命令的执行的；

3. 为对公职人员或者雇员的人身或者财产施以任何憎恨或者报复行为；

4. 为任何政治或者社会目标，对个人或任何社会阶层施以任何憎恨或者报复行为的；及

5. 为任何政治或者社会目的，掠夺个人、市、省或者国家政府（或者美国政府）所有的全部或者部分财产的。

第 140 条　煽动罪之刑罚——对煽动行为之领导者处以最低幅度的监禁和不超过 10000 比索的罚金。

对其他参加者处以最高幅度的监狱矫正和不超过 5000 比索的罚金。（第 187 号总统令恢复适用）

第 141 条　共谋煽动罪——对共谋煽动者，处以中间幅度的监狱矫正并处不超过 2000 比索之罚金。（第 187 号总统令恢复适用）

第 142 条　煽动暴乱罪——不直接参加暴乱犯罪，而通过演讲、宣言、著述、徽章、卡通、标语或者其他追求这种目的的表示方法煽动他人完成所组织的暴乱，或者对他人发出煽动言词或演讲，书写、出版或者散布下流的诽谤言词反对菲律宾政府（美国政府或者联邦政府），或者当局官方，或者有助于干扰者阻碍任何合法行使政府职能的官员，或者有助于鼓动他人为非法目的策划阴谋或者一起集会，或者建议或鼓动反叛阴谋或暴乱，或者导致或意图挑起人民反抗合法政府或者扰乱社会治安、政府安全和秩序，或者故意隐瞒上述恶行的，处以最高幅度的监狱矫正和不超过 2000 比索之罚金。（第 187 号总统令恢复适用）

第二章　侵犯公众代表罪

第一节　侵犯立法机关和类似机关罪

第 143 条　阻止议会和类似团体会议罪——通过暴力或者欺诈手段阻止国会（菲律宾国会）或者任何其委员会、小组委员会、制宪委员会或者常务委员会或者其分会会议，或者任何省、市或者地方委员会之会议的，单处或者并处监狱矫正或 200 至 2000 比索之罚金。（第 187 号总统令恢复适用）

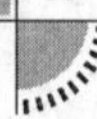

第144条　扰乱会议罪——扰乱国会(菲律宾国会)之会议或者任何其委员会、小组委员会、制宪委员会或者常务委员会或者其分会会议,或者任何省或市或地方委员会之会议,或者在这些团体前表现有关妨碍会议或者损害其应有之尊严的举止的,处以长期禁闭或者处以200至1000比索的罚金。(第187号总统令恢复适用)

第二节　侵犯议员豁免权罪

第145条　侵犯议员豁免权罪——使用暴力、威胁、恐吓,或者欺诈手段阻止国会(菲律宾国会)议员参加议会(国会)会议或者阻止任何其委员会或者小组委员会、制宪委员会或常委会或者其分会的议员发表意见或投票的,处以监禁;任何公职人员或者雇员在议会(国会)进行定期会议或者特别会议期间禁闭或者搜查议员的,应处以监狱矫正,但此议员的犯罪行为应被处以比监禁更重之刑罚的情形除外。

第三章　非法集会罪和非法结社罪

第146条　非法集会罪——任何基于实施本法规定应处以刑罚的犯罪行为的目的,有武装人员参加的集会之组织者或者领导者,或者任何煽动听众犯叛国罪、谋反罪、叛乱罪、煽动罪或攻击政府人员或者其代理人的集会之组织者或者领导者,处以最高幅度的监狱矫正至中间幅度的监禁;仅参加此集会者,处以长期禁闭;如果是武装人员参加此集会的,应处以监狱矫正。

参加集会者非法携带枪支的,在其所涉及的范围内可以推定其集会的目的是本法规定之应处罚的犯罪行为,且被认定为是前款范围内的集会之领导者或者组织者。

本条所使用的"集会"一词应理解为包括无论是在一个固定场所或移动的场所的聚集或者聚合。(第187号总统令恢复适用)

第147条　非法结社罪——为了实施任何本法规定可罚之犯罪行为或者为了一些与公共道德相悖的目的而全部或者部分地参加组织结社的发起人、负责人和会长,处以最低幅度与最高幅度的监狱矫正和不超过1000比索之罚金。仅为上述结社之成员的,处以长期禁闭。(第187号总统令恢复适用)

第四章　威胁、抵抗、违抗政府官员或其代理人罪

第148条　直接威胁政府官员或其代理人罪——行为人为达到任何谋

反罪和暴乱罪定义所列举的目的，但不属于公众叛乱的行为，而使用暴力或者胁迫的；或者殴打、使用暴力，或者严重胁迫或抵抗任何从事公务或者正在执行公务的政府官员或者其代理人员的，使用武器进行威胁或者罪犯是政府官员或者其雇员的，或者罪犯在辅助政府官员的，处以中间幅度与最高幅度的监狱矫正和不超过1000比索之罚金。如果没有发生任何前述情形，处以最低幅度的监狱矫正和不超过500比索之罚金。

第149条　间接威胁政府官员或其代理人罪——在发生前条规定之任何犯罪时，对正在帮助政府机构或其代理人的任何人员施以暴力或者胁迫的，处以其最低幅度和中间幅度的监狱矫正和不超过500比索之罚金。

第150条　不服从国会或其委员会或小组委员会，制宪委员会或其常委会或小组委员会或分会的召集罪——被召集作为证人参加国会（议会）、其特别委员会或常务委员会或小组委员会，制宪委员会或其常务委员会，或者分会，或者在委员会或者常务委员会主任或者委员授权召集作证之前，无法定理由拒绝服从召集；或者正在出席会议时，在任何这些立法或者宪法机关或官员面前，被要求证实或者回答任何合法的质询或者出示任何他们所有的书籍、报纸、文件或者档案，当被他们要求行使这些职责时，拒绝被宣誓或者任命，单处或者并处长期禁闭或者200至1000比索之罚金。阻止他人作为证人参加会议或者诱导他人不服从召集或者拒绝上述机构或官员的召集，处以同样的刑罚。

第151条　抵抗或者违抗政府官员或其代理人员罪——除前条规定的以外，抵抗或者严重违抗正在执行公务的政府官员或者其代理人员的，处以长期禁闭和不超过500比索之罚金。

不服从政府官员的代理人员性质不严重的，处以短期禁闭或10至100比索的罚金。

第152条　政府官员及其代理人员的认定——在适用本法前条和其他条款时，任何不管作为个人或者作为一些法院或者政府团体、部、委的成员之一，只要直接被授予权力的，都是政府官员。镇长和村长[1]也视为政府官员。

任何通过法律直接规定或者选举或者主管当局任命，承担维护公共秩

---

① “barangay”直译为“巴郎盖”，来源于马来语，一个政府的单位，大约由30—100家居民，有的多达2000多家，在古代菲律宾一个“巴郎盖”就是一个国家，因为比镇小，所以译者直接译为村，“a barangay chairman”就直接译为“村长”。

序和保护人身财产安全,比如地方行政区域议员、地方行政区域警察和村领导及任何协助政府官员的人员,都被视为政府官员之代理人员。

适用本法第 148 条和第 151 条的规定时,教师、教授、管理公立或者正式合法的私立学校、学院和大学的负责人和实际在行使本职职责或者正在行使其本职职责的律师都被视为权力机关人员。(经 1973 年 9 月 19 日的第 299 号共和国法案和 1985 年 6 月 12 日通过的第 837 号 BP 修正)

第五章　扰乱公共秩序罪

第 153 条　骚乱罪和其他扰乱公共秩序罪;喧嚣的骚乱罪和容易引起骚乱的妨碍罪——任何在公共场所、政府机关或者部队引起严重骚乱,或者妨碍或者扰乱公众演出、仪式或者集会或者和平会议的,如果此行为不包括在本法第 131 条和第 132 条所规定之情形的,处以中间幅度的长期禁闭至最低幅度的监狱矫正和不超过 1000 比索之罚金。

对引起任何骚乱或者具有动乱特征的妨碍者,处以重一等级的刑罚。

如果骚乱或者妨碍是由 3 人以上携带武器者或者持有暴力工具所引起的,则认为是动乱的。

在集会、结社或公共场所为了叛乱或者骚乱而大声喊叫,或者陈列能煽动公共秩序骚乱的布告或者标志的,处以长期禁闭。

违反第 85 条最后一句之规定,对已被合法执行死刑者举行隆重的葬仪的,处以长期禁闭和不超过 200 比索之罚金。

第 154 条　非法使用出版方法罪和非法发表罪——对实施以下行为者,处以长期禁闭和 200 至 1000 比索之罚金。

1. 通过印刷、平版印刷或其他的出版方法出版或促成危害公共秩序或者导致国家利益和信用受到损害的虚假新闻出版的;

2. 通过同样手段或者言词、话语或者演讲怂恿违抗法律或者现任当局,或者对任何应受处罚的行为加以赞扬、证明其合法或者赞美的;

3. 未经正当授权或者正式出版前,恶意出版或者促使任何官方决议或者文件出版的;或

4. 印刷、出版或者分发或者促使无真正的印刷者名称,或者是匿名分类的书籍、小册子、杂志或者传单被印刷、出版或者分发的。

第 155 条　恐慌罪和公愤罪——对实施以下行为者,处以短期禁闭或者不超过 200 比索之罚金。

1. 任何在一都市或者公共场所开枪放炮、发射火箭、燃放爆竹或者引爆使其他可能引起恐吓或者危险之爆炸物的；

2. 鼓动或者积极参加大嚷闹或者其他侵犯另一集会或者有害于公共安宁的混乱集会的；

3. 在夜间闲逛或参加任何其他夜间娱乐活动而扰乱公共安宁的；或

4. 醉酒或者其他的情形下，在公共场所引起骚动或者公愤的，且这种情形不适用于第153条的规定。

第156条　越狱逃跑罪——通过暴力、胁迫、贿赂等方式脱逃监狱或者羁押场所或者帮助囚犯脱逃的，处以最高幅度的长期禁闭至最低幅度的监狱矫正。使用其他手段脱逃的，处以长期禁闭。

如果囚犯是在上述场所外通过对看守者进行袭击而脱逃的，处以最低幅度的上述刑罚。

第六章　逃避服刑罪

第157条　逃避服刑罪——任何在服终审判决刑罚期间通过逃跑来逃避服刑的，处以中间幅度和最高幅度的监狱矫正。如果这些逃避或者逃跑是通过破坏门、窗、大门、墙、屋顶或者地面，或使用撬锁工具、备用钥匙、欺骗、暴力或者胁迫，或是与其他囚犯或者刑罚机构雇员共谋而得逞的，处以最高幅度的监狱矫正。

第158条　骚乱、火灾、地震或其他灾难时逃避服刑罪——在因火灾、地震、爆炸或者其他类似灾难而引起的混乱时，或者在其所没有参加的暴乱期间，通过逃离其应该被羁押的刑罚机构而逃避服刑的罪犯，如果不在总统发布通告宣布灾难已结束之后48小时内向有关当局自首的，增长其原判刑罚所剩刑期的1/5的刑期，但最长不得超过6个月。

罪犯在前款规定之情形下，在总统发布通告宣布48小时内向有关当局自首的罪犯，有权按本法第98条规定减刑。

第159条　其他逃避服刑罪——获得总统批准的有条件赦免之罪犯，违反了任一赦免条件的，处以最低幅度的监狱矫正。然而，如果罪犯被赦免之刑期超过6年的，将继续执行未执行完毕的原判刑罚。

第七章　服刑期间犯另一新罪

第160条　服刑期间犯新罪及其刑罚——除第62条第5款之规定以

外,任何在被终审宣判有罪以后,在服刑前或服刑期间又犯罪的,处以最高幅度的新罪的法定刑。

本条所涉的这类罪犯不是惯犯的,如果原判刑罚已经执行完毕,或者在70周岁以后才能执行完毕的,在其70周岁时将获得赦免,除非因其品行或其他情形不应得到这种宽恕。

第四编 危害公共利益罪

第一章 伪 造 罪

第一节 伪造菲律宾政府图章、总统签字或者印章罪

第161条 伪造菲律宾政府国玺罪、伪造总统签字或印章罪——对伪造菲律宾政府之国玺或总统之签字或印章的,处以无期徒刑。

第162条 使用伪造的签字或者伪造的图章或印章罪——故意使用前条所述的伪造的图章或者伪造的签名或印章的,处以监禁。

第二节 伪造货币罪

第163条 制造、进口、使用假币罪——任何制造、进口或者使用假币或者纵容造伪币者或进口者的,按以下规定处罚:

1. 如果伪币是菲律宾银币合金或者是10分或10分以上面额的菲律宾中央银行硬币的,处以最低幅度和中间幅度的监狱矫正和不超过10000比索之罚金。

2. 如果是菲律宾较小币值的伪币或者是10分面额以下的菲律宾中央银行伪币的,处以最低幅度和中间幅度的监狱矫正和不超过2000比索的罚金。

3. 如果是当前外国流通的伪币,处以最低监狱矫正和不超过1000比索之罚金。(1965年6月19日通过的第4202号共和国法案修正)

第164条 毁损货币罪、进口和使用毁损的货币罪——毁损美国或者菲律宾合法流通的货币或者进口或者使用损坏的流通货币,或者纵容损坏者或者进口者的,处以最低幅度的监狱矫正和不超过2000比索之罚金。

第165条 无纵容之出售伪造的或者毁损的货币罪——虽没有前条规定之纵容行为,行为人意图使用而故意持有,或已实际使用伪造的或者毁损

的硬币的,处以比前条规定的刑罚轻一等级之刑罚。

第三节　伪造国库券或者银行票据、债务和有价证券罪;进口和使用伪造或伪造票据、债务和有价证券罪

第 166 条　伪造国库券或者银行票据或者其他可支付凭证罪;进口和使用仿造或者伪造的票据和凭证罪——仿造或者伪造国库券,或者银行票据,或证券,或其他债券和可支付的有价证券的和在债券和票据之伪造者或者进口者的默许下进口和使用的,按以下规定处罚:

1. 如果伪造或者变造美国或菲律宾债务或者证券的,则处以最低幅度的有期徒刑和不超过 10000 比索的罚金。

"美国或者菲律宾债券或者证券"是指美国或菲律宾授权的政府官员签发的所有的公债、债务凭证、国家银行票据、辅券、存款单、凭单、支票或现金汇票、以及任何美国国会或者菲律宾议会的法律规定已经或者可能发行的任何有金额面值的价值代表物。

2. 如果伪造或者变造的凭证是经法律正式授权的银行协会发行的流通票据的,则处以最高幅度的监禁和不超过 5000 比索的罚金。

3. 如果伪造或仿造之凭证是外国政府发行的凭证的,则处以中间的监禁和不超过 5000 比索之罚金。

4. 如果伪造或者变造的凭证属于被正式授权的外国银行发行的票据或者凭单的,则处以最低幅度的监禁和不超过 2000 比索之罚金。

第 167 条　伪造、进口和使用不可支付的票据罪——任何在伪造者或者进口者之默许下伪造、进口或者使用凭指示付款之票据或者其他不能支付给持票人的信用凭证的,处以中间幅度和最高监禁和不超过 6000 比索之罚金。

第 168 条　非法持有和使用伪造的国库券或者银行票据和其他信用凭证罪——除非行为属于任一上述条款规定的情形之一,任何人意图使用本节所列的任何虚假的或者已伪造的凭证而故意使用或者持有的,处以比上述条款所规定的刑罚轻一等级之刑罚。

第 169 条　伪造罪的犯罪方法——本节提到的伪造罪通过以下方法犯罪:

1. 提供国库券或者银行票据或者任何可支付的或者凭指示的凭证,或表面是真实票据。

2. 通过任何方法涂擦、替换、伪造或者变造凭证中的数据、字母、文字或签字。

第四节 伪造立法、公用、商业或者秘密文件罪和伪造无线电、电报、电话信息罪

第 170 条 伪造立法文件罪——未经特别授权而修改任何议案、决议，或者立法议会或者任何省政委员会或者市政委员会颁布或通过的或者正在审查中的法律法规的，处以最高幅度监狱矫正和不超过 6000 比索之罚金。

第 171 条 政府官员、雇员、公证人或者牧师伪造罪——对任何利用其职务便利之政府官员、雇员或者公证人，通过以下途径伪造文件的，处以监禁和不超过 5000 比索的罚金：

1. 伪造或者模仿笔迹、签名或者红标题的；

2. 导致事实上并未参与任何行为或者程序的人员看似已参与该行为或者程序的；

3. 将实施者之行为归因于给行为或者程序的参加者的；

4. 陈述事实时作出虚假陈述的；

5. 更改真实日期的；

6. 对真实文件进行更改或添加而改变其意思的；

7. 原文件不存在时，出具鉴别文件来证明其为原件的复印件，或所证明的复印件与原文件相反或者相矛盾的；或

8. 在会谈记录、登记簿或者任职文件中添加有关的文件或者批注的。

牧师犯任何本条以上各项所列的罪行，有关的这些伪造的档案或者文件可能影响国民的法律地位的，将处以同样的刑罚。

第 172 条 个人伪造和使用伪造的文件罪——对实施以下行为者，处以中间幅度和最高幅度的监狱矫正和不超过 5000 比索之罚金：

1. 任何个人在公用或者官方文件，或者换文，或者其他形式的商业文件实施前条所列之各伪造行为的；

2. 任何人实施前条所列之伪造行为造成第三方或者意图造成第三方损害的。

任何以造成损害为目的，在刑事诉讼或者在他人的损害赔偿中，故意提交前条或者本条前两项所包括的虚假文件证据，处以前述刑罚低一级的刑罚。

第 173 条 伪造和使用无线电、海底电报、电报和电话信息罪——任何

从事无线电、电缆或者电话信息接收的政府或者私营公司的职员或者雇员，或者有关从事此类服务的人员，发射虚假的无线电、电报或者电话之系统信息的，处以中间幅度和最高幅度的监狱矫正。

任何人使用这种虚假的急件损害或者意图损害第三方的利益的，处以低一等级的刑罚。

第五节　伪造诊断书、荣誉证书或者服务证书或者类似证书罪

第174条　伪造诊断书、荣誉证书或者其他服务证书罪——对实施下列行为者，处以最高幅度长期禁闭至最低幅度的监狱矫正和不超过1000比索之罚金：

1. 任何利用其职业关系出具虚假证明的医生；
2. 任何出具虚假的荣誉证书、服务证书，或良好品行证明书或者类似证明的公职人员。

对任何故意伪造不属于以上两款规定的其他证明书的个人，处以长期禁闭。

第175条　使用伪造证明书罪——任何故意使用前条所列的各种证明书的，处以短期禁闭。

第六节　制造、进口和持有打算用于伪造犯罪之器具或者工具罪

第176条　制造和持有用于伪造的器具或者工具罪——任何制造或者进口打算用于本章前几节所涉及的伪造或者仿冒犯罪的印章、硬模、标记或其他器具或者工具的，处以中间幅度和最高幅度的监狱矫正和不超过10000比索之罚金。

任何意图使用而持有前款规定之器具或者工具的，处以比前款规定的刑罚轻一等级之刑罚。

第二章　其他伪造罪

第一节　冒用权力、职衔、头衔罪和不正当使用名字、制服和徽章罪

第177条　冒用权力或者官方职能罪——未经法律授权，任何人故意

假冒菲律宾政府或者外国政府机构官员、代理人、代表,以及伪称官衔并行使菲律宾政府、外国政府或者代理机构赋予该职位官员之职能的行为,应处以中间幅度的监狱矫正。

第 178 条　使用假名罪和隐瞒真实姓名罪——为隐藏罪行、规避刑罚或者引发灾害而公开使用假名的,处以 6 个月禁闭和不超过 500 比索之罚金。

任何隐瞒真实姓名或者其他个人情况的,处以 6 个月禁闭或者不超过 200 比索之罚金。

第 179 条　非法使用制服或者徽章罪——公开地和不正当地利用徽章、制服、穿戴某些机关或阶层特定的职业装,应处以长期禁闭。

第二节　伪　证　罪

第 180 条　作不利被告之伪证罪——在刑事案件中作对被告不利之伪证的应追究刑事责任:

1. 使被告被判处死刑的,处以有期徒刑;
2. 使被告被判处有期徒刑或者无期徒刑的,处以监禁;
3. 使被告被判处任何其他重刑的,处以监狱矫正;
4. 使被告被判处矫正刑、罚金或者宣告无罪的,处长期禁闭。

如果属于本条前款第三项和第四项所规定的情形,还应处以 1000 比索以下的罚金。

第 181 条　作有利被告之伪证罪——在刑事案件中,作对被告有利之伪证之行为的,处以最高幅度的长期禁闭至最低幅度的监狱矫正;如被起诉的重罪应被处以重刑的,附加处以 1000 比索以下的罚金,其他情形下附加处以长期禁闭。

第 182 条　民事伪证罪——任何在民事案件中被发现作伪证的,争论数额超过 5000 比索的,处以最低幅度的监狱矫正并处不超过 6000 比索的罚金;争论数额没超过 5000 比索或者难以估计的,处以最高幅度的长期禁闭至最低幅度的监狱矫正并处不超过 1000 比索的罚金。

第 183 条　其他情形的伪证罪和正式宣誓场合的伪誓罪——任何故意作出前三条规定以外的誓言或者宣誓书形式的虚假陈述的行为人,在有关执行案件(法律要求宣誓的案件)宣誓程序的人员前证明任何主要事实的,应处以最高幅度的长期禁闭至最低幅度的监狱矫正。

任何人在正式宣誓场合代替宣誓的,将犯本条或者前三条所规定的罪行,应分别按其相应的规定处罚。

第184条 提供虚假证人证言——任何故意在司法程序或者法定程序中提供虚假证人或者虚假证言的,构成伪证罪并分别按本节各相应规定予以处罚。

第三章 欺 诈 罪

第一节 密谋罪、垄断罪和联合罪

第185条 公开拍卖中密谋罪——任何以获得财物或者承诺为对价而放弃参与公开拍卖,以及任何为降低拍卖物价格而通过威胁、赠送、承诺或者其他欺诈行为使竟买者不能参加拍卖会的,处以最低幅度监狱矫正并处拍卖物价值之10%至50%的罚金。

第186条 贸易管制中垄断罪和联合罪。对犯以下罪行者,单处或者并处最低幅度的监狱矫正或200至600比索之罚金:

1. 任何形成同行业企业之合同或者协议、共谋或联合参与托拉斯或者其他垄断性组织、限制商业贸易或者通过人为手段阻碍市场自由竞争的;

2. 任何垄断商品、贸易或商业物品,或者为调整价格而联合他人对商品或者物品进行垄断,通过散布虚假信息或利用其他商品来抑制市场自由竞争的;

3. 商品或货物的制造者、生产者或者加工者或者进口商,不管其是负责人还是代理商、批发商或者零售商,与该商品或货物的生产、制造、加工、装配或者进口人员联合、共策阴谋或以任何方式达成一致协议的,或者为了让不当交易变为合法商业或者让菲律宾群岛某地之市场价格上涨或者为制造、生产、加工、装配此类商品或者将其引进行菲律宾群岛或者为在生产过程中使用这类商品或者货物品而与其他行业者联合,共策阴谋或达成一致的。

如果上述犯罪行为影响粮食、燃油或者其他主要生活必需品的,处以最高幅度的监禁;如果已经开始实施上述联合行为,处以中间幅度的监禁。

因前述条款中所指的合同或者联合行为而获得的财产,一律没收归菲律宾政府。

上述犯罪主体为法人或者团体、在非律宾的外国法人或者团体的负责人和其代理人或代表故意允许或者不阻止该犯罪行为的,以主犯论处。

第二节　工商业欺诈罪

第187条　进口或者处置假冒商标商品或者金、银或者其他贵重金属或者其合成金属制成品罪——对任何故意进口、出售、转让标有印花、商标、标记的金、银或者其他贵重金属或者合成金属制成物品,而不标明其实际的等级或质量的,单处或者并处监狱矫正或者200至1000比索的罚金。

雕刻、打印、压印、粘贴或者粘附在物品上的印花、商标、标签或者标志的,如果金制品的其余部分纯度比所标明的纯度少了1/2克拉以上时,或银制品的其余部分纯度比所标明的纯度少了4‰克拉以上时,被认为不能说明其真实纯度。但对于黄金制成的表壳和餐具,其黄金纯度不得少于上述标志所示之纯度的3‰克拉。

第188条　替换、更换商标、商号或者服务标志罪——对犯以下罪行者,单处或者并处最低幅度监狱矫正或者50至2000比索之罚金;

1. 用其他生产商、经销商的商号或商标,或者用仿制的商号或商标代替真正生产商或经销商的商品商标并出售的;

2. 明知前项所述商品的商号或者商标是被骗取使用,仍出售或为出售而提供此类商品的;

3. 在销售或者服务广告中,使用、替换成他人服务标志或者仿制他人服务标志的;

4. 明知是某人使用的商号、商标或服务标志,行为人仍为他人印刷、平版印刷或者用其他方法复制这些标志或者其仿造品,使其能在本人所有或者与出售相关的商品,或者服务广告上欺诈使用这些标志。

此处所称商号或者商标是指为了让公众区分商号或商标的使用者和拥有者,作为广告、招牌、标签、招贴或者其他用途而使用的单词或词语、名字、名称、符号、徽章、标记、图案或者其组合。

此处所指的服务标志是指在销售或者服务广告中用来识别某人的服务并且与他人服务相区别的一种标志,包括但不限于标志、名字、符号、牌号、标语、个人姓名和无线电或其他广告中的区别性特征。

第189条　不正当竞争罪,欺诈注册商标、商号或者服务标志,欺诈性原产地标志和虚假说明书——对下列行为按上一条的规定的刑罚处罚:

1. 在不正当竞争中和为欺骗或者欺诈另一合法交易或大众,出售与其他生产商或经销商外形相似产品,该产品与他人产品相似,或者产品的包装、图案、代码或者其他特征与他人产品相似,从而可能导致公众误信所售商品是实际的生产商或者经销商所提供的;或者基于相同之目的,给予他人实施此行为提供条件的;除非基于相同之目的,实际的生产商或者经销商允许他人出售。

2. 在商品、服务、集装箱或者货物集装箱上粘贴、提供、添加、使用虚假标志、虚假说明书或者虚假陈述并出售此类商品和服务的。

3. 任何通过虚假或者欺骗性的口头或者书面之陈述或者声明或者通过其他手段从专利局或者任何其他以后依法确定的机构获得商号、商标或者服务标志的注册或者登记,或者使其本人成为所有者。

第五编　有关鸦片和其他禁止毒品罪

第190条　持有、配制和使用禁止性毒品罪和经营鸦片烟馆罪——对实施下列行为者,处以中间幅度的长期禁闭至最低幅度监狱矫正和300至1000比索之罚金:

1. 未经法律授权,任何持有、配制、管理或者其他方式使用禁止性毒品的。

此处“禁止性毒品”指包括鸦片、可卡因、α-优卡因和β-优卡因、印度大麻,或者其生成物和所有其配制物,和其他天然的或者人工的作为麻醉性物质能引起生理反应的毒品。

“鸦片”包括各种类、各性质的鸦片,无论是天然还是加工的;其废料之灰末;麻醉配制物;吗啡或者任何鸦片生化碱,含有鸦片、吗啡或者任何种类鸦片成分之配制品,也包括鸦片叶或鸦片叶的包装材料,无论用来配制与否。

“印度大哈希什麻”在不同的地方被称为大麻物、大麻脂、美国大麻、哈希什、大麻叶、印度瓜子麻和印度大麻,包括各种类、各性质的印度大麻,不管是干的或新鲜的,雌花枝上顶端的花或果、其树脂未被榨取的大麻植物,包括其他各地不同品种的用作手卷大麻烟,树脂,榨取汁,酊剂或其他诸如此类之物。

麻醉性毒品是指使人的大脑处于一种无知觉和忧郁迟钝的幻觉状态,并可能上瘾的一种毒品。

2. 违法经营任何形式的吸毒场所的。

第191条　管理、看管鸦片烟馆罪——对以下行为者,处以长期禁闭和100至300比索之罚金:

1. 违法鸦片烟馆的任何管理者和看管者；

2. 除前条规定的以外的人员有意地参观上述的鸦片烟馆的。

第 192 条　进口和出售禁止性毒品罪——进口任何禁止性毒品至菲律宾的,处以中间幅度和最高幅度的监狱矫正和 300 至 500 比索的罚金。

非法出售或者提供禁止性毒品给他人的,处以相同的刑罚。

第 193 条　非法持有鸦片烟具或其他用于吸食禁止性毒品的用具罪——未经法律授权,持有鸦片烟具或者其他为吸食、注射、提供或者使用鸦片或者禁止性毒品而使用的工具的,处以长期禁闭和不超过 500 比索之罚金。

非法持有鸦片烟具或者其他用于吸食禁止性毒品的用具的,将作为持有者使用上述毒品之行为的初步证据。

第 194 条　给病人开不必要的鸦片处方罪——医生为身体状况不需要使用鸦片之病人开鸦片处方的,单处或并处监狱矫正和 300 至 10000 比索的罚金。

第六编　危害公共道德犯罪

第一章　游戏罪和赌博罪

第 195 条　赌博罪——(a)对下列行为,处以长期禁闭或者不超过 200 比索之罚金;如果是累犯的,处以长期禁闭或者 200 至 6000 比索之罚金:

1. 除了以下(b)项和(c)项规定之外,以其他任何方式直接或者间接参加纸牌赌博,花档或者其他形式的彩票、波里希彩票、银行业或者比率游戏、赛狗赌博,或者结果完全或者主要靠几率和风险的其他游戏,或者赌注由金钱、有价值物品或价值之代表物构成的游戏;或者利用或使用其他自创的机械或者工具决定输家或者赢家的金钱、价值物品或价值代表物的。

2. 任何故意允许前款规定的赌博活动在其拥有和控制下的建筑物、船只或者其他交通工具上之居住或者非居住地进行的,如进行赌博活动之地是众所周知或者在此经常进行非法赌博的,对其犯罪分子处以最高幅度的本条规定的刑罚。

(b) 对花档等类似赌博的经营者、指挥者和银行业负责人,处以最高幅度监狱矫正刑。

(c) 无合法目的,行为人故意将属于或者附属于用于花档等类似赌博中任何形式的文字、数字、符号、记号,自制到其发球和抽奖的名单、纸牌内的,处以中间幅度的监狱矫正。

第 196 条　进口、出售和持有彩票或者彩票广告罪——任何从外国或者外港进口彩票或者彩票广告至菲律宾,或者在进口者的默许下出售或者分发彩票或者彩票广告的,由法院决定单处或者并处最高幅度的长期禁闭至最低幅度的监狱矫正或者 200 至 2000 比索之罚金。

任何明知并故意持有彩票或彩票广告的,或者不是经过进口者默许而出售或者分发彩票或彩票广告的,由法院决定单处或者并处短期禁闭或者不超过 200 比索之罚金。

在菲律宾内持有彩票或彩票广告之行为是意图出售、分发或者使用彩票或彩票广告的初步证据。

第 197 条　体育竞赛中的赌博罪——任何对拳击或者其他体育比赛结果以金钱或者其他有价之物或者价值代表物下赌注的,单处或并处长期禁闭或者 200 比索以下的罚金。

第 198 条　非法赛马罪——对法律允许的赛马期以外赛马的,单处或并处长期禁闭或者不超过 200 比索的罚金。在同样情况下,对为下赛马赌注或者实现利润而经营或者使用赛马赌金计算器或者其他仪器或者设备的,单处或者并处长期禁闭或 200 至 2000 比索之罚金。

因为本条规定之目的,在同一天同一地点举行赛马的,以并合罪论处;如果是合伙、法人或者社团犯此罪的,对允许或者故意默许犯罪的负责人和董事长或者经理,以主犯论处。

第 199 条　非法斗鸡罪——对下列行为,由法院决定单处或者并处长期禁闭或者不超过 200 比索的罚金:

1. 以金钱或者有价物为赌注直接或者间接参加斗鸡的,或者在法律规定以外的时间组织斗鸡赌博的。
2. 在未经许可的斗鸡场直接或者间接参加斗鸡活动的。

第二章　侵犯公序良俗罪

第 200 条　严重诽谤罪——通过实施不属于本法其他条款特别规定的严重诽谤性行为侵犯公序良俗的,处以长期禁闭和谴责。

第 201 条　宣传不道德的学说罪、出版和展览淫秽作品罪及有伤风化表演罪——对下列行为,单处或并处监禁或者 6000 至 12000 比索之罚金:

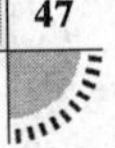

1. 公开阐述或者宣传与社会公共道德背道而驰之学说的；

2. (a) 以任何形式出版的淫秽文学作品之作者；出版此类淫秽文学作品之编辑；和出售此类作品的所有者或者经营者；

(b) 在剧院、展览会、电影院或者其他地方，展出下流的或者不道德的剧本、场景、动作或表演，无论是现场还是电影形式，根据道德标准规定之不同，包括：(1) 赞扬罪犯或者宽容犯罪的；(2) 只为满足暴力、情欲或色情市场的；(3) 侵犯种族或者宗教的；(4) 趋向于唆使他人交易和使用禁止性毒品的；(5) 违反法律、公共秩序、道德、优良习俗、政策、法规、政令和法令的；

3. 出售、分发或者展览违背道德准则的电影、图片、雕刻、雕塑或者文学作品的。(第960号和第969号总统令修正)

第202条　流浪罪和卖淫罪——以下为流浪者：

1. 任何无明确的谋生手段，且具有从事劳动的能力但不专心从事自己的合法职业的；

2. 任何被发现闲荡在公共或半公共建筑物或场所，或游荡在乡下或者街上而无明确谋生手段的；

3. 任何在家里恶名昭彰的游手好闲者或者放荡者；流氓、皮条客以及与经常与妓女联合的人；

4. 任何不属于本法其他条文规定之情形的，被发现无任何合法和正当目的而游荡在任何他人的住所或者非住宿地的；

5. 妓女。

根据本条，以获得金钱和利益为目的，经常从事性交易和有伤风化行为的女性为妓女。

任何被发现犯本条规定之罪行的，处以短期禁闭或者不超过200比索之罚金。如果是累犯的，由法院决定单处或者并处中间幅度的长期禁闭至最低幅度的监狱矫正或者200至2000比索的罚金。

第七编　渎职犯罪

第一章　一般规定

第203条　公职人员的范围——为适用于本编和前面各编之规定，任何直接依照法律规定、公众选举或者当局任命而参与行使菲律宾政府公共职能以及在其各部门之各层和各级作为雇员、代理人或者下属官员而行使公共职能的都是公职人员。

第二章　渎职罪和滥用职权罪

第一节　玩忽职守罪

第 204 条　故意枉法裁判罪——对任何在由其裁决之案件中故意作出枉法裁判的审判人员，处以监禁和终身完全剥夺权利。

第 205 条　疏忽大意枉法裁判罪——对任何在由其作出裁判之案件中，因为不可免责的疏忽或者无知作出明显不公判决的审判人员，处以长期禁闭和临时剥夺特别权利。

第 206 条　不公中间裁决罪——任何审判人员故意作出不公的中间裁决或者判决，处以最低幅度的长期禁闭和中止职务；如果其行为是不可免责的疏忽或者无知行为，并且中间裁决明显不公的，则中止执行其刑罚。

第 207 条　恶意延迟执行判决罪——对任何故意延迟执行判决的审判人员，处以最低幅度的监狱矫正。

第 208 条　失职不起诉罪和默许犯罪罪——因失职而有意避免违法者被起诉或者默许犯罪行为的政府公职人员或者司法人员，处以最低幅度的监狱矫正和中止公职。

第 209 条　律师或者法律顾问背信泄秘罪——对任何因恶意严重失职或者不可宽恕的疏忽或者无知而造成当事人利益受损的，或者泄露其职权范围内的当事人的秘密的律师或者法律顾问（法律事务代理人），除正当的管理行为以外，单处或并处最低幅度监狱矫正或者 200 至 1000 比索之罚金。

在同一案件中担任辩护律师或已知当事人的秘密，未经原当事人同意而担任案件中对方当事人的辩护律师的律师或者法律顾问（法律事务代理人），处相同的刑罚。

第二节　贿　赂　罪

第 210 条　直接受贿罪——公职人员在履行相关公职时，亲自或者通过他人中介接受他人财物、许诺、礼物或者礼品，允许他人实施犯罪行为的，处以中间幅度和最高幅度的监禁和不少于所收礼物价值额之罚金，如有前科，除对其罪行处以刑罚以外，还处以不少于所收礼物价值额三倍的罚金。

如果公职人员已经接受他人财物，但其允许实施的行为不构成犯罪的，处以前款规定之刑罚；如果该行为还未完成的，处以中间幅度的监狱矫正和不超过所收礼物价值额两倍的罚金。

如因接收了礼物或被承诺给予礼物而抑制公职人员实施其工作本职的，对公职人员处以最高幅度监狱矫正和不少于接收礼物之价值额3倍的罚金。

除前几款规定的处罚外，对犯罪分子还应处以临时剥夺特别权利的处罚。

本条前几款之规定同样适用于法官助理、仲裁员、鉴定人员和诉讼委员、专家或其他履行公共职责之人员。（1985年6月10日第872号BP修正）

第211条　间接受贿罪——任何利用职务形成的便利收受他人财物的公职人员，对其处以中间幅度和最高幅度的监狱矫正和谴责。（1985年6月10日第872号BP修正）

第212条　对公职人员行贿罪——任何进行提供、承诺或者赠与以上各条规定的财物或者礼物的，除不处以剥夺权利和中止公职以外，其他刑罚与前几条规定相同。

第三章　公职人员诈骗罪和非法勒索和交易罪

第213条　公职人员骗取公共财产和类似犯罪——对任何实施下列行为的公职人员，单处和并处中间幅度的监狱矫正至最低幅度的监禁或者200至10000比索的罚金：

1. 在职权范围内处理与他人进行涉及公共财产和公共资金的供应物品、签订合同，或者调整或结账过程中，与有关当事人或者投机商订约或通过其他手段欺骗政府的；

2. 被委托收取税款、许可证税、费或者其他关税的公职人员犯罪或者有以下行为或者失职的：

（a）直接或者间接要求对方支付与法律法规不相符的或者大于规定的数额的税费的。

（b）故意不主动出具法律规定的征收税、费的收据的。

（c）直接或者间接征收或者接受法律规定以外的其他物品作为给付税、费的。

犯罪分子是国家税务局或者是海关署的工作人员或雇员的，适用于《行政法》之规定。

第214条　公职人员其他诈骗罪——公职人员利用职务便利实施本法第二册第十编第六章规定所列之诈骗行为的，除处以本法第二册第十编第六章规定的刑罚之外，还处以最高幅度的有期剥夺特别权利至终身剥夺特别权利。

第215条　非法交易罪——任何在任职期间内的公职人员，在其权限范围内直接或间接从其进行的交易或买卖活动中获取利益的，单处或并处最高幅度的监狱矫正或者200至1000比索的罚金。

第216条　公职人员获取非法利益罪——任何直接或间接利用职务便利介入合同或交易而从中获利的公职人员，单处或并处中间幅度的长期禁闭至最低幅度的监狱矫正或200至1000比索的罚金。

本条规定同样适用于担任评估、分配或裁定财产的合同或谈判的专家、仲裁员和私人会计师和有财产保管权之看管者和执行者。

第四章　贪污公款或公共财物罪

第217条　贪污公款或公共财物罪及贪污罪的推定——任何负责管理公款或公共财物的公职人员，利用职务便利挪用、侵吞或盗用公款或公共财物，或者由于放弃或疏忽同意，允许他人将全部或部分公款或公共财物据为己有，或者其他挪用或者贪污公款或公共财产犯罪的，应受处罚：

1. 如果挪用或者贪污的价值金额没有超过200比索的，处以中间幅度和最高幅度的监狱矫正。

2. 如果挪用或者贪污的价值金额超过200比索少于600比索的，处以最低幅度和中间幅度的监禁。

3. 如果挪用或者贪污的价值金额超过600比索少于1200比索的，处以最高幅度的监禁至中间幅度的有期徒刑。

4. 如果挪用或者贪污的价值金额超过1200比索少于24000比索的，处以中间幅度和最高幅度的有期徒刑；如果挪用或者贪污的价值金额超过24000比索的，处以最高幅度的有期徒刑至无期徒刑。

对任何挪用公款者都处以终身剥夺特别权利和与被贪污公款数目或财产价值相等的罚金。

公职人员未能根据授权人的要求提供其管理的公款或财产，可视为该公职人员私人挪用公款或财产的初步证据。（第1060号共和国法案已修

正）

第 218 条　责任人员不提交账目罪——任何在职、因辞职或其他原因不在职的公职人员，法律规定其必须向国家审计人员或省审计人员提交账目，却在规定期满后两个月内没有提交的，单处或者并处最低幅度的监狱矫正或 200 至 6000 比索的罚金。

第 219 条　公职人员出国之前不提交账目罪——任何未从国家审计人员手中得到表明其账目无问题的证明而非法离开或准备离开菲律宾的公职人员，单处或者并处长期禁闭或 200 至 1000 比索的罚金。

第 220 条　非法将公款或公共财产挪作他用罪——公职人员在其职权范围内，擅自将公款或公共财物挪作其他公用的，处以最低幅度的监狱矫正，如果该挪用行为给公务造成损失或妨碍的，处以被挪用的价值金额之1/2 至 1 倍的罚金。在前述任何一种情况下，都处以有期剥夺特别权利。

若对公务行为没有引起损害与妨碍的，处以被挪用的价值金额之5% 至50% 的罚金。

第 221 条　不上交公款或公共财产罪——任何有义务将其持有的公款或公共财产上交给政府而未上交的公职人员，处以长期禁闭并处应上交之价值金额的 5% 至 25% 的罚金。

本条适用于任何拒绝实施主管当局的命令而未将其监管或保管下的公款或公共财物送交的公职人员。

如果财产价值 50 比索以上的，其罚金按财产价值标准来分等级。

第 222 条　前述规定所包括的工作人员——本章各条之规定适用于任何负责国家、省或市的资金、税收或财产的个人和属于政府当局扣押、没收、保管的资金、财产的管理人或保管人，即使该财产属于个人也同样适用。

第五章　公职人员不忠于职守罪

第一节　监管不忠罪

第 223 条　纵容或同意脱逃罪——公职人员同意其监管或负责的被监管人员脱逃的，应追究刑事责任：

1. 如果逃犯是已终审判处刑罚的，处以中间幅度或最高幅度的监狱矫正和最高幅度的有期剥夺特别权利至终身剥夺特别权利。

2. 如果逃犯未被最后定罪，但因犯罪或违反法规或政府规定而被拘禁的，处以最低幅度的监狱矫正和有期剥夺特别权利。

第 224 条　过失致被监管人脱逃罪——由于负责运输或监管的公职人员的过失导致被监管人员逃脱的,对上述人员处以最高幅度的长期禁闭至最低幅度的监狱矫正和有期剥夺特别权利。

第 225 条　其他监管人员致被监管人员逃脱——任何被委托运送或监管被监管人员的个人,犯前两条规定之罪行的,处以比公职人员轻一等级的刑罚。

第二节　保管公文不忠罪

第 226 条　转移、隐藏、毁坏公文罪——公职人员转移、毁坏或隐藏公文或受委托管理的官方文件的,应追究刑事责任:

1. 导致第三方或公共利益遭受严重损失的,处以监禁和不超过 1000 比索的罚金。

2. 对第三方或公共利益未造成严重损失的,处以最低幅度和中间幅度的监狱矫正并处不超过 1000 比索的罚金。

前面两种情形下,都处以最高幅度的有期剥夺特别权利至终身剥夺特别权利的附加刑。

第 227 条　公职人员撕毁封条罪——任何负责保管公文或被有关权力机关密封的财产的公职人员,撕毁或同意他人撕毁封条的,并处最低幅度和中间幅度的监狱矫正、有期剥夺特别权利和不超过 2000 比索的罚金。

第 228 条　私开密封公文罪——除上述各条规定的公职人员之外的其他公职人员,未经正式授权,擅自打开或允许他人打开自己受委托保管的密封公文、文件或物品的,并处监禁、有期剥夺特别权利和不超过 2000 比索的罚金。

第三节　泄露秘密罪

第 229 条　公职人员泄露秘密罪——公职人员泄露其职权范围内的秘密,或不正当的提供其管理但不许公开的文件或复印件的,如果泄露秘密或提供文件的行为对公共利益造成损害的,处以中间幅度和最高监幅度的监狱矫正、有期剥夺特别权利和不超过 2000 比索的罚金。没有造成损害的,则处以最低幅度监狱矫正、有期剥夺特别权利和不超过 50 比索的罚金。

第 230 条　公职人员泄露他人秘密罪——公职人员泄露因其职权而获得的他人秘密的,处以长期禁闭和不超过 1000 比索的罚金。

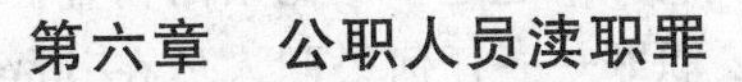

第六章　公职人员渎职罪

第一节　违　抗　罪

第231条　公开违抗罪——司法官员或执行官员公开拒绝执行上级机关在其司法权限内合法制作和颁布的判决、决定或命令的，以中间幅度的长期禁闭至最低幅度的监狱矫正、有期剥夺特别权利和不超过1000比索的罚金。

第232条　不服从、延期执行上级命令罪——任何公职人员有理由要求延期执行上级命令，上级未批准后仍不执行上级命令的，处以最低幅度和中间幅度的监狱矫正和终身剥夺特别权利。

第233条　拒绝协助罪——有关当局的要求提供合作而不提供的公职人员，如果因其不作为而导致公共利益或第三方利益遭受严重损害的，处以中间幅度的长期禁闭至最低幅度的监狱矫正、终身剥夺特别权利和不超过1000比索的罚金；其他情形下处以中间幅度和最高幅度的长期禁闭和不超过500比索的罚金。

第234条　拒绝履行所选任的公职罪——任何被公众选举担任公职的人员，无法定理由拒绝宣誓或拒绝履行上述公职的，单处或者并处长期禁闭或不超过1000比索的罚金。

第235条　虐待被监管人员罪——公职人员或者雇员对其负责矫正或处理的囚犯或拘留犯实施法律法规规定之外的刑罚，或对其实行酷刑或羞辱刑的，除对其身体造成伤害或损害应负刑事责任之外，还应处以中间幅度的长期禁闭至最低幅度的监狱矫正。

如虐待囚犯的目的是逼供或获取一些消息，则除对囚犯身体伤害和损害承担刑事责任以外，还应处以最低幅度的监狱矫正、有期剥夺特别权利和不超过500比索的罚金。

第二节　提前履行、延期履行和放弃公职罪

第236条　提前履行公职罪——任何未经宣誓或者获得法定合同而提前履行公职人员或雇员的职责与权力的，中止其公职直到其履行正式手续时，并处以200至500比索的罚金。

第237条　延期履行公职罪——公职人员在法律、法规、特别条款规定的期限之外继续履行其公共职责和权力的，处以最低幅度的监狱矫正、最低

幅度的有期剥夺特别权利和不超过500比索的罚金。

第238条　放弃公职罪——任何公职人员在其辞职被正式批准之前不履行职责而对公务工作造成损害的,处以长期禁闭。

为了逃避预防、控诉或处罚第二册第三编第一章和本章第一节规定之犯罪而放弃公职的公职人员,处以最低幅度和中间幅度的监狱矫正,为了逃避对其他犯罪控诉或处罚而放弃公职的公职人员,处以长期禁闭。

第三节　篡夺权力和非法任职罪

第239条　篡夺立法权罪——公职人员在其权限之外制定任一一般法律法规,或试图废止某一法律或中止执行某一法律而侵犯政府立法机构之立法权的,处以最低幅度的监狱矫正、有期剥夺特别权利和不超过1000比索的罚金。

第240条　篡夺执行权罪——任何法官篡夺执行当局的执行权或故意阻碍执行当局行使执行权的,处以中间幅度的长期禁闭至最低幅度的监狱矫正。

第241条　篡夺司法权罪——任何政府执行部门的官员篡夺或故意阻碍法官在其有司法权限范围内作出的命令或者判决的执行的,处以中间幅度的长期禁闭至最低幅度的监狱矫正。

第242条　违反管辖权罪——任何公职人员在管辖权作出决定前,在法律要求其禁止诉讼程序后,仍继续进行的,处以长期禁闭和不超过500比索的罚金。

第243条　执行官对司法机关非法作出命令和要求罪——执行官对有关案件或事务享有专有管辖权的司法机关发出命令和提议的,处以长期禁闭和不超过500比索的罚金。

第244条　非法任命罪——任何公职人员故意任命或者委派缺乏法定资格条件的人员到公共机关任职的,处以长期禁闭和不超过1000比索的罚金。

第四节　滥用职权破坏贞操罪

第245条　滥用职权破坏贞操罪——在下列情形中,将被处以中间幅度或最高幅度的监狱矫正和有期剥夺特别权利:

1. 需要由其作出决定,或向上级提交报告或与上级商议的公职人员,对与未定事项有利害关系的女性提出或者进行不道德或下流的性爱行为的；

2. 直接负责囚犯或被捕人员的监管工作的看守人员或其他公职人员对其监管的女性提出或者进行不道德或下流的性爱行为的。

如果被要求的女性是在该看守人员或其他公职人员所监管下的人员之妻子、女儿、血亲或姻亲姐妹的，将被处以最低幅度或中间幅度的监狱矫正和有期剥夺特别权利。

第八编　侵犯人身罪

第一章　侵害生命罪

第一节　杀亲罪、谋杀罪、杀人罪

第 246 条　杀亲罪——杀害自己婚生或私生的父母或子女，或任何直系尊亲或直系卑亲属，或配偶的行为构成杀亲罪，处以无期徒刑至死刑。

第 247 条　特殊杀人罪或者伤害罪——当具有合法婚姻关系的一方发现其配偶与他人发生性行为而当场杀害或严重伤害任何其中一方或双方的，处以流放。

如果仅造成其他身体伤害时，将免于刑事处罚。

在同样情况下，此规定适用于父母对与其共同生活且未满 18 周岁的女儿和其诱奸者。

但任何促进和帮助其妻子或女儿卖淫或同意其配偶与他人通奸的情形不适用本条。

第 248 条　谋杀罪——行为人在第 246 条规定的情形之外杀害他人，如果犯罪伴有下列任何情形之一的属于谋杀，处以最高幅度的有期徒刑至死刑：

1. 行为人背信弃义，利用体力优势以及在其他武装分子的帮助下，或者采取手段削弱被害人的防护能力，或利用其他手段、利用他人使自己不受惩罚的。

2. 基于赏金、报酬或承诺而实施的。

3. 行为人通过决水、放火、投毒、爆炸、海难、使船只搁浅、火车出轨、袭击街车或火车、坠机来犯罪，或利用机动车辆以及利用其他大规模损耗和破坏的方法犯罪的。

4. 行为人在前项所列的灾难发生时实施犯罪行为，或在地震、火山爆发、暴风、流行性疾病或其他社会灾难发生时实施犯罪行为的。

5. 有明显预谋的。

6. 行为极端残酷、故意或残忍地加重受害人的痛苦,或虐待受害人及其尸体的。

第 249 条　杀人罪——行为人在第 246 条所规定的情形下杀害他人且没有出现前条所列的情形的,处以有期徒刑。

第 250 条　对杀亲受阻、谋杀受阻、杀人受阻的处罚——法院基于对案情的考虑,可以根据前述条款对杀亲受阻、谋杀受阻、杀人受阻者进行定罪和处罚,根据第 50 条的规定比应处的刑罚降一等级处罚。

法院基于对案情的考虑,对叛逆未遂、谋杀未遂、杀人未遂的罪犯,根据第 51 条的规定比应处的刑罚降一等级处罚。

第 251 条　混乱斗殴致死罪——多人在事先无组织无目的混乱情况下互相殴打和袭击,在斗殴过程中有人被杀死,具体杀人者无法确定,而致受害人重伤的行为人可以确定时,则对该行为人处以监禁。

如果致受害人重伤的行为人不能确定时,则所有对受害者施加过暴力的行为人将被处以中间幅度和最高幅度的监狱矫正。

第 252 条　混乱斗殴致伤罪——在前条所述的混乱斗殴中,如只导致其他斗殴者严重身体伤害且具体加害人无法确定时,则所有对受害者实施过暴力的行为人将被处以比适用于造成身体伤害的刑罚规定低一等级的刑罚。

如造成轻伤且具体加害人不明时,则所有对受害者实施过暴力的行为人将被处以 5 至 15 天的禁闭。

第 253 条　帮助自杀罪——为他人自杀提供帮助的,处以监禁,如果是其引导并帮助他人自杀则处以有期徒刑,如果自杀未遂的,处以中间幅度和最高幅度的长期紧闭。

第 254 条　持枪杀人罪——对持枪杀人者,处以最低幅度和中间幅度的监狱矫正,但如果该行为构成杀亲罪、谋杀罪、杀人罪的受阻或者未遂,或本法典规定之其他应处以更严重刑罚的犯罪的除外。

第二节　杀婴罪和堕胎罪

第 255 条　杀婴罪——任何杀害出生不到三天的婴儿将被处以第 246 条关于杀亲罪和第 248 条关于谋杀罪的刑罚。

母亲为了隐瞒本人的羞耻而实施上述行为的,处以中间幅度和最高幅

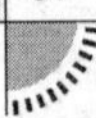

度的监狱矫正，如外祖父母，或外祖父或外祖母基于同样目的实施上述行为的，处以监禁。

第256条　故意堕胎罪——任何人故意导致堕胎的应追究刑事责任：

1. 对孕妇施加暴力导致堕胎的，处以有期徒刑。

2. 虽未施加暴力，但未经孕妇允许而使孕妇堕胎的，处以监禁。

3. 经孕妇允许帮助堕胎的，处以中间幅度和最高幅度的监狱矫正。

第257条　过失堕胎罪——行为人无堕胎故意，因实施暴力行为而导致堕胎的，处以最低幅度和中间幅度的监狱矫正。

第258条　自己堕胎罪或父母帮助堕胎罪——孕妇自己堕胎或允许他人帮助堕胎的，处以中间幅度和最高幅度的监狱矫正。

孕妇为隐瞒自己羞耻而堕胎，处以最低幅度和中间幅度的监狱矫正。

为隐瞒女儿的羞耻行为，孕妇的父母、父亲或母亲，经孕妇同意而帮助堕胎的，处以中间幅度和最高幅度送监狱矫正。

第259条　医生或接生员帮助堕胎罪和药物早产罪——医生或接生员利用其医学知识或技术实施堕胎或协助堕胎，处以最高幅度的第256条规定的相应刑罚。

药剂师在没有医生正确处方的情况下配药流产，处以长期禁闭和不超过1000比索的罚金。

第三节　决　斗　罪

第260条　决斗罪——在决斗中杀害对手的，处以有期徒刑。

如果只是造成对手身体伤害的，根据性质处以相应的刑罚。

其他虽未造成对手身体伤害之情形，处以长期禁闭。

整个事件的帮助者以共犯论处。

第261条　挑起决斗罪——任何挑战他人、煽动他人进行或接受挑起决斗，或因对方拒绝决斗而公然嘲弄和诋毁的，处以最低幅度监狱矫正。

第二章　伤　害　罪

第262条　伤残罪——故意毁伤他人，使他人丧失部分或者全部器官，或者毁伤他人重要生殖器官的，处以有期徒刑至无期徒刑。

其他故意造成他人伤残的，处以中间幅度和最高幅度的监禁。

第263条　重伤罪——伤害、殴打、袭击他人而造成他人重伤的构成重

伤罪,应追究刑事责任:

1. 致使被害人成为精神病人、弱智者、性无能者或盲人的,处以监禁;

2. 致使被害人丧失说话、听觉、嗅觉功能,或失去一眼、一手、一脚、一胳膊、一腿,或上述部分失去效用或丧失日常工作能力的,处以中间幅度和最高幅度的监狱矫正;

3. 致使被害人残疾或失去身体某一部分、身体某部分功能丧失、生病或 90 天以上不能从事日常工作的,处以最低幅度和中间幅度的监狱矫正;

4. 致使被害人生病或失去劳动能力 30 天以上的,处以最高幅度的禁闭至最低幅度的监狱矫正。

对第 246 条所列的人犯罪,或具有第 248 条规定之情形,符合本条第一项所包括的情形的,处以中间幅度和最高幅度的有期徒刑;符合本条第二项所包括的情形的,处以最高幅度的监狱矫正至最低幅度的监禁;符合本条第三项所包括的情形的,处以中间幅度和最高幅度的监狱矫正;符合本条第四项所包含的情形的,处以最低幅度和中间幅度的监狱矫正。

前款规定不适用于父母对孩子的严惩而造成的身体受伤的情形。

第 264 条　给予有害食品或饮料罪——无杀人之故意,故意给予他人有害食物、饮料,或利用对方的弱智或轻信实施该行为,造成他人严重身体伤害的,分别适用前条规定的刑罚。

第 265 条　次重伤害罪——造成被害人的伤害不属于前条所规定的伤害之内,但导致被害人丧失劳动能力 10 天以上或需要 10 天以上的医护期的,构成次重伤害罪,处以长期禁闭。

有明显的杀害或故意伤害被害人之动机,或对被害人有羞辱行为,而造成他人轻伤的,除处以长期禁闭之外,并处以不超过 500 比索的罚金。

行为人使其父母、直系尊亲、监护人、保护人、教师或军人或权力机关人员受轻微伤的,处以最低幅度和中间幅度的监狱矫正,如果权力机关人员实施同样行为时不构成此罪。

第 266 条　轻微伤害罪和虐待罪——对轻微伤害行为应追究刑事责任:

1. 造成被害人丧失劳动能力 1 至 9 天,或需要医护 1 至 9 天的,处以短期禁闭。

2. 既未对被害人的劳动能力造成影响也不需医护的,处以短期禁闭或不超过 20 比索的罚金和谴责。

3. 虐待他人而未造成任何伤害的,处以最低幅度的长期禁闭或不超过

50 比索的罚金。

第九编　侵犯人身自由与安全罪

第一章　侵犯人身自由罪

第 267 条　绑架罪和严重非法拘禁罪——绑架、拘禁或通过其他手段剥夺他人人身自由的，处以无期徒刑至死刑：

1. 绑架或拘禁期超过 5 天的。
2. 冒充政府当局犯此罪行的。
3. 对被绑架者或被拘禁者造成重伤或以杀害相威胁的。
4. 绑架或拘禁未成年人、女性或公职人员的。

不具有上述任何一种情形，但以从被绑架者或被拘禁者或其他人手中诈取赎金的为目的而实施绑架或拘禁行为的，同样处以死刑。

第 268 条　轻微非法拘禁罪——任何个人触犯上一条没有列举的各种情形的，处以有期徒刑。

为罪犯提供犯罪场所的，处相同刑罚。

未达到犯罪目的，于绑架或拘禁后的 3 天内，且在刑事诉讼程序启动之前主动释放被害人的罪犯，处以最低幅度和中间幅度的监禁和不超过 700 比索的罚金。

第 269 条　非法逮捕罪——未经法律授权或无合法理由，为将他人转交有关权力机关而对其进行逮捕或拘留的，处以长期禁闭和不超过 500 比索的罚金。

第 270 条　拐骗和不交还未成年人罪——未成年人的委托监护人故意不将未成年人交还其父母或监护人的，处以有期徒刑。

第 271 条　劝诱未成年人出走罪——任何劝诱未成年人离开其父母、监护人或委托监护人，对其处以监狱矫正和不超过 700 比索的罚金。

未成年人之父母犯前两条规定的罪行的，单处或并处长期禁闭或不超过 300 比索的罚金。

第 272 条　使他人沦为奴隶罪——任何为使他人成为奴隶而购买、出售、绑架或拘禁他人的，处以监禁和不超过 10000 比索的罚金。

为将被害人进行不道德交易而实施该行为的，处以最高幅度的刑罚。

第 273 条　剥削童工罪——任何以偿还未成年人直系尊亲、监护人或委托监护人债务为借口,违背未成年人意志而强迫其劳动的,处以最低幅度和中间幅度的监狱矫正和不超过500比索的罚金。

第274条　强迫他人劳动以偿还债务罪——为使强迫偿还债务而违背他人意愿强迫债务人作为家庭仆人或者农场劳动者为其工作的,处以最高幅度的有期禁闭至最低幅度的监狱矫正。

第二章　侵犯人身安全罪

第一节　遗弃无助者和剥削未成年人罪

第275条　遗弃处于危险中的人员罪和遗弃受害人罪——对下列行为,处以长期禁闭:

1. 发现处在无人居住地受伤或处于死亡危险之中的人员,能实施不伤及其身的救助行为却不实施救助行为的,但如果此行为构成更严重之犯罪情况除外。

2. 对意外受伤者未给予帮助或未提供援助的。

3. 发现未满7周岁的被遗弃的儿童,未将其交送至相关机构或其家人或未将其带到安全地方的。

第276条　遗弃未成年人罪——负有监护责任的监护人遗弃未满7周岁未成年人的,处以长期禁闭和不超过500比索的罚金。

如果该遗弃行为造成未成年人死亡的,对犯罪分子处以中间幅度和最高幅度的监狱矫正;如果其遗弃行为让未成年人生命处于危险之中的,则对犯罪分子处以最低幅度和中间幅度的监狱矫正。

当上述行为构成更严重的其他犯罪时,以上两款所包括的规定不影响其他的应处的刑罚。

第277条　委托监护人遗弃未成年人罪、父母不关心子女罪——任何对未成年人负有培养、教育义务的行为人,未经委托人同意或在委托人不在时,未经相关机关同意,将未成年交送公共机构或者他人的,处以长期禁闭刑和不超过500比索的罚金。

在生活和物质条件允许的情况下,却不让未成年人受教育的父母,处同样刑罚。

第278条　剥削未成年人罪——对下列犯罪处以最低幅度和中间幅度的监狱矫正和不超过500比索的罚金:

1. 使未满16周岁的未成年人实施危险的平衡表演、体力或柔功的。

2. 任何杂技演员、体操员、钢丝演员、野生动物驯养者、马戏团负责人或从事类似行业的人员,雇佣未满16周岁的非其亲生后代或其晚辈血亲的未成年人从事类似职业的。

3. 从事前项规定的各种行业的人员,雇佣自己的12周岁以下的晚辈血亲表演上述危险动作的。

4. 任何被委托照顾未满16周岁未成年人的直系尊亲、监护人、老师,无任何理由将未成年人交送给本条第二项规定之人员、流浪者或乞丐的。

如果是出于金钱、赔偿或承诺之目的而交送的,任何情形下处以最高幅度的刑罚。

对被定罪的监护人或保护人作为监护人或保护人之权利由政府取消;孩子之父母犯上述罪行的,由法院裁定暂时或终身剥夺其作为父母之权利。

5. 任何诱使16周岁以下的未成年人离开直系尊亲、监护人、保护人或老师,而让其从事本条第二项规定的工作的或让其陪伴流浪者或乞丐的。

第279条　对其他犯罪之额外刑——本章各条规定的刑罚的实施,不影响对同一行为人根据本法的规定的对其他犯罪进行定罪和处罚。

第二节　非法侵入他人住宅罪

第280条　非法侵入他人住宅罪——任何违背他人意愿强行进入他人住宅的,处以长期禁闭和不超过1000比索的罚金。

如果使用暴力或恐吓侵入他人住宅的,处以中间幅度和最高幅度的监禁和不超过1000比索的罚金。

本条之规定不适用于为阻止房主或第三人对其本人进行严重伤害而进入他人住所、为实施人道或正义而进入他人住所以及进入餐馆、酒店、客栈和其他公共建筑的情形。

第281条　其他非法侵入住宅罪——任何未获主人或管理者允许,进入明显不准进入的他人的封闭建筑物或有围墙的庄园,该建筑物或庄园都是非居住地的,单处或并处长期禁闭和不超过200比索的罚金。

第三节　威胁罪和胁迫罪

第282条　严重威胁罪——任何以他人或他人的亲属之名誉、财产的不测作为威胁而构成犯罪的,应受处罚:

1. 犯罪分子为了获得金钱或者满足其他条件(即使该条件合法)而威胁他人,如果目的已达到,对其处以比法律对威胁他人犯罪之规定的刑罚轻一等级的刑罚。如果目的未达到,对其处以轻两等级的刑罚。

如果威胁行为是通过书面材料或中间人完成的,对其处以最高幅度刑罚。

2. 由于情势所迫而作出威胁的,处以长期禁闭和不超过500比索的罚金。

第283条　轻微威胁罪——任何以前条第1款规定的方式实施违法行为但不构成犯罪的,处以长期禁闭。

第284条　保证良好表现——属于前两条规定的任何情形的,威胁者可以被要求保证其不再妨碍被威胁者,如果该威胁者未提供保证的,处以流放。

第285条　其他的轻微威胁罪——对以下任一情形,将处以最低幅度的短期禁闭和不超过200比索的罚金:

1. 不包括在前条规定的行为人使用武器威胁他人或在争吵中出示武器的,除非是正当防卫。

2. 如果威胁行为不属于本法第282条规定的情形,任何在最激烈时口头威胁他人,对他人造成一定的危害但不构成犯罪,且其后面的行为表明其没有坚持于有关威胁的想法的。

3. 口头威胁对他人造成一定的危害但不构成重罪的。

第286条　严重强迫罪——未经法律授权,通过暴力阻止他人实施法律并未禁止之行为,或不管正确与否,暴力强迫他人实施违背本人意愿的事情的,处以长期禁闭和不超过500比索的罚金。

如果胁迫的目的是迫使或阻止他人实施某一宗教行为的,处以情节重一等级的刑罚。

第287条　轻微强迫罪——为迫使债务人偿还债务而使用暴力扣押债务人的任何物品的,处以最低幅度的长期禁闭和与债务价值金额相等的罚金。

对其他强迫或不当行为之犯罪,单处或并处长期禁闭和5至200比索的罚金。

第288条　其他类似强迫罪(强迫他人购物或强行使用代币支付工资罪)——任何公司或合伙的个人、代理商或高级职员直接或间接强制、强迫或故意让其职员或雇员强制或被迫购买其任何商品的,单处或并处长期禁闭和200至500比索的罚金。

任何用代币或物品作为工资给付其职员或雇员而非给付现行使用的法

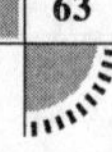

定货币的，处相同刑罚。

第289条　使用暴力或威胁促使、保持和禁止资金或劳动力结合罪——为组织、维持、阻止资金结合、劳动力结合、工人罢工、雇员停工，而实施暴力或威胁手段，足以迫使或强制职工或雇工自由合法从事生产工作的，如果依照本法规定尚不构成更严重犯罪的，处以长期禁闭和不超过300比索的罚金。

第三章　发现和泄露秘密罪

第290条　通过扣押信件发现秘密罪——任何人为发现他人秘密而扣押他人文件或信件，并泄露信件或文件内容的，处以最低幅度和中间幅度的监狱矫正和不超过500比索的罚金。

如果该行为人不泄露信件或文件内容，则处以长期禁闭和不超过500比索的罚金。

本条规定不适用于父母、监护人或未成年人的委托监护人对其照管和教育下的小孩或未成年人的文件或信件内容的泄露，也不适用于拥有文件或信件者的配偶实施这些行为的情形。

第291条　滥用职权泄露秘密罪——获悉其秘密的管理人员、雇员或仆人泄露其负责人或主人秘密的，处以长期禁闭和不超过500比索的罚金。

第292条　泄露工业秘密罪——制造业或工业机构的负责人、雇员或工人泄露工业秘密而损害所有者利益的，处以最低幅度和中间幅度的监狱矫正和不超过500比索的罚金。

第十编　侵犯财产罪

第一章　抢劫罪的一般规定

第293条　抢劫罪的定义——抢劫罪是指以获取财物为目的，通过对他人实施暴力或胁迫的手段，或使用暴力强加于任何财物而夺取他人所有的财物的行为。

第一节　对人实施暴力或胁迫之抢劫罪

第294条　对人实施暴力或胁迫之抢劫罪——任何对人实施暴力或胁迫进行抢劫的，按下列规定处罚：

1. 由于实行抢劫行为或者在抢劫时犯杀人罪的,处以无期徒刑至死刑。

2. 抢劫伴有强奸或故意伤害,或由于实施抢劫行为或在抢劫时造成本法第263条第一项规定之应受处罚之身体伤害的,处以中间幅度的有期徒刑至无期徒刑;但是,如果强奸时使用了致命武器或两人或者两人以上实施强奸的,处以无期徒刑至死刑。(第767号总统令修正)

3. 由于实施抢劫行为或在抢劫时,造成被害人遭受第263条第二项规定应受处罚之身体伤害的,处以有期徒刑。

4. 抢劫所实施的暴力或胁迫达到犯罪所明显不必要的程度或实施造成任何对犯罪无责任的人遭受第263条第三项和第四项所包括之身体伤害的,处以最高幅度的监禁至中间幅度的有期徒刑。

5. 对其他情形之抢劫,处以最高幅度监狱矫正至中间幅度的有期徒刑。(第18号共和国法案修正)

第295条　在无人居住地抢劫或团伙抢劫致人伤害罪;拦路持枪抢劫罪——在无人居住地,或团伙实施前条第三项、第四项、第五项规定之抢劫行为的,或侵袭行驶中的火车、客车或机动车辆或飞机,或进入火车乘客车厢以任何方式偷袭乘客,或在街道、公路、高速公路或小巷使用枪支相胁迫的,以相关刑罚的最高幅度刑罚处罚。

在同样情形下,对团伙之首要分子处以情节重一等级的处罚。

第296条　团伙的定义及其成员应处的刑罚——三人以上的携有武器的犯罪分子参加同一抢劫的,视为团伙抢劫。犯罪过程中所使用的武器是非法枪支的,对所有犯罪分子应处以相应的法定最高刑罚,不影响对非法持有枪支行为的处罚。

任何参加抢劫团伙的成员都以团伙的主犯论处,除非能证明其努力阻止过犯罪。

第297条　某些情形下的抢劫未遂和抢劫受阻——由于抢劫未遂或抢劫受阻的原因,或者在抢劫未遂或抢劫受阻时而犯杀人罪的,对其处以最高幅度的有期徒刑至无期徒刑,除非本法规定对其杀人罪处以更重的刑罚。

第298条　暴力或胁迫订契约之抢劫罪——任何为诈取他人,通过暴力或胁迫强迫他人签名、盖章或出具公开的契约或者文书的行为构成抢劫罪,分别按本章相应的规定进行处罚。

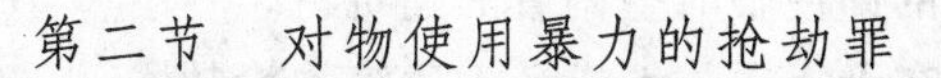

第二节　对物使用暴力的抢劫罪

第299条　进入他人住所或公共建筑物或宗教建筑物抢劫罪——携带凶器在他人住所或公共建筑物或宗教信仰之建筑物内实施抢劫的,如果抢劫的财产价值超过250比索的,且如果符合下列情形的,处以有期徒刑:

(a)罪犯通过任何以下途径进入被抢劫的住所或者建筑物的:

1. 通过并非作为出入口的通道进入的。

2. 通过破坏墙壁、天花板、地板或门窗进入的。

3. 通过使用仿制钥匙、撬锁工具或类似工具进入的。

4. 通过使用假名或假装行使公共职权而进入的。

或者如果——

(b)在下列任一情形下犯抢劫罪的:

1. 打破门、柜子、箱子或其已被锁上或被密封的家具或者贮藏间。

2. 将其家具或物件带到抢劫地之外将其打破或者强行打开。

罪犯未携带凶器,但被抢劫之财产价值超过250比索的,处以情节轻一等级的刑罚。

上述规定同样适用于罪犯携带了凶器,但其抢劫财产之价值不超过250比索的情形。

罪犯未携带凶器且其所抢之财产的价值不超过250比索的,处以最低幅度的前两款规定的刑罚。

抢劫行为是在住所、公共建筑物、宗教信仰之建筑物的附属建筑之一进行的,处以情节轻一等级的刑罚。

第300条　在无人居住地团伙抢劫罪——前条所论及的抢劫是一团伙在无人居住地进行的,处以最高幅度的以上规定的刑罚。

第301条　住所、公共建筑物或宗教信仰建筑物和其附属建筑之范围——住所是指任一居住了一人或多人的遮蔽物、船舶或者船只,即使抢劫时居住者临时不在也属于住所。

所有的内部庭院、蓄栏、水房、粮仓、畜棚、车库、马厩或者其他与建筑物连接一起被封闭起来的地方,有内部连接的入口构成总体的一部分的相临的地方,视为住所、公共建筑或者宗教信仰之建筑物的附属建筑。

前两款不包括果园或者其他用来开发或生产之地,即使是临近建筑物或者与其有直接联系的被隔离开来之地,也不构成附属建筑。

"公共建筑物"包括任何政府或者私人所有的建筑物,但不包括政府使用过的或者出租的即使临时空闲着的建筑物。

第302条　在无人居住地或私人建筑物抢劫罪——任何在无人居住地或者除第299条第1款规定之外的建筑物实施抢劫，抢劫财产之价值超过250比索，并符合下列任一情形的，处以监狱矫正：

1. 如果通过不作为进出口的通道进入的。

2. 如果墙壁、屋顶、地板或者外门或窗户被打破的。

3. 如果通过使用伪造钥匙、撬锁工具或者其他类似工具进入的。

4. 如果任何宿舍、柜子、箱子或者被封上和锁上的家具或者保管箱被打破的。

5. 如果任何上一款所论及的被锁或者被密封的保管箱被带走或在别处被强行打开的。

抢劫财产不超过250比索的，处以轻一等级的刑罚。

在本法第294条、第295条、第297条、第299条、第300条和第302条规定的情形下，被抢劫的财产是邮件或者大型牲畜的，对罪犯处以比上述条款规定的刑罚重一等级的刑罚。

第303条　抢劫无人居住地或者私人建筑物的谷物、水果或柴火罪——在第299条和第302条所列的情形下，所抢劫的财物为谷物、水果或者柴火的，对犯罪分子处以比上述条款规定的刑罚轻一等级的刑罚。

第304条　持有撬锁工具和类似工具罪——无正当理由持有撬锁工具或者类似用来犯抢劫犯罪的工具，处以最高幅度的长期禁闭至最低幅度的监狱矫正。

制造上述犯罪工具者，处以同样的刑罚。如果罪犯为修锁工，则处以中间幅度至最高幅度的监狱矫正。

第305条　仿造钥匙的认定——“仿造钥匙”被认为包括：

1. 前条提及的工具。

2. 从所有者手中盗取的真正的钥匙。

3. 除所有者用于开锁之外的任何犯罪分子用来强行开锁的钥匙。

第二章　强　盗　罪

第306条　强盗罪的认定和处罚——由三人以上的武器携带者，为了通过使用武力和暴力的方法拦路抢劫，或者为敲诈勒索或其他目的而绑架他人的而组成一抢劫团伙的，视为拦路抢劫犯或强盗。

行为人犯这种罪行的,处以中间幅度的监禁至最低幅度的有期徒刑;如果犯罪行为不应判处更重的刑罚的,则处以同样的刑罚。

如果上述罪犯携带的是非法枪支的,则推定其为拦路抢劫犯或强盗,如果被宣告有罪则处以最高幅度的刑罚。

第 307 条　帮助或者教唆强盗团伙罪——故意以任何方式帮助、教唆或者保护前条规定的强盗团伙,或者当公安机关或其他正在行使辅助行为的政府治安官(或美国军事机关)采取行动时通风报信,或者获得或接收强盗所抢之财产的,处以中间幅度的监狱矫正至最低幅度的监禁。

除非有相反的证据证明,行为人实行了本条规定之任何行为的推定为故意行为。

第三章　盗　窃　罪

第 308 条　盗窃罪的认定——行为人以获取财产为目的,对他人不实施暴力或者胁迫也不对财物实施暴力,未经他人同意取走他人财产的,构成盗窃罪。

下列行为同样构成盗窃罪:

1. 行为人发现他人丢失的财产未交给当地政府或者其主人的;

2. 行为人恶意毁坏他人财产后,转移或使用其所损坏之物的;

3. 未经他人许可,行人人进入他人禁止进入的已被圈围的庄园或牧场,进行打猎或者捕鱼或者收取谷物或其他林产品或农产品的。

第 309 条　盗窃罪的处罚——对任何犯盗窃罪按以下规定处罚:

1. 被盗物价值为 12000 比索以上但不超过 20000 比索的,处以最低幅度和中间幅度的监禁;如果被盗物的价值超过 20000 比索的,处以最高幅度的监禁,且每超过 10000 比索就判处 1 年的额外刑,但是所判处的刑期总和不得超过 20 年;在这种情形下,连同可能判处的本法其他条款所规定的附加刑,应根据不同情况将刑罚限定为监禁或有期徒刑。

2. 被盗物的价值为 6000 比索以上但不超过 12000 比索的,处以中间幅度和最高监狱矫正。

3. 被盗物的价值为 200 比索以上但不超过 6000 比索的处以最低幅度和中间幅度的监狱矫正。

4. 被盗物价值为 50 比索以上但不超过 200 比索的,处以中间幅度的长期禁闭至最低幅度的监狱矫正。

5. 被盗物价值为5比索以上但不超过50比索的,处以最长的长期禁闭。

6. 被盗物价值不超过5比索的,处以最低幅度或者中间幅度的长期禁闭。

7. 盗窃罪行在前条第3款所列举的情形下,且被盗物价值不超过5比索的,处以短期禁闭或者不超过200比索的罚金;如果被盗物价值超过5比索的,适用本条前五项中的相应规定。

8. 被盗物价值不超过5比索的,且犯罪分子实施犯罪行为是由于饥饿、贫穷、自己或者其家人生活困难的,处以最低幅度的短期禁闭或者不超过50比索的罚金。

第310条　利用条件盗窃罪——如果盗窃罪是家庭仆人所为或严重滥用信任进行犯罪,或者如果被盗物是机动车辆、邮件或者大型牲畜,或者包括从种植地偷椰子或者从鱼池或渔场偷鱼,或者趁火灾、地震、台风、火山爆发或者其他灾难、车祸或者内乱而窃取他人财产的,处以比前条相应各款刑罚重两等级的处罚。(1980年5月1日第120号共和国法案和第71号BP修正)

第311条　盗窃国家图书馆和国家博物馆罪——对盗取国家图书馆或者国家博物馆之任何财物的,单处或者并处长期禁闭或者200至500比索的罚金,除非如果本法其他条款对其规定更重的刑罚,则处以更重的刑罚。

第四章　侵　占　罪

第312条　占有不动产或者侵占不动产财产权罪——任何通过对他人使用暴力或者胁迫,占有他人任何不动产或者侵占他人不动产财产权的,除对其暴力行为处以刑罚之外,还处以其侵占财产价值的50%至100%的罚金,但罚金不得少于75比索。

不能确定其非法所得财产的价值的,处以200至500比索的罚金。

第313条　改动分界线或界标罪——任何擅自改动镇、省或者房产或者其他指明分界的界址点或者界碑的,单处或者并处短期禁闭或者不超过100比索的罚金。

第五章　逃　债　罪

第314条　欺诈逃债罪——任何携带财产潜逃损害债权人利益的行

为，如果行为人是商人的，处以监禁，如果行为人不是商人的，处以最高幅度的监狱矫正至中间幅度的监禁。

第六章　诈骗罪和其他欺骗罪

第315条　诈骗罪——以下列任何方式骗取他人财产的行为，按以下规定处罚：

第一，所骗取的金额在12000比索以上但不超过22000比索的，处以最高幅度的监狱矫正至最低幅度的有期徒刑，但是如果超过22000比索的，处以本款规定的最高幅度的刑罚，且每增加10000比索就增加1年刑期，但总刑期数不得超过20年。在这些情形下，与本法其他条款之规定，应根据不同情况将刑罚限定为监禁或有期徒刑；

第二，所骗金额在6000比索以上但不超过12000比索的，处以最低幅度和中间幅度的监狱矫正；

第三，骗取的金额在200比索以上但不超过6000比索的，处以中间幅度的长期禁闭至最低幅度的监狱矫正；

第四，按照这四种情形的规定，如果骗取的金额没有超过200比索，通过任一下列手段诈骗的，处以最高幅度的长期禁闭：

1. 不忠或者滥用信任的行为，即：

(a) 对其负责运送的物质、物质的数量或者质量或者其他价值进行改动的行为，即使这种职责的滥用是建立于不道德或者非法的报酬基础之上的。

(b) 盗用或者更换货币、货物或者其他个人财产，给他人造成损害的，而这些财产是犯罪分子基于信任，或委托，或管理或在其他包括交付或归还的职责下所接收的财产，即使上述职责全部或者部分被担保人保证或者否认债权人已收到这些金钱、货物或者其他财产的情形，也构成犯罪。

(c) 不当地利用被害人之签名或者在任何文件上的空白处签被害人姓名，给受害人或者第三人造成损害的。

2. 犯罪之前或者犯罪时，使用任一以下虚假身份或者欺诈行为进行诈骗的：

(a) 使用假名，或者假装拥有权力、影响力、法定资格、财产、信誉、代理权、商业或者虚假的业务，或者使用其他类似欺骗方法。

(b) 改变其行业所规定的质量、纯度或者重量。

(c) 假装已向政府官员行贿而欺骗对方,而这种行为并未影响受害人对犯罪人的诽谤行为提起诉讼,在这种情况下,应对犯罪人处以最高幅度的刑罚。

(d) 在支票上迟签日期或者开空头支票的行为。从收到银行或/或者收款人或者持票人发出的通知起 3 天之内不给付必需的支票金额,而因金额不足使支票遭到银行拒付将作为构成诈骗罪或者欺诈犯罪的初步证据。(1967 年 6 月 17 日通过的第 4885 号共和国法案修正)

(e) 在旅馆、客栈、餐馆、寄宿处、出租公寓或者公寓建筑物和类似地方欺诈经营者或者管理人员而获得未支付费用的食物、饮料或者住宿,或者用利用虚假借口在旅馆、客栈、餐馆、寄宿处、出租公寓或者公寓建筑物取得信任,或者从旅馆、客栈、餐馆、寄宿处、出租公寓或者公寓建筑物免费取得食物、饮料或者住宿。放弃或者秘密地携带部分行李暗自离开的行为。

3. 通过任一下列欺诈手段的:

(a) 欺骗性诱使他人在文件上签字的。

(b) 在赌博游戏中靠欺诈赢取的。

(c) 转移、隐藏或者毁坏全部或者部分法院记录、办公文件、档案或其他文件的。

第 316 条　诈骗罪的其他形式——对下列犯罪行为处以最低幅度和中间幅度的长期禁闭和处以相当于所造成的损失的 1 倍至 3 倍的罚金。

1. 任何冒充不动产的所有者而转让、出卖、抵债或抵押其财产的。

2. 行为人明知不动产已抵押但仍然进行处置的,即使该抵押没有登记。

3. 财产的合法所有人非法从财产持有人取走财产,给持有人或者第三人利造成损害的。

4. 签订虚假合同损害他人利益的。

5. 行为人实际没有给他人从事过某种服务或劳动,而他人误给其报酬仍然接受的。

6. 任何作为有关刑事或者民事诉讼的担保人,未经法院明示授权或在撤销合同之前或解除合同义务之前,出卖、抵押或者以其他方式妨碍履行担保责任下的不动产或者财产的。

第 317 条　诈骗未成年人罪——任何利用未成年人的不成熟或情感或同情使他人造成损害,以贷款或者他人私有财产为借口诱使其承担债务或使其让与财产或者转移财产权利的,不管贷款以书面形式或是以其他形式明确表示，对犯罪分子处以长期禁闭和处以与未成年人承当的合同债务的价值之10%至50%的罚金。

第318条　其他欺骗罪——通过前两条未提及其他欺诈手段损害他人利益的，处以长期禁闭和所造成的损失价值之1倍至2倍的罚金。

为获取利益或财物进行解梦、预测和算命或利用公众轻信的其他类似方式的，处以长期禁闭或者不超过200比索的罚金。

第七章　转移、出售或者抵押已被抵押的动产罪

第319条　转移、出售或者抵押已被抵押的动产罪——对下列犯罪行为处以监禁或者处以财产价值金额2倍的罚金：

1. 除了执行动产抵押，任何未经抵押权人，或执行官，或管理人或受让人之书面同意，故意将已经按《动产抵押法》规定抵押的个人财产转移至其他省或市的。

2. 未经抵押权人背书同意或在财产所在地的合同登记机关登记而全部或者部分出售或抵押已经按《动产抵押法》抵押的个人财产的。

第八章　纵火罪和其他毁坏性犯罪

第320条　毁灭性纵火罪——对任何纵火烧毁下列标的物的行为，处以最高幅度的有期徒刑至无期徒刑：

1. 任何兵工厂、造船所、仓库或者军事炸药厂或者鞭炮厂、法规库、档案馆和政府综合博物馆。

2. 任何正在运行的客运列车或者机动车辆，或已起航的船只。

3. 任何居住地、仓库或者易燃易爆或生产爆炸性物质的工厂。

第321条　其他纵火罪——纵火存在烧毁其他财产并且符合下列规定情形的，应受追究刑事责任：

1. 对下列行为，处以有期徒刑或者无期徒刑：

(a) 明知任一建筑物、农舍、仓库、棚舍、遮蔽物或者港口的船只当时有一人或多人居住，还对其纵火的；

(b) 烧毁公共建筑且其损失价值超过6000比索的；

(c) 出于毁灭证据之目的而烧毁保存诉讼证据的公共建筑物的，不管是否造成损失；

(d) 出于毁灭证据之目的而烧毁保存立法、司法或者行政程序之证据

的公共建筑物的,不管是否造成损失;毁灭的证据是用来追究犯罪刑事责任的证据的,则处以无期徒刑;

(e) 以火灾造成损失或损害而获取保险赔偿金的目的纵火的。

2. 对下列行为,处以有期徒刑:

(a) 烧毁住房或人们通常用来集会的其他建筑物,且犯罪时对建筑物里是否有人并不知情的;或纵火烧毁正在运行的货运火车或者机动车辆且造成损失超过6000比索的;

(b) 符合上一款(b)项规定的情形且损失不超过6000比索的;

(c) 纵火烧毁农场、食糖厂、蔗糖厂、制造中心、竹林或者类似种植园且造成损失超过6000比索的;

(d) 对粮田、牧场或者森林或者种植物纵火,且造成损失超过6000比索的。

3. 对下列行为,处以监禁;

(a) 符合上一款(a)、(c)和(d)项规定的情形且造成的损失不超过6000比索的;

(b) 纵火的建筑物位于居住区而非住所或集会场所且造成损失超过6000比索的。

4. 对下列行为,处以最高幅度的监狱矫正至中间幅度的有期徒刑:

(a) 对非居民区的居住建筑物纵火且所造成的损失超过1000比索的;

(b) 符合本条第2款(c)和(d)项的所规定的情形且所造成的损失不超过200比索的。

5. 所造成的损失在200比索以上但没超过1000比索,且是对第4款(a)项所指的财产纵火的,处以中间幅度的监狱矫正至最低幅度的监禁。但造成财产损失不超过200比索的,处以轻一等级的刑罚。

6. 符合本条第3款(b)项规定的情形下,且造成的损失在200比索以上不超过6000比索的,处以中间幅度和最高幅度的监狱矫正。

7. 符合第3款(b)项规定的情形且造成的损失不超过200比索的,处以最低幅度和中间幅度的监狱矫正。

8. 纵火损失的财产包括粮食场、牧场、森林或者种植物等价值不超过200比索的,处以长期禁闭并处所造成损失之金额的50%至1倍的罚金。(1969年5月12日通过的第5467号总统令修正)

第322条　以上各条规定之外的纵火罪——对不属于以上各条规定的纵火犯罪,应追究刑事责任:

1. 所造成的损失没超过50比索的,处以中间幅度和最高幅度的长期禁闭;

2. 所造成的损失超过50比索的,处以最高幅度的长期禁闭至最低幅度的监狱矫正;

3. 所造成的损失为200比索以上但没超过1000比索的,处以最低幅度和中间幅度的监狱矫正;

4. 所造成的损失超过1000比索的,处以中间幅度和最高幅度的监狱矫正。

第323条　纵火小额财产罪——对无人居住的棚屋、仓库、畜舍、工棚,或者其他价值不超过25比索的财产纵火且每次犯罪时明显没有火势蔓延的危险的,不按本章各规定进行处罚,而是根据所造成的损失依照下一章各相关规定进行处罚。

第324条　破坏罪——任何通过爆炸、放电、洪水、沉没或者搁浅船只、故意损坏船只的发动机、拿走铁轨、恶意替换行驶中的火车的安全标志、破坏电信线路和电信线杆或者其他类似系统,或者通过其他与上述所列的破坏效果大体相同的工具或手段的,对他人安全有生命危险的,处以有期徒刑;其他情形下处以监禁。

第325条　以烧毁自己的财产作为纵火的手段的处罚——纵火或者造成他人财产严重破坏的,按本章的规定处罚,即使对自己的财产进行纵火或破坏。

第326条　纵火自己财产罪——烧毁属于自己的财产,如果犯罪目的是为欺骗他人或者使他人造成损失的,或已实际造成损害的,或如果被烧物是在居住区内的建筑物的,对其处以最高幅度的长期禁闭至最低幅度的监狱矫正。

第326-A条　纵火致人死亡罪——对任何财产纵火或者在前面各条规定的情形下纵火致人死亡的,处以死刑。

第326-B条　纵火罪的初步证据——下列情形构成纵火罪的初步证据:

1. 火灾发生后,发现浸有汽油、煤油、石油或其他可燃物的原料或者物质,或者机械的、电的化学物品或者痕迹或任何一种前述物质的。

2. 被告人藏有相当数量的并非其业务所需的易燃物质或者原料。

3. 在建筑物或者场所的几个地方同时起火的,一般不可能是意外的或非故意的原因引起的情形:然而,如果在任何上述三种情形中出现下列其中至少一种情形的就有可能出现：

(a) 发生火灾时，对建筑物和(或)物品的总保险额超过其价值的80%的；

(b) 被告在火灾后提出欺诈性的索赔。

任何为了犯罪或者作为敲诈或者胁迫的手段而谋划上述条款所规定的情形的，处以监狱矫正。(1969年5月12日通过的第5467号共和国法案修正)

第九章 故意损害他人财产罪

第327条 故意损害他人财产罪的认定——除上一章规定的罪行之外，任何故意造成他人财产损害的，构成故意损害财产罪。

第328条 特殊故意损害他人财产罪——任何妨碍公共职能的行使，或使用有毒或者腐蚀性物质；或者传播传染病或者病毒给牲畜而造成损失的；或者破坏国家博物馆或者国家图书馆，或者对档案文件或登记处、供水系统、公路、公共场所或者其他公共使用的场所的，应当追究刑事责任：

1. 所造成的损失价值超过1000比索的，处以最低幅度和中间幅度的监狱矫正；

2. 所造成的损失价值在200比索以上但不超过1000比索的，处以长期禁闭；

3. 所造成的损失价值不超过200比索的，处以短期禁闭。

第329条 其他损害他人财产罪——不包括在上一条规定的损害应追究刑事责任：

1. 所造成的损失价值超过1000比索的，处以中间幅度和最高幅度的监禁；

2. 所造成的损失价值为200比索以上不超过1000比索的，处以最低幅度和中间幅度的长期禁闭；

3. 所造成的有关损失价值不超过200比索或者无法估价的，处以短期禁闭或者处以所造成的损失额以上不低于200比索的罚金。

第330条 破坏或者妨碍交通通讯工具罪——任何损害铁路、电报或者电话线的，处以中间幅度和最高幅度的监狱矫正。

如果破坏行为导致车辆出轨、碰撞或者其他事故的，处以监禁，不影响追究犯罪分子所造成的其他犯罪结果所应承担的刑事责任。

根据本条的立法目的，电线、牵索、信号系统和其他与铁路有关的其他事物都视为铁路系统的组成部分。

第 331 条　毁坏或破坏雕像、公共场所纪念碑或者公共场所画罪——任何毁坏或者破坏雕像或其他有用的或者装饰性的公共场所的纪念碑的，处以中间幅度的长期禁闭至最低幅度的监狱矫正。

任何毁坏或者破坏有用的或者装饰性的公共场所画的，由法院决定单处或者并处长期禁闭或者不超过 200 比索的罚金。

第十章　侵犯财产罪之刑事责任的免除

第 332 条　被免除刑事责任的行为人——下列行为人单独或者共同犯盗窃罪、诈骗罪或者故意损害财产罪的，不承担刑事责任，仅承担民事责任：

1. 配偶、血亲或者姻亲的直系血亲、直系卑亲；
2. 寡居的配偶将有关属于死者的财产在其死亡后转让给他人的；
3. 共同生活的兄弟、姐妹、姐夫、妹夫、大伯子、小叔子、嫂子和弟妹。

本条规定的免除刑事责任不适用于除上述人员以外的其他犯罪参与者。

第十一编　侵犯贞节罪

第一章　通奸和姘居

第 333 条　通奸罪——任何已婚妇女与其丈夫之外的男人发生性关系和与其发生性关系之男人明知对方为已婚的妇女，均犯通奸罪，即使婚姻后来被宣布无效。

对通奸罪处以中间幅度或最高幅度的监狱矫正。

通奸罪的犯罪分子是其配偶无正当理由将其抛弃的，则比较前款的规定处以情节轻一等级的刑罚。

第 334 条　姘居罪——任何丈夫在令人产生反感的情况下留宿妻子以外的其他女性于夫妻共同住处或者与妻子以外的女性发生性关系或者在其他的地方同居的，处以最低幅度和重价幅度的监狱矫正。

对姘妇处以流放。

第二章　强奸罪和猥亵罪

第 335 条　强奸罪——在下列情形下与女性发生性交的行为构成强奸罪：

1. 使用暴力或胁迫；
2. 在女性失去理智或失去知觉时；
3. 即使不具备上述两项规定的情形，但女性未满 12 周岁的。

对强奸罪处以无期徒刑。

只要犯罪时使用致命武器或者是两人或者两人以上犯罪的，处以无期徒刑至死刑。

因强奸或者在强奸时致被害人精神失常的，处以死刑。

强奸未遂或强奸受阻和因强奸或在强奸时犯杀人罪的，同样处以死刑。

由于强奸行为或者在实施强奸行为时犯杀人罪的，处以死刑。（该款已由 1960 年 6 月 18 日通过的 2632 号共和国法案和 1964 年 6 月 20 日通过的 4111 号共和国法案修正）

第 336 条　猥亵罪——在上一条规定的任一情形下对异性作出猥亵行为的，处以监狱矫正。

第三章　诱奸罪、堕落未成年人罪和卖淫罪

第 337 条　利用条件的诱奸罪——任何公职人员、牧师、家仆、佣人、监护人、老师或者其他有能力被委托对被诱奸的女性进行教育或监管的受托人，对 12 周岁以上未满 18 周岁的少女进行诱奸的，对其处以最低幅度和中间幅度的监狱矫正。

任何对其姐妹或者晚辈女性血亲进行诱奸的，不管该女性是少女还是年满 18 周岁，对犯罪者一律处以情节重一等级的刑罚。

本章规定的诱奸，是指犯罪分子已与被害人发生了性关系和已完成本章所述的各种行为。

第 338 条　普通诱奸罪——通过欺骗方法诱奸年满 12 周岁但未满 18 周岁的单身女性或者有良好声誉的寡妇的，处以长期禁闭。

第 339 条　被害人同意的猥亵罪——经被害人同意，与第 337 条和第 338 条规定相同的行为人，在相同的情形下实施其他猥亵行为的，处以长期禁闭。

第 340 条 堕落未成年人罪——对任何促使或者便利未成年人卖淫或者堕落专为满足他人性欲的行为，处以监禁；如果犯罪分子是公职人员或者雇员，包括国有和控股企业人员的，还应对其处以临时完全剥夺权利。（第 92 号 BP 修正）

第 341 条 卖淫罪——以任何手段或者任何托辞从事卖淫活动或者获利于卖淫或者协助他人从事卖淫的，处以中间幅度和最高幅度的监禁。（第 186 号 BP 修正）

第四章 诱拐妇女罪

第 342 条 强行诱拐妇女罪——具有猥亵的目的强行诱拐妇女的，处以有期徒刑。

被诱拐的女性未满 12 周岁的，无论哪种情形下，都处以有期徒刑。

第 343 条 被害人同意的诱拐罪——具有猥亵的目，经年满 12 周岁而未满 18 周岁的少女同意而进行诱拐的，处以最低幅度和中间幅度的监狱矫正。

第五章 本编前述各章相关的规定

第 344 条 对通奸罪、姘居罪、诱奸罪、诱拐妇女罪、强奸罪和猥亵罪的起诉——除非被告配偶提起控诉，否则对通奸罪和姘居罪不起诉。

在任何情况下，如果被害人已同意或宽恕罪犯的，被害人不能提起刑事自诉，但如果有罪的当事人均活着，则不包括另一犯罪人。

对于诱奸罪、诱拐妇女罪、强奸罪或者猥亵罪，除非被害人或其父母或其祖父母或其监护人告发，否则，对犯罪分子不予起诉；如果在上述人员明确表明对犯罪分子宽恕的情形下，也不予追究责任。

在诱奸罪、诱拐妇女罪、猥亵罪或者强奸罪的情形下，犯罪人与被害人结婚的行为将终止刑事诉讼或者免除对犯罪分子已判处的刑罚。本款规定也适用于上述犯罪的共同主犯、共犯和从犯。

第 345 条 侵犯贞节罪的民事责任——犯强奸、诱奸或诱拐妇女罪的，同时判处：

1. 对受害妇女进行赔偿；
2. 除法律不允许的情况之外，认领其子女；
3. 任何情况下，抚养子女。

通过同样的程序或者通过单独的民事诉讼,判处第 333 条和第 334 条规定的通奸者和姘居者对遭受损害的配偶进行赔偿。

第 346 条　被害人的直系尊亲、监护人、老师或者其他受托人的责任——直系尊亲、监护人、老师或者其他受托人滥用其权利或信任关系,作为同谋者共同实施本编第二、第三、第四章规定之行为的,以主犯论处。

对老师或者其他被委托教育和辅导青少年之责任人,处以最高幅度的有期剥夺特别权利至终身剥夺特定权利。

本条规定的各犯罪分子和其他为他人利益而堕落未成年人的犯罪人,处以取消其担任监护官的权利。

第十二编　侵犯个人公民身份罪

第一章　假冒出生罪和冒用公民身份罪

第 347 条　假冒出生罪、交换子女罪以及隐瞒或遗弃婚生子女罪——假冒出生和交换子女的,处以监禁和不超过 1000 比索的罚金。

故意隐瞒或遗弃婚生子女而使其丧失公民身份的,处以同样的刑罚。

任何医生或政府官员违反职责或工作职能,为前两款所述犯罪的实施提供帮助的,处以上述刑罚并处以有期剥夺特别资格。

第 348 条　冒用公民身份罪——冒用他人公民身份,如果是出于骗取被害人或其继承人财物为目的的,处以监禁;其他情形下处以中间幅度和最高幅度的监狱矫正。

第二章　非法婚姻罪

第 349 条　重婚罪——行为人在前一婚姻还未依法解除前,或在其失踪配偶按正当程序被宣布死亡前,再次缔结婚姻或重婚的,处以监禁。

第 350 条　非法缔结婚姻罪——行为人不按法律规定缔结婚姻或者无视法定的结婚障碍[①],则处以中间幅度和最高幅度的监狱矫正,但不包括在上述条款中规定的情形。

---

① 法定的结婚障碍(相当于我国婚姻法规定禁止结婚的条件)具体包括:先前婚姻的存许;禁止结婚的血亲或者姻亲的关系;暴力、欺诈或误解;未达法定婚龄、智力或身体的能力缺陷——译者注。

如果任一婚姻缔结方是通过暴力、胁迫或诈骗来获取另一方同意的，处以最高幅度的前款规定的刑罚。

第351条　过早婚姻罪——丧偶的妇女在其丈夫死亡后301天内再婚或在其丈夫死时已怀孕而未分娩再婚的，处以长期禁闭并处不超过500比索的罚金。

婚姻被取消或解除后的妇女，在分娩前或是在婚姻合法解除后期满301天之前再婚的，处以同样的刑罚。

第352条　举行非法婚姻仪式罪——任何宗派、教派的牧师或教士或民间权威机构执行或批准非法婚姻之仪式的，将依据《婚姻法》相关规定给予处罚。

第十三编　侵犯名誉罪

第一章　诽　谤　罪

第一节　诽谤罪的定义、形式和处罚

第353条　诽谤罪的定义——诽谤罪是指公开和恶意地诋毁犯罪，或真实的或者虚构的缺陷或缺点，或任何行为、疏忽、地位、身份，或其他意在使他人遭到名誉玷污、耻辱的情形，或者侮辱自然人或者法人，或诋毁死者的名声的行为。

第354条　公开的要件——任何诽谤行为如果出于不良目的和不正当动机而公开的，即使其内容真实，都假定其是怀有恶意的，但下列情形除外：

1. 任何两人之间在法律、道德和社会责任允许范围内的私人交流；

2. 在司法、立法或其他官方行为中作出的非机密性的、诚意的未加任何注解和评论的公正且真实的报道，或是在上述行为中作出的声明、报告或演讲或是公职人员在其职权范围内的行为。

第355条　通过著述或其他类似方法诽谤罪——通过著述、印刷、平版印刷、雕版、收音机、留声机、图画、戏剧表演和电影显示以及其他类似方法进行诽谤的，处以最低幅度和中间幅度的监狱矫正或者单处或并处200比索至6000比索的罚金。

第356条　威胁他人出版诽谤物罪和为获取报酬而提供诽谤出版物罪——威胁他人出版与他人本人或他人之父母、配偶、子女或其他家庭成员有关的诽谤物，或者出于补偿或金钱考虑而提供这些诽谤出版物的，单处或

并处长期禁闭或者200至2000比索的罚金。

第357条　发表禁止发表的公务行为罪——任何报纸、日报或杂志的记者、编辑或管理人员，公开发表他人私生活和对他人的荣誉、美德和名誉进行攻击，即使该报道与司法或行政程序中的所涉及的事实相关或者以其论述的必要为托辞的，单处或者并处长期拘役或者20至2000比索的罚金。

第358条　诽谤罪——口头诽谤情节严重且带有侮辱性质的，处以最高幅度的长期禁闭至最低幅度的监狱矫正；用其他方式口头诽谤的，处以短期禁闭或者处以不超过200比索的罚金。

第359条　事实诽谤罪——本编所包含和处罚以外的诽谤他人名誉、信用或名声的行为，处以最高幅度的长期禁闭至最低幅度的监狱矫正，或处以200至1000比索的罚金，如果上述行为性质不严重则处以长期禁闭或处以不超过200比索的罚金。

第二节　总　　则

第360条　责任主体——发表、展示或是用著述或类似方法形成诽谤出版物或展示品的人员同样承担刑事责任。

书或小册子的作者或编辑，日报、杂志或连载出版物的主编或业务经理如是诽谤文章的作者时，将在同样范围内对其出版物中诽谤内容负责。

本章所规定的书面诽谤的刑事和民事损害赔偿诉讼应同时或分别在诽谤文章印刷和首次出版地的省或市所在地法院或犯罪时被害人实际居住地法院提起诉讼。然而，如果犯诽谤罪时被害人中有人在马尼拉任公职，则该案件应被提交到马尼拉或是该诽谤文章的印刷地和首次出版地的省、市所在地一审法院；如果该公职人员不在马尼拉任职，则此案件应被提交到其被诽谤时任职的省、市所在地或是该诽谤文章的印刷地和首次出版地的一审法院；如果被害人是个人，则该案件应被提交到犯罪时被害人实际居住地的法院或者该诽谤文章印刷和首次出版地的一审法院。民事案件应被提交至受理刑事案件的同一法院，反之亦然。此外，最先受理损害赔偿的刑事案件或民事案件的法院取得排他管辖权。再次，最先受理刑事案件或民事损害赔偿案件的法院取得排他管辖权。最后，这些修正案不适用于本法生效时书面诽谤的民事或刑事案件已被法院受理的情形。

本章关于书面诽谤的刑事案件由省或市的检查官或者依照本法规定可以向其提起诉讼的较大市或者省会城市法院进行初步调查。

诋毁犯罪行为不能提起诽谤罪的刑事公诉，除非是被害人明确控诉。

(由1955年6月15日生效的1289号共和国法案和1965年6月19日生效的4363号共和国法案修正)

第361条　事实证据——在每件诽谤罪的刑事诉讼中,有足够证据证明诽谤内容属实且是处于良好动机和有理由的目的,则法院将宣判被告人无罪。

作为或不作为的诽谤行为不构成有效的事实证据,除非诽谤行为是不利于政府官员与履行公务相关的事实。

若被告在上述情形中能证明诽谤内容属实,将被宣判无罪。

第362条　诽谤性的评论——恶意作出与第354条规定下的例外情形相关的损害名誉的评论或意见的作者或报纸的编辑或责任编辑,都不能被免除刑事责任。

第二章　阴　谋　罪

第363条　诬告罪——任何人通过非伪证的行为直接控告或归罪于某一无罪人的,处以短期禁闭。

第364条　阴谋损害荣誉罪——对任何阴谋损害他人荣誉或者名誉为主要目的的行为,处以短期拘禁或不超过200比索的罚金。

第十四编　准　犯　罪

单独一章　过失犯罪

第365条　轻率和疏忽行为——行为人不计后果的轻率行为,如果是有意地违反法律行为,将构成重罪,处以最高幅度的长期禁闭至中间幅度的监狱矫正;如果构成次重罪时,处以最低幅度和中间幅度的长期禁闭;构成轻罪时,处以最高幅度的短期禁闭。

行为人由于轻微地轻率或疏忽行为而另外构成重罪时,处以中间幅度和最高幅度的长期禁闭;如果构成次重罪时,处以最低幅度的长期禁闭。

实行本条中包括的犯罪行为仅导致他人财产造成损害时,处以受损财产价值的1倍至3倍的罚金,但其罚金额最低不得少于25比索。

如果行为人故意实施轻微的轻率或疏忽的不法行为的,构成轻罪,应处以不超过200比索的罚金以及谴责。

在判处刑罚时,法院应不考虑第64条的有关规定进行合理的自由裁量。

本条有关规定不适用于以下情形：

1. 当行为人的刑罚相同于或低于本条1、2款规定的刑罚时，法院处以比他们认为合理的刑罚幅度低一等级的刑罚。

2. 行为人的轻率或疏忽行为违反汽车法，造成一人死亡的，处以中间幅度和最高幅度的监狱矫正。

轻率行为存在于自由意志的选择而非恶意蓄谋，是因行为人不可宽赦的缺乏应有的谨慎而给他人造成物质损害的作为或不作为，认定时应考虑到行为人的职业、智力水平、身体状况和其他关于人物、时间和地点因素。

存在于因缺乏预防措施的轻微的轻率行为显示即将发生的损害不是直接地也不是明显的危险造成的。

当罪犯在现场能为受害方提供其所能提供的帮助而未提供的，处以比本条规定重一等级的刑罚。

附　则

第366条　本法典颁布前的法律的适用——在本法典生效之前所犯的重罪和轻罪，在没有损害本法典第22条规定的情形的，按照犯罪时的法典或法律予以处罚。

第367条　废止条款——除前条规定的情形外，现行刑法典和其适用本法的临时实施法律以及第277、282、480、518、519、899、1121、1438、1523、1559、1692、1754、1955、1733、2020、2036、2071、2142、2212、2293、2298、2300、2364、2549、2557、2595、2609、2718、3103、3195、3244、3298、3309、3313、3397、3559和3586号法案因此废止。

以下所列法案中的相关条款同样被废止：

第666号法案第6节和第18节。

第1508号法案第9、10、11、12节。

第1524号法案第1、2、6节。

第1697号法案第3、4节。

第1757号法案第1、2、3、3、5、6、7、11、12节。

第2381号法案第2、3、4、6、8、9节。

第2711号法案第102、2670、2671、2672节。

第3247号法案第1、2、3、5节以及1900年系列的第58号通用规则第106节。

以上所列各法案的全部或部分条款与本法典有冲突的由此予以废止。

1930年12月8日通过

《修正刑法典》所废止的法案

1. 第 277 号法案，即关于诽谤以及威胁发表诽谤等法律。本法第 353 条、第 362 条现已规定。

2. 第 282 号法案(第 1692 号法案作了修正)，即关于对叛国、叛乱、煽动暴乱等犯罪的详细说明和处罚的法律。本法第 114 条至第 116 条以及第 134 条至第 142 条已有规定。

3. 第 480 号法案，即管理斗鸡和斗鸡场的法律，由现行本法第 199 条和特别法管理。

4. 第 518 号法案(第 1121 号和第 2036 号法案修正)，即关于高速公路上的抢劫和团伙抢劫的详细定义和处罚法律，现包含在本法第 306 条至第 307 条之规定。

5. 第 519 号法案，即关于流浪的法律，按照本法第 202 条处罚。

6. 第 666 号法案的第六节和第十八节，即关于商标和商号的法律，现依本法第 188 条至第 189 条之规定。

7. 第 899 号法案，即关于延迟判决美国公民等法律。

8. 第 1438 号法案(第 3203 号、第 3309 号和第 3559 号修正)，即关于管理少年犯和违法儿童的规定，他们的监管，按照本法第 80 条的规定管理。

9. 第 1508 号法案第 9 节至第 12 节，即财产抵押法，现按本法第 319 条处罚。

10. 第 1523 号法案，即有关禁止彩票的进口、出售等法案，现按本法第 195 条至第 196 条处罚。

11. 第 1524 号法案第四节有关规定总督有条件赦免的决定的法律，现本法第 159 条已经包括。

12. 第1553号法案第1节、第2节和第6节(第1559号法案修正),即有关表现良好和积极的罪犯减刑的法律,现本法第97条已规定。

13. 第1697号法案第3节、第4节,即有关对在公务调查中作伪证的处罚法律,现本法第180条至第183条已规定。

14. 第1754号法案,即关于对伪造和伪造物的法律,现本法第160条至第169条已规定。

15. 第1775号法案,即关于对侵犯立法机关犯罪的处罚的法律,现本法第143条至第145条已规定。

16. 第1757号法案的第1条至第7条、第11条、第12条(第3242号法案修正),即关于禁止赌博法,现本法第195条至第199条已规定。

17. 第1173号法案,即关于通奸、姘居、强奸、猥亵、诽谤、侵犯他人权利等犯罪的规定,现本法第333条至第346条已规定。

18. 第2071号法案和第2300号法案,即有关规定劳役、强制劳役、劳役偿债以及买卖人口的规定,现按照本法第272条至第274条处罚。

19. 第2212号法案,即关于货币、艺术品、工具、器具和赌博设备的没收和处理的规定,现本法第45条已规定。

20. 第293号法案,即对故意破坏、损害、占有或者带走任何菲律宾图书馆的财物的法律,现本法第311条已规定。

21. 第2364号法案,即关于在监管被羁押的犯罪嫌疑人或罪犯时不忠的处罚的法律,现本法第223条至第225条已规定。

22. 第2381号法案第2条至第9条,即关于对鸦片使用的限制等的法律,现本法第190条至第194条已经规定。

23. 第2549号法案,即有关禁止强迫、逼迫或责成劳工或其他雇员购买商品、日用品或特定情况下的个人财产以及用代币或物品而非合法货币来支付劳工或其他雇员的工资的处罚的法律,现按照本法第288条处罚以及受第303号法案和第602号法案的《最低工资法》(第812号共和国法案修正)的约束。

24. 第2557号法案,即规定防止性羁押的犯罪人的奖励的法律,现包含在本法第29条。

25. 第2595号法案,即确定诽谤罪的追诉时效以及发生民事诉讼的诉讼时效的法律,现本法第90条已规定。

26. 第2711号法案第102条和第2670号至第2672号法案,即修正行政法典的修正法案。

27. 第3104号法案对2726号法案的修正,即关于死刑的执行方式的法律,现具体包含在本法第18条至第85条。

28. 第3586号和第3397号法案,即法律关于惯犯的法律,现本法第62条第5款中已规定。

29. 1900年系列的第58号通则的第106条,即刑事诉讼法典。

30. 被《修正刑法典》废止的其他法律仅是旧刑法典的修正法律,包括第2030、2142、2298、2712、3195、3244、3298和3313号法案。

其他刑事法案

第 1602 号总统令

对违反菲律宾赌博法行为处以更严厉处罚的简要规定

尽管有菲律宾赌博法,特别是《修正刑法典》第 195 条至第 199 条、第 3063 号共和国法案(赛马编)、第 499 号总统令(斗鸡)、第 483 号总统令(赌博设备)、第 519 号总统令(老虎机)和第 1036 号总统令(回力球编)以及全国各地城市赌博条例,但由于对违法犯罪行为的处罚制度混乱不当,这些法律已经变得无能为力了,犯罪分子也易于逃避处罚。

因而,迫切需要修正这些赌博法,使之简单明了,易于理解和标准化,对这些违法行为规定更严厉的处罚,使这些处罚对当前人们的行为举止标准更有效且作出更强烈的响应。

所以,现在我费迪南德·埃·马科斯,作为菲律宾共和国的现任总统,基于宪法赋予我的权力和为了实现我们社会和经济体制所渴望的和必需的转变或改革,据此制定以下法律并宣布其作为本国法律的组成部分:

第 1 条　违法行为和刑罚——对以下罪犯处以中间幅度的监禁或处 500 至 2000 比索的罚金;如果是累犯,将处以中间幅度的监狱矫正或处 1000 至 6000 比索的罚金:

(a) 除下一项规定的方式以外任何直接或间接参与斗鸡、花档、赌彩(包括回力球或赛马)或其他彩票游戏,硬币正反或金属球和类似赌博、黑杰克牌,幸运 9、扑克 2 或俄罗斯扑克、西班牙纸牌赌博、巴卡拉特纸牌赌博或其他纸牌赌博、扑克、骨牌、麻将、王牌、老虎机、轮盘赌、弹球或其他机器项目或设备、赛狗、赛船、赛车或其他比赛、篮球、排球、拳击、7—11 骰子游戏和其他类似游戏以及包括赌博设备、刮分或其他阴谋庄家或百分比游戏，或其他未经政府授权的，无论按机会还是论技能的任何其他赌博或配置，其赌资包括金钱和其他有价物。

(b) 故意允许上述(a)规定的各种赌博在居住地或非居住地或任一建筑物、船只或其他归其所有或控制的交通工具里进行的。如进行赌博之地以赌博著称或被禁止的赌博在此经常进行或者其是在公共和政府的建筑或集会所，对罪犯处以最高幅度的规定刑罚和 6000 比索的罚金。

上述赌博设备的维护人员、管理人员将被处以最高幅度的监狱矫正和 6000 比索的罚金。

如维护人员、管理人员或庄家是政府官员或赌博设备、刮分机或其他赌博机器中的玩家、赞助者、调解人员、仲裁人员、鉴定人员或指导人员是政府官员的将被处以中间幅度的监禁和有期剥夺全部权利以及 6000 比索的罚金。

任何故意的且出于非法目的在某时段拥有发生或者将发生的彩票记录、票据或其他用于花档、回力球或赛马和类似赌博游戏或彩票赌博的信件、数字、标记或者符号的材料将被处以中间幅度的监狱矫正和 500 至 2000 比索的罚金。

第 2 条　村官——任何村官在其管辖权限内设有赌场或有以赌博著称的地点将被处以中间幅度的监狱矫正和 500 至 2000 比索的罚金以及有期剥夺全部权利。

第 3 条　举报者的奖金——任何人若提供相关信息而使犯罪分子被逮捕和被最后定罪的将获得相当于所没收到的赌资的 20% 的奖金。

第 4 条　废止条款——《修正刑法典》第 196 条至第 199 条，第 3063 号共和国法案，第 483 号、第 499 号、第 510 号、第 1306 号总统令、指令、法律、行政命令、规则和规章，以及与本法令不一致的城市和市政法令据此废止并作出相应的修改。

第 5 条　生效——本法令于公共信息部部长在出版物至少曾经是全国发行的报纸上公布后马上生效。

上议院全体成员于 1978 年 6 月 11 日于马尼拉制定。

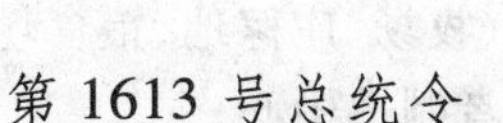

第 1613 号总统令

纵火罪的修正案

警察和政府情报机构调查结果显示:犯罪组织使纵火和包括其他破坏性犯罪在马尼拉和国内其他的城市中心永存,有的犯罪还与国外有关联。

然而,由于现行法关于纵火罪的法律规定的某些不完整性妨碍对纵火犯的有效地控制和控诉。

因此,为保护国民经济并保持国家的社会经济和政治稳定,阻止因纵火罪和其他破坏性犯罪造成的严重影响已迫在眉睫。

现在,我费迪南德·埃·马科斯作为菲律宾总统,基于宪法赋予我的权力而制定以下命令和法令作为国家法律的一部分:

第 1 条　纵火罪——任何烧毁或者纵火烧他人财物的,处以监禁。

行为人对自己的财产放火,但是危及到他人生命和财产的,处以同样的刑罚。

第 2 条　破坏性纵火罪——被烧毁的财产是下列任一情形的,处以最高幅度有期徒刑至无期徒刑:

1. 所有兵工厂和其他存储易爆、易燃或可燃物质的设施;

2. 任何公用或者私人档案文件室、博物馆或者任何用于文化、教育或社会服务的建筑物;

3. 任何教堂或礼拜堂或者其他人们经常集会的建筑物;

4. 任何火车、飞机或者航行器、船舰或者船只,或者运送乘客和财产的运输工具;

5. 任何用来保存立法、司法、行政或者其他公务行为证据的建筑物;

6. 任何医院、旅馆、宿舍、公寓、住宅房、购物中心、公共或者私人商业中心,剧院或者影院或者类似的地方或者建筑物;

7. 任何位于居住区或者人口密集区的建筑物,不管是居所与否。

第 3 条　其他纵火情形——被烧毁物是下列任一情形的,处以有期徒刑至无期徒刑:

1. 任何政府机关或其代理机构作为办公的建筑物;

2. 任何无人居住的房屋或者寓所;

3. 任何工业建筑,造船厂、油井、矿井、站台或者隧道;

4. 任何种植园、农场、牧场、庄稼地、粮食场、果园、竹林或者森林；

5. 任何米厂、糖厂或者制造中心；

6. 任何火车站或者汽车站、飞机场、码头或者仓库。

第4条　纵火罪的特别加重情节——对任何以下情形的纵火犯处以最高幅度的刑罚：

1. 为获取某物而犯罪的；

2. 为他人之利益而犯罪的；

3. 犯罪分子出于对被烧毁财产的主人有怨恨和仇恨的动机而犯罪的；

4. 团伙犯罪的。

有三人或三人以上的人员策划或者实施犯罪即构成团伙犯罪。

第5条　纵火致人死亡——因纵火或者在纵火时致人死亡的，处以有期徒刑至死刑。

第6条　纵火罪的初步证据——任一下列情形构成纵火罪的初步证据：

1. 同时从建筑物之两处或者两处以上起火；

2. 建筑物里藏有犯罪者所不必需或者家庭不用之可燃物质或原料；

3. 在废墟或者被烧的建筑物的地基或者财产里发现浸湿的汽油、煤油、石油或其他可燃或易燃物质或者原料或容器，或者用来生火的机械、电的、化学的、电子装置，或者任何一前述物质的灰烬和痕迹；

4. 在签发保险单时，对建筑物或者财产投保的价值比其实际价值大的；

5. 在对应的火灾保险单期间，已经发生过两次同样火灾的或其罪犯或被保险人所有或者在其控制下的房屋；

6. 火灾发生之前不久一部分已投保或存放在建筑物或者财产里的有价值的财物被撤走，除非是正常业务需要；

7. 在火灾前为了作出金钱或者与受益价值相等的回报的需要或为了受害人的人身或其财产安全而交换罪犯的财产的。

第7条　纵火罪的共犯——共谋犯纵火罪者，处以最低监禁刑。

第8条　纵火对象的没收——纵火对象之建筑包括其所在的土地应该被没收和收归国有，除非所有者能证明其并未参加纵火行为且尽了应有的义务仍对纵火行为不知情。

第9条　废止条款——《修正刑法典》的第320条至第326-B条和部分或者部分与本法令不一致的法律、总统令、规定和规章因此相应地废止或修改。

第10条　生效——本法令在其中至少曾经全国发行的报纸上公布之日立即生效。

1979年3月7日于马尼拉制定。

第1744号总统令

对《修正刑法典》第320条关于纵火罪的修改

鉴于罪犯对居民住房、公共建筑、商场、酒店和其他商业设施猖獗和肆意纵火。

为了有力地打击纵火犯罪,防止破坏财产和保护无辜人员的生命安全,对纵火犯必须处以死刑。

因此,我费迪南德·马科斯作为菲律宾现任总统,基于宪法赋予我的权力而制定命令和法令对《修正刑法典》的第320条进行修正:

第1条 《修正刑法典》第320条及其内涵——第320条,毁灭性纵火。任何人如对以下目标纵火将被处以最高幅度的监禁至死刑:

1. 一座或多座房屋或者建筑物由于某单一纵火行为而燃烧或同时燃烧作为结果或由于多个不同场合纵火而燃烧。

2. 任何公共或私所有的建筑,通常作为公共场所或人们为了明确的目的但是不限于政府官方的职能或者事务的经常聚会,如个人事务、商业、贸易、集会和会议,或是人们出于明确目的偶然聚会,比如但不限于酒店、汽车旅馆、临时寓所、公共运输工具或车站或其机场候车室,不管罪犯是否明知放火时有人在该建筑物里,也不管是该建筑物里是否有人居住。

3. 任何用于运送公用、休闲或娱乐的火车、机车、轮船、飞船或者飞机。

4. 任何作为公用事业的建筑物、工厂、仓库设备或是其附属物。

5. 出于隐瞒或破坏另一违法犯罪证据或出于隐瞒破产或欺骗债权人或出于骗取保险金的目的而纵火的建筑物。

不管对上述情形如何实施,当犯纵火罪或者两人或两人以上或团伙纵火,不管他们的目的是否仅仅是燃烧或破坏该建筑物,或者纵火明显是一种犯罪行为或者触犯另一个法律,同样处以死刑。

任何人对下列目标纵火的处以最高幅度的有期徒刑至死刑:

1. 任何军兵工厂、造船厂、仓库、军事火药或烟花厂、军械库、档案室或政府博物馆。

2. 任何位于居民区的易燃易爆的仓库或工厂。

如果罪犯的任一纵火行为造成他人伤亡,或有价值的文件、设备、机器、仪器及其他有价值财产遭到烧毁,将依本条处以死刑。

第2条　修正案法典第320条,第321条和第322条中与此不一致的规定因此被废止。

第3条　生效——本法令立即生效。

上议院全体成员于1980年1月11日于马尼拉制定。

第3019号共和国法案

反渎职和腐败法案

（由菲律宾国会代表所组成的参议院和众议院制定）

第1条　政策声明——菲律宾政府的政策，与公务行为是一种公众信任的原则相一致，约束公务人员或非公务人员的某些诸如腐败或渎职行为或可能由此导致的行为。

第2条　术语界定——本法案中的术语：

（a）“政府”包括中央政府、地方政府、政府所有和政府控股企业和其他菲律宾共和国的政府机构与代理及其分支机构。

（b）“公务人员”是指选举和任命的终身或临时的政府官员和雇员，无论是有级别的还是没有级别的，或者在前项规定的政府部门领取津贴，但不需上班的甚至是挂名的。

（c）“接受任何礼物”是指公务人员为本人或其任何家庭成员或四代以内的亲戚，直接或间接接受他人而不是其直系亲属的礼物，也包括接受具有血亲或姻亲关系的人，甚至是在家庭庆祝或全国性节日如圣诞节时其所赠礼物，且明显超过正常价值的礼物。

（d）“人”包括自然人和法人，除非本法案有其他规定。

第3条　公务人员的腐败行为——根据现行法律，公务人员的作为和不作为都应受处罚，下列情形的任何公务人员的腐败行为都被认为是非法的：

（a）劝说、劝诱或感化其他政府官员违反当局正式公布的规则和条例或者违背公务职责，或是愿意接收他人劝说、劝诱或感化而违法或犯罪。

（b）在政府和其他团体之间的合同或交易中，为自己或他人直接或间接地索取或接受礼物、礼品、分股、分成或利益，包括公务人员利用其职权干涉法律。

（c）公务人员为自己或他人直接或间接地索取或接受他人礼物、礼品或其他金钱或物质利益，而利用因其帮助或将提供的帮助，以任何方式或地位保证或者获得或愿意保证或者获得政府的批准或许可，不影响本法案第13条的规定。

（d）公务人员在任职期间或期满后一年以内，接受或让家庭中的其他成员接受与官方有商业活动的私有企业的聘用。

(e) 给予任何私人团体未经批准的利益、优势或是利用其拥有的政府行政权给予优先权或明显的司法偏袒和明显不诚实或严重的不可辩解的疏忽,而造成任何一方包括对政府的不正当的伤害。本条适用的主体是政府官员和雇员或掌管执照或许可证或其他特许权的政府团体。

(f) 为达到某种目的,在合理时间内应解决待决事情之前,且在到期需求或者请求之后没有足够理由而忽视或者拒绝,直接或者间接地从他人获利的事物中获得一些金钱和物质利益或利益,或给予不适当的利益或区别对待其他应获得利益者。

(g) 公务人员代表政府在合同或者交易事物处理过程中有明显和严重不利于政府的行为,不管是已经获益或者将因此获益。

(h) 直接或间接地在商业、合同或交易事物中利用职权进行干预或参与而获得金钱利益,或从宪法或其他任何法律所禁止的行为中获利。

(i) 为了获得个人利益,直接或间接地存在利害关系,或是在交易中获得物质利益或主动要求成为董事会、专门小组或小组中的一员,即使在批准过程中进行了谨慎考虑,甚至对此投票反对或没有参与董事会、委员会、专门小组和小组的活动。

公务人员有明显不合法的、不公平的或不合常规的批准或认可他们所在的董事会、专门小组或小组的行为而获得的个人利益通常被认为是与其工作职责相悖。

(j) 故意批准或者准许任何执照、许可证、特权或利益,有利于没有资格者或未经合法授权的人获得这些执照、许可证、特权或利益,或者仅使之成为没有资格或授权的人的代表或虚假人员。

(k) 因为其公职或地位而获取的机密性有价值信息泄露给未经授权的人,或在被允许泄漏日期之前泄漏该信息的。

以任何形式与政府进行商业活动的人,据上述(b) 和(c)项给予公务人员礼物、礼品、分股、分成或利益;或提供或给予公务人员在上述(d)项中提到的职位;或据本部分(k)项说服公务人员泄露或过早地泄漏机密,将据本法案第 9 条的规定与犯罪的公务人员一起受到处罚并且由法院斟酌处以终身或有期剥夺权利。

第 4 条　关于个人的禁止——(a) 任何公务人员让其家属或关系密切的人与任何公务人员进行投资或开发,或利用其家属或关系密切的人,直接或间接地向其他与政府有商业、交易、申请、请求或合同关系的人索取或接受任何礼物、礼品或物质或金钱利益。在此过程中，该公务人员进行干预的行为是违法的。家属是指配偶或三代以内的血亲或姻亲。“关系密切的人”是指亲密朋友、社交朋友和有兄弟般关系的人，或给予了这些公务人员升迁之便的具有特殊职位的关系隐秘的人。

(b) 任何故意引诱或导致公务人员犯本法案第3条规定的犯罪行为之一的行为是违法的。

第5条　关于亲属的禁止——对于菲律宾总统、副总统、参议院或众议院院长之配偶或三代以内的血亲或姻亲，直接或间接地干预任何与政府有关的商业、交易、合同或申请的行为是非法的：假若本部分不适用于一直沿用同样的方式处理的政府事务，即与其有关联的上述政府官员之工作是在此假设之前作出的，也在不包括在此假设的时间内该公共事务已经存在或是待决的交易、合同或申请，但不包括由他签署的申请，该申请就其职责或与职责相关但遵从法律或与法律相符的规则或章程所规定的要求内考虑不周，也不是指在其工作职权范围内实施的合法行为或专业性行为。

第6条　关于国会成员的禁止——以后，任何国会成员在其被选举成为议员的任期内，任何特殊的商业活动直接和特别地被支持或受益于由其事先起草的、同期由国会通过或采纳的法律或议案，并从中索取或接受任何个人金钱利益的行为是违法的。

该条款适用于其他任何公务人员，其介绍相似的行为促使国会颁布或采纳任何法律或议案，且在其任期内索取或接受诸如此类的利益。

对于这些议员或其他公务人员，在其起草或推荐的这些法律或议案被通过之前就已得到了某种利益，在通过之后的30天内又获得某些利益的，同样被认为是违法的。

第7条　财产和债务声明——每个公务人员在本法案生效30天内或在从事公务后，此后每隔1年的1月及其工作期满时，向部门负责人准备和提交相应的真实详细且经宣誓的财产和债务声明，包括其收入的数额和来源、个人和家庭开支数量及支上年度支付的所得税额，如果是部门负责人或独立部门的负责人，则向总统办公室提交，如果是国会成员或官员和雇员，则提交给相应的议院秘书办公室：如果公务人员是在公历年年底前工作不足2个月的，就在二月份之内提交第一份声明。

第8条　因未申报财产而免职——如果根据第1379号共和国法案的规定，公务人员在任职期间被发现以本人名义或他人名义获得一定数量的财产和/或金钱，明显超出其工资水平和其他合法收入，该事实将作为免职

或离职的依据。该公务人员的配偶或未婚子女名义上的财产没有令人满意的说明,即使是通过合法方式取得,也可以考虑这一点。执行本条时,银行存款将会被考虑,尽管法律的有其他相反的规定。

第 9 条　刑罚——(a) 任何公务人员或非公务人员实施本法案第 3 条至第 6 条规定的任何违法或疏忽行为,处 1 年以上 10 年以下的监禁、终身剥夺从事公务资格,和充公或没收政府禁止的任何利益和不能解释的明显与其薪水和其他合法收入不符的财产。

(b) 如果被告人被指控有罪,任何控告人在被告人被提起诉讼时就有权在刑事诉讼过程中对被控金钱数额或财物,或与价值相当的财物享有优先于政府罚款的权利,任何公务人员违反本法案第 7 条的规定,由法院酌情单处或者并处 100 比索以上 1000 比索以下的罚金或处以不超过 1 年的监禁。

上述违法行为在适当的行政诉讼中被证实,将是公务人员开除或免职的充分理由,即使对该公务人员没有提起刑事诉讼。

第 10 条　管辖法院——除非法律另有规定,本法案所有的诉讼由相应的一审法院享有初审管辖权。

第 11 条　追诉期限的规定——本法案规定的所有犯罪行为的追诉时效为 10 年。

第 12 条　公职的终止——任何公职人员依本法案规定的犯罪或《修正刑法典》有关贿赂罪的规定在刑事或者行政调查未决期间,或被起诉未决期间不许辞职或退休。

第 13 条　暂停公职和利益的丧失——任何公务人员依本法案规定或依《修正刑法典》有关贿赂罪的规定,被提起刑事诉讼,法院尚未审结期间,应当被暂停公职。如果终身判决有罪,将丧失任何法定的退休金或养老金,但如果被赦免,将有资格复职并获得在审判未决期间丧失的薪金和津贴,除非同时被提起行政诉讼。

第 14 条　例外规定——非索取的礼物,或数额小的或价值不大的礼物,或根据当地的习俗或习惯纯粹是出于感激或友情馈赠的一般礼物,应该被排除在本法案规定之外。本法案不能被认为是损害或禁止任何私人或公务人员在其任职期间,并在法定范围内实施的合法的职业、贸易或副业行为,除非是其职业、贸易或副业行为涉及与他人或公务员合谋触犯了本法案规定的应受处罚的违法行为。

第 15 条　可分性条款——本法案的任何规定或这些规定的适用对任

何人或任何情况将不会因此声明而受影响。

第 16 条　生效——本法案通过后生效，但为了确定未经说明的财产，对其任职后所获得的全部财产都应当考虑。

1960 年 8 月 17 日通过。

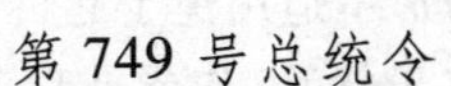

第 749 号总统令

批准在贿赂和其他渎职案件中的行贿人和其礼品及其共犯免予起诉的决定

然而,公务行为是一种公信力:公务人员只是人民的公仆,应当全心全意为人民服务。

但是,因为缺乏证人,不可能保证对不忠诚的公仆定罪和免职:行贿人或送礼者总是不愿意对腐败作证,因为他们害怕他们自己的贿赂和腐败行为被起诉和判刑。

但是,行贿人或送礼者被批准免予起诉,因此他可以就政府官员的腐败自由地作证,比起接受贿赂和礼物的官员逍遥法外且自傲的留在机关继续进行目无法纪及腐败行为,使公共事务和公共利益受到大量的损害来,应该更符合社会的需要。

因此,现在我费迪南德·马科斯作为菲律宾总统,基于宪法赋予我的权力制定命令和法令:

第 1 条 任何人自愿地对《修正刑法典》第 210 条、第 211 条和第 212 条;修正的共和国第 3019 号法案;《国内税收法》第 345 条和《关税和海关法》第 3604 条以及已颁布法典的其他有关公务人员滥用或不诚实行为的处罚规定;和其他法律、法规和条例对渎职、腐败和其他滥用公职规定的行为控告;并愿对公务官员或雇员的这些违法行为作证,其与提控告和证词有关的犯罪行为将免予起诉或处罚,并且在此诉讼中可以辩护或证明:首先,如果该控告和证词针对的不是公务人员而是上述违法行为的主犯、共犯或从犯,即使是在此种情形下也可以有权;其次,如果这些控告者或证人提供或给予行贿或送礼或他的助手实施这些行为,这样的被免予起诉还是有权享有的;最后,如果下列情形同时发生:

1. 所控告的内容必须涉及上述法律、法规和条例规定的违法行为的完成;

2. 该控告和证词对追究公务人员的罪责是必要的;

3. 国家法律还没有规定这样的举报和证词的;

4. 这样的控告和证词所涵盖的内容能够被确证;

5. 而且该控告或证词以前没有证明涉及道德卑劣行为为有罪行为。

第2条 下面提到的情形不适用免予起诉:随后证明其控告和/或证词是错误的和恶意的或仅仅出于扰乱、作弄或以其他任何方式侵害公务人员为目的而捏造的,因上述控告或证词使其遭受民事或刑事起诉。

第3条 所有提起公诉的检察官、法官或委员会所引起的初步调查和所有引起的相关诉讼,为了保护政府官员的名声将被极其秘密地或不公开地进行,在对事件的调查中查明该报告的证据是没有根据的或不作为主要证据。

第4条 所有与本法令不一致的法案、法令和规则及章程据此废止或修正。

第5条 本法令即日起生效。

上议院全体成员于1975年7月18日于马尼拉制定。

第 8353 号共和国法案

为修改 3815 号法案(即《修正刑法典》)和其他目的,扩大解释强奸罪、将强奸罪重新归类到对人身犯罪一编中的法案

(由菲律宾国会代表组成的参议院和众议院制定)

第 1 条　短标题——本法案也称为“1997 年反强奸法案”。

第 2 条　强奸作为对人的犯罪——强奸犯罪从此将根据 3815 号共和国法案(即《修正刑法典》)第八编分类为对人身的犯罪。相应地,将其并入该法的八编另立新的一章——第三章强奸罪,解释如下:

第三章　强　奸　罪

第 266-A 条　强奸罪——强奸罪是:

1. 男人在下列情形下与女人性交:

(a) 通过暴力、恐吓或者威胁;

(b) 当被害人处于丧失理智或其他无意识状态;

(c) 通过欺诈性的诡计或者严重滥用权力;

(d) 即使不具有上述情形,但是被害人未满 12 周岁或者是精神病人。

2. 任何人在任何前项规定的情形下将他的阴茎插入他人的嘴巴或者肛门,或者用任何工具或者物体插入他人的性器官或者肛门。

第 266-B 条　刑罚——犯前条第一项规定的强奸罪的,处以无期徒刑。

如果犯罪是携带致命的武器或者二人或者二人以上轮奸的,处以无期徒刑至死刑。

由于强奸的原因或者强奸使被害人成为精神病人的,处以无期徒刑至死刑。

由于强奸未遂的原因或者强奸而杀人的,处以无期徒刑至死刑。

由于强奸的原因或者在强奸时杀人的,处以死刑。

如果具有下列加重(规定)的情节的,将处以死刑:

(1) 被害人未满 18 周岁,且犯罪人是父亲、直系尊亲、继父、监护人、三代以内的血亲和姻亲,或者被害人母亲的习惯法上的配偶的;

(2) 被害人是在警察、军事机构或者任何法律执行或刑事机构的监管

下的；

(3) 强奸是在被害人的配偶、父母、任何子女或者其他三代以内的血亲的能够看见下进行的；

(4) 犯罪人在强奸前或强奸时，明知被害人是从事合法的宗教职业或者行业的尼姑的；

(5) 被害人未满 7 周岁的；

(6) 犯罪人知道自己患有艾滋病或者任何其他能传染的性病且病毒和传染病已经传染给被害人的；

(7) 是菲律宾武装部队或者准武装部队人员，或菲律宾国家警察或法法律执行机构或刑事机构人员利用职务便利犯强奸罪的；

(8) 由于强奸的原因或者强奸时，造成被害人终身身体毁损或者残疾的；

(9) 犯罪人在犯罪时知道被害人是孕妇的；

(10) 犯罪人在犯罪时知道被害人精神障碍、情感混乱和（或）身体障碍的。

第 266-C 条　宽恕的效力——后来被害人与罪犯的合法结婚将消灭刑事诉讼或已判处的刑罚。

如果犯罪人成为合法的丈夫，被害人成为妻子，其后来的宽恕将消灭刑事诉讼或刑罚；如果婚姻是无效的则犯罪不可以消灭或者刑罚不能被免除。

第 266-D 条　推定——任何程度的被害人任何身体外在的自卫行为证明反抗强奸的行为，或者被害人处于不能给予有效的同意的情形，可以被认为 266-A 条应受处罚行为的起诉的证据。

第 3 条　可分离条款——如果本法案的任何部分或者章节的规定被宣布无效或者违宪，不影响其他部分继续有效。

第 4 条　废止条款——修正的 3815 法案的第 336 条和所有法律、法案、总统令、行政命令、规则和规章与本法案不一致或者相违背的被认为相应地已经修正、修改或废止。

第 5 条　生效——本法案在两种全国发行的报纸公布后 15 天生效。

批准：

众议院院长（SGD.）JOSE DE VENECIA，JR.

参议院院长（SGD.）ERNESTO M. MACEDA

本法案是合并参议院第 950 号议案和众议院第 6265 号议案，最后由参议院和众议院分别于 1997 年 6 月 5 日和 1997 年 9 月 3 日通过。

众议院秘书(SGD.) ROBERTO P. NAZARENO

参议院秘书(SGD.) LORENZO E. LEYNES, JR.

批准:1997 年 9 月 30 日

菲律宾总统 (SGD.) FIDEL V. RAMOS

第8177号共和国法案

指定用注射方法适用死刑的法案

（修正被第7659号共和国法案第24条修改的
《修正刑法典》第81条的法案）

第1条 被第7659号共和国法案第24条修改的《修正刑法典》第81条，现修改如下：

"第81条 死刑执行的时间与方式——死刑判决执行应优先于其他刑罚的执行，统一用注射方式执行死刑。死刑判决应由矫正局长授权执行，在注射及注射前的程序中，尽可能减轻被执行人的痛苦。

矫正局长应按步骤保证注射的执行能够足以使罪犯在瞬间死亡。

依照规定，所有执行注射死刑的部门的人员都要在执行此项任务前进行培训。

矫正局被授权的医生，通过全面的检查后，作一个罪犯死亡的正式证明且在矫正局的档案中签名。

死刑判决终审宣判生效后，不能在1年内也不能超过18个月才执行，不影响总统在此期间行使赦免权。"

第2条 经可执行的终审判决宣判的、等待通过电刑或毒气来执行死刑的罪犯，在本法案生效后，应遵守本法案的相关规定。为此目的，上述判决将自动修正。

第3条 执行条款——司法部长协同卫生部长和矫正局长，在本法案生效后30日内，公布此执行条款的规定。

第4条 废止条款——与本法案的规定不一致的所有或者部分的法律，总统令和公布、实施的规则和规章据此相应的废止和修改。

第5条 生效——本法案在政府公报或者至少在2份全面发行的国家级报纸（在先公布的任何一个）公布后15日后生效。不能在通过后10日后才公布。

1996年3月20日通过

第9262号共和国法案

定义暴虐妇女儿童的行为，为受害人提供保护性措施以及其他目的，规定相应的刑罚的法案

菲律宾国会议员组成的参议院和众议院制定颁布

第1条　短标题——本法案称为“2004年反暴虐妇女儿童法案”。

第2条　政策声明——据此宣布国家重视妇女儿童的尊严和保证充分尊重人权。国家也要承认保护家庭及其成员特别是妇女和儿童的人身安全免受暴力和威胁是必需的。

朝着这个目标，国家应该尽力宣传暴虐妇女儿童是违反《宪法》、《世界人权宣言》、《消除妇女歧视公约》、《儿童权利公约》和其他菲律宾加入的国际人权公约所承诺的基本自由的。

第3条　术语解释——本法所使用的(a)“暴虐妇女儿童”是指任何人对妇女或者儿童实施的导致或者可能导致其身体的、性有关的、或者心理上的伤害或者痛苦，或包括恐吓、殴打、攻击、强迫、折磨或任意剥夺自由的行为，经济上的虐待的行为，行为对象是他的妻子、前妻、性伙伴或者情人关系或与其有共同的小孩的妇女，或者对其婚生或者非婚生的子女，这些行为不管是家庭内还是家庭外，包括但是不限于下列行为：

A. “身体暴虐”是指身体或者肉体的伤害；

B. “性暴虐”是指对妇女或者儿童所实施的实际上的性侵害，包括但是不限于：

a. 对妇女或儿童实施强奸、性骚扰、挑逗行为，做一些下流或者挑逗性的言行举止，对受害者的性感区实施身体上侵害，强迫受害者观看淫秽出版物和下流的表演，或者强迫妇女或儿童做淫秽动作和(或)拍摄淫秽影片，强迫其妻子和情妇与性虐待者在他们的住所共同生活；

b. 通过暴力、暴力相威胁，或者其他伤害或强迫，造成或者企图造成受害者实施任何性行为的；

c. 使妇女或者儿童卖淫的。

C. “心理上的暴虐”是指造成和可能造成受害者精神上或者情感上的痛苦，诸如但不限于胁迫、折磨、跟踪、财产损失、公众嘲笑或羞辱、反复谩骂

和精神错乱。它包括导致或允许受害者目击家庭成员身体、性或心理的虐待，或者观看任何形式的色情文学或者目击对宠物的虐待性伤害或剥夺共同的孩子的监护权和（或）探望权。

D. “经济虐待”是指使或企图使一名妇女的经济依靠包括但不限于下列行为：

1. 取消经济支持或阻止受害者参与任何合法的行业、职业、事务或活动，除非如果在另一方配偶或性伙伴对象存在有《家庭法》第 73 条所规定的有依据的、严重的道德原因；

2. 剥夺或者威胁剥夺经济来源、收益权、夫妻权和共同拥有的夫妻财产；

3. 毁坏家庭财产；

4. 控制受害者的自己的金钱或财物，或单独控制夫妻金钱或财产。

（b）“殴打”是指使妇女或儿童造成身体伤害因而导致身心或者精神痛苦。

（c）“被虐妇女综合症”是指妇女由于长期生活在虐待的殴打关系中，被发现具有科学确定的心理上和行为上的症状。

（d）“跟踪”是指行为人故意且没有合法的理由跟随妇女或儿童，或直接或间接地使他们处于监视下，或两种行为都有。

（e）“情人关系”是指作为丈夫和妻子生活的一方没有得到结婚的利益或是在关系期间所有时间和一个持续的期间烂漫。在商业或社会交往中两人之间偶然相识或普通的社会交往不属于情人关系。

（f）“性关系”是指一种单独的性行为，可能或可能不生出一个共同的孩子。

（g）“安全住所或庇护所”是指社会福利和发展部或其代理机构维持和管理的，或以本法为目的经社会福利和发展部认可的其他自愿组织，维持和管理的任何家园和机构，任何其他自愿接收受害者的适当的居住地。

（h）“儿童”是指那些在 18 周岁以下或依照第 7610 号共和国法案规定的生活不能自理的大于 18 周岁的人，它包括受害者的亲生子女和其他由其监管的孩子。

第 4 条　解释——为促进对受暴虐的妇女和儿童的保护和安全，本法将不受限制的解释。

第 5 条　暴虐妇女和儿童——暴虐妇女儿童罪是通过以下行为犯罪：

（a）造成妇女或儿童身体伤害；

(b) 威胁导致妇女或儿童身体伤害;

(c) 企图使妇女或儿童身体造成伤害;

(d) 使妇女或儿童担心将造成身体伤害;

(e) 企图强迫或强迫妇女或儿童参与有权不实施的行为,或不许妇女或儿童实施有权实施的行为,或通过暴力或者以身体暴力或者其他伤害威胁,企图制约或制约妇女或儿童的行动自由,或者直接胁迫命令妇女或者儿童。包括但不限于通过以下行为来控制或制约妇女或儿童的活动和行为:

1. 威胁剥夺或实际上剥夺妇女或其家庭对小孩的监管;

2. 剥夺或威胁剥夺妇女或儿童法律上应当给予的经济支持;或故意给妇女和儿童提供不足的经济支持;

3. 剥夺或威胁剥夺妇女或儿童的合法权利;

4. 阻止妇女从事任何合法的行业、职业、事务或活动,或控制受害者本人的钱物,或单一地控制夫妻共同的钱物;

(f) 为控制她的行动或决定,造成或威胁要对行为人本人造成身体伤害;

(g) 通过暴力或身体伤害相威胁,造成或企图造成妇女或儿童参与不构成强奸的任何性活动, 或通过胁迫控制妇女或儿童或其直系亲属;

(h) 亲自或通过他人从事有目的、故意或轻率的行为,来恐吓或实际上造成妇女或儿童情感上或者心理上创伤,包括但不限于以下行为:

1. 在公开或私人场所潜围或跟踪妇女或儿童的;

2. 在窗户偷窥或在妇女或她的孩子的住所之外逗留不走的;

3. 违反妇女或儿童的意愿,进入或留在妇女或儿童的住所或所有物的;

4. 毁坏妇女或儿童个人财产或对她们所有的动物或宠物进行伤害的;

5. 实施任何形式的骚扰或暴力的;

(i) 造成妇女或儿童精神或情感痛苦,被公开嘲笑或屈辱,包括但不限于反复的谩骂和情感虐待和对妇女的孩子拒绝经济支持或对未成年儿童拒绝监护。

第6条　刑罚——第5条规定的暴虐妇女儿童犯罪,应按下列规定处罚:

(a) 触犯第5条(a)项的规定,构成杀亲罪或者谋杀罪或者杀人罪的未遂、受阻或者既遂的,依照《修正刑法典》的相应规定处罚。

如果这些行为导致身体毁损的,依照《修正刑法典》的相应规定处罚;构成严重的身体伤害的,处以监狱矫正;构成轻伤的,处以长期禁闭。

触犯第5条(b)项的规定,处以比前款对犯罪既遂所规定的刑罚低两等级的刑罚,但在任何情形下不得低于长期禁闭。

(b) 触犯第5条(c)项和(d)项的规定的,处以长期禁闭;

(c) 触犯第5条(e)项的规定的,处以监狱矫正;

(d) 触犯第5条(f)项的规定的,处以长期禁闭;

(e) 触犯第5条(g)项的规定的,处以监禁;

(f) 触犯第5条(h)项和(i)项的规定的,处以监禁。

如果在妇女或儿童怀孕时或她的孩子在场时实施犯罪行为的;处以最高幅度的本条规定的刑罚。

除羁押之外,罪犯应:(a) 支付不少于10万比索(100000菲元) 但不超过30万比索(300,000菲元)的罚金;(b) 必须强制接受心理咨询或精神治疗并且向法院报告。

第7条　审判地点——地方审判法院应建立一个家事法庭,对本法规定的暴虐妇女儿童的案件享有最初和排他的裁判权。在没有这种法庭的地方,案件将被移送到控诉方所选择的犯罪或任何犯罪要素所在地的地方审判法院。

第8条　保护命令——保护命令是为了进一步防止本法案第5条规定的暴虐妇女儿童行为的发生和给予其他必需的救济,依照本法发布的命令。保护命令所给予的救济是为了维护受害者免受进一步的伤害,使受害者的日常生活的干扰最小化,为受害者重新独立驾驭生命的机会和能力提供便利。可以依照本法案发布的保护命令是村保护令,临时保护令和终身保护令;可以依照本法发布保护令的,包括任何部分或者所有的下列救济:

(a) 禁止被告本人或者通过他人威胁将触犯或者触犯本法第5条规定的行为;

(b) 禁止被告直接或间接地骚扰、懊恼、打电话、接触或以其他方式与申请人接触;

(c) 被申请人从申请人的住所迁出和被驱逐的,不管住所的所有权是谁,还是为了临时或终身保护申请人,财产权均不可侵犯,并且如果被申请人必须从住所带走私人用品,法院将指定一个执法人员陪伴被申请人收拾他的东西并护送离开住所;

(d) 法院命令被告在一定的时间离开申请者和所指定的家庭或家庭成员,和离开住所、学校、工作场所,或任何申请人指定经常出入的地方和任何指定的家庭或家庭成员；

(e) 命令合法拥有和使用的汽车和其他私人必需用品，不管所有权属于谁，法院将指定一个适当的执法人员陪伴申请人至配偶对方的住所，保证申请人安全地归还汽车和其他私人必需用品，或监督申请人或被申请人转移个人所有物；

(f) 同意申请人对孩子的临时或永久监护权；

(g) 如果具有合法的抚养权，则命令被告对妇女和或她的孩子提供支持。尽管其他法律有相反规定，法院将确定被申请人的收入或薪金的适当的比例，由被申请人的雇主按期扣除，并直接主动交给此妇女。无正当理由不交付和(或)扣除，或者任何延迟将抚养费交给妇女和(或)她的孩子，将判处被申请人或他的雇主承担蔑视法庭的法律负责；

(h) 禁止被申请人使用和持有任何枪支或致命武器，命令被申请人将这些武器交给法院进行适当的处理，包括许可证的撤回和剥夺使用和持有武器的资格。如果犯罪者是执法人员，法院命令其交出武器并命令有关当局调查犯罪者和对此事件采取适当的措施；

(i) 赔偿因为暴力造成的实际损失，包括但不限于财产损失、医疗费用、子女的开支和和收入损失；

(j) 命令社会福利和发展部或任一适合的代理机构给申请人提供可能的需要；

(k) 如果申请人和任何指定的家庭或家庭成员同意，则提供法院认为为保护和防止他们的安全所必需的其他形式的救济。

即使没有合法分居的判决，或者法院判决婚姻无效或宣布为无效婚姻，也要提供本条规定的任何救济。

村保护令的发布或者终身保护令的申请未决不能影响申请人的申请，或不能影响法院同意临时保护令或终身保护令。

第9条　可以提出保护命令请求的主体——任何下列人员可以提交保护命令请求：

(a) 受害者；

(b) 受害者的父母或监护人；

(c) 长辈、晚辈或四代以内旁系血亲或者姻亲；

(d) 政府官员或社会福利和发展部的社会工作者或地方政府部门的社会工作者；

(e) 警察，负责妇女和儿童的部门；

(f) 村上尉或村委委员

(g) 申请人的律师、法律顾问、或临床医学家或卫生保健师;

(h) 在发生暴虐妇女儿童的城市或者自治市有至少两名可靠且具有犯罪学方面的知识的市民。

第10条 申请保护令的地点——保护令的申请将遵循1991年《地方政府法》第409条规定的规则和其执行规章和规则。对临时保护令或终身保护令的申请可以提交到申请人居住地有属地管辖权的地方审判法院、大城市审判法院、自治区审判法院、自治区巡回审判法院;但是,如果在申请人住所地有家事法庭的,申请将提交给此法院。

第11条 申请保护命令的方式——对保护命令的申请必须是书面的、申请人签字和证明已宣誓的。它可以作为一种单独的行为或在带有本法所述的暴力问题或者争论的任何民事或者刑事案件中的附带救济。一份标准保护命令申请表,应该用英文书写且翻译成主要的地方语言,使其有利于促进对保护命令的申请,并且在其中应包含以下信息:

(a) 申请人和被申请人姓名和地址;

(b) 写明申请人和被申请人之间的关系;

(c) 虐待情况的陈述;

(d) 本法第8条所规定的申请人要写明救济的要求;

(e) 请求的建议和原因;

(f) 请求申请费用缓交到听证时;

(g) 保证在其他法院没有未决的保护命令申请。

如果申请人不是受害者,申请书必须附有申请人的宣誓书证明(a) 受害者所遭受的虐待情况和(b) 受害者同意授权提交申请的情形。何时受害者的地址被透露将面临生命危险,将在此陈述中声明。在这种情况下,申请人应该证实受害者居住在法院有属地管辖权的自治市或城市,并且为了服务程序将提供一个邮寄地址。

提交给法院的保护命令申请将被认为临时保护令或终身保护令的申请。

村干部和法院人员在申请准备时应协助申请人。如果执法人员在保护命令申请属于应该由他们负责时也应提供协助。

第12条 保护命令的执行——所有根据本法发布的临时保护令或终身保护令在菲律宾任何地方可以强制执行,并且违者将单处或者并处5000比索(5000菲元) 至5万比索(50000菲元)的罚金或6个月的监禁。

第 13 条　保护命令申请的代理——如果妇女或儿童在保护命令申请中要求聘请律师,但因缺乏经济的原因没有聘请,法院应立即指定公职律师事务所在申请听证程序中代理申请人。如果公职律师事务所确定申请人能支付律师服务费用的,则由一个律师为申请人的法律代理提供便利。申请人不能取得家庭或夫妻财产,譬如当被罪犯所控制,申请人将有资格将公职律师事务所作为其法律代理。

但是,私人律师提供的免费为申请人代理法律事务不受禁止。

第 14 条　发布村保护命令的主体和方式—— 村保护命令是指由村上尉发布的,命令犯罪人停止本法第 5 条(a)项和(b)项所规定犯罪行为。村上尉收到村保护命令申请的主要要件后的确定一个日期发布保护命令。如果村上尉是不能对申请人的发出村保护命令的,则申请由任一有资格的村委委员签发。如果村委委员发布村保护命令,命令必须附有由村委委员的证明,村上尉无权发布村保护命令。村保护命令的有效期为 15 天。发行村保护命令之后, 村上尉或村委委员将立即亲自将提供一份副本给被申请人,或命令任一村官员亲自提供。

在村上尉前的任何程序中当事人可以由一位非律师辩护人陪同。

第 15 条　临时保护命令——临时保护命令是指在确定应该发布命令后,在提交申请后的一定期间由法院发布的保护命令。法院可以批准临时保护命令中有任何部分或者全部本法案所规定的救济,有效期为 30 天。法院应在临时保护命令期满前或者期满日确定一个听证的时间。法院命令法院法警为被申请人安排临时保护命令的直接个人服务,在服务中法院法警可获得执法人员的协助。临时保护命令包括发布终身保护命令的听证日期的布告。

第 16 条　终身保护命令——终身保护命令是指法院在公告和听证后发布的保护命令。

被申请人尽管已经合法通知后未在法定期限到庭,或没有聘请律师,或律师没有发挥作用都不是重新安排或者推迟发布终身保护命令听证的理由。如果被申请人在举行终身保护命令听证时发现没有聘请律师,法院将为被申请人指定一位律师并继续进行听证。如果被申请人尽管给予适当的通知仍然缺席,法院允许申请人单方面提供证据并将主要证据提交给法院。法院将允许申请人对曾经发生的暴虐行为进行陈述,即使被申请人没有直接指向申请人或申请人所聘请的人员。

法院将尽最大限度的可能在 1 天之内完成发布终身保护命令听证会。

如果在1天之内无法完成听证会并且发布的临时保护命令该到期，法院将延长或在每次特殊时期对临时保护命令重新确定30天的期间直到终身裁判已经发布。如果必要或申请人的要求可以采用，则法院可以变更临时保护命令延长期限或重新起算期限。

法院可能在终身保护命令中批准第8条所指定的部分或者全部救济。终身保护命令在法院根据所发布的命令的受益人提出的申请予以撤回前都是有效的。法院要确保受益人能得到终身保护命令所确定的被申请人的直接个人服务。

法院不能因为暴行和提交申请之间的时间已经失效而拒绝发布保护命令。

不管被申请人被宣告有罪还是无罪，法院必须要判决终身保护命令是否为终身判决。被批准的终身保护命令的有效期应该至命令可能发生的暴虐行为明显不存在时止。

第17条　批准保护令的通知——在村上尉或者法院发布的保护命令中，以下内容应该用粗体字或者大写印刷：

“违反本命令将受法律处罚”。

第18条　保护命令申请行为的强制性期限——在前条规定的期限内无正当理由不能完成保护命令申请行为的，将提交给有管理责任的官员或法官。

第19条　法律分离情形——在法律分离的情形，本法案所特别规定的暴虐行为不适用《家庭法》第58条。法院应尽可能地对主要诉讼和其他事件进行诉讼。申请人提交的任何保护命令申请的听证程序在本法案规定的强制期限内必须要举行。

第20条　申请保护命令的优先权——本法规定的保护命令申请的主要要件已经确定，单方面和双方的听证程序将有优先于所有其他程序。村官员和法院将确定和举行保护命令申请听证会，如果需要，为了听证保护命令的申请将中止其他程序。

第21条　违反保护命令——违反根据本法发布的村保护命令的控告，必须直接向对村发布保护命令由属地管辖权的任何市政审判法院，大城市审判法院，或市巡回法院提出。违反村保护命令的，处以30天的监禁，不影响受害者提起的任何刑事或者民事诉讼。

违反村保护命令的判决根据法院规则可以提起上诉。在审理期间，审判法庭认为必要时，可以无需申请就主动依职权发布保护命令。

违反依照本法发布的临时保护命令或终身保护命令的任何规定，将构成蔑视法庭，根据《法院规则》第 71 条规则的规定处罚，不影响受害者提起的任何刑事或者民事诉讼。

第 22 条　保护命令在刑事案件中的适用——前面关于保护命令的规定可以推定适用于提起包括暴虐妇女儿童在内的刑事诉讼。

第 23 条　不再犯保证——法院可以要求任何发布的保护命令之违者提交不再犯的保证，提供两个有保证能力的保证人，此保证人要保证防止违反者再实施暴虐行为。

被申请人不能按照要求提供保证，如果根据第 5 条(a)项到(f)项的规定被提起刑事诉讼，将处以不超过 6 个月的拘留，如果根据第 5 条(g)项到(i)项的规定被提起刑事诉讼，则处以不超过 30 天的拘留。

保护命令再本条中仅指法院发布的临时保护命令和终身保护命令。

第 24 条　时效——本法案第 5 条(a)项到(f)项的时效为 20 年。第 5 条(g)项到(i)项的时效为 10 年。

第 25 条　公罪——暴虐妇女儿童将被认为是公罪，可以由任何知道此犯罪有关情况的公民提起控告。

第 26 条　被虐妇女综合症辩护理由——法院发现幸存的受害者患有被虐妇女综合症，尽管缺乏符合《修正刑法典》的正当防卫的要件，也不承担任何刑事和民事责任。

对犯罪时患有被虐妇女综合症的妇女的判决过程中，由专门的精神病专家或心理学家协助法院照管。

第 27 条　被禁止的辩护——是在酒精、任何违禁麻醉药品、或其他改变意志物质的影响下，不作为本法案的辩护理由。

第 28 条　对子女的监护——被暴虐的妇女受害者有权获得她的子女的监护和抚养权。孩子在 7 岁以下但有精神病或身体伤残的，抚养权将自动地归母亲，除非法院发现非常有说服性的理由就可以安排其他抚养方式。

患有被虐妇女综合症的受害者无资格监护其孩子。在任何情况下，未成年人的监护权都不能给患有被虐妇女综合症的妇女。

第 29 条　公诉人员和(或)审判人员之职责——公诉人员和审判人员在处理本法规定的受害者时应该履行以下义务：

(a) 使用受害者的妇女或儿童能听懂的语言；

(b) 通知受害者包括可用的法律补救办法和程序以及贫困当事人的特权。

第30条　村官员和执法者责任——村官员和执法者应该履行以下义务：

(a) 无论保护命令是否已经发布，一旦受害者电话要求帮助或请求援助或保护，就必需立刻作出反应并保证受害者的安全；

(b) 没收罪犯持有的任何致命武器或探视器；

(c) 护送受害者到他们所选择的安全地方，或门诊或医院；

(d) 协助受害者从房子搬出个人用品；

(e) 协助对电话请求帮助作出反应的村官员和其他政府官员和雇员；

(f) 保证村上尉或法院发布的保护令的执行；

(g) 当任何本法规定的暴虐行为发生时，或当他(她)凭借个人知识认为任一暴虐行为刚刚发生，和本法规定受害者的生命危险即将发生或处于困境时，无需授权就可拘捕犯罪嫌疑人；

(h) 立刻报告请求社会福利和发展部，地方政府部门或合格的非政府组织的社会保障部门评估或协助。

任何村官员或执法者不报告这些事件的，将处以不超出1万比索(10,000菲元)的罚款，或随时承当刑事、民事或行政责任。

第31条　医疗保健服务者对虐待的反应——任何医疗保健服务者，包括但不限于怀疑存在暴虐行为或被暴虐受害者告知存在暴虐的主治医师、护士、临床医生、村公共卫生工作者、临床医学专家或顾问，应该：

(a) 如实证明任何受害者的身体、情感或心理上的伤害；

(b) 如实记录任何受害者的不确定状态、观察报告和检查或者视察的情况；

(c) 自动免费为受害者提供关于检查或视察的医生证明；

(d) 保护纪录和使记录在受害者请求时实际有效；

(e) 为受害者直接和充分地提供本法规定的权利和补救措施，并且提供有效的服务。

第32条　其他政府机构和地方政府部门的责任——其他政府机构和地方政府部门将建立系统的计划，诸如但不限于关于这些暴虐行为的性质、原因、发生和后果的活动和研讨会或座谈会的教育和信息，特别倾向于在教育公众是要产生社会效果。

保证政府官员和职员关于预防本法规定的暴虐妇女儿童行为发生的持续教育和培训，是有关政府机构和地方政府部门的职责。

第33条　被禁止的行为——审理保护命令申请的村上尉、村委委员或法院，不能命令、指挥、强制或以任何形式影响保护命令申请人妥协或放弃任何本法规定保护申请救济的寻求。1997 年《家事法院发法》第 7 条，1991 年《地方政府法》第 410 条、第 411 条、第 412 条和第 413 条在根据本法寻求救济的程序不再适用。

不遵守本条的规定的官员或法官承担相应的行政责任。

第 34 条　个人干预的责任豁免——在本法规定的每种暴虐妇女儿童的情形，履行法律的任何人，个人或警察当局或村官员，在保证受害者安全时，使用暴力或者约束时没有过分的超出必要限度的，对因此产生的后果无需承担任何刑事、民事或行政责任。

第 35 条　受害者的权利——除现有法律规定的权利之外，受暴虐的妇女儿童将享有以下权利：

(a) 受到尊敬和尊重；

(b) 得到司法部的公职律师事务所或任何公众法律协助机构的法律援助；

(c) 有权获得社会福利和发展部和地方政府部门的支援；

(d) 有资格获得所有《家庭法》规定的赔偿和抚养；

(e) 被告知他们的权利和有用的帮助包括他们申请保护命令的权利。

第 36 条　赔偿金——任何本法规定下的暴虐受害者有权获得实际的、补偿性的、道德的和惩戒性的赔偿金。

第 37 条　强制离境令——法院在根据本法起诉的案件中将加快强制离境令的签发程序。

第 38 条　立案费和其他费用的免交——如果受害者贫困或由于即将发生的危险或危险的威胁而申请保护命令的直接需要，法院在没有交纳申请费和其他费用和速记本副本时应接受申请。

第 39 条　反暴虐妇女儿童内部机构委员会——为贯彻上述政策，因此特成立一个反暴虐妇女儿童内部机构委员会，以下称为委员会，由以下机构组成：

(a) 社会福利和发展部(DSWD)；

(b) 菲律宾妇女地位委员会 (NCRFW)；

(c) 民间服务委员会(CSC)；

(d) 儿童福利委员会(CWC)；

(e) 司法部(DOJ)；

(f) 内政和地方政府部(DILG)；

(g) 菲律宾国家警署(PNP);

(h) 卫生部 (DOH);

(i) 教育部(DepEd);

(j) 劳动就业部(DOLE);

(k) 国家调查局(NBI)。

这些机构承担编制纲要和计划根据他们的要求消除暴虐妇女,又提高他们职员的能力使其变得更满足当事人的需要。委员会并且将担当主动反暴虐妇女的管理机构。

委员也可以指定一位级别不低于助理书记员或相当级别的正当授权的代表。这些代表将代表他们参加委员会会议,并且将领取由委员会根据现有的预算和财会规章制度确定的薪水。

第 40 条　为受害者提供的必要方案和服务——社会福利和发展部地方何政府部门将提供受害者临时庇护所、提供咨询服务、社会心理服务和(或)恢复、康复计划和生活补助。

卫生部将为受害者提供医疗帮助。

第 41 条　罪犯的咨询服务和治疗——社会福利和发展部将为罪犯提供使其恢复的咨询服务和治疗,使犯人学会指定的应付愤怒和情感爆发的方式和革新他们的方法。如果必要,罪犯将由法院命令使其接受精神病治疗或禁闭。

第 42 条　有关对暴虐妇女儿童案件作出反应人员的训练——所有对暴虐妇女儿童事件作出反应的机构将必须接受教育和训练,使他们熟悉:

a. 暴虐妇女儿童的性质、范围和原因;

b. 受暴虐的妇女儿童的法定权利、有效的治疗;

c. 对受害者或幸存者有用的服务和设施;

d. 进行拘捕和提供保护和协助是警察的强制义务;

e. 处理暴虐妇女儿童事件的技巧,使对政府官员的伤害可能减少到最小和促进受害者或幸存者的安全。

菲律宾国家警署协同地方政府机构,建立一个教育和训练计划,使警察和村官员完全能处理暴虐妇女儿童事件。

第 43 条　休假权——除《劳动法》和《公民服务规则和规章》规定的其他带薪休假之外,本法之受害者有权带薪休假 10 天,如果保护命令确定需要延长的情形出现时将延长。

任何雇主侵犯本条规定的权利,将根据《劳动法》和《公民服务规则和规章》的规定处罚。同样,雇主不许雇员帮助本法规定的受害同事的,同样承担歧视责任。

第 44 条　机密性——所有有关暴虐妇女儿童案件的记录,包括那些在村里的记录,将要保密,并且所有公职人员和雇员以及公立或私人诊所医院,应尊重受害者的隐私权。没有经过受害者或其家庭成员同意,任何人以任何形式出版或使出版受害者或者家庭成员的名字、地址、电话号码、学校、商务地址、雇主、或其他可识别信息的,将承担蔑视法庭权威的责任。

任何人违犯本条将被处以 1 年的监禁和不超过 50 万比索(500000 菲元)的罚金。

第 45 条　资助——实施本法案所必需的费用应将被包含在每年的《一般拨款法案》中。

被托管的代办处和地方政府部门的性和发展预算将被用于为受暴虐的妇女儿童服务。

第 46 条　执行规则和章程——从本法案通过之日起 6 个月内,司法部、菲律宾妇女地位委员会、社会福利和发展部、内政和地方政府部、卫生部、菲律宾国家警署和由菲律宾妇女地位委员会从非政府组织中确定的三个代表,将公布执行本法案的规则和章程。

第 47 条　补充适用——为本法案的目的,《修正刑法典》和其他可适用的法律,将补充适用。

第 48 条　可分离条款——如果本法案的任一条款或规定违反宪法或无效,其他条款或规定不受影响。

第 49 条　废止条款——所有或部分的法律、总统令、行政命令和规则章程,与本法不一致的,据此相应地被废止或修改。

第 50 条　生效——本法案从至少在全面发行的两份报纸上全面出版之日起 15 天生效。

批准:

众议院议长:何塞·德贝内西亚(Jose De Venecia)

参议院议长:富兰克林·德里隆(Franklin Drilon)

本法案是第 2723 号参议院议院第 5516 号和第 6054 号众议院议案的合并,最后由参议院和众议院分别于 2004 年 1 月 29 日和 2004 年 2 月 2 日通过。

众议院秘书:ROBERTO P. NAZARENO

参议院秘书:OSCAR G. YABES

批准:2004 年 3 月 8 日

菲律宾总统:格洛丽亚·马卡帕加尔·阿罗约(Gloria Macapagal Arroyo)

菲律宾反对恐怖主义议案[①]

2005 年 5 月 25 日

本法案于2005年5月制定,以此应对2月发生的恐怖袭击。

本法案将所有为应对已发生的那些恐怖袭击而提交的草案编纂成整体。

总统将本法案和其姐妹篇"身份证法案"称为"紧急地",并已批准,因而本法案不需要经过议会的严格审查。

于2005年5月4日起草

本法案由司法委员会和外事委员会提出

确定恐怖主义范围,为了预防和打击恐怖犯罪

建立反恐机制、规定刑罚和其他的目的法案

在菲律宾国会召开时经参议院和众议院制定:

第1条　简短标题——本法被称为"2005年反对恐怖主义法案"。

第2条　政策声明——政策声明:为保护人民的生命、财产以及环境,提高人民的尊严,强烈谴责恐怖主义这一违反国家和人类法律的犯罪行为。国家应该采取一切必要的措施来预防、打击和惩罚任何形式的恐怖主义,同时应该继续尊重和提升铭记在菲律宾宪法的神圣的价值、权利和自由。为了与外交政策保持一致,国家应该在对有关恐怖分子进行调查、逮捕、起诉上和其他国家和国际组织扩展合作和相互提供帮助。

第3条　恐怖主义——恐怖主义是指为了在普通公众、人民团体或特定的人中制造或散布一系列的危险、恐慌、畏惧或混乱,或者为了通过强迫或恐吓政府做出或放弃某种行为为目的,而预谋、威胁、实际使用暴力、武力或其他毁灭性手段对人身、财产或环境实施犯罪的行为。

第4条　恐怖主义的实施方式——恐怖主义是对自然的或法定的个体或团体,为了在普通公众、人民团体或特定的人中制造或散布一系列的危险、恐慌、畏惧或混乱,或者为了通过强迫或恐吓政府做出或放弃某种行为为目的,而预谋、威胁、实际使用暴力、武力或其他毁灭性手段对人身、财产或社会环境实施任一下列行为:

---

① 该法案在众议长德贝西亚的敦促下,菲律宾众议院于2006年4月5日通过,但因为遭到参议院的质疑,参议院提出了修改较大的新法案,目前两院正在僵持,所以该法案尚未正式生效。

(1) 对一人或多人进行威胁,或造成死亡或严重的身体伤害的;

(2) 对社会公众或部分公众健康或安全进行威胁或造成严重危险;

(3) 对公共或私人的重要基础设施或财产进行威胁或造成实质损害、或肆意破坏或放火的;

(4) 对公共的或私人的重要部门、设施或系统进行威胁或造成严重的妨碍或破坏,而不是合法的建议、主张、异议或罢工的;

(5) 劫持或威胁劫持任何飞机、电车、火车、机车、公共汽车或其他大型交通工具、或公共运输工具,或劫持船舶或船只的;

(6) 绑架或威胁绑架他人或剥夺他人的自由;

(7) 暗杀或威胁暗杀,或者绑架或威胁绑架菲律宾总统、副总统、参议院主席,众议院发言人,或最高法院首席大法官的;

(8) 违反《防止和惩处侵害应受国际保护人员包括外交代表的罪行的公约》和其他国际协定,杀害或暴力袭击国际保护人物或剥夺其自由的;

(9) 通过毁坏信息的实际运行机制和通讯基础设施,破坏政府或私人的网络或系统运行必需的信息技术,来攻击或威胁攻击电脑空间,或者对网络、服务器、计算机或其他信息系统或通讯系统进行非法破坏的;

(10) 蓄意破坏陆地、水中和空气中的自然资源,诸如森林资源、海洋资源和矿产资源,或者故意造成石油和毒气的泄露或其他类似的将威胁生态安全的破坏环境的行为;

(11) 非法制造、加工、出售、获取、持有、使用、转移、提供或运输用于生产、销售、发行和传播的化学的、生物的、放射性的或核的物质、设备和器具,而将直接或间接的威胁到一人或数人安全,或对财产造成重大破坏或损害的;

(12) 非法制造、出售、获取、提供、处置、使用、拥有用于或者打算用于促使、或易于发生本法规定的恐怖活动的或与其相关的爆炸物、炸弹、手榴弹、射弹、设备或者其他有毒的武器、物质或机器;

从事恐怖活动的,应该处以终身监禁和1千万比索(10,000,000 菲元)的罚金。如果恐怖行为致人死亡的,或者行为人使用军用或者执法部门专用的制服、随身用具、通讯设备或其他工具的,或者犯罪人是政府官员或雇员,或已经退休、辞职、被开除或其他原因脱离政府部门的人,应该判处死刑。

第5条　共谋或建议实施恐怖行为——恐怖行为的共谋是指两人或两人以上达成实施本法规定的恐怖行为的合意并且决定实施的行为。

恐怖行为的建议是指决定实施本法规定的恐怖行为的行为人建议他人

实施该恐怖活动的行为。

共谋或建议实施恐怖行为的行为人应该被处以6年零1天至12年的监禁和五百万比索(5,000,000 菲元)的罚金;如果行为人在职的或已经退休、辞职、被解雇或其他原因与政府部门脱离关系的政府官员或雇员,应该处以最高幅度的刑罚,并附加终生剥夺担任公职的资格。

第6条　煽动实施恐怖行为——任何自然人或法人通过演讲、宣言、著述、标志、标语或其他能够煽动他人从事恐怖活动的代表物,来煽动他人实施本法第4条所列举的任何一种行为均为非法。

煽动他人实施恐怖行为的行为人应该被处以6年零1天至12年的监禁和五百万比索(5,000,000 菲元)的罚款;如果行为人在职的或已经退休、辞职、被解雇或其他原因与政府部门脱离关系的政府官员或雇员,应该处以最高幅度的刑罚,并附加终生剥夺担任公职的资格。

第7条　帮助、促成、推动实施恐怖行为——任何自然人或法人明知、故意和自愿的通过实施下列任一行为来帮助、促成、推动实施恐怖行为均为非法:

(1) 与实施或正在实施恐怖行为的个人、群体或组织建立、保持、或提供联系的行为;

(2) 明知两人或两人以上的集会是支持恐怖活动或为了实施恐怖活动,而为集会提供安排或帮助的行为;

(3) 参加恐怖训练行为并且为任何进行恐怖活动的个人、群体或组织提供训练设备的行为;

(4) 为了进行恐怖活动而提供训练、技能或专门技术的行为;

(5) 为了帮助或实施恐怖行为的招募行为;

(6) 明知外国人实施过或正在实施恐怖行为,而为外国人进入或停留在菲律宾境内提供帮助的行为;

(7) 推动、提供、请求或鼓励为实施恐怖行为提供财政或物质支持的行为;

(8) 知道或基于合理理由相信他人是实施了本条规定的行为或者是实施了或可能实施任何恐怖行为的行为人,而包庇或窝藏的行为。

实施本条规定的恐怖行为的行为人应该处以终身监禁和1千万比索(100,000,000 菲元)的罚款;如果恐怖行为致人死亡,或者行为人使用军用或者执法部门专用的制服、随身用具、通讯设备或其他工具的,或者犯罪人是政府官员或雇员,或已经退休、辞职、被开除或其他原因脱离政府部门的人，应该判处死刑。

第 8 条　恐怖组织的宣布禁止——本法的立法目的是，司法部长根据由本法产生的反恐委员会的建议，将符合下列情形之一的组织宣布为禁止的恐怖组织：

(1) 何成员公开宣布、认可、承认已经实施本法规定的任何应受处罚的行为；

(2) 任何成员实施过一种或者一种以上的本法第 4、5、6、7 条所规定的恐怖行为；

(3) 已经被联合国或其他国际组织宣布禁止的恐怖组织。

宣布禁止应该在政府公报和主要报纸上公布。被禁止的组织或成员将向司法部争取不被禁止或不被列入，而且被禁止的组织或成员对司法部的决定有权向上诉法院提起上诉。

第 9 条　参与恐怖组织——当一个组织已经被宣布为恐怖组织时，行为人明知、故意或通过公开的行为使其自己成为或保持为该恐怖组织成员，除非行为人能够证明自己对该组织的活动缺乏认知；或当一个组织已经被宣布为恐怖组织时自己没有参与任何活动；或在其被宣布为恐怖组织后一有机会就退出该组织；或当行为人成为或开始声称是其成员时该组织尚未被宣布为恐怖组织，否则行为人的行为违法。

根据本条定罪的行为人应该被判处 6 年零 1 天至 12 年的监禁；如果行为人在职的或已经退休、辞职、被解雇或其他原因与政府部门脱离关系的政府官员或雇员，应该处以最高幅度的刑罚，并附加终生剥夺担任公职的资格。

第 10 条　制造虚假恐怖活动威胁——行为人实施下列行为之一的均为非法：

(1) 过任何方式故意将自己知道或认为是虚假的恐怖行为已经发生、正在发生或即将发生的信息传播给他人或使他人知晓的行为；

(2) 将任何物品放置在任何地方，或通过邮寄或其他运送方式发送物品，由此导致他人的错误认为：

(i) 该物品可能爆炸或燃烧，因而导致人身伤害或财产损失的；

(ii) 该物品含有可能导致死亡、疾病或人身伤害或财产损失的任何危险物质、放射性物质或有害物质；或任何有毒化学药品；或微生物物质或其他生物物质、或毒菌的；

本条第一、二项的目的是：判断行为人引发他人错误认识的标准并不需要行为人在决定引起错误认识时是针对特定人的。根据本条定罪的行为人应该被处以6年零1天至12年的监禁和五百万比索(5,000,000菲元)的罚款;如果行为人在职的或已经退休、辞职、被解雇或其他原因与政府部门脱离关系的政府官员或雇员,应该处以最高幅度的刑罚,并附加终生剥夺担任公职的资格。

第11条　不揭发恐怖行为——行为人知道根据本条规定的任何应受处罚的恐怖行为而隐瞒或不揭发和不尽快向政府或其他有权的机构报告,应该被处以6年零1天至12年的监禁和5万至10万比索(50,000至10,000菲元)的罚款。如果行为人是政府官员、雇员、或已经退休、辞职、被解雇或脱离政府部门的人,可以判处死刑并且附加终生剥夺担任公职的资格。

第12条　看守失职——公职人员在履行看守职务期间故意允许或默许其负责看守的,因实施本法规定的任何应受处罚行为而被指控的被告人或被终审判决的罪犯逃脱,应该处以10年零1天至12年的监禁;此外,附加终生剥夺担任公职的资格。

如果是负责押运和看管的公职人员在履行职务期间的过失行为导致被告人或罪犯的逃脱的,应处以8年零1天至10年的监禁,并附加终生剥夺担任公职的资格。

第13条　合伙组织、公司、社团和其他法人负责人的刑事责任——在合伙组织、公司、社团、基金会和任何其他法人违反本法情况下,股东、董事长、董事或经理同意或明知而容忍该行为的,应该被认定为共同主犯。在此情况下,法院对违法的合伙组织、公司、社团和其他法人进行自由裁量,单处或并处10万比索(100000菲元)以上50万比索(500000菲元)以下的罚款或解散。

第14条　逮捕和拘留——治安官或个人在下列情况下未经授权也可以逮捕下列人员:(a)在现场发现被逮捕的人已经实施、正在实施或将实施本法规定的任何犯罪行为;或者(b)被逮捕的行为人事实上已经实施犯罪行为或有正当理由相信其可能已经实施犯罪行为的。

根据本条被逮捕的行为人拘留期限自其逮捕之日起不得超过15天。

在被逮捕的行为人没有批准要求初步调查且在其律师在场书面表示同意的情况下,拘留期限可以超过15日。被逮捕的行为人有权享有第7438号共和国法案(即《关于被逮捕、拘留、或羁押调查者的权利法案》)所规定的任何其他权利。

移民局专员不需要保证就可以拘留被指控实施本法规定的恐怖犯罪行

为的任何外国人。

第 15 条　对外国人的附加刑——对于违反本法案规定的外国人，除了适用本法案所规定的刑罚种类外，在判决执行完毕以后无需其他程序就可以驱逐出境。

第 16 条　免予起诉——行为人为有关违反本法的刑事案件而为政府作证或提供证据，或者自愿地或因为作证传票或者要求提出，鉴别或提供证词的传票，但并非限于含有文字、声音、图画或图像、照片、地图、图表、略表、录音带、唱片或任何其他形式的文字证据、录制证据或原始证据的书籍、报纸、文件、磁带；根据第 1732 号总统令（即《为对政府证人免于刑事起诉的法令》）的条款和《法庭证据规则》的相关条款规定，应该免于刑事起诉。

第 17 条　证人保护；导致恐怖分子被捕和定罪的报告——行为人以证明书或纪录片形式对因实施本法规定的任何违法行为而被指控犯罪的个人、群体或组织提供调查或起诉所必需的实质性资料，应该受到保护，并应该履行依照第 6981 号共和国法案的《证人保护纲要》规定的义务。

第 18 条　第 9160 号共和国法案（第 9194 号共和国法案已修正）的适用——根据第 9160 号共和国法案，即修正后的《2001 年反洗钱法》规定的恐怖行为和其他违反本法的行为均为非法。

反洗钱委员会可以决定基于合理理由怀疑存在运用货币工具或财产进行恐怖活动和其他违法活动的行为并签发冻结财产的命令，该命令应该在 90 日内对货币工具或财产立即有效执行，上诉法院有权延长该期限。告知自称的所有人其货币工具或财产已被冻结的通知应该和冻结令一同发布。货币工具或财产的自称的所有人有权在收到通知之日起 3 个工作日内进行申辩。反洗钱委员会有权在收到自称的所有人申辩之日起 3 个工作日内进行审查决定。如果反洗钱委员会在收到自称的所有人申辩之日起 3 个工作日内没有采取任何行动的，冻结令将自动失效。

冻结令可以停止所有货币工具或财产的活动或交易或涉及到货币工具或财产的活动或交易。如果在冻结令发布之日前 15 日内关系到冻结令的银行账户的支票被开出，冻结令可以导致支票的自动撤销和停止支付。任何在同一期间发生的活动或交易，不论涉案金额大小，应该向反洗钱委员会报告。

如果银行机构或非银行的金融机构的存款或投资可能在没有依据修正的第 9160 共和国法案而发布的法庭命令被询问或检查；另外，被关闭机构的人员明知任何货币、工具或财产或其收益，代表、包括或涉及恐怖主义或其高级形式，但是没有像处理可疑交易行为一样向反洗钱委员会报告，都应该根据本法第13条承担刑事责任。

第19条　通讯协助机构或执法机构——(a) 相反的，第4200号共和国法案(或称为"反窃听法")规定：在地方法院行政法官发出命令或决定延长命令的期间之前，治安官可以依一方要求提出申请，要求电线、电子通讯设备的提供方来提供截取的通讯内容并且把尚待确认的信息报告给执法机构，或授权或批准对根据本法规定的可罚行为的调查相关的监视装置的安装、使用和撤销。

(b) 本法认为，监视装置应该包括但是不限于下列情形：

1) 能够用来记录或监控计算机信息的流入或流出数据的监视装置或程序；

2) 能够用来偷听、记录、监控或偷听他人谈话内容的窃听装置，但是不包括助听器或相似装置，这些相似装置可以被听力障碍人用来克服听力障碍和听到一般能听到的声音；

3) 能够用来视觉上记录或观察行为的视觉监视装置，但是不包括眼镜、隐形眼镜或被视力障碍人用来克服视力障碍的相似装置；

4) 能够用来确定或监控人或物位置或物体形状的电子跟踪器；

5) 能够记录或解码可以确定已拨号码或在装置所附电话线上传送号码的电子脉冲或其他脉冲的铅笔寄存器，但是不包括电线、电子通讯设备装置的提供商或用户使用的任何装置，这些装置被用来开账或记录开账或在一般商务行为中被用来计费或其他相似目的；

6) 能够捕捉进入的电子脉冲或其他脉冲的陷阱装置和跟踪装置，这些脉冲能够确定通讯仪器或装置的原始号码；

7) 本款第一项至第六项涉及到的两种或两种以上装置的联合装置；

(c) 当治安官已经鉴定可能通过截取、安装或使用得到的信息与对根据本法规定为可罚的违法行为所正在进行的调查有关时，法庭应该签发一个依单方申请的命令，要求电线或电子通讯服务的提供商或授权提供商在60日内安装、使用或撤销使用的装置。法庭有权将期限再延长60日。

这种命令应该规定一种以上的下列情形：

(1) 被监视的房屋；

(2) 对特定物体或一类物体使用监视装置；

(3) 对特定人或身份不明者的谈话、活动、位置使用监视装置；

(4) 法庭许可时才签发命令；

(5) 除非法庭命令,使用监视装置所附属的电线的人或已经被法院命令给请求者提供帮助的公司不得向任何人泄露该装置或对被列入名单订户的调查的存在;

(6) 电线或电子通讯装置的提供商提供截取的通讯内容和把尚未确认信息报告给治安官;或者

(7) 为了安装或撤销监视装置而进入房屋和进入相邻的特定房屋或为进入房屋提供通道;

(d) 电线或电子通讯的提供商、房东、管理员或其他人应该安装或为安装提供立即的帮助和为治安官提供谨慎完成安装、使用和撤销装置所必需的所有信息、设备、技术帮助,并且尽可能不干涉法庭命令提供的这些帮助,如果这种帮助是法庭所要求的,当事人应对进行安装、使用和撤销的人表示尊敬;

(e) 除非法庭命令,由窃听装置得到的信息应该在命令有效期内的正常营业时间的合理间隔期提供给法庭指派的治安官;

(f) 行为人未经授权泄漏依据本条取得、收集或获得的信息,应该判处6月零1天以上6年以下的监禁。如果行为人是政府官员、雇员、或已经退休、辞职、被解雇或脱离政府部门的人,可以判处死刑并且附加判处终生剥夺其从事公务的资格;

(g) 当与根据本法为可罚行为的调查有关的治安官得到一方当事人对与根据本法为可罚行为有关的通讯可以被监控或录制的书面同意时,授权安装、使用或撤销监视装置的行为无需经过法庭命令;

(h) 原告的起诉理由不得针对那些提供与根据本法规定和法庭命令术语相一致的信息、设备或帮助的任何电线或电子通讯装置的提供商、经理人员、雇员、中介人或特定的人。善意的相信根据本法产生的法庭命令就没有必要根据本法或其他法提起民事诉讼或刑事诉讼;

(I) 任何违反本条规定获得的书面形式或口头形式的通讯、谈话、讨论、信息、照片或数据均不得在司法的、准司法的、立法的或行政的听证或调查中被采纳为证据。行为人阻碍或防止治安官履行本法第20条规定义务的,应该判处6月零1天以上6年以下的监禁。如果行为人在职的或已经退休、辞职、被解雇或其他原因与政府部门脱离关系的政府官员或雇员,应该处以最高幅度的刑罚,并附加终生剥夺担任公职的资格。

第20条　没收车辆、船舶、飞机、设备或其他财产或工具——被用来推动本法规定的恐怖行为、附属于恐怖行为或与恐怖行为相关的车辆、船舶、飞机、工具应该被推定为实施了推动本法规定的恐怖行为、附属于恐怖行为或与恐怖行为相关的行为的初步证据,并且应该予以没收、上缴国库,包括但是不限于诸如犯罪所得的货币和其他资产等犯罪所得,以及犯罪工具,除非它们是非故意授权、容忍或同意其使用的无刑事责任第三人的财产。

第21条　涉及恐怖主义的案件和恐怖行为的案件的起诉权限和管辖权限——地区法院应该有权审判本法规定的所有可罚行为。

被指控或被判决实施有本法第4、第5、第6、第7条规定的可罚犯罪行为的行为人,如果其行为没有被包括在被指控行为中时,不影响对《修正刑法典》或特别法规定为犯罪的这些行为起诉。

当刑事起诉书指控的罪行和证据证明或确定的罪行不同时,如果在审判过程中对行为人在普通公众或群体或特定人中制造或引发危险、恐慌或混乱的犯罪意图不能得到证明时,被告人应该以被指控行为中已经被证明的行为定罪。任何人都不得因一个犯罪行为受到两次处罚。

第22条　缓刑和辩诉交易的不适用——修正的《缓刑法》条款(即第908号总统法令)都不得适用于本法规定的可罚行为。同样,《法庭规则》中有关辩诉交易的条款也不得适用于本法规定的可罚行为。

第23条　菲律宾和其他国家或国际组织之间的相互协助与合作——如果菲律宾政府对其他国家或国际组织的请求需要通过根据本法第24条所设立的委员会,当其他国家或国际组织请求菲律宾政府对与恐怖行为有关的事项进行协助时,该委员会应该采取适当措施。

第24条　反对恐怖主义委员会——据此设立的附属于总统办公室的反对恐怖主义委员会应该作为国内外恐怖主义所有事务的政策制定、协调、管理、监控的关键机构。反对恐怖主义委员会应该由以下成员组成:

主　席:行政秘书长;

副主席:国家安全顾问;

其他成员:a 外事秘书;

b 司法秘书;

c 国防秘书;

d 内国政府和地方政府秘书;

e 总统和平进程顾问;

f 国家情报协调处处长;

g 其他总统指派的人员。

反对恐怖主义委员会应该建立反对恐怖主义指挥中心,对反对恐怖主义各项措施的执行进行指挥、协调、管理、监控。该指挥中心应该由国家安全顾问担任国家协调员,并从各个政府机构抽调人手组成。

下列机构除了履行正常职能以外,还应该为反对恐怖主义委员会提供技术和其他必要的支持:菲律宾武装力量;菲律宾国际警察局;国家调查局;菲律宾禁毒处;移民局;民权办公室;菲律宾打击跨国犯罪中心;反洗钱委员会;外交部咨询办公室;交通安全办公室;突发性卫生事件管理中心;菲律宾核研究机构;环境管理局;安全与交流委员会;海关局;国家检察院;国家电讯委员会;投资部;信息和通讯技术委员会;贸易管理局;国家土著居民委员会;以及反对恐怖主义委员会认为必要的其他机构。

第25条　反对恐怖主义委员会的职能——为了实现上一条的要求,反对恐怖主义委员会应该具有以下职能:

a. 必要时制定全面的计划和建立制度性机制来阻止和预防恐怖主义,使政府和国家准备应对恐怖袭击的原始形式和其后果,包括但是不限于使用化学武器、生物武器、放射性武器或核武器,或其他带来灾难性后果的武器;

b. 监督和协调政府政策、计划、措施的执行,以防止和抑制恐怖主义;

c. 在应对恐怖主义中进行政策的研究和学习;

d. 指导和监控防止恐怖主义的进行,反对恐怖主义的行为以及处理恐怖主义后果的行为;

e. 指导和监控对涉及恐怖主义的案件进行即时调查和迅速起诉,并监控这些案件的进程;

f. 将对特定案件的调查从一个执法机构转移到另一机构;

g. 建立一个综合性资料库信息系统和建立预防恐怖主义和反对恐怖主义的行动和恐怖事件发生后的处理行动的连接机制;

h. 批准给予同意为逮捕实施恐怖行为的罪犯提供关键信息的知情人金钱奖励和表彰;

i. 推荐《证人保护、安全和受益纲要》规定的关键证人;

j. 保存审理和判决的档案,这些档案应该进行安全级别的分类,正如反对恐怖主义委员会基于合理裁量所做的命令保护国家利益一样;

k. 向司法部推荐恐怖组织的上榜名单和除名名单;

l. 号召任何部门、机构、办事处或其他行政机关进行协助;

m. 履行总统指派的其他任务。

第26条　修正刑法典和其他普通法或特别法的补充适用——《修正刑

法典》和其他普通法或特别法的条款可以补充本法条款适用。

第27条　规则和规定的执行——反对恐怖主义委员会应该在本法生效之日起60日内,公布确保本法条文有效执行所必需的规则和规章。

第28条　本法的域外适用——《修正刑法典》的第2条第5款由于本法第4条、第5条、第6条、第7条规定的犯罪因而得到修正。

第29条　独立性条款——如果本法的任何条款或部分条款,对任何人任何情形下的适用被宣布违宪或违法,本法案的任何其他条款或其他部分对任何其他人或任何其他情形下的适用并不因此受影响。

第30条　修正条款——第9160号共和国法案(已被第9194号共和国法案修正),第4200号共和国法案(已被第613号联邦法案修正)和968号总统令,据此应进行相应的修正或修改。

第31条　失效条款——所有法律、法令、行政命令、规则、规定的全部或部分与本法案相冲突的,要进行相应的撤销、修正或修改。

第32条　生效——在政府公报或两份全面发行的报纸上公布后15天,本法开始生效。

ACT NO. 3815

AN ACT REVISING THE PENAL CODE

(December 8, 1930)

Preliminary Article—This law shall be known as "*The Revised Penal Code.*"

BOOK ONE GENERAL PROVISIONS

Regarding the Date of Enforcement and Application of the Provisions of this Code, and Regarding the Offenses, the Persons Liable and the Penal Ties.

Preliminary Title
DATE OF EFFECTIVENESS AND APPLICATION OF THE PROVISIONS OF THIS CODE

Article 1. Time when Act takes effect. —This Code shall take effect on the first day of January, nineteen hundred and thirty-two.

Art. 2. Application of its provisions. —Except as provided in the treaties and laws of preferential application, the provisions of this Code shall be enforced not only within the Philippine Archipelago, including its atmosphere, its interior waters and maritime zone, but also outside of its jurisdiction, against those who:

1. Should commit an offense while on a Philippine ship or airship

2. Should forge or counterfeit any coin or currency note of the Philippine Islands or obligations and securities issued by the Government of the Philippine Islands;

3. Should be liable for acts connected with the introduction into these islands of the obligations and securities mentioned in the presiding number;

4. While being public officers or employees, should commit an offense in the exercise of their functions; or

5. Should commit any of the crimes against national security and the law of nations, defined in Title One of Book Two of this Code.

Title One

FELONIES AND CIRCUMSTANCES WHICH AFFECT CRIMINAL LIABILITY

Chapter One FELONIES

Art. 3. Definitions. —Acts and omissions punishable by law are felonies (*delitos*).

Felonies are committed not only be means of deceit (*dolo*) but also by means of fault (*culpa*).

There is deceit when the act is performed with deliberate intent and there is fault when the wrongful act results from imprudence, negligence, lack of foresight, or lack of skill.

Art. 4. Criminal liability. —Criminal liability shall be incurred:

1. By any person committing a felony (*delito*) although the wrongful act done be different from that which he intended.

2. By any person performing an act which would be an offense against persons or property, were it not for the inherent impossibility of its accomplishment or an account of the employment of inadequate or ineffectual means.

Art. 5. Duty of the court in connection with acts which should be repressed but which are not covered by the law, and in cases of excessive penalties. —Whenever a court has knowledge of any act which it may deem proper to repress and which is not punishable by law, it shall render the proper decision, and shall report to the Chief Executive, through the Department of Justice, the reasons which induce the court to believe that said act should be made the subject of legislation.

In the same way, the court shall submit to the Chief Executive, through the Department of Justice, such statement as may be deemed proper, without suspending the execution of the sentence, when a strict enforcement of the provisions of this Code would result in the imposition of a clearly excessive penalty, taking into consideration the degree of malice and the injury caused by the offense.

Art. 6. Consummated, frustrated, and attempted felonies. —Consummated felonies as well as those which are frustrated and attempted, are punishable.

A felony is consummated when all the elements necessary for its execution and accomplishment are present; and it is frustrated when the offender performs all the acts of execution which would produce the felony as a consequence but which, nevertheless, do not produce it by reason of causes independent of the will of the perpetrator.

There is an attempt when the offender commences the commission of a felony directly or over acts, and does not perform all the acts of execution which should produce the felony by reason of some cause or accident other than this own spontaneous desistance.

Art. 7. When light felonies are punishable. —Light felonies are punishable only when they have been consummated, with the exception of those committed against person or property.

Art. 8. Conspiracy and proposal to commit felony. —Conspiracy and proposal to commit felony are punishable only in the cases in which the law specially provides a penalty therefor.

A conspiracy exists when two or more persons come to an agreement concerning the commission of a felony and decide to commit it.

There is proposal when the person who has decided to commit a felony proposes its execution to some other person or persons.

Art. 9. Grave felonies, less grave felonies and light felonies. —Grave felonies are those to which the law attaches the capital punishment or penalties which in any of their periods are afflictive, in accordance with Art. 25 of this Code.

Less grave felonies are those which the law punishes with penalties which in their maximum period are correctional, in accordance with the above-mentioned Art.

Light felonies are those infractions of law for the commission of which a penalty of arrest menor or a fine not exceeding 200 pesos or both; is provided.

Art. 10. Offenses not subject to the provisions of this Code. —Offenses which are or in the future may be punishable under special laws are not subject to the provisions of this Code. This Code shall be supplementary to such laws, unless the latter should specially provide the contrary.

Chapter Two
JUSTIFYING CIRCUMSTANCES AND CIRCUMSTANCES WHICH EXEMPT FROM CRIMINAL LIABILITY

Art. 11. Justifying circumstances. —The following do not incur any criminal liability:

1. Anyone who acts in defense of his person or rights, provided that the following circumstances concur;

First. Unlawful aggression.

Second. Reasonable necessity of the means employed to prevent or repel it.

Third. Lack of sufficient provocation on the part of the person defending himself.

2. Any one who acts in defense of the person or rights of his spouse, ascendants, descendants, or legitimate, natural or adopted brothers or sisters, or his relatives by affinity in the same degrees and those consanguinity within the fourth civil degree, provided that the first and second requisites prescribed in the next preceding circumstance are present, and the further requisite, in case the revocation was given by the person attacked, that the one making defense had no part therein.

3. Anyone who acts in defense of the person or rights of a stranger, provided that the first and second requisites mentioned in the first circumstance of this

Art. are present and that the person defending be not induced by revenge, resentment, or other evil motive.

4. Any person who, in order to avoid an evil or injury, does not act which causes damage to another, provided that the following requisites are present;

First. That the evil sought to be avoided actually exists;

Second. That the injury feared be greater than that done to avoid it;

Third. That there be no other practical and less harmful means of preventing it.

5. Any person who acts in the fulfillment of a duty or in the lawful exercise of a right or office.

6. Any person who acts in obedience to an order issued by a superior for some lawful purpose.

Art. 12. Circumstances which exempt from criminal liability. —the following are exempt from criminal liability:

1. An imbecile or an insane person, unless the latter has acted during a lucid interval.

When the imbecile or an insane person has committed an act which the law defines as a felony (delito), the court shall order his confinement in one of the hospitals or asylums established for persons thus afflicted, which he shall not be permitted to leave without first obtaining the permission of the same court.

2. A person under nine years of age.

3. A person over nine years of age and under fifteen, unless he has acted with discernment, in which case, such minor shall be proceeded against in accordance with the provisions of Art. 80 of this Code.

When such minor is adjudged to be criminally irresponsible, the court, in conformably with the provisions of this and the preceding paragraph, shall commit him to the care and custody of his family who shall be charged with his surveillance and education otherwise, he shall be committed to the care of some institution or person mentioned in said Art. 80.

4. Any person who, while performing a lawful act with due care, causes an injury by mere accident without fault or intention of causing it.

5. Any person who act under the compulsion of irresistible force.

6. Any person who acts under the impulse of an uncontrollable fear of an e-

qual or greater injury.

7. Any person who fails to perform an act required by law, when prevented by some lawful insuperable cause.

Chapter Three
CIRCUMSTANCES WHICH MITIGATE CRIMINAL LIABILITY

Art. 13. Mitigating circumstances. —The following are mitigating circumstances;

1. Those mentioned in the preceding chapter, when all the requisites necessary to justify or to exempt from criminal liability in the respective cases are not attendant.

2. That the offender is under eighteen year of age or over seventy years. In the case of the minor, he shall be proceeded against in accordance with the provisions of Art. 80.

3. That the offender had no intention to commit so grave a wrong as that committed.

4. That sufficient provocation or threat on the part of the offended party immediately preceded the act.

5. That the act was committed in the immediate vindication of a grave offense to the one committing the felony (*delito*), his spouse, ascendants, or relatives by affinity within the same degrees.

6. That of having acted upon an impulse so powerful as naturally to have produced passion or obfuscation.

7. That the offender had voluntarily surrendered himself to a person in authority or his agents, or that he had voluntarily confessed his guilt before the court prior to the presentation of the evidence for the prosecution;

8. That the offender is deaf and dumb, blind or otherwise suffering some physical defect which thus restricts his means of action, defense, or communications with his fellow beings.

9. Such illness of the offender as would diminish the exercise of the willpower of the offender without however depriving him of the consciousness of his acts.

10. And, finally, any other circumstances of a similar nature and analogous to those above mentioned.

Chapter Four
CIRCUMSTANCE WHICH AGGRAVATE CRIMINAL LIABILITY

Art. 14. Aggravating circumstances. —The following are aggravating circumstances:

1. That advantage be taken by the offender of his public position.

2. That the crime be committed in contempt or with insult to the public authorities.

3. That the act be committed with insult or in disregard of the respect due the offended party on account of his rank, age, or sex, or that is be committed in the dwelling of the offended party, if the latter has not given provocation.

4. That the act be committed with abuse of confidence or obvious ungratefulness.

5. That the crime be committed in the palace of the Chief Executive or in his presence, or where public authorities are engaged in the discharge of their duties, or in a place dedicated to religious worship.

6. That the crime be committed in the night time, or in an uninhabited place, or by a band, whenever such circumstances may facilitate the commission of the offense.

Whenever more than three armed malefactors shall have acted together in the commission of an offense, it shall be deemed to have been committed by a band.

7. That the crime be committed on the occasion of a conflagration, shipwreck, earthquake, epidemic or other calamity or misfortune.

8. That the crime be committed with the aid of armed men or persons who insure or afford impunity.

9. That the accused is a recidivist.

A recidivist is one who, at the time of his trial for one crime, shall have been previously convicted by final judgment of another crime embraced in the same title of this Code.

10. That the offender has been previously punished by an offense to which the law attaches an equal or greater penalty or for two or more crimes to which it attaches a lighter penalty.

11. That the crime be committed in consideration of a price, reward, or promise.

12. That the crime be committed by means of inundation, fire, poison, explosion, stranding of a vessel or international damage thereto, derailment of a locomotive, or by the use of any other artifice involving great waste and ruin.

13. That the act be committed with evidence premeditation.

14. That the craft, fraud or disguise be employed.

15. That advantage be taken of superior strength, or means be employed to weaken the defense.

16. That the act be committed with treachery (*alevosia*).

There is treachery when the offender commits any of the crimes against the person, employing means, methods, or forms in the execution thereof which tend directly and specially to insure its execution, without risk to himself arising from the defense which the offended party might make.

17. That means be employed or circumstances brought about which add ignominy to the natural effects of the act.

18. That the crime be committed after an unlawful entry.

There is an unlawful entry when an entrance of a crime a wall, roof, floor, door, or window be broken.

19. That the crime be committed with the aid of persons under fifteen years of age or by means of motor vehicles, motorized watercraft, airships, or other similar means. (As amended by RA 5438).

20. That the wrong done in the commission of the crime be deliberately augmented by causing other wrong not necessary for its commissions.

Chapter Five
ALTERNATIVE CIRCUMSTANCES

Art. 15. Their concept. —Alternative circumstances are those which must be taken into consideration as aggravating or mitigating according to the nature and effects of the crime and the other conditions attending its commission. They are the relationship, intoxication and the degree of instruction and education of the offender.

The alternative circumstance of relationship shall be taken into consideration when the offended party in the spouse, ascendant, descendant, legitimate, natural, or adopted brother or sister, or relative by affinity in the same degrees of the offender.

The intoxication of the offender shall be taken into consideration as a mitigating circumstances when the offender has committed a felony in a state of intoxication, if the same is not habitual or subsequent to the plan to commit said felony but when the intoxication is habitual or intentional, it shall be considered as an aggravating circumstance.

Title Two
PERSONS CRIMINALLY LIABLE FOR FELONIES

Art. 16. Who are criminally liable. —The following are criminally liable for grave and less grave felonies:

1. Principals.
2. Accomplices.
3. Accessories.

The following are criminally liable for light felonies:

1. Principals
2. Accomplices.

Art. 17. Principals. —The following are considered principals:

1. Those who take a direct part in the execution of the act;
2. Those who directly force or induce others to commit it;
3. Those who cooperate in the commission of the offense by another act without which it would not have been accomplished.

Art. 18. Accomplices. —Accomplices are those persons who, not being included in Art. 17, cooperate in the execution of the offense by previous or simultaneous acts.

Art. 19. Accessories. —Accessories are those who, having knowledge of the commission of the crime, and without having participated therein, either as principals or accomplices, take part subsequent to its commission in any of the following manners:

1. By profiting themselves or assisting the offender to profit by the effects of the crime.

2. By concealing or destroying the body of the crime, or the effects or instruments thereof, in order to prevent its discovery.

3. By harboring, concealing, or assisting in the escape of the principals of the crime, provided the accessory acts with abuse of his public functions or whenever the author of the crime is guilty of treason, parricide, murder, or an attempt to take the life of the Chief Executive, or is known to be habitually guilty of some other crime.

Art. 20. Accessories who are exempt from criminal liability.—The penalties prescribed for accessories shall not be imposed upon those who are such with respect to their spouses, ascendants, descendants, legitimate, natural, and adopted brothers and sisters, or relatives by affinity within the same degrees, with the single exception of accessories falling within the provisions of paragraph 1 of the next preceding article.

Title Three
PENALTIES

Chapter One
PENALTIES IN GENERAL

Art. 21. Penalties that may be imposed.—No felony shall be punishable by any penalty not prescribed by law prior to its commission.

Art. 22. Retroactive effect of penal laws.—Penal Laws shall have a retroactive effect insofar as they favor the persons guilty of a felony, who is not a habitual criminal, as this term is defined in Rule 5 of Article 62 of this Code, although at the time of the publication of such laws a final sentence has been pronounced and the convict is serving the same.

Art. 23. Effect of pardon by the offended party.—A pardon of the offended party does not extinguish criminal action except as provided in Article 344 of this Code; but civil liability with regard to the interest of the injured party is extinguished by his express waiver.

Art. 24. Measures of prevention or safety which are nor considered penalties. —The following shall not be considered as penalties:

1. The arrest and temporary detention of accused persons, as well as their detention by reason of insanity or imbecility, or illness requiring their confinement in a hospital.

2. The commitment of a minor to any of the institutions mentioned in Article 80 and for the purposes specified therein.

3. Suspension from the employment of public office during the trial or in order to institute proceedings.

4. Fines and other corrective measures which, in the exercise of their administrative disciplinary powers, superior officials may impose upon their subordinates.

5. Deprivation of rights and the reparations which the civil laws may establish in penal form.

Chapter Two
CLASSIFICATION OF PENALTIES

Art. 25. Penalties which may be imposed. —The penalties which may be imposed according to this Code, and their different classes, are those included in the following:

Scale **PRINCIPAL PENALTIES**

Capital punishment: Death.

Afflictive penalties: Reclusion perpetua,
Reclusion temporal,
Perpetual or temporary absolute disqualification,
Perpetual or temporary special disqualification,
Prision mayor.

Correctional penalties: Prision correccional,
Arresto mayor,
Suspension,

Destierro.

Light penalties: Arresto menor,

Public censure.

Penalties common to the three preceding classes:

Fine,

and Bond to keep the peace.

ACCESSORY PENALTIES

Perpetual or temporary absolute disqualification,

Perpetual or temporary special disqualification,

Suspension from public office, the right to vote and be voted for, the profession or calling.

Civil interdiction,

Indemnification,

Forfeiture or confiscation of instruments and proceeds of the offense,

Payment of costs.

Art. 26. When afflictive, correctional, or light penalty.—A fine, whether imposed as a single of as an alternative penalty, shall be considered an afflictive penalty, if it exceeds 6,000 pesos; a correctional penalty, if it does not exceed 6,000 pesos but is not less than 200 pesos; and a light penalty if it less than 200 pesos.

Chapter Three
DURATION AND EFFECTS OF PENALTIES

Section One Duration of Penalties

Art. 27. Reclusion perpetua.—Any person sentenced to any of the perpetual penalties shall be pardoned after undergoing the penalty for thirty years, unless such person by reason of his conduct or some other serious cause shall be considered by the Chief Executive as unworthy of pardon.

Reclusion temporal.—The penalty of reclusion temporal shall be from twelve years and one day to twenty years.

Prision mayor and temporary disqualification.—The duration of the penalties of prision mayor and temporary disqualification shall be from six years and one day to twelve years, except when the penalty of disqualification is imposed as an accessory penalty, in which case its duration shall be that of the principal penalty.

Prision correccional, suspension, and destierro. —The duration of the penalties of prision correccional, suspension and destierro shall be from six months and one day to six years, except when suspension is imposed as an accessory penalty, in which case, its duration shall be that of the principal penalty.

Arresto mayor. —The duration of the penalty of arresto mayor shall be from one month and one day to six months.

Arresto menor. —The duration of the penalty of arresto menor shall be from one day to thirty days.

Bond to keep the peace. —The bond to keep the peace shall be required to cover such period of time as the court may determine.

Art. 28. Computation of penalties. —If the offender shall be in prison, the term of the duration of the temporary penalties shall be computed from the day on which the judgment of conviction shall have become final.

If the offender be not in prison, the term of the duration of the penalty consisting of deprivation of liberty shall be computed from the day that the offender is placed at the disposal of the judicial authorities for the enforcement of the penalty. The duration of the other penalties shall be computed only from the day on which the defendant commences to serve his sentence.

Art. 29. Period of preventive imprisonment deducted from term of imprisonment. —Offenders who have undergone preventive imprisonment shall be credited in the service of their sentence consisting of deprivation of liberty, with the full time during which they have undergone preventive imprisonment, if the detention prisoner agrees voluntarily in writing to abide by the same disciplinary rules imposed upon convicted prisoners, except in the following cases:

1. When they are recidivists or have been convicted previously twice or more times of any crime; and

2. When upon being summoned for the execution of their sentence they have failed to surrender voluntarily.

If the detention prisoner does not agree to abide by the same disciplinary rules imposed upon convicted prisoners, he shall be credited in the service of his sentence with four-fifths of the time during which he has undergone preventive imprisonment. (As amended by Republic Act 6127, June 17, 1970).

Whenever an accused has undergone preventive imprisonment for a period equal to or more than the possible maximum imprisonment of the offense charged to which he may be sentenced and his case is not yet terminated, he shall be released immediately without prejudice to the continuation of the trial thereof or the proceeding on appeal, if the same is under review. In case the maximum penalty to which the accused may be sentenced is destierro, he shall be released after thirty (30) days of preventive imprisonment. (As amended by E. O. No. 214, July 10, 1988).

Section Two Effects of the penalties according to their respective nature

Art. 30. Effects of the penalties of perpetual or temporary absolute disqualification. —The penalties of perpetual or temporary absolute disqualification for public office shall produce the following effects:

1. The deprivation of the public offices and employments which the offender may have held even if conferred by popular election.

2. The deprivation of the right to vote in any election for any popular office or to be elected to such office.

3. The disqualification for the offices or public employments and for the exercise of any of the rights mentioned.

In case of temporary disqualification, such disqualification as is comprised in paragraphs 2 and 3 of this article shall last during the term of the sentence.

4. The loss of all rights to retirement pay or other pension for any office formerly held.

Art. 31. Effect of the penalties of perpetual or temporary special disqualification. —The penalties of perpetual or temporal special disqualification for public office, profession or calling shall produce the following effects:

1. The deprivation of the office, employment, profession or calling affected;

2. The disqualification for holding similar offices or employments either per-

petually or during the term of the sentence according to the extent of such disqualification.

Art. 32. Effect of the penalties of perpetual or temporary special disqualification for the exercise of the right of suffrage. —The perpetual or temporary special disqualification for the exercise of the right of suffrage shall deprive the offender perpetually or during the term of the sentence, according to the nature of said penalty, of the right to vote in any popular election for any public office or to be elected to such office. Moreover, the offender shall not be permitted to hold any public office during the period of his disqualification.

Art. 33. Effects of the penalties of suspension from any public office, profession or calling, or the right of suffrage. —The suspension from public office, profession or calling, and the exercise of the right of suffrage shall disqualify the offender from holding such office or exercising such profession or calling or right of suffrage during the term of the sentence.

The person suspended from holding public office shall not hold another having similar functions during the period of his suspension.

Art. 34. Civil interdiction. —Civil interdiction shall deprive the offender during the time of his sentence of the rights of parental authority, or guardianship, either as to the person or property of any ward, of marital authority, of the right to manage his property and of the right to dispose of such property by any act or any conveyance inter vivos.

Art. 35. Effects of bond to keep the peace. —It shall be the duty of any person sentenced to give bond to keep the peace, to present two sufficient sureties who shall undertake that such person will not commit the offense sought to be prevented, and that in case such offense be committed they will pay the amount determined by the court in the judgment, or otherwise to deposit such amount in the office of the clerk of the court to guarantee said undertaking.

The court shall determine, according to its discretion, the period of duration of the bond.

Should the person sentenced fail to give the bond as required he shall be detained for a period which shall in no case exceed six months, is he shall have been prosecuted for a grave or less grave felony, and shall not exceed thirty days, if for a light felony.

Art. 36. Pardon; its effect.—A pardon shall not work the restoration of the right to hold public office, or the right of suffrage, unless such rights be expressly restored by the terms of the pardon.

A pardon shall in no case exempt the culprit from the payment of the civil indemnity imposed upon him by the sentence.

Art. 37. Cost; What are included.—Costs shall include fees and indemnities in the course of the judicial proceedings, whether they be fixed or unalterable amounts previously determined by law or regulations in force, or amounts not subject to schedule.

Art. 38. Pecuniary liabilities; Order of payment.—In case the property of the offender should not be sufficient for the payment of all his pecuniary liabilities, the same shall be met in the following order:

1. The reparation of the damage caused.
2. Indemnification of consequential damages.
3. The fine.
4. The cost of the proceedings.

Art. 39. Subsidiary penalty.—If the convict has no property with which to meet the fine mentioned in the paragraph 3 of the nest preceding article, he shall be subject to a subsidiary personal liability at the rate of one day for each eight pesos, subject to the following rules:

1. If the principal penalty imposed be prision correccional or arresto and fine, he shall remain under confinement until his fine referred to in the preceding paragraph is satisfied, but his subsidiary imprisonment shall not exceed one-third of the term of the sentence, and in no case shall it continue for more than one year, and no fraction or part of a day shall be counted against the prisoner.

2. When the principal penalty imposed be only a fine, the subsidiary imprisonment shall not exceed six months, if the culprit shall have been prosecuted for a grave or less grave felony, and shall not exceed fifteen days, if for a light felony.

3. When the principal imposed is higher than prision correccional, no subsidiary imprisonment shall be imposed upon the culprit.

4. If the principal penalty imposed is not to be executed by confinement in a penal institution, but such penalty is of fixed duration, the convict, during the

period of time established in the preceding rules, shall continue to suffer the same deprivations as those of which the principal penalty consists.

5. The subsidiary personal liability which the convict may have suffered by reason of his insolvency shall not relieve him, from the fine in case his financial circumstances should improve. (As amended by RA 5465, April 21, 1969).

Section Three Penalties in which other accessory penalties are inherent

Art. 40. Death; Its accessory penalties. —The death penalty, when it is not executed by reason of commutation or pardon shall carry with it that of perpetual absolute disqualification and that of civil interdiction during thirty years following the date sentence, unless such accessory penalties have been expressly remitted in the pardon.

Art. 41. Reclusion perpetua and reclusion temporal; Their accessory penalties. —The penalties of reclusion perpetua and reclusion temporal shall carry with them that of civil interdiction for life or during the period of the sentence as the case may be, and that of perpetual absolute disqualification which the offender shall suffer even though pardoned as to the principal penalty, unless the same shall have been expressly remitted in the pardon.

Art. 42. Prision mayor; Its accessory penalties. —The penalty of prision mayor, shall carry with it that of temporary absolute disqualification and that of perpetual special disqualification from the right of suffrage which the offender shall suffer although pardoned as to the principal penalty, unless the same shall have been expressly remitted in the pardon.

Art. 43. Prision correccional; Its accessory penalties. —The penalty of prision correccional shall carry with it that of suspension from public office, from the right to follow a profession or calling, and that of perpetual special disqualification from the right of suffrage, if the duration of said imprisonment shall exceed eighteen months. The offender shall suffer the disqualification provided in the article although pardoned as to the principal penalty, unless the same shall have been expressly remitted in the pardon.

Art. 44. Arresto; Its accessory penalties. —The penalty of arresto shall carry with it that of suspension of the right to hold office and the right of suffrage during the term of the sentence.

Art. 45. Confiscation and forfeiture of the proceeds or instruments of the crime. —Every penalty imposed for the commission of a felony shall carry with it the forfeiture of the proceeds of the crime and the instruments or tools with which it was committed.

Such proceeds and instruments or tools shall be confiscated and forfeited in favor of the Government, unless they be property of a third person not liable for the offense, but those articles which are not subject of lawful commerce shall be destroyed.

Chapter Four
APPLICATION OF PENALTIES

Section One Rules for the application of penalties to the persons criminally liable and for the graduation of the same

Art. 46. Penalty to be imposed upon principals in general. —The penalty prescribed by law for the commission of a felony shall be imposed upon the principals in the commission of such felony.

Whenever the law prescribes a penalty for a felony is general terms, it shall be understood as applicable to the consummated felony.

Art. 47. In what cases the death penalty shall not be imposed. —The death penalty shall be imposed in all cases in which it must be imposed under existing laws, except in the following cases:

1. When the guilty person be more than seventy years of age.

2. When upon appeal or revision of the case by the Supreme court, all the members thereof are not unanimous in their voting as to the propriety of the imposition of the death penalty. For the imposition of said penalty or for the confirmation of a judgment of the inferior court imposing the death sentence, the Supreme Court shall render its decision per curiam, which shall be signed by all justices of said court, unless some member or members thereof shall have been disqualified from taking part in the consideration of the case, in which even the unanimous vote and signature of only the remaining justices shall be required.

Art. 48. Penalty for complex crimes. —When a single act constitutes two or more grave or less grave felonies, or when an offense is a necessary means for committing the other, the penalty for the most serious crime shall be imposed, the same to be applied in its maximum period.

Art. 49. Penalty to be imposed upon the principals when the crime committed is different from that intended. —In cases in which the felony committed is different from that which the offender intended to commit, the following rules shall be observed:

1. If the penalty prescribed for the felony committed be higher than that corresponding to the offense which the accused intended to commit, the penalty corresponding to the latter shall be imposed in its maximum period.

2. If the penalty prescribed for the felony committed be lower than that corresponding to the one which the accused intended to commit, the penalty for the former shall be imposed in its maximum period.

3. The rule established by the next preceding paragraph shall not be applicable if the acts committed by the guilty person shall also constitute an attempt or frustration of another crime, if the law prescribes a higher penalty for either of the latter offenses, in which case the penalty provided for the attempted or the frustrated crime shall be imposed in its maximum period.

Art. 50. Penalty to be imposed upon principals of a frustrated crime. —The penalty next lower in degree than that prescribed by law for the consummated felony shall be imposed upon the principal in a frustrated felony.

Art. 51. Penalty to be imposed upon principals of attempted crimes. —A penalty lower by two degrees than that prescribed by law for the consummated felony shall be imposed upon the principals in an attempt to commit a felony.

Art. 52. Penalty to be imposed upon accomplices in consummated crime. —The penalty next lower in degree than that prescribed by law for the consummated shall be imposed upon the accomplices in the commission of a consummated felony.

Art. 53. Penalty to be imposed upon accessories to the commission of a consummated felony. —The penalty lower by two degrees than that prescribed by law for the consummated felony shall be imposed upon the accessories to the commission of a consummated felony.

Art. 54. Penalty to imposed upon accomplices in a frustrated crime. —The penalty next lower in degree than prescribed by law for the frustrated felony

shall be imposed upon the accomplices in the commission of a frustrated felony.

Art. 55. Penalty to be imposed upon accessories of a frustrated crime. —The penalty lower by two degrees than that prescribed by law for the frustrated felony shall be imposed upon the accessories to the commission of a frustrated felony.

Art. 56. Penalty to be imposed upon accomplices in an attempted crime. —The penalty next lower in degree than that prescribed by law for an attempt to commit a felony shall be imposed upon the accomplices in an attempt to commit the felony.

Art. 57. Penalty to be imposed upon accessories of an attempted crime. —The penalty lower by two degrees than that prescribed by law for the attempted felony shall be imposed upon the accessories to the attempt to commit a felony.

Art. 58. Additional penalty to be imposed upon certain accessories. —Those accessories falling within the terms of paragraphs 3 of Article 19 of this Code who should act with abuse of their public functions, shall suffer the additional penalty of absolute perpetual disqualification if the principal offender shall be guilty of a grave felony, and that of absolute temporary disqualification if he shall be guilty of a less grave felony.

Art. 59. Penalty to be imposed in case of failure to commit the crime because the means employed or the aims sought are impossible. —When the person intending to commit an offense has already performed the acts for the execution of the same but nevertheless the crime was not produced by reason of the fact that the act intended was by its nature one of impossible accomplishment or because the means employed by such person are essentially inadequate to produce the result desired by him, the court, having in mind the social danger and the degree of criminality shown by the offender, shall impose upon him the penalty of arresto mayor or a fine from 200 to 500 pesos.

Art. 60. Exception to the rules established in Articles 50 to 57. —The provisions contained in Articles 50 to 57, inclusive, of this Code shall not be applicable to cases in which the law expressly prescribes the penalty provided for a frustrated or attempted felony, or to be imposed upon accomplices or accessories.

Art. 61. Rules for graduating penalties. —For the purpose of graduating the penalties which, according to the provisions of Articles 50 to 57, inclusive, of this Code, are to be imposed upon persons guilty as principals of any frustrated or attempted felony, or as accomplices or accessories, the following rules shall be observed:

1. When the penalty prescribed for the felony is single and indivisible, the penalty next lower in degrees shall be that immediately following that indivisible penalty in the respective graduated scale prescribed in Article 71 of this Code.

2. When the penalty prescribed for the crime is composed of two indivisible penalties, or of one or more divisible penalties to be impose to their full extent, the penalty next lower in degree shall be that immediately following the lesser of the penalties prescribed in the respective graduated scale.

3. When the penalty prescribed for the crime is composed of one or two indivisible penalties and the maximum period of another divisible penalty, the penalty next lower in degree shall be composed of the medium and minimum periods of the proper divisible penalty and the maximum periods of the proper divisible penalty and the maximum period of that immediately following in said respective graduated scale.

4. when the penalty prescribed for the crime is composed of several periods, corresponding to different divisible penalties, the penalty next lower in degree shall be composed of the period immediately following the minimum prescribed and of the two next following, which shall be taken from the penalty prescribed, if possible; otherwise from the penalty immediately following in the above mentioned respective graduated scale.

5. When the law prescribes a penalty for a crime in some manner not especially provided for in the four preceding rules, the courts, proceeding by analogy, shall impose corresponding penalties upon those guilty as principals of the frustrated felony, or of attempt to commit the same, and upon accomplices and accessories.

TABULATION OF THE PROVISIONS OF THE CHAPTER

	Penalty Prescribe for the crime	Penalty to be imposed upon the principal in a frustrated crime, and accomplice in a consummated crime	Penalty to be imposed upon the principal in an attempted crime, the accessory in the consummated crime and the accomplices in a frustrated crime.	Penalty to be imposed upon the accessory in a frustrated crime, and the accomplices in an attempted crime	Penalty to be imposed upon the accessory in an attempted crime
First Case	Death	Reclusion Perpetua	Reclusion Temporal	Prision Mayor	Prision Correccional
Second Case	Reclusion Perpetua to Death	Reclusion Temporal	Prision Mayor	Prision Correccional	Arresto Mayor
Third Case	Reclusion Temporal in its maximum period to death	Prision Mayor in its maximum period to reclusion temporal in its medium period	Prision correccional in its maximum period to prision mayor in its medium period	Arresto Mayor in it s maximum period to prision correccional in its medium period	Fine and Arresto Mayor in its minimum and medium periods
Fourth Case	Prision Mayor in its maximum period to reclusion temporal in its medium period.	Prision correccional in its maximum period to prision mayor in its medium period.	Arresto mayor in its maximum period to prision correccional in its medium period.	Fine and Arresto Mayor in its minimum and medium periods	Fine.

Section Two Rules for the application of penalties with regard to the mitigating and aggravating circumstances, and habitual delinquency

Art. 62. Effect of the attendance of mitigating or aggravating circumstances and of habitual delinquency. —Mitigating or aggravating circumstances and habitual delinquency shall be taken into account for the purpose of diminishing or increasing the penalty in conformity with the following rules:

1. Aggravating circumstances which in themselves constitute a crime specially punishable by law or which are included by the law in defining a crime and prescribing the penalty therefor shall not be taken into account for the purpose of increasing the penalty.

2. The same rule shall apply with respect to any aggravating circumstance inherent in the crime to such a degree that it must of necessity accompany the

commission thereof.

3. Aggravating or mitigating circumstances which arise from the moral attributes of the offender, or from his private relations with the offended party, or from any other personal cause, shall only serve to aggravate or mitigate the liability of the principals, accomplices and accessories as to whom such circumstances are attendant.

4. The circumstances which consist in the material execution of the act, or in the means employed to accomplish it, shall serve to aggravate or mitigate the liability of those persons only who had knowledge of them at the time of the execution of the act or their cooperation therein.

5. Habitual delinquency shall have the following effects:

(a) Upon a third conviction the culprit shall be sentenced to the penalty provided by law for the last crime of which he be found guilty and to the additional penalty of prision correccional in its medium and maximum periods;

(b) Upon a fourth conviction, the culprit shall be sentenced to the penalty provided for the last crime of which he be found guilty and to the additional penalty of prision mayor in its minimum and medium periods; and

(c) Upon a fifth or additional conviction, the culprit shall be sentenced to the penalty provided for the last crime of which he be found guilty and to the additional penalty of prision mayor in its maximum period to reclusion temporal in its minimum period.

Notwithstanding the provisions of this article, the total of the two penalties to be imposed upon the offender, in conformity herewith, shall in no case exceed 30 years.

For the purpose of this article, a person shall be deemed to be habitual delinquent, is within a period of ten years from the date of his release or last conviction of the crimes of serious or less serious physical injuries, *robo*, *hurto*, estafa or falsification, he is found guilty of any of said crimes a third time or oftener.

Art. 63. Rules for the application of indivisible penalties. —In all cases in which the law prescribes a single indivisible penalty, it shall be applied by the courts regardless of any mitigating or aggravating circumstances that may have attended the commission of the deed.

In all cases in which the law prescribes a penalty composed of two indivisible penalties, the following rules shall be observed in the application thereof:

1. When in the commission of the deed there is present only one aggravating circumstance, the greater penalty shall be applied.

2. When there are neither mitigating nor aggravating circumstances and there is no aggravating circumstance, the lesser penalty shall be applied.

3. When the commission of the act is attended by some mitigating circumstances and there is no aggravating circumstance, the lesser penalty shall be applied.

4. When both mitigating and aggravating circumstances attended the commission of the act, the court shall reasonably allow them to offset one another in consideration of their number and importance, for the purpose of applying the penalty in accordance with the preceding rules, according to the result of such compensation.

Art. 64. Rules for the application of penalties which contain three periods. —In cases in which the penalties prescribed by law contain three periods, whether it be a single divisible penalty or composed of three different penalties, each one of which forms a period in accordance with the provisions of Articles 76 and 77, the court shall observe for the application of the penalty the following rules, according to whether there are or are not mitigating or aggravating circumstances:

1. When there are neither aggravating nor mitigating circumstances, they shall impose the penalty prescribed by law in its medium period.

2. When only a mitigating circumstances is present in the commission of the act, they shall impose the penalty in its minimum period.

3. When an aggravating circumstance is present in the commission of the act, they shall impose the penalty in its maximum period.

4. When both mitigating and aggravating circumstances are present, the court shall reasonably offset those of one class against the other according to their relative weight.

5. When there are two or more mitigating circumstances and no aggravating circumstances are present, the court shall impose the penalty next lower to that prescribed by law, in the period that it may deem applicable, according to the

number and nature of such circumstances.

6. Whatever may be the number and nature of the aggravating circumstances, the courts shall not impose a greater penalty than that prescribed by law, in its maximum period.

7. Within the limits of each period, the court shall determine the extent of the penalty according to the number and nature of the aggravating and mitigating circumstances and the greater and lesser extent of the evil produced by the crime.

Art. 65. Rule in cases in which the penalty is not composed of three periods. —In cases in which the penalty prescribed by law is not composed of three periods, the courts shall apply the rules contained in the foregoing articles, dividing into three equal portions of time included in the penalty prescribed, and forming one period of each of the three portions.

Art. 66. Imposition of fines. —In imposing fines the courts may fix any amount within the limits established by law; in fixing the amount in each case attention shall be given, not only to the mitigating and aggravating circumstances, but more particularly to the wealth or means of the culprit.

Art. 67. Penalty to be imposed when not all the requisites of exemption of the fourth circumstance of Article 12 are present. —When all the conditions required in circumstances Number 4 of Article 12 of this Code to exempt from criminal liability are not present, the penalty of arresto mayor in its maximum period to prision correccional in its minimum period shall be imposed upon the culprit if he shall have been guilty of a grave felony, and arresto mayor in its minimum and medium periods, if of a less grave felony.

Art. 68. Penalty to be imposed upon a person under eighteen years of age. —When the offender is a minor under eighteen years and his case is one coming under the provisions of the paragraphs next to the last of Article 80 of this Code, the following rules shall be observed:

1. Upon a person under fifteen but over nine years of age, who is not exempted from liability by reason of the court having declared that he acted with discernment, a discretionary penalty shall be imposed, but always lower by two degrees at least than that prescribed by law for the crime which he committed.

2. Upon a person over fifteen and under eighteen years of age the penalty

next lower than that prescribed by law shall be imposed, but always in the proper period.

Art. 69. Penalty to be imposed when the crime committed is not wholly excusable.—A penalty lower by one or two degrees than that prescribed by law shall be imposed if the deed is not wholly excusable by reason of the lack of some of the conditions required to justify the same or to exempt from criminal liability in the several cases mentioned in Article 11 and 12, provided that the majority of such conditions be present. The courts shall impose the penalty in the period which may be deemed proper, in view of the number and nature of the conditions of exemption present or lacking.

Art. 70. Successive service of sentence.—When the culprit has to serve two or more penalties, he shall serve them simultaneously if the nature of the penalties will so permit otherwise, the following rules shall be observed:

In the imposition of the penalties, the order of their respective severity shall be followed so that they may be executed successively or as nearly as may be possible, should a pardon have been granted as to the penalty or penalties first imposed, or should they have been served out.

For the purpose of applying the provisions of the next preceding paragraph the respective severity of the penalties shall be determined in accordance with the following scale:

1. Death,
2. Reclusion perpetua,
3. Reclusion temporal,
4. Prision mayor,
5. Prision correccional,
6. Arresto mayor,
7. Arresto menor,
8. Destierro,
9. Perpetual absolute disqualification,
10. Temporal absolute disqualification.
11. Suspension from public office, the right to vote and be voted for, the right to follow a profession or calling, and
12. Public censure.

Notwithstanding the provisions of the rule next preceding, the maximum duration of the convict's sentence shall not be more than three-fold the length of time corresponding to the most severe of the penalties imposed upon him. No other penalty to which he may be liable shall be inflicted after the sum total of those imposed equals the same maximum period.

Such maximum period shall in no case exceed forty years.

In applying the provisions of this rule the duration of perpetual penalties (pena perpetua) shall be computed at thirty years. (As amended).

Art. 71. Graduated scales. —In the case in which the law prescribed a penalty lower or higher by one or more degrees than another given penalty, the rules prescribed in Article 61 shall be observed in graduating such penalty.

The lower or higher penalty shall be taken from the graduated scale in which is comprised the given penalty.

The courts, in applying such lower or higher penalty, shall observe the following graduated scales:

SCALE NO. 1

1. Death,
2. Reclusion perpetua,
3. Reclusion temporal,
4. Prision mayor,
5. Prision correccional,
6. Arresto mayor,
7. Destierro,
8. Arresto menor,
9. Public censure,
10. Fine.

SCALE NO. 2

1. Perpetual absolute disqualification,
2. Temporal absolute disqualification
3. Suspension from public office, the right to vote and be voted for, the right to follow a profession or calling,

4. Public censure,

5. Fine.

Art. 72. Preference in the payment of the civil liabilities. —The civil liabilities of a person found guilty of two or more offenses shall be satisfied by following the chronological order of the dates of the judgments rendered against him, beginning with the first in order of time.

Section Three Provisions common in the last two preceding sections

Art. 73. Presumption in regard to the imposition of accessory penalties. —Whenever the courts shall impose a penalty which, by provision of law, carries with it other penalties, according to the provisions of Articles 40, 41, 42, 43 and 44 of this Code, it must be understood that the accessory penalties are also imposed upon the convict.

Art. 74. Penalty higher than reclusion perpetua in certain cases. —In cases in which the law prescribes a penalty higher than another given penalty, without specially designating the name of the former, if such higher penalty should be that of death, the same penalty and the accessory penalties of Article 40, shall be considered as the next higher penalty.

Art. 75. Increasing or reducing the penalty of fine by one or more degrees. —Whenever it may be necessary to increase or reduce the penalty of fine by one or more degrees, it shall be increased or reduced, respectively, for each degree, by one-fourth of the maximum amount prescribed by law, without however, changing the minimum.

The same rules shall be observed with regard of fines that do not consist of a fixed amount, but are made proportional.

Art. 76. Legal period of duration of divisible penalties. —The legal period of duration of divisible penalties shall be considered as divided into three parts, forming three periods, the minimum, the medium, and the maximum in the manner shown in the following table:

TABLE SHOWING THE DURATION OF DIVISIBLE PENALTIES AND THE TIME INCLUDED IN EACH OF THEIR PERIODS

Penalties	Time included in the penalty in its entirety	Time included in its imum period	Time included in its edium period	Time included in its maximum period
Reclusion temporal	From 12 years And 1 day to 20 years	From 12 years and 1 day to 14 years and 8 months	From 14 years, 8 months and 1 day to 17 years and 4 months.	From 17 years, 4 months and 1 day to 20 years.
Prision mayor, absolute disqualification and special temporary disqualification	From 6 years and 1 day to 12 years.	From 6 years and 1 day to 8 years	From 8 years and 1 day to 10 years.	From 10 years and 1 day to 12 years.
Prision correccional suspension and destierro	From 6 months and 1 day to 6 years.	From 6 months and 1 day to 2 years and 4 months.	From 2 years, 4 months and 1 day to 4 years and 2 months	From 4 years, 2 months and 1 day to 6 years.
Arresto mayor	From 1 month and 1 day to 6 months	From 1 to 2 months.	From 2 months and 1 day to 4 months.	From 4 months and 1 day to 6 months.
Arresto menor	From 1 to 30 days	From 1 to 10 days.	From 11 to 20 days.	From 21 to 30 days.

Art. 77. When the penalty is a complex one composed of three distinct penalties. —In cases in which the law prescribes a penalty composed of three distinct penalties, each one shall form a period; the lightest of them shall be the minimum the next the medium, and the most severe the maximum period.

Whenever the penalty prescribed does not have one of the forms specially provided for in this Code, the periods shall be distributed, applying by analogy the prescribed rules.

Chapter Five
EXECUTION AND SERVICE OF PENALTIES

Section One General Provisions

Art. 78. When and how a penalty is to be executed. —No penalty shall be executed except by virtue of a final judgment.

A penalty shall not be executed in any other form than that prescribed by law, nor with any other circumstances or incidents than those expressly authorized thereby.

In addition to the provisions of the law, the special regulations prescribed for the government of the institutions in which the penalties are to be suffered shall be observed with regard to the character of the work to be performed, the time of its performance, and other incidents connected therewith, the relations of the convicts among themselves and other persons, the relief which they may receive, and their diet.

The regulations shall make provision for the separation of the sexes in different institutions, or at least into different departments and also for the correction and reform of the convicts.

Art. 79. Suspension of the execution and service of the penalties in case of insanity. —When a convict shall become insane or an imbecile after final sentence has been pronounced, the execution of said sentence shall be suspended only with regard to the personal penalty, the provisions of the second paragraph of circumstance number 1 of Article 12 being observed in the corresponding cases.

If at any time the convict shall recover his reason, his sentence shall be executed, unless the penalty shall have prescribed in accordance with the provisions of this Code.

The respective provisions of this section shall also be observed if the insanity or imbecility occurs while the convict is serving his sentence.

Art. 80. Suspension of sentence of minor delinquents. —Whenever a minor of either sex, under sixteen years of age at the date of the commission of a grave or less grave felony, is accused thereof, the court, after hearing the evidence in the proper proceedings, instead of pronouncing judgment of conviction, shall suspend all further proceedings and shall commit such minor to the custody or care of a public or private, benevolent or charitable institution, established under the law of the care, correction or education of orphaned, homeless, defective, and delinquent children, or to the custody or care of any other responsible person in any other place subject to visitation and supervision by the Director of Public Welfare or any of his agents or representatives, if there be any, or otherwise by the superintendent of public schools or his representatives, subject to such conditions as are prescribed hereinbelow until such minor shall have reached his majority age or for such less period as the court may deem proper.

The court, in committing said minor as provided above, shall take into consideration the religion of such minor, his parents or next of kin, in order to avoid his commitment to any private institution not under the control and supervision of the religious sect or denomination to which they belong.

The Director of Public Welfare or his duly authorized representatives or agents, the superintendent of public schools or his representatives, or the person to whose custody or care the minor has been committed, shall submit to the court every four months and as often as required in special cases, a written report on the good or bad conduct of said minor and the moral and intellectual progress made by him.

The suspension of the proceedings against a minor may be extended or shortened by the court on the recommendation of the Director of Public Welfare or his authorized representative or agents, or the superintendent of public schools or his representatives, according as to whether the conduct of such minor has been good or not and whether he has complied with the conditions imposed upon him, or not. The provisions of the first paragraph of this article shall not, however, be affected by those contained herein.

If the minor has been committed to the custody or care of any of the institutions mentioned in the first paragraph of this article, with the approval of the Director of Public Welfare and subject to such conditions as this official in accordance with law may deem proper to impose, such minor may be allowed to stay elsewhere under the care of a responsible person.

If the minor has behaved properly and has complied with the conditions imposed upon him during his confinement, in accordance with the provisions of this article, he shall be returned to the court in order that the same may order his final release.

In case the minor fails to behave properly or to comply with the regulations of the institution to which he has been committed or with the conditions imposed upon him when he was committed to the care of a responsible person, or in case he should be found incorrigible or his continued stay in such institution should be inadvisable, he shall be returned to the court in order that the same may render the judgment corresponding to the crime committed by him.

The expenses for the maintenance of a minor delinquent confined in the institution to which he has been committed, shall be borne totally or partially by his parents or relatives or those persons liable to support him, if they are able to do so, in the discretion of the court; Provided, that in case his parents or relatives or those persons liable to support him have not been ordered to pay said expenses or are found indigent and cannot pay said expenses, the municipality in which the offense was committed shall pay one-third of said expenses; the province to which the municipality belongs shall pay one-third; and the remaining one-third shall be borne by the National Government: Provided, however, That whenever the Secretary of Finance certifies that a municipality is not able to pay its share in the expenses above mentioned, such share which is not paid by said municipality shall be borne by the National Government. Chartered cities shall pay two-thirds of said expenses; and in case a chartered city cannot pay said expenses, the internal revenue allotments which may be due to said city shall be withheld and applied in settlement of said indebtedness in accordance with section five hundred and eighty-eight of the Administrative Code.

Section Two Execution of principal penalties

Art. 81. When and how the death penalty is to be executed. —The death sentence shall be executed with reference to any other and shall consist in putting the person under sentence to death by electrocution. The death sentence shall be executed under the authority of the Director of Prisons, endeavoring so far as possible to mitigate the sufferings of the person under sentence during electrocution as well as during the proceedings prior to the execution.

If the person under sentence so desires, he shall be anaesthetized at the moment of the electrocution.

Art. 82. Notification and execution of the sentence and assistance to the culprit. —The court shall designate a working day for the execution but not the hour thereof; and such designation shall not be communicated to the offender before sunrise of said day, and the execution shall not take place until after the expiration of at least eight hours following the notification, but before sunset. During the interval between the notification and the execution, the culprit shall, in so far as possible, be furnished such assistance as he may request in order to be attended in his last moments by priests or ministers of the religion he professes and to consult lawyers, as well as in order to make a will and confer with members of his family or persons in charge of the management of his business, of the administration of his property, or of the care of his descendants.

Art. 83. Suspension of the execution of the death sentence. —The death sentence shall not be inflicted upon a woman within the three years next following the date of the sentence or while she is pregnant, nor upon any person over seventy years of age. In this last case, the death sentence shall be commuted to the penalty of reclusion perpetua with the accessory penalties provided in Article 40.

Art. 84. Place of execution and persons who may witness the same. — The execution shall take place in the penitentiary of Bilibid in a space closed to the public view and shall be witnessed only by the priests assisting the offender and by his lawyers, and by his relatives, not exceeding six, if he so request, by the physician and the necessary personnel of the penal establishment, and by such persons as the Director of Prisons may authorize.

Art. 85. Provisions relative to the corpse of the person executed and its burial. —Unless claimed by his family, the corpse of the culprit shall, upon the completion of the legal proceedings subsequent to the execution, be turned over to the institute of learning or scientific research first applying for it, for the purpose of study and investigation, provided that such institute shall take charge of the decent burial of the remains. Otherwise, the Director of Prisons shall order the burial of the body of the culprit at government expense, granting permission to be present thereat to the members of the family of the culprit and the friends of the latter. In no case shall the burial of the body of a person sentenced to death be held with pomp.

Art. 86. Reclusion perpetua, reclusion temporal, prision mayor, pri-

sion correccional and arresto mayor. —The penalties of reclusion perpetua, reclusion temporal, prision mayor, prision correccional and arresto mayor, shall be executed and served in the places and penal establishments provided by the Administrative Code in force or which may be provided by law in the future.

Art. 87. Destierro. —Any person sentenced to destierro shall not be permitted to enter the place or places designated in the sentence, nor within the radius therein specified, which shall be not more than 250 and not less than 25 kilometers from the place designated.

Art. 88. Arresto menor. —The penalty of arresto menor shall be served in the municipal jail, or in the house of the defendant himself under the surveillance of an officer of the law, when the court so provides in its decision, taking into consideration the health of the offender and other reasons which may seem satisfactory to it.

Title Four
EXTINCTION OF CRIMINAL LIABILITY

Chapter One
TOTAL EXTINCTION OF CRIMINAL LIABILITY

Art. 89. How criminal liability is totally extinguished. —Criminal liability is totally extinguished:

1. By the death of the convict, as to the personal penalties and as to pecuniary penalties, liability therefor is extinguished only when the death of the offender occurs before final judgment;

2. By service of the sentence;

3. By amnesty, which completely extinguishes the penalty and all its effects;

4. By absolute pardon;

5. By prescription of the crime;

6. By prescription of the penalty;

7. By the marriage of the offended woman, as provided in Article 344 of this Code.

Art. 90. Prescription of crime. —Crimes punishable by death, reclusion perpetua or reclusion temporal shall prescribe in twenty years.

Crimes punishable by other afflictive penalties shall prescribe in fifteen years.

Those punishable by a correctional penalty shall prescribe in ten years; with the exception of those punishable by arresto mayor, which shall prescribe in five years.

The crime of libel or other similar offenses shall prescribe in one year.

The crime of oral defamation and slander by deed shall prescribe in six months.

Light offenses prescribe in two months.

When the penalty fixed by law is a compound one, the highest penalty shall be made the basis of the application of the rules contained in the first, second and third paragraphs of this article. (As amended by RA 4661, approved June 19, 1966)

Art. 91. Computation of prescription of offenses. —The period of prescription shall commence to run from the day on which the crime is discovered by the offended party, the authorities, or their agents, and shall be interrupted by the filing of the complaint or information, and shall commence to run again when such proceedings terminate without the accused being convicted or acquitted, or are unjustifiably stopped for any reason not imputable to him.

The term of prescription shall not run when the offender is absent from the Philippine Archipelago.

Art. 92. When and how penalties prescribe. —The penalties imposed by final sentence prescribe as follows:

1. Death and reclusion perpetua, in twenty years;

2. Other afflictive penalties, in fifteen years;

3. Correctional penalties, in ten years; with the exception of the penalty of arresto mayor, which prescribes in five years;

4. Light penalties, in one year.

Art. 93. Computation of the prescription of penalties. —The period of prescription of penalties shall commence to run from the date when the culprit should evade the service of his sentence, and it shall be interrupted if the defendant should give himself up, be captured, should go to some foreign country with which this Government has no extradition treaty, or should commit another crime before the expiration of the period of prescription.

Chapter Two

PARTIAL EXTINCTION OF CRIMINAL LIABILITY

Art. 94. Partial Extinction of criminal liability. —Criminal liability is extinguished partially:

1. By conditional pardon;
2. By commutation of the sentence; and
3. For good conduct allowances which the culprit may earn while he is serving his sentence.

Art. 95. Obligation incurred by person granted conditional pardon. — Any person who has been granted conditional pardon shall incur the obligation of complying strictly with the conditions imposed therein otherwise, his non-compliance with any of the conditions specified shall result in the revocation of the pardon and the provisions of Article 159 shall be applied to him.

Art. 96. Effect of commutation of sentence. —The commutation of the original sentence for another of a different length and nature shall have the legal effect of substituting the latter in the place of the former.

Art. 97. Allowance for good conduct. —The good conduct of any prisoner in any penal institution shall entitle him to the following deductions from the period of his sentence:

1. During the first two years of his imprisonment, he shall be allowed a deduction of five days for each month of good behavior;
2. During the third to the fifth year, inclusive, of his imprisonment, he shall be allowed a deduction of eight days for each month of good behavior;
3. During the following years until the tenth year, inclusive, of his imprisonment, he shall be allowed a deduction of ten days for each month of good behavior; and
4. During the eleventh and successive years of his imprisonment, he shall be allowed a deduction of fifteen days for each month of good behavior.

Art. 98. Special time allowance for loyalty. —A deduction of one-fifth of the period of his sentence shall be granted to any prisoner who, having evaded the service of his sentence under the circumstances mentioned in Article 58 of this Code, gives himself up to the authorities within 48 hours following the issuance of a proclamation announcing the passing away of the calamity or catastrophe to in said article.

Art. 99. Who grants time allowances. —Whenever lawfully justified, the Director of Prisons shall grant allowances for good conduct. Such allowances once granted shall not be revoked.

Title Five

CIVIL LIABILITY

Chapter One

PERSON CIVILLY LIABLE FOR FELONIES

Art. 100. Civil liability of a person guilty of felony. —Every person criminally liable for a felony is also civilly liable.

Art. 101. Rules regarding civil liability in certain cases. —The exemption from criminal liability established in subdivisions 1, 2, 3, 5 and 6 of Article 12 and in subdivision 4 of Article 11 of this Code does not include exemption from civil liability, which shall be enforced subject to the following rules:

First. In cases of subdivisions 1, 2, and 3 of Article 12, the civil liability for acts committed by an imbecile or insane person, and by a person under nine years of age, or by one over nine but under fifteen years of age, who has acted without discernment, shall devolve upon those having such person under their legal authority or control, unless it appears that there was no fault or negligence on their pArt.

Should there be no person having such insane, imbecile or minor under his authority, legal guardianship or control, or if such person be insolvent, said insane, imbecile, or minor shall respond with their own property, excepting property exempt from execution, in accordance with the civil law.

Second. In cases falling within subdivision 4 of Article 11, the persons for whose benefit the harm has been prevented shall be civilly liable in proportion to the benefit which they may have received.

The courts shall determine, in sound discretion, the proportionate amount for which each one shall be liable.

When the respective shares cannot be equitably determined, even approximately, or when the liability also attaches to the Government, or to the majority of the inhabitants of the town, and, in all events, whenever the damages have been caused with the consent of the authorities or their agents, indemnification shall be made in the manner prescribed by special laws or regulations.

Third. In cases falling within subdivisions 5 and 6 of Article 12, the persons using violence or causing the fears shall be primarily liable and secondarily, or, if there be no such persons, those doing the act shall be liable, saving always to the latter that part of their property exempt from execution.

Art. 102. Subsidiary civil liability of innkeepers, tavernkeepers and proprietors of establishments. —In default of the persons criminally liable, innkeepers, tavernkeepers, and any other persons or corporations shall be civilly liable for crimes committed in their establishments, in all cases where a violation of municipal ordinances or some general or special police regulation shall have been committed by them or their employees.

Innkeepers are also subsidiarily liable for the restitution of goods taken by robbery or theft within their houses from guests lodging therein, or for the payment of the value thereof, provided that such guests shall have notified in advance the innkeeper himself, or the person representing him, of the deposit of such goods within the inn; and shall furthermore have followed the directions which such innkeeper or his representative may have given them with respect to the care and vigilance over such goods. No liability shall attach in case of robbery with violence against or intimidation of persons unless committed by the innkeeper's employees.

Art. 103. Subsidiary civil liability of other persons. —The subsidiary liability established in the next preceding article shall also apply to employers, teachers, persons, and corporations engaged in any kind of industry for felonies committed by their servants, pupils, workmen, apprentices, or employees in the discharge of their duties.

Chapter Two
WHAT CIVIL LIABILITY INCLUDES

Art. 104. What is included in civil liability. —The civil liability established in Articles 100, 101, 102, and 103 of this Code includes:

1. Restitution;
2. Reparation of the damage caused;
3. Indemnification for consequential damages.

Art. 105. Restitution; How made. —The restitution of the thing itself must be made whenever possible, with allowance for any deterioration, or diminution of value as determined by the court.

The thing itself shall be restored, even though it be found in the possession of a third person who has acquired it by lawful means, saving to the latter his action against the proper person, who may be liable to him.

This provision is not applicable in cases in which the thing has been acquired by the third person in the manner and under the requirements which, by law, bar an action for its recovery.

Art. 106. Reparation; How made. —The court shall determine the amount of damage, taking into consideration the price of the thing, whenever possible, and its special sentimental value to the injured party, and reparation shall be made accordingly.

Art. 107. Indemnification; What is included. —Indemnification for consequential damages shall include not only those caused the injured party, but also those suffered by his family or by a third person by reason of the crime.

Art. 108. Obligation to make restoration, reparation for damages, or indemnification for consequential damages and actions to demand the same; Upon whom it devolves. —The obligation to make restoration or reparation for damages and indemnification for consequential damages devolves upon the heirs of the person liable.

The action to demand restoration, reparation, and indemnification likewise descends to the heirs of the person injured.

Art. 109. Share of each person civilly liable. —If there are two or more persons civilly liable for a felony, the courts shall determine the amount for which each must respond.

Art. 110. Several and subsidiary liability of principals, accomplices and accessories of a felony; Preference in payment.—Notwithstanding the provisions of the next preceding article, the principals, accomplices, and accessories, each within their respective class, shall be liable severally (in solidum) among themselves for their quotas, and subsidiaries for those of the other persons liable.

The subsidiary liability shall be enforced, first against the property of the principals; next, against that of the accomplices, and, lastly, against that of the accessories.

Whenever the liability in solidum or the subsidiary liability has been enforced, the person by whom payment has been made shall have a right of action against the others for the amount of their respective shares.

Art. 111. Obligation to make restitution in certain cases.—Any person who has participated gratuitously in the proceeds of a felony shall be bound to make restitution in an amount equivalent to the extent of such participation.

Chapter Three
EXTINCTION AND SURVIVAL OF CIVIL LIABILITY

Art. 112. Extinction of civil liability.—Civil liability established in Articles 100, 101, 102, and 103 of this Code shall be extinguished in the same manner as obligations, in accordance with the provisions of the Civil Law.

Art. 113. Obligation to satisfy civil liability.—Except in case of extinction of his civil liability as provided in the next preceding article the offender shall continue to be obliged to satisfy the civil liability resulting from the crime committed by him, notwithstanding the fact that he has served his sentence consisting of deprivation of liberty or other rights, or has not been required to serve the same by reason of amnesty, pardon, commutation of sentence or any other reason.

BOOK TWO CRIMES AND PENALTIES

Title One
CRIMES AGAINST NATIONAL SECURITY AND THE LAW OF NATIONS

Chapter One
CRIMES AGAINST NATIONAL SECURITY

Section One Treason and espionage

Art. 114. Treason. —Any person who, owing allegiance to (the United States or) the Government of the Philippine Islands, not being a foreigner, levies war against them or adheres to their enemies, giving them aid or comfort within the Philippine Islands or elsewhere, shall be punished by reclusion temporal to death and shall pay a fine not to exceed P20,000 pesos.

No person shall be convicted of treason unless on the testimony of two witnesses at least to the same overt act or on confession of the accused in open court.

Likewise, an alien, residing in the Philippine Islands, who commits acts of treason as defined in paragraph 1 of this Article shall be punished by prision mayor to death and shall pay a fine not to exceed P20,000 pesos. (As amended by E. O. No. 44, May 31, 1945).

Art. 115. Conspiracy and proposal to commit treason; Penalty. —The conspiracy or proposal to commit the crime of treason shall be punished respectively, by prision mayor and a fine not exceeding P10,000 pesos, and prision correccional and a fine not exceeding P5,000 pesos.

Art. 116. Misprision of treason. —Every person owing allegiance to (the United States) the Government of the Philippine Islands, without being a foreigner, and having knowledge of any conspiracy against them, conceals or does not disclose and make known the same, as soon as possible to the governor or fiscal of the province, or the mayor or fiscal of the city in which he resides, as the case may be, shall be punished as an accessory to the crime of treason.

Art. 117. Espionage. —The penalty of prision correccional shall be inflicted upon any person who:

1. Without authority therefor, enters a warship, fort, or naval or military establishment or reservation to obtain any information, plans, photographs, or other data of a confidential nature relative to the defense of the Philippine Archipelago; or

2. Being in possession, by reason of the public office he holds, of the articles, data, or information referred to in the preceding paragraph, discloses their contents to a representative of a foreign nation.

The penalty next higher in degree shall be imposed if the offender be a public officer or employee.

Section Two Provoking war and disloyalty in case of war

Art. 118. Inciting to war or giving motives for reprisals. —The penalty of reclusion temporal shall be imposed upon any public officer or employee, and that of prision mayor upon any private individual, who, by unlawful or unauthorized acts provokes or gives occasion for a war involving or liable to involve the Philippine Islands or exposes Filipino citizens to reprisals on their persons or property.

Art. 119. Violation of neutrality. —The penalty of prision correccional shall be inflicted upon anyone who, on the occasion of a war in which the Government is not involved, violates any regulation issued by competent authority for the purpose of enforcing neutrality.

Art. 120. Correspondence with hostile country. —Any person who in time of war, shall have correspondence with an enemy country or territory occupied by enemy troops shall be punished:

1. By prision correccional, if the correspondence has been prohibited by the Government;

2. By prision mayor, if such correspondence be carried on in ciphers or conventional signs; and

3. By reclusion temporal, if notice or information be given thereby which might be useful to the enemy. If the offender intended to aid the enemy by giving such notice or information, he shall suffer the penalty of reclusion temporal to death.

Art. 121. Flight to enemy country. —The penalty of arresto mayor shall be inflicted upon any person who, owing allegiance to the Government, attempts to flee or go to an enemy country when prohibited by competent authority.

Section Three Piracy and mutiny on the high seas

Art. 122. Piracy in general and mutiny on the high seas. —The penalty of reclusion temporal shall be inflicted upon any person who, on the high seas, shall attack or seize a vessel or, not being a member of its complement nor a passenger, shall seize the whole or part of the cargo of said vessel, its equipment, or personal belongings of its complement or passengers.

The same penalty shall be inflicted in case of mutiny on the high seas.

Art. 123. Qualified piracy. —The penalty of reclusion temporal to death shall be imposed upon those who commit any of the crimes referred to in the preceding article, under any of the following circumstances:

1. Whenever they have seized a vessel by boarding or firing upon the same;
2. Whenever the pirates have abandoned their victims without means of saving themselves; or
3. Whenever the crime is accompanied by murder, homicide, physical injuries or rape.

Title Two
CRIMES AGAINST THE FUNDAMENTAL LAWS OF THE STATE

Chapter One
ARBITRARY DETENTION OR EXPULSION, VIOLATION OF DWELLING, PROHIBITION, INTERRUPTION, AND DISSOLUTION OF PEACEFUL MEETINGS AND CRIMES AGAINST RELIGIOUS WORSHIP

Section One Arbitrary detention and expulsion

Art. 124. Arbitrary detention. —Any public officer or employee who, without legal grounds, detains a person, shall suffer;

1. The penalty of arresto mayor in its maximum period to prision correccional in its minimum period, if the detention has not exceeded three days;

2. The penalty of prision correccional in its medium and maximum periods, if the detention has continued more than three but not more than fifteen days;

3. The penalty of prision mayor, if the detention has continued for more than fifteen days but not more than six months; and

4. That of reclusion temporal, if the detention shall have exceeded six months.

The commission of a crime, or violent insanity or any other ailment requiring the compulsory confinement of the patient in a hospital, shall be considered legal grounds for the detention of any person.

Art. 125. Delay in the delivery of detained persons to the proper judicial authorities. —The penalties provided in the next preceding article shall be imposed upon the public officer or employee who shall detain any person for some legal ground and shall fail to deliver such person to the proper judicial authorities within the period of; twelve (12) hours, for crimes or offenses punishable by light penalties, or their equivalent; eighteen (18) hours, for crimes or offenses punishable by correctional penalties, or their equivalent and thirty-six (36) hours, for crimes, or offenses punishable by afflictive or capital penalties, or their equivalent.

In every case, the person detained shall be informed of the cause of his detention and shall be allowed upon his request, to communicate and confer at any time with his attorney or counsel. (As amended by E. O. Nos. 59 and 272, Nov. 7, 1986 and July 25, 1987, respectively)

Art. 126. Delaying release. —The penalties provided for in Article 124 shall be imposed upon any public officer or employee who delays for the period of time specified therein the performance of any judicial or executive order for the release of a prisoner or detention prisoner, or unduly delays the service of the notice of such order to said prisoner or the proceedings upon any petition for the liberation of such person.

Art. 127. Expulsion. —The penalty of prision correccional shall be imposed upon any public officer or employee who, not being thereunto authorized by law, shall expel any person from the Philippine Islands or shall compel such person to change his residence.

Section Two Violation of domicile

Art. 128. Violation of domicile. —The penalty of prision correccional in its minimum period shall be imposed upon any public officer or employee who, not being authorized by judicial order, shall enter any dwelling against the will of the owner thereof, search papers or other effects found therein without the previous consent of such owner, or having surreptitiously entered said dwelling, and being required to leave the premises, shall refuse to do so.

If the offense be committed in the night-time, or if any papers or effects not constituting evidence of a crime be not returned immediately after the search made by the offender, the penalty shall be prision correccional in its medium and maximum periods.

Art. 129. Search warrants maliciously obtained and abuse in the service of those legally obtained. —In addition to the liability attaching to the offender for the commission of any other offense, the penalty of arresto mayor in its maximum period to prision correccional in its minimum period and a fine not exceeding P1,000 pesos shall be imposed upon any public officer or employee who shall procure a search warrant without just cause, or, having legally procured the same, shall exceed his authority or use unnecessary severity in executing the same.

Art. 130. Searching domicile without witnesses. —The penalty of arresto mayor in its medium and maximum periods shall be imposed upon a public officer or employee who, in cases where a search is proper, shall search the domicile, papers or other belongings of any person, in the absence of the latter, any member of his family, or in their default, without the presence of two witnesses residing in the same locality.

Section Three Prohibition, interruption and dissolution of peaceful meetings

Art. 131. Prohibition, interruption and dissolution of peaceful meetings. —The penalty of prision correccional in its minimum period shall be imposed upon any public officer or employee who, without legal ground, shall prohibit or interrupt the holding of a peaceful meeting, or shall dissolve the same.

The same penalty shall be imposed upon a public officer or employee who shall hinder any person from joining any lawful association or from attending any of its meetings.

The same penalty shall be imposed upon any public officer or employee who shall prohibit or hinder any person from addressing, either alone or together with others, any petition to the authorities for the correction of abuses or redress of grievances.

Section Four Crimes against religious worship

Art. 132. Interruption of religious worship. —The penalty of prision correccional in its minimum period shall be imposed upon any public officer or employee who shall prevent or disturb the ceremonies or manifestations of any religion.

If the crime shall have been committed with violence or threats, the penalty shall be prision correccional in its medium and maximum periods.

Art. 133. Offending the religious feelings. —The penalty of arresto mayor in its maximum period to prision correccional in its minimum period shall be imposed upon anyone who, in a place devoted to religious worship or during the celebration of any religious ceremony shall perform acts notoriously offensive to the feelings of the faithful.

Title Three
CRIMES AGAINST PUBLIC ORDER

Chapter One
REBELLION, SEDITION AND DISLOYALTY

Art. 134. Rebellion or insurrection; How committed. —The crime of rebellion or insurrection is committed by rising publicly and taking arms against the Government for the purpose of removing from the allegiance to said Government or its laws, the territory of the Philippine Islands or any part thereof, of any body of land, naval or other armed forces, depriving the Chief Executive or the Legislature, wholly or partially, of any of their powers or prerogatives. (As amended by R. A. 6968)

Article 134-A. Coup d'etat; How committed. —The crime of coup d'etat is a swift attack accompanied by violence, intimidation, threat, strategy or stealth, directed against duly constituted authorities of the Republic of the Philippines, or any military camp or installation, communications network, public utilities or other facilities needed for the exercise and continued possession of power, singly or simultaneously carried out anywhere in the Philippines by any person or persons, belonging to the military or police or holding any public office of employment with or without civilian support or participation for the purpose of seizing or diminishing state power. (As amended by R. A. 6968)

Art. 135. Penalty for rebellion, insurrection or coup d'etat.—Any person who promotes, maintains, or heads rebellion or insurrection shall suffer the penalty of reclusion perpetua.

Any person merely participating or executing the commands of others in a rebellion shall suffer the penalty of reclusion temporal.

Any person who leads or in any manner directs or commands others to undertake a coup d'etat shall suffer the penalty of reclusion perpetua.

Any person in the government service who participates, or executes directions or commands of others in undertaking a *coup d'etat* shall suffer the penalty of prision mayor in its maximum period.

Any person not in the government service who participates, or in any manner supports, finances, abets or aids in undertaking a *coup d'etat* shall suffer the penalty of reclusion temporal in its maximum period.

When the rebellion, insurrection, or *coup d'etat* shall be under the command of unknown leaders, any person who in fact directed the others, spoke for them, signed receipts and other documents issued in their name, as performed similar acts, on behalf or the rebels shall be deemed a leader of such a rebellion, insurrection, or *coup d'etat*. (As amended by R. A. 6968, approved on October 24, 1990)

Art. 136. Conspiracy and proposal to commit coup d'etat, rebellion or insurrection.—The conspiracy and proposal to commit *coup d'etat* shall be punished by prision mayor in minimum period and a fine which shall not exceed eight thousand pesos (P8,000.00).

The conspiracy and proposal to commit rebellion or insurrection shall be punished respectively, by prision correccional in its maximum period and a fine which shall not exceed five thousand pesos (P5,000.00) and by prision correccional in its medium period and a fine not exceeding two thousand pesos (P2,000.00). (As amended by R. A. 6968, approved October 24, 1990)

Art. 137. Disloyalty of public officers or employees. —The penalty of prision correccional in its minimum period shall be imposed upon public officers or employees who have failed to resist a rebellion by all the means in their power, or shall continue to discharge the duties of their offices under the control of the rebels or shall accept appointment to office under them. (Reinstated by E. O. No. 187)

Art. 138. Inciting a rebellion or insurrection. —The penalty of prision mayor in its minimum period shall be imposed upon any person who, without taking arms or being in open hostility against the Government, shall incite others to the execution of any of the acts specified in article 134 of this Code, by means of speeches, proclamations, writings, emblems, banners or other representations tending to the same end. (Reinstated by E. O. No. 187)

Art. 139. Sedition; How committed. —The crime of sedition is committed by persons who rise publicly and tumultuously in order to attain by force, intimidation, or by other means outside of legal methods, any of the following objects:

1. To prevent the promulgation or execution of any law or the holding of any popular election;

2. To prevent the National Government, or any provincial or municipal government or any public officer thereof from freely exercising its or his functions, or prevent the execution of any administrative order;

3. To inflict any act of hate or revenge upon the person or property of any public officer or employee;

4. To commit, for any political or social end, any act of hate or revenge against private persons or any social class; and

5. To despoil, for any political or social end, any person, municipality or province, or the National Government (or the Government of the United States), of all its property or any part thereof.

Art. 140. Penalty for sedition. —The leader of a sedition shall suffer the penalty of prision mayor in its minimum period and a fine not exceeding 10,000 pesos.

Other persons participating therein shall suffer the penalty of prision correccional in its maximum period and a fine not exceeding 5,000 pesos. (Reinstated by E. O. No. 187)

Art. 141. Conspiracy to commit sedition. —Persons conspiring to commit the crime of sedition shall be punished by prision correccional in its medium period and a fine not exceeding 2,000 pesos. (Reinstated by E. O. No. 187)

Art. 142. Inciting to sedition. —The penalty of prision correccional in its maximum period and a fine not exceeding 2,000 pesos shall be imposed upon any person who, without taking any direct part in the crime of sedition, should incite others to the accomplishment of any of the acts which constitute sedition, by means of speeches, proclamations, writings, emblems, cartoons, banners, or other representations tending to the same end, or upon any person or persons who shall utter seditious words or speeches, write, publish, or circulate scurrilous libels against the Government (of the United States or the Government of the Commonwealth) of the Philippines, or any of the duly constituted authorities thereof, or which tend to disturb or obstruct any lawful officer in executing the functions of his office, or which tend to instigate others to cabal and meet together for unlawful purposes, or which suggest or incite rebellious conspiracies or riots, or which lead or tend to stir up the people against the lawful authorities or to disturb the peace of the community, the safety and order of the Government, or who shall knowingly conceal such evil practices. (Reinstated by E. O. No. 187)

Chapter Two
CRIMES AGAINST POPULAR REPRESENTATION

Section One Crimes against legislative bodies and similar bodies

Art. 143. Act tending to prevent the meeting of the Assembly and similar bodies. —The penalty of prision correccional or a fine ranging from 200 to 2,000 pesos, or both, shall be imposed upon any person who, by force or fraud, prevents the meeting of the National Assembly (Congress of the Philippines) or of any of its committees or subcommittees, constitutional commissions or committees or divisions thereof, or of any provincial board or city or municipal council or board. (Reinstated by E. O. No. 187)

Art. 144. Disturbance of proceedings. —The penalty of arresto mayor or a fine from 200 to 1,000 pesos shall be imposed upon any person who disturbs the meetings of the National Assembly (Congress of the Philippines) or of any of its committees or subcommittees, constitutional commissions or committees or divisions thereof, or of any provincial board or city or municipal council or board, or in the presence of any such bodies should behave in such manner as to interrupt its proceedings or to impair the respect due it. (Reinstated by E. O. No. 187)

Section Two Violation of parliamentary immunity

Art. 145. Violation of parliamentary immunity. —The penalty of prision mayor shall be imposed upon any person who shall use force, intimidation, threats, or fraud to prevent any member of the National Assembly (Congress of the Philippines) from attending the meetings of the Assembly (Congress) or of any of its committees or subcommittees, constitutional commissions or committees or divisions thereof, from expressing his opinions or casting his vote; and the penalty of prision correccional shall be imposed upon any public officer or employee who shall, while the Assembly (Congress) is in regular or special session, arrest or search any member thereof, except in case such member has committed a crime punishable under this Code by a penalty higher than prision mayor.

Chapter Three
ILLEGAL ASSEMBLIES AND ASSOCIATIONS

Art. 146. Illegal assemblies. —The penalty of prision correccional in its maximum period to prision mayor in its medium period shall be imposed upon the organizers or leaders of any meeting attended by armed persons for the purpose of committing any of the crimes punishable under this Code, or of any meeting in which the audience is incited to the commission of the crime of treason, rebellion or insurrection, sedition or assault upon a person in authority or his agents. Persons merely present at such meeting shall suffer the penalty of arresto mayor, unless they are armed, in which case the penalty shall be prision correccional.

If any person present at the meeting carries an unlicensed firearm, it shall be presumed that the purpose of said meeting, insofar as he is concerned, is to commit acts punishable under this Code, and he shall be considered a leader or organizer of the meeting within the purview of the preceding paragraph.

As used in this article, the word "*meeting*" shall be understood to include a gathering or group, whether in a fixed place or moving. (Reinstated by E. O. No. 187)

Art. 147. Illegal associations.—The penalty of prision correccional in its minimum and medium periods and a fine not exceeding 1,000 pesos shall be imposed upon the founders, directors, and presidents of associations totally or partially organized for the purpose of committing any of the crimes punishable under this Code or for some purpose contrary to public morals. Mere members of said associations shall suffer the penalty of arresto mayor. (Reinstated by E. O. No. 187)

Chapter Four
ASSAULT UPON, AND RESISTANCE AND DISOBEDIENCE TO, PERSONS IN AUTHORITY AND THEIR AGENTS

Art. 148. Direct assaults.—Any person or persons who, without a public uprising, shall employ force or intimidation for the attainment of any of the purpose enumerated in defining the crimes of rebellion and sedition, or shall attack, employ force, or seriously intimidate or resist any person in authority or any of his agents, while engaged in the performance of official duties, or on occasion of such performance, shall suffer the penalty of prision correccional in its medium and maximum periods and a fine not exceeding P1,000 pesos, when the assault is committed with a weapon or when the offender is a public officer or employee, or when the offender lays hands upon a person in authority. If none of these circumstances be present, the penalty of prision correccional in its minimum period and a fine not exceeding P500 pesos shall be imposed.

Art. 149. Indirect assaults.—The penalty of prision correccional in its minimum and medium periods and a fine not exceeding P500 pesos shall be im-

posed upon any person who shall make use of force or intimidation upon any person coming to the aid of the authorities or their agents on occasion of the commission of any of the crimes defined in the next preceding article.

Art. 150. Disobedience to summons issued by the National Assembly, its committees or subcommittees, by the Constitutional Commissions, its committees, subcommittees or divisions.—The penalty of arresto mayor or a fine ranging from two hundred to one thousand pesos, or both such fine and imprisonment shall be imposed upon any person who, having been duly summoned to attend as a witness before the National Assembly, (Congress), its special or standing committees and subcommittees, the Constitutional Commissions and its committees, subcommittees, or divisions, or before any commission or committee chairman or member authorized to summon witnesses, refuses, without legal excuse, to obey such summons, or being present before any such legislative or constitutional body or official, refuses to be sworn or placed under affirmation or to answer any legal inquiry or to produce any books, papers, documents, or records in his possession, when required by them to do so in the exercise of their functions. The same penalty shall be imposed upon any person who shall restrain another from attending as a witness, or who shall induce disobedience to a summon or refusal to be sworn by any such body or official.

Art. 151. Resistance and disobedience to a person in authority or the agents of such person.—The penalty of arresto mayor and a fine not exceeding 500 pesos shall be imposed upon any person who not being included in the provisions of the preceding articles shall resist or seriously disobey any person in authority, or the agents of such person, while engaged in the performance of official duties.

When the disobedience to an agent of a person in authority is not of a serious nature, the penalty of arresto menor or a fine ranging from 10 to P100 pesos shall be imposed upon the offender.

Art. 152. Persons in authority and agents of persons in authority; Who shall be deemed as such.—In applying the provisions of the preceding and other articles of this Code, any person directly vested with jurisdiction, whether as an individual or as a member of some court or governmental corporation, board, or commission, shall be deemed a person in authority. A barrio captain and a barangay chairman shall also be deemed a person in authority.

A person who, by direct provision of law or by election or by appointment by competent authority, is charged with the maintenance of public order and the protection and security of life and property, such as a barrio councilman, barrio policeman and barangay leader and any person who comes to the aid of persons in authority, shall be deemed an agent of a person in authority.

In applying the provisions of Articles 148 and 151 of this Code, teachers, professors and persons charged with the supervision of public or duly recognized private schools, colleges and universities, and lawyers in the actual performance of their professional duties or on the occasion of such performance, shall be deemed persons in authority. (As amended by PD No. 299, Sept. 19, 1973 and Batas Pambansa Blg. 873, June 12, 1985)

Chapter Five
PUBLIC DISORDERS

Art. 153. Tumults and other disturbance of public orders; Tumultuous disturbance or interruption liable to cause disturbance. —The penalty of arresto mayor in its medium period to prision correccional in its minimum period and a fine not exceeding 1,000 pesos shall be imposed upon any person who shall cause any serious disturbance in a public place, office, or establishment, or shall interrupt or disturb public performances, functions or gatherings, or peaceful meetings, if the act is not included in the provisions of Articles 131 and 132.

The penalty next higher in degree shall be imposed upon persons causing any disturbance or interruption of a tumultuous character.

The disturbance or interruption shall be deemed to be tumultuous if caused by more than three persons who are armed or provided with means of violence.

The penalty of arresto mayor shall be imposed upon any person who in any meeting, association, or public place, shall make any outcry tending to incite rebellion or sedition or in such place shall display placards or emblems which provoke a disturbance of the public order.

The penalty of arresto menor and a fine not to exceed P200 pesos shall be imposed upon these persons who in violation of the provisions contained in the

last clause of Article 85, shall bury with pomp the body of a person who has been legally executed.

Art. 154. Unlawful use of means of publication and unlawful utterances.—The penalty of arresto mayor and a fine ranging from P200 to P1,000 pesos shall be imposed upon:

1. Any person who by means of printing, lithography, or any other means of publication shall publish or cause to be published as news any false news which may endanger the public order, or cause damage to the interest or credit of the State;

2. Any person who by the same means, or by words, utterances or speeches shall encourage disobedience to the law or to the constituted authorities or praise, justify, or extol any act punished by law;

3. Any person who shall maliciously publish or cause to be published any official resolution or document without proper authority, or before they have been published officially; or

4. Any person who shall print, publish, or distribute or cause to be printed, published, or distributed books, pamphlets, periodicals, or leaflets which do not bear the real printer's name, or which are classified as anonymous.

Art. 155. Alarms and scandals.—The penalty of arresto menor or a fine not exceeding P200 pesos shall be imposed upon:

1. Any person who within any town or public place, shall discharge any firearm, rocket, firecracker, or other explosives calculated to cause alarm or danger;

2. Any person who shall instigate or take an active part in any charivari or other disorderly meeting offensive to another or prejudicial to public tranquility;

3. Any person who, while wandering about at night or while engaged in any other nocturnal amusements, shall disturb the public peace; or

4. Any person who, while intoxicated or otherwise, shall cause any disturbance or scandal in public places, provided that the circumstances of the case shall not make the provisions of Article 153 applicable.

Art. 156. Delivery of prisoners from jails.—The penalty of arresto mayor in its maximum period of prision correccional in its minimum period shall be imposed upon any person who shall remove from any jail or penal establishment any person confined therein or shall help the escape of such person, by means of violence, intimidation, or bribery. If other means are used, the penalty of arresto mayor shall be imposed.

If the escape of the prisoner shall take place outside of said establishments by taking the guards by surprise, the same penalties shall be imposed in their minimum period.

Chapter Six
EVASION OF SERVICE OF SENTENCE

Art. 157. Evasion of service of sentence. —The penalty of prision correccional in its medium and maximum periods shall be imposed upon any convict who shall evade service of his sentence by escaping during the term of his imprisonment by reason of final judgment. However, if such evasion or escape shall have taken place by means of unlawful entry, by breaking doors, windows, gates, walls, roofs, or floors, or by using picklocks, false keys, deceit, violence or intimidation, or through connivance with other convicts or employees of the penal institution, the penalty shall be prision correccional in its maximum period.

Art. 158. Evasion of service of sentence on the occasion of disorder, conflagrations, earthquakes, or other calamities. —A convict who shall evade the service of his sentence, by leaving the penal institution where he shall have been confined, on the occasion of disorder resulting from a conflagration, earthquake, explosion, or similar catastrophe, or during a mutiny in which he has not participated, shall suffer an increase of one-fifth of the time still remaining to be served under the original sentence, which in no case shall exceed six months, if he shall fail to give himself up to the authorities within forty-eight hours following the issuance of a proclamation by the Chief Executive announcing the passing away of such calamity.

Convicts who, under the circumstances mentioned in the preceding paragraph, shall give themselves up to the authorities within the above mentioned period of 48 hours, shall be entitled to the deduction provided in Article 98.

Art. 159. Other cases of evasion of service of sentence. —The penalty of prision correccional in its minimum period shall be imposed upon the convict who, having been granted conditional pardon by the Chief Executive, shall violate any of the conditions of such pardon. However, if the penalty remitted by the granting of such pardon be higher than six years, the convict shall then suffer the unexpired portion of his original sentence.

Chapter Seven
COMMISSION OF ANOTHER CRIME DURING SERVICE OF PENALTY IMPOSED FOR ANOTHER PREVIOUS OFFENSE

Art. 160. Commission of another crime during service of penalty imposed for another offense; Penalty. —Besides the provisions of Rule 5 of Article 62, any person who shall commit a felony after having been convicted by final judgment, before beginning to serve such sentence, or while serving the same, shall be punished by the maximum period of the penalty prescribed by law for the new felony.

Any convict of the class referred to in this article, who is not a habitual criminal, shall be pardoned at the age of seventy years if he shall have already served out his original sentence, or when he shall complete it after reaching the said age, unless by reason of his conduct or other circumstances he shall not be worthy of such clemency.

Title Four
CRIMES AGAINST PUBLIC INTEREST

Chapter One
FORGERIES

Section One Forging the seal of the Government of the Philippine Islands, the signature or stamp of the Chief Executive

Art. 161. Counterfeiting the great seal of the Government of the Philippine Islands, forging the signature or stamp of the Chief Executive. — The penalty of reclusion temporal shall be imposed upon any person who shall forge the Great Seal of the Government of the Philippine Islands or the signature or stamp of the Chief Executive.

Art. 162. Using forged signature or counterfeit seal or stamp. —The penalty of prision mayor shall be imposed upon any person who shall knowingly make use of the counterfeit seal or forged signature or stamp mentioned in the preceding article.

Section Two Counterfeiting Coins

Art. 163. Making and importing and uttering false coins. —Any person who makes, imports, or utters, false coins, in connivance with counterfeiters, or importers, shall suffer:

1. Prision mayor in its minimum and medium periods and a fine not to exceed P10,000 pesos, if the counterfeited coin be silver coin of the Philippines or coin of the Central Bank of the Philippines of ten centavo denomination or above.

2. Prision correccional in its minimum and medium periods and a fine of not to exceed P2,000 pesos, if the counterfeited coins be any of the minor coinage of the Philippines or of the Central Bank of the Philippines below ten-centavo denomination.

3. Prision correccional in its minimum period and a fine not to exceed P1,000 pesos, if the counterfeited coin be currency of a foreign country. (As amended by R. A. No. 4202, approved June 19, 1965)

Art. 164. Mutilation of coins; Importation and utterance of mutilated coins. —The penalty of prision correccional in its minimum period and a fine not to exceed P2,000 pesos shall be imposed upon any person who shall mutilate coins of the legal currency of the United States or of the Philippine Islands or import or utter mutilated current coins, or in connivance with mutilators or importers.

Art. 165. Selling of false or mutilated coin, without connivance. —The person who knowingly, although without the connivance mentioned in the preceding articles, shall possess false or mutilated coin with intent to utter the same, or shall actually utter such coin, shall suffer a penalty lower by one degree than that prescribed in said articles.

Section Three Forging treasury or bank notes, obligations and securities; importing and uttering false or forged notes, obligations and securities

Art. 166. Forging treasury or bank notes on other documents payable to bearer; importing, and uttering such false or forged notes and documents. —The forging or falsification of treasury or bank notes or certificates or other obligations and securities payable to bearer and the importation and uttering in connivance with forgers or importers of such false or forged obligations or notes, shall be punished as follows:

1. By reclusion temporal in its minimum period and a fine not to exceed P10,000 pesos, if the document which has been falsified, counterfeited, or altered, is an obligations or security of the United States or of the Philippines Islands.

The word "*obligation or security of the United States or of the Philippine Islands*" shall be held to mean all bonds, certificates of indebtedness, national bank notes, fractional notes, certificates of deposit, bills, checks, or drafts for money, drawn by or upon authorized officers of the United States or of the Philippine Islands, and other representatives of value, of whatever denomination, which have been or may be issued under any act of the Congress of the United States or of the Philippine Legislature.

2. By prision mayor in its maximum period and a fine not to exceed P5,000 pesos, if the falsified or altered document is a circulating note issued by any banking association duly authorized by law to issue the same.

3. By prision mayor in its medium period and a fine not to exceed P5,000 pesos, if the falsified or counterfeited document was issued by a foreign government.

4. By prision mayor in its minimum period and a fine not to exceed P2,000 pesos, when the forged or altered document is a circulating note or bill issued by a foreign bank duly authorized therefor.

Art. 167. Counterfeiting, importing and uttering instruments not payable to bearer. —Any person who shall forge, import or utter, in connivance with the forgers or importers, any instrument payable to order or other document of credit not payable to bearer, shall suffer the penalties of prision correccional in its medium and maximum periods and a fine not exceeding P6,000 pesos.

Art. 168. Illegal possession and use of false treasury or bank notes and other instruments of credit. —Unless the act be one of those coming under the provisions of any of the preceding articles, any person who shall knowingly use or have in his possession, with intent to use any of the false or falsified instruments referred to in this section, shall suffer the penalty next lower in degree than that prescribed in said articles.

Art. 169. How forgery is committed. —The forgery referred to in this section may be committed by any of the following means:

1. By giving to a treasury or bank note or any instrument, payable to bearer or order mentioned therein, the appearance of a true genuine document.

2. By erasing, substituting, counterfeiting or altering by any means the figures, letters, words or signs contained therein.

Section Four Falsification of legislative, public, commercial, and privatedocuments, and wireless, telegraph, and telephone message

Art. 170. Falsification of legislative documents. —The penalty of prision correccional in its maximum period and a fine not exceeding P6,000 pesos shall be imposed upon any person who, without proper authority therefor alters any bill, resolution, or ordinance enacted or approved or pending approval by either House of the Legislature or any provincial board or municipal council.

Art. 171. Falsification by public officer, employee or notary or ecclesiastic minister. —The penalty of prision mayor and a fine not to exceed P5,000 pesos shall be imposed upon any public officer, employee, or notary who, taking advantage of his official position, shall falsify a document by committing any of the following acts:

1. Counterfeiting or imitating any handwriting, signature or rubric;

2. Causing it to appear that persons have participated in any act or proceeding when they did not in fact so participate;

3. Attributing to persons who have participated in an act or proceeding statements other than those in fact made by them;

4. Making untruthful statements in a narration of facts;

5. Altering true dates;

6. Making any alteration or intercalation in a genuine document which changes its meaning;

7. Issuing in an authenticated form a document purporting to be a copy of an original document when no such original exists, or including in such a copy a statement contrary to, or different from, that of the genuine original; or

8. Intercalating any instrument or note relative to the issuance thereof in a protocol, registry, or official book.

The same penalty shall be imposed upon any ecclesiastical minister who shall commit any of the offenses enumerated in the preceding paragraphs of this article, with respect to any record or document of such character that its falsification may affect the civil status of persons.

Art. 172. Falsification by private individual and use of falsified documents. —The penalty of prision correccional in its medium and maximum periods and a fine of not more than P5,000 pesos shall be imposed upon:

1. Any private individual who shall commit any of the falsifications enumerated in the next preceding article in any public or official document or letter of exchange or any other kind of commercial document; and

2. Any person who, to the damage of a third party, or with the intent to cause such damage, shall in any private document commit any of the acts of falsification enumerated in the next preceding article.

Any person who shall knowingly introduce in evidence in any judicial proceeding or to the damage of another or who, with the intent to cause such damage, shall use any of the false documents embraced in the next preceding article, or in any of the foregoing subdivisions of this article, shall be punished by the penalty next lower in degree.

Art. 173. Falsification of wireless, cable, telegraph and telephone messages, and use of said falsified messages. —The penalty of prision correccional in its medium and maximum periods shall be imposed upon officer or employee of the Government or of any private corporation or concern engaged in the service of sending or receiving wireless, cable or telephone message who utters a fictitious wireless, telegraph or telephone message of any system or falsifies the same.

Any person who shall use such falsified dispatch to the prejudice of a third party or with the intent of cause such prejudice, shall suffer the penalty next lower in degree.

Section Five Falsification of medical certificates, certificates of merit or services and the like

Art. 174. False medical certificates, false certificates of merits or service, etc. —The penalties of arresto mayor in its maximum period to prision correccional in its minimum period and a fine not to exceed P1,000 pesos shall be imposed upon:

1. Any physician or surgeon who, in connection, with the practice of his profession, shall issue a false certificate; and

2. Any public officer who shall issue a false certificate of merit of service, good conduct or similar circumstances.

The penalty of arresto mayor shall be imposed upon any private person who shall falsify a certificate falling within the classes mentioned in the two preceding subdivisions.

Art. 175. Using false certificates. —The penalty of arresto menor shall be imposed upon any one who shall knowingly use any of the false certificates mentioned in the next preceding article.

Section Six Manufacturing, importing and possession of instruments or implements intended for the commission of falsification

Art. 176. Manufacturing and possession of instruments or implements for falsification. —The penalty of prision correccional in its medium and maximum periods and a fine not to exceed P10,000 pesos shall be imposed upon any person who shall make or introduce into the Philippine Islands any stamps, dies, marks, or other instruments or implements intended to be used in the commission of the offenses of counterfeiting or falsification mentioned in the preceding sections of this Chapter.

Any person who, with the intention of using them, shall have in his possession any of the instruments or implements mentioned in the preceding paragraphs, shall suffer the penalty next lower in degree than that provided therein.

Chapter Two
OTHER FALSIFICATIONS

Sec. One Usurpation of authority, rank, title, and improper use of names, uniforms and insignia

Art. 177. Usurpation of authority or official functions. —Any person who shall knowingly and falsely represent himself to be an officer, agent or representative of any department or agency of the Philippine Government or of any foreign government, or who, under pretense of official position, shall perform any act pertaining to any person in authority or public officer of the Philippine Government or any foreign government, or any agency thereof, without being lawfully entitled to do so, shall suffer the penalty of prision correccional in its minimum and medium periods.

Art. 178. Using fictitious name and concealing true name. —The penalty of arresto mayor and a fine not to exceed 500 pesos shall be imposed upon any person who shall publicly use a fictitious name for the purpose of concealing a crime, evading the execution of a judgment or causing damage.

Any person who conceals his true name and other personal circumstances shall be punished by arresto menor or a fine not to exceed 200 pesos.

Art. 179. Illegal use of uniforms or insignia. —The penalty of arresto mayor shall be imposed upon any person who shall publicly and improperly make use of insignia, uniforms or dress pertaining to an office not held by such person or to a class of persons of which he is not a member.

Section Two False testimony

Art. 180. False testimony against a defendant. —Any person who shall give false testimony against the defendant in any criminal case shall suffer:

1. The penalty of reclusion temporal, if the defendant in said case shall have been sentenced to death;

2. The penalty of prision mayor, if the defendant shall have been sentenced to reclusion temporal or reclusion perpetua;

3. The penalty of prision correccional, if the defendant shall have been sentenced to any other afflictive penalty; and

4. The penalty of arresto mayor, if the defendant shall have been sentenced

to a correctional penalty or a fine, or shall have been acquitted.

In cases provided in subdivisions 3 and 4 of this article the offender shall further suffer a fine not to exceed 1,000 pesos.

Art. 181. False testimony favorable to the defendants.—Any person who shall give false testimony in favor of the defendant in a criminal case, shall suffer the penalties of arresto mayor in its maximum period to prision correccional in its minimum period a fine not to exceed 1,000 pesos, if the prosecution is for a felony punishable by an afflictive penalty, and the penalty of arresto mayor in any other case.

Art. 182. False testimony in civil cases.—Any person found guilty of false testimony in a civil case shall suffer the penalty of prision correccional in its minimum period and a fine not to exceed 6,000 pesos, if the amount in controversy shall exceed 5,000 pesos, and the penalty of arresto mayor in its maximum period to prision correccional in its minimum period and a fine not to exceed 1,000 pesos, if the amount in controversy shall not exceed said amount or cannot be estimated.

Art. 183. False testimony in other cases and perjury in solemn affirmation.—The penalty of arresto mayor in its maximum period to prision correccional in its minimum period shall be imposed upon any person, who knowingly makes untruthful statements and not being included in the provisions of the next preceding articles, shall testify under oath, or make an affidavit, upon any material matter before a competent person authorized to administer an oath in cases in which the law so requires.

Any person who, in case of a solemn affirmation made in lieu of an oath, shall commit any of the falsehoods mentioned in this and the three preceding articles of this section, shall suffer the respective penalties provided therein.

Art. 184. Offering false testimony in evidence.—Any person who shall knowingly offer in evidence a false witness or testimony in any judicial or official proceeding, shall be punished as guilty of false testimony and shall suffer the respective penalties provided in this section.

Chapter Three
FRAUDS

Section One Machinations, monopolies and combinations

Art. 185. Machinations in public auctions.—Any person who shall solicit any gift or promise as a consideration for refraining from taking part in any public auction, and any person who shall attempt to cause bidders to stay away fróm an auction by threats, gifts, promises, or any other artifice, with intent to cause the reduction of the price of the thing auctioned, shall suffer the penalty of prision correccional in its minimum period and a fine ranging from 10 to 50 per centum of the value of the thing auctioned.

Art. 186. Monopolies and combinations in restraint of trade.—The penalty of prision correccional in its minimum period or a fine ranging from 200 to 6,000 pesos, or both, shall be imposed upon:

1. Any person who shall enter into any contract or agreement or shall take part in any conspiracy or combination in the form of a trust or otherwise, in restraint of trade or commerce or to prevent by artificial means free competition in the market;

2. Any person who shall monopolize any merchandise or object of trade or commerce, or shall combine with any other person or persons to monopolize and merchandise or object in order to alter the price thereof by spreading false rumors or making use of any other article to restrain free competition in the market;

3. Any person who, being a manufacturer, producer, or processor of any merchandise or object of commerce or an importer of any merchandise or object of commerce from any foreign country, either as principal or agent, wholesaler or retailer, shall combine, conspire or agree in any manner with any person likewise engaged in the manufacture, production, processing, assembling or importation of such merchandise or object of commerce or with any other persons not so similarly engaged for the purpose of making transactions prejudicial to lawful commerce, or of increasing the market price in any part of the Philippines, of any such merchandise or object of commerce manufactured, produced, processed, assembled in or imported into the Philippines, or of any article in the manufacture of which such manufactured, produced, or imported merchandise or

object of commerce is used.

If the offense mentioned in this article affects any food substance, motor fuel or lubricants, or other articles of prime necessity, the penalty shall be that of prision mayor in its maximum and medium periods it being sufficient for the imposition thereof that the initial steps have been taken toward carrying out the purposes of the combination.

Any property possessed under any contract or by any combination mentioned in the preceding paragraphs, and being the subject thereof, shall be forfeited to the Government of the Philippines.

Whenever any of the offenses described above is committed by a corporation or association, the president and each one of its agents or representatives in the Philippines in case of a foreign corporation or association, who shall have knowingly permitted or failed to prevent the commission of such offense, shall be held liable as principals thereof.

Section Two Frauds in commerce and industry

Art. 187. Importation and disposition of falsely marked articles or merchandise made of gold, silver, or other precious metals or their alloys. —The penalty of prision correccional or a fine ranging from 200 to 1,000 pesos, or both, shall be imposed on any person who shall knowingly import or sell or dispose of any article or merchandise made of gold, silver, or other precious metals, or their alloys, with stamps, brands, or marks which fail to indicate the actual fineness or quality of said metals or alloys.

Any stamp, brand, label, or mark shall be deemed to fail to indicate the actual fineness of the article on which it is engraved, printed, stamped, labeled or attached, when the rest of the article shows that the quality or fineness thereof is less by more than one-half karat, if made of gold, and less by more than four one-thousandth, if made of silver, than what is shown by said stamp, brand, label or mark. But in case of watch cases and flatware made of gold, the actual fineness of such gold shall not be less by more than three one-thousandth than the fineness indicated by said stamp, brand, label, or mark.

Art. 188. Subsisting and altering trade-mark, trade-names, or service marks. —The penalty of prision correccional in its minimum period or a fine ranging from 50 to 2,000 pesos, or both, shall be imposed upon:

1. Any person who shall substitute the trade name or trade-mark of some other manufacturer or dealer or a colorable imitation thereof, for the trademark of the real manufacturer or dealer upon any article of commerce and shall sell the same;

2. Any person who shall sell such articles of commerce or offer the same for sale, knowing that the trade-name or trade-mark has been fraudulently used in such goods as described in the preceding subdivision;

3. Any person who, in the sale or advertising of his services, shall use or substitute the service mark of some other person, or a colorable imitation of such mark; or

4. Any person who, knowing the purpose for which the trade-name, trade-mark, or service mark of a person is to be used, prints, lithographs, or in any way reproduces such trade-name, trade-mark, or service mark, or a colorable imitation thereof, for another person, to enable that other person to fraudulently use such trade-name, trade-mark, or service mark on his own goods or in connection with the sale or advertising of his services.

A trade-name or trade-mark as herein used is a word or words, name, title, symbol, emblem, sign or device, or any combination thereof used as an advertisement, sign, label, poster, or otherwise, for the purpose of enabling the public to distinguish the business of the person who owns and uses said trade-name or trade-mark.

A service mark as herein used is a mark used in the sale or advertising of services to identify the services of one person and distinguish them from the services of others and includes without limitation the marks, names, symbols, titles, designations, slogans, character names, and distinctive features of radio or other advertising.

Art. 189. Unfair competition, fraudulent registration of trade-mark, trade-name or service mark, fraudulent designation of origin, and false description. —The penalty provided in the next proceeding article shall be imposed upon:

1. Any person who, in unfair competition and for the purposes of deceiving or defrauding another of his legitimate trade or the public in general, shall sell his goods giving them the general appearance of goods of another manufacturer or

dealer, either as to the goods themselves, or in the wrapping of the packages in which they are contained or the device or words thereon or in any other features of their appearance which would be likely to induce the public to believe that the goods offered are those of a manufacturer or dealer other than the actual manufacturer or dealer or shall give other persons a chance or opportunity to do the same with a like purpose.

2. Any person who shall affix, apply, annex or use in connection with any goods or services or any container or containers for goods a false designation of origin or any false description or representation and shall sell such goods or services.

3. Any person who by means of false or fraudulent representation or declarations orally or in writing or by other fraudulent means shall procure from the patent office or from any other office which may hereafter be established by law for the purposes the registration of a trade-name, trade-mark or service mark or of himself as the owner of such trade-name, trade-mark or service mark or an entry respecting a trade-name, trade-mark or service mark.

Title Five

CRIMES RELATIVE TO OPIUM AND OTHER PROHIBITED DRUGS

Art. 190. Possession, preparation and use of prohibited drugs and maintenance of opium dens. —The penalty of arresto mayor in its medium period to prision correccional in its minimum period and a fine ranging from 300 to 1,000 pesos shall be imposed upon:

1. Anyone who unless lawfully authorized shall possess, prepare, administer, or otherwise use any prohibited drug.

"Prohibited drug," as used herein includes opium, cocaine, alpha and beta eucaine, Indian hemp, their derivatives, and all preparations made from them or any of them, and such other drugs, whether natural or synthetic, having physiological action as a narcotic drug.

"Opium" embraces every kind, class, and character of opium, whether crude or prepared; the ashes on refuse of the same; narcotic preparations thereof or therefrom; morphine or any alkaloid of opium, preparation in which opium, morphine or any kind of opium, enter as an ingredient, and also opium leaves or wrappings of opium leaves, whether prepared or not for their use.

"Indian hemp" otherwise known as marijuana, cannabis, Americana, hashish, bhang, guaza, churruz, and ganjah embraces every kind, class and character of Indian hemp, whether dried or fresh, flowering or fruiting tops of the pistillate plant cannabis satival, from which the resin has not been extracted, including all other geographic varieties whether used as reefers, resin, extract, tincture or in any other form whatsoever.

By narcotic drug is meant a drug that produces a condition of insensibility and melancholy dullness of mind with delusions and may be habit-forming.

2. Anyone who shall maintain a dive or resort where any prohibited drug is used in any form, in violation of the law.

Art. 191. Keeper, watchman and visitor of opium den. —The penalty of arresto mayor and a fine ranging from 100 to 300 pesos shall be imposed upon:

1. Anyone who shall act as a keeper or watchman of a dive or resort where any prohibited drug is used in any manner contrary to law; and

2. Any person who, not being included in the provisions of the next preceding article, shall knowingly visit any dive or resort of the character referred to above.

Art. 192. Importation and sale of prohibited drugs. —The penalty of prision correccional in its medium and maximum periods and a fine ranging from 300 to 10,000 pesos shall be imposed upon any person who shall import or bring into the Philippine Islands any prohibited drug.

The same penalty shall be imposed upon any person who shall unlawfully sell or deliver to another prohibited drug.

Art. 193. Illegal possession of opium pipe or other paraphernalia for the use of any prohibited drug. —The penalty of arresto mayor and a fine not exceeding 500 pesos shall be imposed upon any person who, not being authorized by law, shall possess any opium pipe or other paraphernalia for smoking, injecting, administering or using opium or any prohibited drug.

The illegal possession of an opium pipe or other paraphernalia for using any other prohibited drug shall be prima facie evidence that its possessor has used said drug.

Art. 194. Prescribing opium unnecessary for a patient. —The penalty of prision correccional or a fine ranging from 300 to 10,000 pesos, or both shall be imposed upon any physician or dentist who shall prescribe opium for any person whose physical condition does not require the use of the same.

Title Six

CRIMES AGAINST PUBLIC MORALS

Chapter One

GAMBLING AND BETTING

Art. 195. What acts are punishable in gambling. —(a) The penalty of arresto mayor or a fine not exceeding two hundred pesos, and, in case of recidivism, the penalty of arresto mayor or a fine ranging from two hundred or six thousand pesos, shall be imposed upon:

1. Any person other than those referred to in subsections (b) and (c) who, in any manner shall directly, or indirectly take part in any game of monte, jueteng or any other form of lottery, policy, banking, or percentage game, dog races, or any other game of scheme the result of which depends wholly or chiefly upon chance or hazard; or wherein wagers consisting of money, articles of value or representative of value are made; or in the exploitation or use of any other mechanical invention or contrivance to determine by chance the loser or winner of money or any object or representative of value.

2. Any person who shall knowingly permit any form of gambling referred to in the preceding subdivision to be carried on in any unhabited or uninhabited place of any building, vessel or other means of transportation owned or controlled by him. If the place where gambling is carried on has the reputation of a gambling place or that prohibited gambling is frequently carried on therein, the culprit shall be punished by the penalty provided for in this article in its maximum period.

(b) The penalty of prision correccional in its maximum degree shall be imposed upon the maintainer, conductor, or banker in a game of jueteng or any similar game.

(c) The penalty of prision correccional in its medium degree shall be imposed upon any person who shall, knowingly and without lawful purpose, have in his possession and lottery list, paper or other matter containing letters, figures, signs or symbols which pertain to or are in any manner used in the game of jueteng or any similar game which has taken place or about to take place.

Art. 196. Importation, sale and possession of lottery tickets or advertisements. —The penalty of arresto mayor in its maximum period to prision correccional in its minimum period or a fine ranging from 200 to 2,000 pesos, or both, in the discretion of the court, shall be imposed upon any person who shall import into the Philippine Islands from any foreign place or port any lottery ticket or advertisement or, in connivance with the importer, shall sell or distribute the same.

Any person who shall knowingly and with intent to use them, have in his possession lottery tickets or advertisements, or shall sell or distribute the same without connivance with the importer of the same, shall be punished by arresto menor, or a fine not exceeding 200 pesos, or both, in the discretion of the court.

The possession of any lottery ticket or advertisement shall be prima facie evidence of an intent to sell, distribute or use the same in the Philippine Islands.

Art. 197. Betting in sports contests. —The penalty of arresto menor or a fine not exceeding 200 pesos, or both, shall be imposed upon any person who shall bet money or any object or article of value or representative of value upon the result of any boxing or other sports contests.

Art. 198. Illegal betting on horse race. —The penalty of arresto menor or a fine not exceeding 200 pesos, or both, shall be imposed upon any person who except during the period allowed by law, shall be on horse races. The penalty of arresto mayor or a fine ranging from 200 to 2,000 pesos, or both, shall be imposed upon any person who, under the same circumstances, shall maintain or employ a totalizer or other device or scheme for betting on horse races or realizing any profit therefrom.

For the purposes of this article, any race held in the same day at the same place shall be held punishable as a separate offense, and if the same be committed by any partnership, corporation or association, the president and the directors or managers thereof shall be deemed to be principals in the offense if they have consented to or knowingly tolerated its commission.

Art. 199. Illegal cockfighting. —The penalty of arresto menor or a fine not exceeding 200 pesos, or both, in the discretion of the court, shall be imposed upon:

1. Any person who directly or indirectly participates in cockfights, by betting money or other valuable things, or who organizes cockfights at which bets are made, on a day other than those permitted by law.

2. Any person who directly or indirectly participates in cockfights, at a place other than a licensed cockpit.

Chapter Two
OFFENSES AGAINST DECENCY AND GOOD CUSTOMS

Art. 200. Grave scandal. —The penalties of arresto mayor and public censure shall be imposed upon any person who shall offend against decency or good customs by any highly scandalous conduct not expressly falling within any other article of this Code.

Art. 201. Immoral doctrines, obscene publications and exhibitions and indecent shows. —The penalty of prision mayor or a fine ranging from six thousand to twelve thousand pesos, or both such imprisonment and fine, shall be imposed upon:

1. Those who shall publicly expound or proclaim doctrines openly contrary to public morals;

2. (a) the authors of obscene literature, published with their knowledge in any form; the editors publishing such literature; and the owners/operators of the establishment selling the same;

(b) Those who, in theaters, fairs, cinematographs or any other place, exhibit, indecent or immoral plays, scenes, acts or shows, whether live or in film, which are prescribed by virtue hereof, shall include those which (1) glorify criminals or condone crimes; (2) serve no other purpose but to satisfy the market for violence, lust or pornography; (3) offend any race or religion; (4) tend to abet traffic in and use of prohibited drugs; and (5) are contrary to law, public order, morals, and good customs, established policies, lawful orders, decrees and edicts;

3. Those who shall sell, give away or exhibit films, prints, engravings, sculpture or literature which are offensive to morals. (As amended by PD Nos. 960 and 969)

Art. 202. Vagrants and prostitutes; penalty.—The following are vagrants:

1. Any person having no apparent means of subsistence, who has the physical ability to work and who neglects to apply himself or herself to some lawful calling;

2. Any person found loitering about public or semi-public buildings or places or trampling or wandering about the country or the streets without visible means of support;

3. Any idle or dissolute person who ledges in houses of ill fame; ruffians or pimps and those who habitually associate with prostitutes;

4. Any person who, not being included in the provisions of other articles of this Code, shall be found loitering in any inhabited or uninhabited place belonging to another without any lawful or justifiable purpose;

5. Prostitutes.

For the purposes of this article, women who, for money or profit, habitually indulge in sexual intercourse or lascivious conduct, are deemed to be prostitutes.

Any person found guilty of any of the offenses covered by this articles shall be punished by arresto menor or a fine not exceeding 200 pesos, and in case of recidivism, by arresto mayor in its medium period to prision correccional in its minimum period or a fine ranging from 200 to 2,000 pesos, or both, in the discretion of the court.

Title Seven
CRIMES COMMITTED BY PUBLIC OFFICERS

Chapter One
PRELIMINARY PROVISIONS

Art. 203. Who are public officers. —For the purpose of applying the provisions of this and the preceding titles of this book, any person who, by direct provision of the law, popular election or appointment by competent authority, shall take part in the performance of public functions in the Government of the Philippine Islands, of shall perform in said Government or in any of its branches public duties as an employee, agent or subordinate official, of any rank or class, shall be deemed to be a public officer.

Chapter Two
MALFEASANCE AND MISFEASANCE IN OFFICE

Section One Dereliction of duty

Art. 204. Knowingly rendering unjust judgment. —Any judge who shall knowingly render an unjust judgment in any case submitted to him for decision, shall be punished by prision mayor and perpetual absolute disqualification.

Art. 205. Judgment rendered through negligence. —Any judge who, by reason of inexcusable negligence or ignorance shall render a manifestly unjust judgment in any case submitted to him for decision shall be punished by arresto mayor and temporary special disqualification.

Art. 206. Unjust interlocutory order. —Any judge who shall knowingly render an unjust interlocutory order or decree shall suffer the penalty of arresto mayor in its minimum period and suspension; but if he shall have acted by reason of inexcusable negligence or ignorance and the interlocutory order or decree be manifestly unjust, the penalty shall be suspension.

Art. 207. Malicious delay in the administration of justice. —The penalty of prision correccional in its minimum period shall be imposed upon any judge guilty of malicious delay in the administration of justice.

Art. 208. Prosecution of offenses; negligence and tolerance. —The penalty of prision correccional in its minimum period and suspension shall be imposed upon any public officer, or officer of the law, who, in dereliction of the duties of his office, shall maliciously refrain from instituting prosecution for the punishment of violators of the law, or shall tolerate the commission of offenses.

Art. 209. Betrayal of trust by an attorney or solicitor. —Revelation of secrets. —In addition to the proper administrative action, the penalty of prision correccional in its minimum period, or a fine ranging from 200 to 1,000 pesos, or both, shall be imposed upon any attorney-at-law or solicitor (procurador judicial) who, by any malicious breach of professional duty or of inexcusable negligence or ignorance, shall prejudice his client, or reveal any of the secrets of the latter learned by him in his professional capacity.

The same penalty shall be imposed upon an attorney-at-law or solicitor (*procurador judicial*) who, having undertaken the defense of a client or having received confidential information from said client in a case, shall undertake the defense of the opposing party in the same case, without the consent of his first client.

Section Two Bribery

Art. 210. Direct bribery. —Any public officer who shall agree to perform an act constituting a crime, in connection with the performance of this official duties, in consideration of any offer, promise, gift or present received by such officer, personally or through the mediation of another, shall suffer the penalty of prision mayor in its medium and maximum periods and a fine [of not less than the value of the gift and] not less than three times the value of the gift in addition to the penalty corresponding to the crime agreed upon, if the same shall have been committed.

If the gift was accepted by the officer in consideration of the execution of an act which does not constitute a crime, and the officer executed said act, he shall suffer the same penalty provided in the preceding paragraph; and if said act shall not have been accomplished, the officer shall suffer the penalties of prision correccional, in its medium period and a fine of not less than twice the value of such gift.

If the object for which the gift was received or promised was to make the public officer refrain from doing something which it was his official duty to do, he shall suffer the penalties of prision correccional in its maximum period and a fine [of not less than the value of the gift and] not less than three times the value of such gift.

In addition to the penalties provided in the preceding paragraphs, the culprit shall suffer the penalty of special temporary disqualification.

The provisions contained in the preceding paragraphs shall be made applicable to assessors, arbitrators, appraisal and claim commissioners, experts or any other persons performing public duties. (As amended by Batas Pambansa Blg. 872, June 10, 1985)

Art. 211. Indirect bribery. —The penalties of prision correccional in its medium and maximum periods, and public censure shall be imposed upon any public officer who shall accept gifts offered to him by reason of his office. (As amended by Batas Pambansa Blg. 872, June 10, 1985)

Art. 212. Corruption of public officials. —The same penalties imposed upon the officer corrupted, except those of disqualification and suspension, shall be imposed upon any person who shall have made the offers or promises or given the gifts or presents as described in the preceding articles.

Chapter Three
FRAUDS AND ILLEGAL EXACTIONS AND TRANSACTIONS

Art. 213. Frauds against the public treasury and similar offenses. — The penalty of prision correccional in its medium period to prision mayor in its minimum period, or a fine ranging from 200 to 10,000 pesos, or both, shall be imposed upon any public officer who:

1. In his official capacity, in dealing with any person with regard to furnishing supplies, the making of contracts, or the adjustment or settlement of accounts relating to public property or funds, shall enter into an agreement with any interested party or speculator or make use of any other scheme, to defraud the Government;

2. Being entrusted with the collection of taxes, licenses, fees and other imposts, shall be guilty or any of the following acts or omissions:

(a) Demanding, directly, or indirectly, the payment of sums different from or larger than those authorized by law.

(b) Failing voluntarily to issue a receipt, as provided by law, for any sum of money collected by him officially.

(c) Collecting or receiving, directly or indirectly, by way of payment or otherwise things or objects of a nature different from that provided by law.

When the culprit is an officer or employee of the Bureau of Internal Revenue or the Bureau of Customs, the provisions of the Administrative Code shall be applied.

Art. 214. Other frauds. —In addition to the penalties prescribed in the provisions of Chapter Six, Title Ten, Book Two, of this Code, the penalty of temporary special disqualification in its maximum period to perpetual special disqualification shall be imposed upon any public officer who, taking advantage of his official position, shall commit any of the frauds or deceits enumerated in said provisions.

Art. 215. Prohibited transactions. —The penalty of prision correccional in its maximum period or a fine ranging from 200 to 1,000 pesos, or both, shall be imposed upon any appointive public officer who, during his incumbency, shall directly or indirectly become interested in any transaction of exchange or speculation within the territory subject to his jurisdiction.

Art. 216. Possession of prohibited interest by a public officer. —The penalty of arresto mayor in its medium period to prision correccional in its minimum period, or a fine ranging from 200 to 1,000 pesos, or both, shall be imposed upon a public officer who directly or indirectly, shall become interested in any contract or business in which it is his official duty to intervene.

This provisions is applicable to experts, arbitrators and private accountants who, in like manner, shall take part in any contract or transaction connected with the estate or property in appraisal, distribution or adjudication of which they shall have acted, and to the guardians and executors with respect to the property belonging to their wards or estate.

Chapter Four
MALVERSATION OF PUBLIC FUNDS OR PROPERTY

Art. 217. Malversation of public funds or property; Presumption of malversation. —Any public officer who, by reason of the duties of his office, is accountable for public funds or property, shall appropriate the same or shall take or misappropriate or shall consent, through abandonment or negligence, shall permit any other person to take such public funds, or property, wholly or partially, or shall otherwise be guilty of the misappropriation or malversation of such funds or property, shall suffer:

1. The penalty of prision correccional in its medium and maximum periods, if the amount involved in the misappropriation or malversation does not exceed two hundred pesos.

2. The penalty of prision mayor in its minimum and medium periods, if the amount involved is more than two hundred pesos but does not exceed six thousand pesos.

3. The penalty of prision mayor in its maximum period to reclusion temporal in its minimum period, if the amount involved is more than six thousand pesos but is less than twelve thousand pesos.

4. The penalty of reclusion temporal, in its medium and maximum periods, if the amount involved is more than twelve thousand pesos but is less than twenty-two thousand pesos. If the amount exceeds the latter, the penalty shall be reclusion temporal in its maximum period to reclusion perpetua.

In all cases, persons guilty of malversation shall also suffer the penalty of perpetual special disqualification and a fine equal to the amount of the funds malversed or equal to the total value of the property embezzled.

The failure of a public officer to have duly forthcoming any public funds or property with which he is chargeable, upon demand by any duly authorized officer, shall be prima facie evidence that he has put such missing funds or property to personal use. (As amended by RA 1060)

Art. 218. Failure of accountable officer to render accounts. —Any public officer, whether in the service or separated therefrom by resignation or any other cause, who is required by law or regulation to render account to the Insular Auditor, or to a provincial auditor and who fails to do so for a period of two months after such accounts should be rendered, shall be punished by prision correccional in its minimum period, or by a fine ranging from 200 to 6,000 pesos, or both.

Art. 219. Failure of a responsible public officer to render accounts before leaving the country. —Any public officer who unlawfully leaves or attempts to leave the Philippine Islands without securing a certificate from the Insular Auditor showing that his accounts have been finally settled, shall be punished by arresto mayor, or a fine ranging from 200 to 1,000 pesos or both.

Art. 220. Illegal use of public funds or property. —Any public officer who shall apply any public fund or property under his administration to any public use other than for which such fund or property were appropriated by law or ordinance shall suffer the penalty of prision correccional in its minimum period or a fine ranging from one-half to the total of the sum misapplied, if by reason of such misapplication, any damages or embarrassment shall have resulted to the public service. In either case, the offender shall also suffer the penalty of temporary special disqualification.

If no damage or embarrassment to the public service has resulted, the penalty shall be a fine from 5 to 50 per cent of the sum misapplied.

Art. 221. Failure to make delivery of public funds or property. —Any public officer under obligation to make payment from Government funds in his possession, who shall fail to make such payment, shall be punished by arresto mayor and a fine from 5 to 25 per cent of the sum which he failed to pay.

This provision shall apply to any public officer who, being ordered by competent authority to deliver any property in his custody or under his administration, shall refuse to make such delivery.

The fine shall be graduated in such case by the value of the thing, provided that it shall not less than 50 pesos.

Art. 222. Officers included in the preceding provisions. —The provisions of this chapter shall apply to private individuals who in any capacity whatever, have charge of any insular, provincial or municipal funds, revenues, or property and to any administrator or depository of funds or property attached, seized or deposited by public authority, even if such property belongs to a private individual.

Chapter Five
INFIDELITY OF PUBLIC OFFICERS

Section One Infidelity in the custody of prisoners

Art. 223. Conniving with or consenting to evasion. —Any public officer who shall consent to the escape of a prisoner in his custody or charge, shall be punished:

1. By prision correccional in its medium and maximum periods and temporary special disqualification in its maximum period to perpetual special disqualification, if the fugitive shall have been sentenced by final judgment to any penalty.

2. By prision correccional in its minimum period and temporary special disqualification, in case the fugitive shall not have been finally convicted but only held as a detention prisoner for any crime or violation of law or municipal ordinance.

Art. 224. Evasion through negligence. —If the evasion of the prisoner shall have taken place through the negligence of the officer charged with the conveyance or custody of the escaping prisoner, said officer shall suffer the penalties of arresto mayor in its maximum period to prision correccional in its minimum period and temporary special disqualification.

Art. 225. Escape of prisoner under the custody of a person not a public officer. —Any private person to whom the conveyance or custody or a prisoner or person under arrest shall have been confided, who shall commit any of the offenses mentioned in the two preceding articles, shall suffer the penalty next lower in degree than that prescribed for the public officer.

Section Two Infidelity in the custody of document

Art. 226. Removal, concealment or destruction of documents. —Any public officer who shall remove, destroy or conceal documents or papers officially entrusted to him, shall suffer:

1. The penalty of prision mayor and a fine not exceeding 1,000 pesos, whenever serious damage shall have been caused thereby to a third party or to

the public interest.

2. The penalty of prision correccional in its minimum and medium period and a fine not exceeding 1,000 pesos, whenever the damage to a third party or to the public interest shall not have been serious.

In either case, the additional penalty of temporary special disqualification in its maximum period to perpetual disqualification shall be imposed.

Art. 227. Officer breaking seal. —Any public officer charged with the custody of papers or property sealed by proper authority, who shall break the seals or permit them to be broken, shall suffer the penalties of prision correccional in its minimum and medium periods, temporary special disqualification and a fine not exceeding 2,000 pesos.

Art. 228. Opening of closed documents. —Any public officer not included in the provisions of the next preceding article who, without proper authority, shall open or shall permit to be opened any closed papers, documents or objects entrusted to his custody, shall suffer the penalties or arresto mayor, temporary special disqualification and a fine of not exceeding 2,000 pesos.

Section Three Revelation of secrets

Art. 229. Revelation of secrets by an officer. —Any public officer who shall reveal any secret known to him by reason of his official capacity, or shall wrongfully deliver papers or copies of papers of which he may have charge and which should not be published, shall suffer the penalties of prision correccional in its medium and maximum periods, perpetual special disqualification and a fine not exceeding 2,000 pesos if the revelation of such secrets or the delivery of such papers shall have caused serious damage to the public interest; otherwise, the penalties of prision correccional in its minimum period, temporary special disqualification and a fine not exceeding 50 pesos shall be imposed.

Art. 230. Public officer revealing secrets of private individual. —Any public officer to whom the secrets of any private individual shall become known by reason of his office who shall reveal such secrets, shall suffer the penalties of arresto mayor and a fine not exceeding 1,000 pesos.

Chapter Six
OTHER OFFENSES OR IRREGULARITIES BY PUBLIC OFFICERS

Section One Disobedience

Art. 231. Open disobedience. —Any judicial or executive officer who shall openly refuse to execute the judgment, decision or order of any superior authority made within the scope of the jurisdiction of the latter and issued with all the legal formalities, shall suffer the penalties of arresto mayor in its medium period to prision correccional in its minimum period, temporary special disqualification in its maximum period and a fine not exceeding 1,000 pesos.

Art. 232. Disobedience to order of superior officers, when said order was suspended by inferior officer. —Any public officer who, having for any reason suspended the execution of the orders of his superiors, shall disobey such superiors after the latter have disapproved the suspension, shall suffer the penalties of prision correccional in its minimum and medium periods and perpetual special disqualification.

Art. 233. Refusal of assistance. —The penalties of arresto mayor in its medium period to prision correccional in its minimum period, perpetual special disqualification and a fine not exceeding 1,000 pesos, shall be imposed upon a public officer who, upon demand from competent authority, shall fail to lend his cooperation towards the administration of justice or other public service, if such failure shall result in serious damage to the public interest, or to a third party; otherwise, arresto mayor in its medium and maximum periods and a fine not exceeding 500 pesos shall be imposed.

Art. 234. Refusal to discharge elective office. —The penalty of arresto mayor or a fine not exceeding 1,000 pesos, or both, shall be imposed upon any person who, having been elected by popular election to a public office, shall refuse without legal motive to be sworn in or to discharge the duties of said office.

Art. 235. Maltreatment of prisoners. —The penalty of arresto mayor in its medium period to prision correccional in its minimum period, in addition to his liability for the physical injuries or damage caused, shall be imposed upon any public officer or employee who shall overdo himself in the correction or handling of a prisoner or detention prisoner under his charge, by the imposition of punishment not authorized by the regulations, or by inflicting such punishment in a cruel and humiliating manner.

If the purpose of the maltreatment is to extort a confession, or to obtain some information from the prisoner, the offender shall be punished by prision correccional in its minimum period, temporary special disqualification and a fine not exceeding 500 pesos, in addition to his liability for the physical injuries or damage caused.

Section Two Anticipation, prolongation and abandonment of the duties and powers of public office

Art. 236. Anticipation of duties of a public office. —Any person who shall assume the performance of the duties and powers of any public officer or employment without first being sworn in or having given the bond required by law, shall be suspended from such office or employment until he shall have complied with the respective formalities and shall be fined from 200 to 500 pesos.

Art. 237. Prolonging performance of duties and powers. —Any public officer shall continue to exercise the duties and powers of his office, employment or commission, beyond the period provided by law, regulation or special provisions applicable to the case, shall suffer the penalties of prision correccional in its minimum period, special temporary disqualification in its minimum period and a fine not exceeding 500 pesos.

Art. 238. Abandonment of office or position. —Any public officer who, before the acceptance of his resignation, shall abandon his office to the detriment of the public service shall suffer the penalty of arresto mayor.

If such office shall have been abandoned in order to evade the discharge of the duties of preventing, prosecuting or punishing any of the crime falling within Title One, and Chapter One of Title Three of Book Two of this Code, the offender shall be punished by prision correccional in its minimum and medium periods, and by arresto mayor if the purpose of such abandonment is to evade the duty of preventing, prosecuting or punishing any other crime.

Section Three Usurpation of powers and unlawful appointments

Art. 239. Usurpation of legislative powers. —The penalties of prision correccional in its minimum period, temporary special disqualification and a fine not exceeding 1,000 pesos, shall be imposed upon any public officer who shall encroach upon the powers of the legislative branch of the Government, either by making general rules or regulations beyond the scope of his authority, or by attempting to repeal a law or suspending the execution thereof.

Art. 240. Usurpation of executive functions. —Any judge who shall assume any power pertaining to the executive authorities, or shall obstruct the latter in the lawful exercise of their powers, shall suffer the penalty of arresto mayor in its medium period to prision correccional in its minimum period.

Art. 241. Usurpation of judicial functions. —The penalty of arresto mayor in its medium period to prision correccional in its minimum period and shall be imposed upon any officer of the executive branch of the Government who shall assume judicial powers or shall obstruct the execution of any order or decision rendered by any judge within its jurisdiction.

Art. 242. Disobeying request for disqualification. —Any public officer who, before the question of jurisdiction is decided, shall continue any proceeding after having been lawfully required to refrain from so doing, shall be punished by arresto mayor and a fine not exceeding 500 pesos.

Art. 243. Orders or requests by executive officers to any judicial authority. —Any executive officer who shall address any order or suggestion to any judicial authority with respect to any case or business coming within the exclusive jurisdiction of the courts of justice shall suffer the penalty of arresto mayor and a fine not exceeding 500 pesos.

Art. 244. Unlawful appointments. —Any public officer who shall knowingly nominate or appoint to any public office any person lacking the legal qualifications therefor, shall suffer the penalty of arresto mayor and a fine not exceeding 1,000 pesos.

Section Four Abuses against chastity

Art. 245. Abuses against chastity; Penalties. —The penalties of prision correccional in its medium and maximum periods and temporary special disqualification shall be imposed:

1. Upon any public officer who shall solicit or make immoral or indecent advances to a woman interested in matters pending before such officer for decision, or with respect to which he is required to submit a report to or consult with a superior officer;

2. Any warden or other public officer directly charged with the care and custody of prisoners or persons under arrest who shall solicit or make immoral or indecent advances to a woman under his custody.

If the person solicited be the wife, daughter, sister of relative within the same degree by affinity of any person in the custody of such warden or officer, the penalties shall be prision correccional in its minimum and medium periods and temporary special disqualification.

Title Eight
CRIMES AGAINST PERSONS

Chapter One
DESTRUCTION OF LIFE

Section One Parricide, murder, homicide

Art. 246. Parricide. —Any person who shall kill his father, mother, or child, whether legitimate or illegitimate, or any of his ascendants, or descendants, or his spouse, shall be guilty of parricide and shall be punished by the penalty of reclusion perpetua to death.

Art. 247. Death or physical injuries inflicted under exceptional circumstances. —Any legally married person who having surprised his spouse in the act of committing sexual intercourse with another person, shall kill any of them or both of them in the act or immediately thereafter, or shall inflict upon them any serious physical injury, shall suffer the penalty of destierro.

If he shall inflict upon them physical injuries of any other kind, he shall be exempt from punishment.

These rules shall be applicable, under the same circumstances, to parents with respect to their daughters under eighteen years of age, and their seducer, while the daughters are living with their parents.

Any person who shall promote or facilitate the prostitution of his wife or daughter, or shall otherwise have consented to the infidelity of the other spouse shall not be entitled to the benefits of this article.

Art. 248. Murder. —Any person who, not falling within the provisions of Article 246 shall kill another, shall be guilty of murder and shall be punished by reclusion temporal in its maximum period to death, if committed with any of the following attendant circumstances:

1. With treachery, taking advantage of superior strength, with the aid of armed men, or employing means to weaken the defense or of means or persons to insure or afford impunity.

2. In consideration of a price, reward, or promise.

3. By means of inundation, fire, poison, explosion, shipwreck, stranding of a vessel, derailment or assault upon a street car or locomotive, fall of an airship, by means of motor vehicles, or with the use of any other means involving great waste and ruin.

4. On occasion of any of the calamities enumerated in the preceding paragraph, or of an earthquake, eruption of a volcano, destructive cyclone, epidemic or other public calamity.

5. With evident premeditation.

6. With cruelty, by deliberately and inhumanly augmenting the suffering of the victim, or outraging or scoffing at his person or corpse.

Art. 249. Homicide. —Any person who, not falling within the provisions of Article 246, shall kill another without the attendance of any of the circumstances enumerated in the next preceding article, shall be deemed guilty of homicide and be punished by reclusion temporal.

Art. 250. Penalty for frustrated parricide, murder or homicide. —The courts, in view of the facts of the case, may impose upon the person guilty of the frustrated crime of parricide, murder or homicide, defined and penalized in the preceding articles, a penalty lower by one degree than that which should be imposed under the provision of Article 50.

The courts, considering the facts of the case, may likewise reduce by one degree the penalty which under Article 51 should be imposed for an attempt to commit any of such crimes.

Art. 251. Death caused in a tumultuous affray.—When, while several persons, not composing groups organized for the common purpose of assaulting and attacking each other reciprocally, quarrel and assault each other in a confused and tumultuous manner, and in the course of the affray someone is killed, and it cannot be ascertained who actually killed the deceased, but the person or persons who inflicted serious physical injuries can be identified, such person or persons shall be punished by prision mayor.

If it cannot be determined who inflicted the serious physical injuries on the deceased, the penalty of prision correccional in its medium and maximum periods shall be imposed upon all those who shall have used violence upon the person of the victim.

Art. 252. Physical injuries inflicted in a tumultuous affray.—When in a tumultuous affray as referred to in the preceding article, only serious physical injuries are inflicted upon the participants thereof and the person responsible thereof cannot be identified, all those who appear to have used violence upon the person of the offended party shall suffer the penalty next lower in degree than that provided for the physical injuries so inflicted.

When the physical injuries inflicted are of a less serious nature and the person responsible therefor cannot be identified, all those who appear to have used any violence upon the person of the offended party shall be punished by arresto mayor from five to fifteen days.

Art. 253. Giving assistance to suicide.—Any person who shall assist another to commit suicide shall suffer the penalty of prision mayor; if such person leads his assistance to another to the extent of doing the killing himself, he shall suffer the penalty of reclusion temporal. However, if the suicide is not consummated, the penalty of arresto mayor in its medium and maximum periods, shall be imposed.

Art. 254. Discharge of firearms.—Any person who shall shoot at another with any firearm shall suffer the penalty of prision correccional in its minimum and medium periods, unless the facts of the case are such that the act can be held to constitute frustrated or attempted parricide, murder, homicide or any other crime for which a higher penalty is prescribed by any of the articles of this

Code.

Section Two Infanticide and abortion

Art. 255. Infanticide. —The penalty provided for parricide in Article 246 and for murder in Article 248 shall be imposed upon any person who shall kill any child less than three days of age.

If the crime penalized in this article be committed by the mother of the child for the purpose of concealing her dishonor, she shall suffer the penalty of prision correccional in its medium and maximum periods, and if said crime be committed for the same purpose by the maternal grandparents or either of them, the penalty shall be prision mayor.

Art. 256. Intentional abortion. —Any person who shall intentionally cause an abortion shall suffer:

1. The penalty of reclusion temporal, if he shall use any violence upon the person of the pregnant woman.

2. The penalty of prision mayor if, without using violence, he shall act without the consent of the woman.

3. The penalty of prision correccional in its medium and maximum periods, if the woman shall have consented.

Art. 257. Unintentional abortion. —The penalty of prision correccional in its minimum and medium period shall be imposed upon any person who shall cause an abortion by violence, but unintentionally.

Art. 258. Abortion practiced by the woman herself of by her parents. —The penalty of prision correccional in its medium and maximum periods shall be imposed upon a woman who shall practice abortion upon herself or shall consent that any other person should do so.

Any woman who shall commit this offense to conceal her dishonor, shall suffer the penalty of prision correccional in its minimum and medium periods.

If this crime be committed by the parents of the pregnant woman or either of them, and they act with the consent of said woman for the purpose of concealing her dishonor, the offenders shall suffer the penalty of prision correccional in its medium and maximum periods.

Art. 259. Abortion practiced by a physician or midwife and dispensing of abortives. —The penalties provided in Article 256 shall be imposed in its maximum period, respectively, upon any physician or midwife who, taking advantage of their scientific knowledge or skill, shall cause an abortion or assist in causing the same.

Any pharmacist who, without the proper prescription from a physician, shall dispense any abortive shall suffer arresto mayor and a fine not exceeding 1,000 pesos.

Section Three Duel

Art. 260. Responsibility of participants in a duel.—The penalty of reclusion temporal shall be imposed upon any person who shall kill his adversary in a duel.

If he shall inflict upon the latter physical injuries only, he shall suffer the penalty provided therefor, according to their nature.

In any other case, the combatants shall suffer the penalty of arresto mayor, although no physical injuries have been inflicted.

The seconds shall in all events be punished as accomplices.

Art. 261. Challenging to a duel.—The penalty of prision correccional in its minimum period shall be imposed upon any person who shall challenge another, or incite another to give or accept a challenge to a duel, or shall scoff at or decry another publicly for having refused to accept a challenge to fight a duel.

Chapter Two
PHYSICAL INJURIES

Art. 262. Mutilation.—The penalty of reclusion temporal to reclusion perpetua shall be imposed upon any person who shall intentionally mutilate another by depriving him, either totally or partially, or some essential organ of reproduction.

Any other intentional mutilation shall be punished by prision mayor in its medium and maximum periods.

Art. 263. Serious physical injuries.—Any person who shall wound, beat, or assault another, shall be guilty of the crime of serious physical injuries and shall suffer:

1. The penalty of prision mayor, if in consequence of the physical injuries inflicted, the injured person shall become insane, imbecile, impotent, or blind;

2. The penalty of prision correccional in its medium and maximum periods, if in consequence of the physical injuries inflicted, the person injured shall have lost the use of speech or the power to hear or to smell, or shall have lost an eye, a hand, a foot, an arm, or a leg or shall have lost the use of any such member, or shall have become incapacitated for the work in which he was therefor habitually engaged;

3. The penalty of prision correccional in its minimum and medium periods, if in consequence of the physical injuries inflicted, the person injured shall have become deformed, or shall have lost any other part of his body, or shall have lost the use thereof, or shall have been ill or incapacitated for the performance of the work in which he as habitually engaged for a period of more than ninety days;

4. The penalty of arresto mayor in its maximum period to prision correccional in its minimum period, if the physical injuries inflicted shall have caused the illness or incapacity for labor of the injured person for more than thirty days.

If the offense shall have been committed against any of the persons enumerated in Article 246, or with attendance of any of the circumstances mentioned in Article 248, the case covered by subdivision number 1 of this Article shall be punished by reclusion temporal in its medium and maximum periods; the case covered by subdivision number 2 by prision correccional in its maximum period to prision mayor in its minimum period; the case covered by subdivision number 3 by prision correccional in its medium and maximum periods; and the case covered by subdivision number 4 by prision correccional in its minimum and medium periods.

The provisions of the preceding paragraph shall not be applicable to a parent who shall inflict physical injuries upon his child by excessive chastisement.

Art. 264. Administering injurious substances or beverages. —The penalties established by the next preceding article shall be applicable in the respective case to any person who, without intent to kill, shall inflict upon another any serious, physical injury, by knowingly administering to him any injurious substance or beverages or by taking advantage of his weakness of mind or credulity.

Art. 265. Less serious physical injuries. —Any person who shall inflict upon another physical injuries not described in the preceding articles, but which shall incapacitate the offended party for labor for ten days or more, or shall require medical assistance for the same period, shall be guilty of less serious physical injuries and shall suffer the penalty of arresto mayor.

Whenever less serious physical injuries shall have been inflicted with the manifest intent to kill or offend the injured person, or under circumstances adding ignominy to the offense in addition to the penalty of arresto mayor, a fine not exceeding 500 pesos shall be imposed.

Any less serious physical injuries inflicted upon the offender's parents, ascendants, guardians, curators, teachers, or persons of rank, or persons in authority, shall be punished by prision correccional in its minimum and medium periods, provided that, in the case of persons in authority, the deed does not constitute the crime of assault upon such person.

Art. 266. Slight physical injuries and maltreatment.—The crime of slight physical injuries shall be punished:

1. By arresto menor when the offender has inflicted physical injuries which shall incapacitate the offended party for labor from one to nine days, or shall require medical attendance during the same period.

2. By arresto menor or a fine not exceeding 20 pesos and censure when the offender has caused physical injuries which do not prevent the offended party from engaging in his habitual work nor require medical assistance.

3. By arresto menor in its minimum period or a fine not exceeding 50 pesos when the offender shall ill-treat another by deed without causing any injury.

Title Nine
CRIMES AGAINST PERSONAL LIBERTY AND SECURITY

Chapter One
CRIMES AGAINST LIBERTY

Art. 267. Kidnapping and serious illegal detention.—Any private individual who shall kidnap or detain another, or in any other manner deprive him of his liberty, shall suffer the penalty of reclusion perpetua to death:

1. If the kidnapping or detention shall have lasted more than five days.

2. If it shall have been committed simulating public authority.

3. If any serious physical injuries shall have been inflicted upon the person kidnapped or detained; or if threats to kill him shall have been made.

4. If the person kidnapped or detained shall be a minor, female or a public officer.

The penalty shall be death where the kidnapping or detention was committed for the purpose of extorting ransom from the victim or any other person, even if none of the circumstances above-mentioned were present in the commission of the offense.

Art. 268. Slight illegal detention. —The penalty of reclusion temporal shall be imposed upon any private individual who shall commit the crimes described in the next preceding article without the attendance of any of circumstances enumerated therein.

The same penalty shall be incurred by anyone who shall furnish the place for the perpetration of the crime.

If the offender shall voluntarily release the person so kidnapped or detained within three days from the commencement of the detention, without having attained the purpose intended, and before the institution of criminal proceedings against him, the penalty shall be prision mayor in its minimum and medium periods and a fine not exceeding seven hundred pesos.

Art. 269. Unlawful arrest. —The penalty of arresto mayor and a fine not exceeding 500 pesos shall be imposed upon any person who, in any case other than those authorized by law, or without reasonable ground therefor, shall arrest or detain another for the purpose of delivering him to the proper authorities.

Art. 270. Kidnapping and failure to return a minor. —The penalty of reclusion perpetua shall be imposed upon any person who, being entrusted with the custody of a minor person, shall deliberately fail to restore the latter to his parents or guardians.

Art. 271. Inducing a minor to abandon his home. —The penalty of prision correccional and a fine not exceeding seven hundred pesos shall be imposed upon anyone who shall induce a minor to abandon the home of his parent or guardians or the persons entrusted with his custody.

If the person committing any of the crimes covered by the two preceding articles shall be the father or the mother of the minor, the penalty shall be arresto mayor or a fine not exceeding three hundred pesos, or both.

Art. 272. Slavery. —The penalty of prision mayor and a fine of not exceeding 10,000 pesos shall be imposed upon anyone who shall purchase, sell, kidnap or detain a human being for the purpose of enslaving him.

If the crime be committed for the purpose of assigning the offended party to some immoral traffic, the penalty shall be imposed in its maximum period.

Art. 273. Exploitation of child labor. —The penalty of prision correccional in its minimum and medium periods and a fine not exceeding 500 pesos shall be imposed upon anyone who, under the pretext of reimbursing himself of a debt incurred by an ascendant, guardian or person entrusted with the custody of a minor, shall, against the latter's will, retain him in his service.

Art. 274. Services rendered under compulsion in payment of debt. — The penalty of arresto mayor in its maximum period to prision correccional in its minimum period shall be imposed upon any person who, in order to require or enforce the payment of a debt, shall compel the debtor to work for him, against his will, as household servant or farm laborer.

Chapter Two
CRIMES AGAINST SECURITY

Section One Abandonment of helpless persons and exploitation of minors

Art. 275. Abandonment of person in danger and abandonment of one's own victim. —The penalty of arresto mayor shall be imposed upon:

1. Any one who shall fail to render assistance to any person whom he shall find in an uninhabited place wounded or in danger of dying, when he can render such assistance without detriment to himself, unless such omission shall constitute a more serious offense.

2. Anyone who shall fail to help or render assistance to another whom he has accidentally wounded or injured.

3. Anyone who, having found an abandoned child under seven years of age, shall fail to deliver said child to the authorities or to his family, or shall fail

to take him to a safe place.

Art. 276. Abandoning a minor. —The penalty of arresto mayor and a fine not exceeding 500 pesos shall be imposed upon any one who shall abandon a child under seven years of age, the custody of which is incumbent upon him.

When the death of the minor shall result from such abandonment, the culprit shall be punished by prision correccional in its medium and maximum periods; but if the life of the minor shall have been in danger only, the penalty shall be prision correccional in its minimum and medium periods.

The provisions contained in the two preceding paragraphs shall not prevent the imposition of the penalty provided for the act committed, when the same shall constitute a more serious offense.

Art. 277. Abandonment of minor by person entrusted with his custody; indifference of parents. —The penalty of arresto mayor and a fine not exceeding 500 pesos shall be imposed upon anyone who, having charge of the rearing or education of a minor, shall deliver said minor to a public institution or other persons, without the consent of the one who entrusted such child to his care or in the absence of the latter, without the consent of the proper authorities.

The same penalty shall be imposed upon the parents who shall neglect their children by not giving them the education which their station in life require and financial conditions permit.

Art. 278. Exploitation of minors. —The penalty of prision correccional in its minimum and medium periods and a fine not exceeding 500 pesos shall be imposed upon:

1. Any person who shall cause any boy or girl under sixteen years of age to perform any dangerous feat of balancing, physical strength, or contortion.

2. Any person who, being an acrobat, gymnast, rope-walker, diver, wild-animal tamer or circus manager or engaged in a similar calling, shall employ in exhibitions of these kinds children under sixteen years of age who are not his children or descendants.

3. Any person engaged in any of the callings enumerated in the next paragraph preceding who shall employ any descendant of his under twelve years of age in such dangerous exhibitions.

4. Any ascendant, guardian, teacher or person entrusted in any capacity

with the care of a child under sixteen years of age, who shall deliver such child gratuitously to any person following any of the callings enumerated in paragraph 2 hereof, or to any habitual vagrant or beggar.

If the delivery shall have been made in consideration of any price, compensation, or promise, the penalty shall in every case be imposed in its maximum period.

In either case, the guardian or curator convicted shall also be removed from office as guardian or curator; and in the case of the parents of the child, they may be deprived, temporarily or perpetually, in the discretion of the court, of their parental authority.

5. Any person who shall induce any child under sixteen years of age to abandon the home of its ascendants, guardians, curators, or teachers to follow any person engaged in any of the callings mentioned in paragraph 2 hereof, or to accompany any habitual vagrant or beggar.

Art. 279. Additional penalties for other offenses. —The imposition of the penalties prescribed in the preceding articles, shall not prevent the imposition upon the same person of the penalty provided for any other felonies defined and punished by this Code.

Section Two Trespass to dwelling

Art. 280. Qualified trespass to dwelling. —Any private person who shall enter the dwelling of another against the latter's will shall be punished by arresto mayor and a fine not exceeding 1,000 pesos.

If the offense be committed by means of violence or intimidation, the penalty shall be prision correccional in its medium and maximum periods and a fine not exceeding 1,000 pesos.

The provisions of this article shall not be applicable to any person who shall enter another's dwelling for the purpose of preventing some serious harm to himself, the occupants of the dwelling or a third person, nor shall it be applicable to any person who shall enter a dwelling for the purpose of rendering some service to humanity or justice, nor to anyone who shall enter cafes, taverns, inn and other public houses, while the same are open.

Art. 281. Other forms of trespass. —The penalty of arresto menor or a fine not exceeding 200 pesos, or both, shall be imposed upon any person who shall enter the closed premises or the fenced estate of another, while either or them are uninhabited, if the prohibition to enter be manifest and the trespasser has not secured the permission of the owner or the caretaker thereof.

Section Three Threats and coercion

Art. 282. Grave threats. —Any person who shall threaten another with the infliction upon the person, honor or property of the latter or of his family of any wrong amounting to a crime, shall suffer:

1. The penalty next lower in degree than that prescribed by law for the crime be threatened to commit, if the offender shall have made the threat demanding money or imposing any other condition, even though not unlawful, and said offender shall have attained his purpose. If the offender shall not have attained his purpose, the penalty lower by two degrees shall be imposed.

If the threat be made in writing or through a middleman, the penalty shall be imposed in its maximum period.

2. The penalty of arresto mayor and a fine not exceeding 500 pesos, if the threat shall not have been made subject to a condition.

Art. 283. Light threats. —Any threat to commit a wrong not constituting a crime, made in the manner expressed in subdivision 1 of the next preceding article, shall be punished by arresto mayor.

Art. 284. Bond for good behavior. —In all cases falling within the two next preceding articles, the person making the threats may also be required to give bail not to molest the person threatened, or if he shall fail to give such bail, he shall be sentenced to destierro.

Art. 285. Other light threats. —The penalty of arresto menor in its minimum period or a fine not exceeding 200 pesos shall be imposed upon:

1. Any person who, without being included in the provisions of the next preceding article, shall threaten another with a weapon or draw such weapon in a quarrel, unless it be in lawful self-defense.

2. Any person who, in the heat of anger, shall orally threaten another with some harm not constituting a crime, and who by subsequent acts show that he did not persist in the idea involved in his threat, provided that the circumstances of the offense shall not bring it within the provisions of Article 282 of this Code.

3. Any person who shall orally threaten to do another any harm not constituting a felony.

Art. 286. Grave coercions.—The penalty of arresto mayor and a fine not exceeding 500 pesos shall be imposed upon any person who, without authority of law, shall, by means of violence, prevent another from doing something not prohibited by law, or compel him to do something against his will, whether it be right or wrong.

If the coercion be committed for the purpose of compelling another to perform any religious act or to prevent him from so doing, the penalty next higher in degree shall be imposed.

Art. 287. Light coercions.—Any person who, by means of violence, shall seize anything belonging to his debtor for the purpose of applying the same to the payment of the debt, shall suffer the penalty of arresto mayor in its minimum period and a fine equivalent to the value of the thing, but in no case less than 75 pesos.

Any other coercions or unjust vexations shall be punished by arresto menor or a fine ranging from 5 pesos to 200 pesos, or both.

Art. 288. Other similar coercions; (Compulsory purchase of merchandise and payment of wages by means of tokens.)—The penalty of arresto mayor or a fine ranging from 200 to 500 pesos, or both, shall be imposed upon any person, agent or officer, of any association or corporation who shall force or compel, directly or indirectly, or shall knowingly permit any laborer or employee employed by him or by such firm or corporation to be forced or compelled, to purchase merchandise or commodities of any kind.

The same penalties shall be imposed upon any person who shall pay the wages due a laborer or employee employed by him, by means of tokens or objects other than the legal tender currency of the laborer or employee.

Art. 289. Formation, maintenance and prohibition of combination of capital or labor through violence or threats.—The penalty of arresto mayor and a fine not exceeding 300 pesos shall be imposed upon any person who, for the purpose of organizing, maintaining or preventing coalitions or capital or labor, strike of laborers or lock-out of employees, shall employ violence or threats in such a degree as to compel or force the laborers or employers in the free and legal exercise of their industry or work, if the act shall not constitute a more serious offense in accordance with the provisions of this Code.

Chapter Three
DISCOVERY AND REVELATION OF SECRETS

Art. 290. Discovering secrets through seizure of correspondence. —The penalty of prision correccional in its minimum and medium periods and a fine not exceeding 500 pesos shall be imposed upon any private individual who in order to discover the secrets of another, shall seize his papers or letters and reveal the contents thereof.

If the offender shall not reveal such secrets, the penalty shall be arresto mayor and a fine not exceeding 500 pesos.

The provision shall not be applicable to parents, guardians, or persons entrusted with the custody of minors with respect to the papers or letters of the children or minors placed under their care or study, nor to spouses with respect to the papers or letters of either of them.

Art. 291. Revealing secrets with abuse of office. —The penalty of arresto mayor and a fine not exceeding 500 pesos shall be imposed upon any manager, employee, or servant who, in such capacity, shall learn the secrets of his principal or master and shall reveal such secrets.

Art. 292. Revelation of industrial secrets. —The penalty of prision correccional in its minimum and medium periods and a fine not exceeding 500 pesos shall be imposed upon the person in charge, employee or workman of any manufacturing or industrial establishment who, to the prejudice of the owner thereof, shall reveal the secrets of the industry of the latter.

Title Ten
CRIMES AGAINST PROPERTY

Chapter One
ROBBERY IN GENERAL

Art. 293. Who are guilty of robbery. —Any person who, with intent to

gain, shall take any personal property belonging to another, by means of violence or intimidation of any person, or using force upon anything shall be guilty of robbery.

Section One Robbery with violence or intimidation of persons

Art. 294. Robbery with violence against or intimidation of persons; Penalties. —Any person guilty of robbery with the use of violence against or intimidation of any person shall suffer:

1. The penalty of reclusion perpetua to death, when by reason or on occasion of the robbery, the crime of homicide shall have been committed.

2. The penalty of reclusion temporal in its medium period to reclusion perpetua when the robbery shall have been accompanied by rape or intentional mutilation, or if by reason or on occasion of such robbery, any of the physical injuries penalized in subdivision 1 of Article 263 shall have been inflicted; Provided, however, that when the robbery accompanied with rape is committed with a use of a deadly weapon or by two or more persons, the penalty shall be reclusion perpetua to death. (As amended by PD No. 767)

3. The penalty of reclusion temporal, when by reason or on occasion of the robbery, any of the physical injuries penalized in subdivision 2 of the article mentioned in the next preceding paragraph, shall have been inflicted.

4. The penalty of prision mayor in its maximum period to reclusion temporal in its medium period, if the violence or intimidation employed in the commission of the robbery shall have been carried to a degree clearly unnecessary for the commission of the crime, or when the course of its execution, the offender shall have inflicted upon any person not responsible for its commission any of the physical injuries covered by sub-divisions 3 and 4 of said Article 263.

5. The penalty of prision correccional in its maximum period to prision mayor in its medium period in other cases. (As amended by R. A. 18)

Art. 295. Robbery with physical injuries, committed in an uninhabited place and by a band, or with the use of firearm on a street, road or alley. —If the offenses mentioned in subdivisions three, four, and five of the next preceding article shall have been committed in an uninhabited place or by a band, or by attacking a moving train, street car, motor vehicle or airship, or by entering the passenger's compartments in a train or, in any manner, taking the passengers thereof by surprise in the respective conveyances, or on a street, road, highway, or alley, and the intimidation is made with the use of a firearm, the offender shall be punished by the maximum period of the proper penalties.

In the same cases, the penalty next higher in degree shall be imposed upon the leader of the band.

Art. 296. Definition of a band and penalty incurred by the members thereof. —When more than three armed malefactors take part in the commission of a robbery, it shall be deemed to have been committed by a band. When any of the arms used in the commission of the offense be an unlicensed firearm, the penalty to be imposed upon all the malefactors shall be the maximum of the corresponding penalty provided by law, without prejudice of the criminal liability for illegal possession of such unlicensed firearms.

Any member of a band who is present at the commission of a robbery by the band, shall be punished as principal of any of the assaults committed by the band, unless it be shown that he attempted to prevent the same.

Art. 297. Attempted and frustrated robbery committed under certain circumstances. —When by reason or on occasion of an attempted or frustrated robbery a homicide is committed, the person guilty of such offenses shall be punished by reclusion temporal in its maximum period to reclusion perpetua, unless the homicide committed shall deserve a higher penalty under the provisions of this Code.

Art. 298. Execution of deeds by means of violence or intimidation. — Any person who, with intent to defraud another, by means of violence or intimidation, shall compel him to sign, execute or deliver any public instrument or documents, shall be held guilty of robbery and punished by the penalties respectively prescribed in this Chapter.

Section Two Robbery by the use of force upon things

Art. 299. Robbery in an inhabited house or public building or edifice devoted to worship. —Any armed person who shall commit robbery in an inhabited house or public building or edifice devoted to religious worship, shall be punished by reclusion temporal, if the value of the property taken shall exceed 250 pesos, and if:

(a) The malefactors shall enter the house or building in which the robbery was committed, by any of the following means:

1. Through a opening not intended for entrance or egress.

2. By breaking any wall, roof, or floor or breaking any door or window.

3. By using false keys, picklocks or similar tools.

4. By using any fictitious name or pretending the exercise of public authority.

Or if —

(b) The robbery be committed under any of the following circumstances:

1. By the breaking of doors, wardrobes, chests, or any other kind of locked or sealed furniture or receptacle.

2. By taking such furniture or objects to be broken or forced open outside the place of the robbery.

When the offenders do not carry arms, and the value of the property taken exceeds 250 pesos, the penalty next lower in degree shall be imposed.

The same rule shall be applied when the offenders are armed, but the value of the property taken does not exceed 250 pesos.

When said offenders do not carry arms and the value of the property taken does not exceed 250 pesos, they shall suffer the penalty prescribed in the two next preceding paragraphs, in its minimum period.

If the robbery be committed in one of the dependencies of an inhabited house, public building, or building dedicated to religious worship, the penalties next lower in degree than those prescribed in this article shall be imposed.

Art. 300. Robbery in an uninhabited place and by a band. —The robbery mentioned in the next preceding article, if committed in an uninhabited place and by a band, shall be punished by the maximum period of the penalty provided therefor.

Art. 301. What is an inhabited house, public building or building dedicated to religious worship and their dependencies. —Inhabited house means any shelter, ship or vessel constituting the dwelling of one or more persons, even though the inhabitants thereof shall temporarily be absent therefrom when the robbery is committed.

All interior courts, corrals, waterhouses, granaries, barns, coach-houses, stables or other departments or inclosed places contiguous to the building or edifice, having an interior entrance connected therewith, and which form part of the whole, shall be deemed dependencies of an inhabited house, public building or building dedicated to religious worship.

Orchards and other lands used for cultivation or production are not included in the terms of the next preceding paragraph, even if closed, contiguous to the building and having direct connection therewith.

The term "*public building*" includes every building owned by the Government or belonging to a private person not included used or rented by the Government, although temporarily unoccupied by the same.

Art. 302. Robbery is an uninhabited place or in a private building. — Any robbery committed in an uninhabited place or in a building other than those mentioned in the first paragraph of Article 299, if the value of the property taken exceeds 250 pesos, shall be punished by prision correccional if any of the following circumstances is present:

1. If the entrance has been effected through any opening not intended for entrance or egress.

2. If any wall, roof, flour or outside door or window has been broken.

3. If the entrance has been effected through the use of false keys, picklocks or other similar tools.

4. If any dorm, wardrobe, chest or by sealed or closed furniture or receptacle has been broken.

5. If any closed or sealed receptacle, as mentioned in the preceding paragraph, has been removed even if the same to broken open elsewhere.

When the value of the property takes does not exceed 250 pesos, the penalty next lower in degree shall be imposed.

In the cases specified in Articles 294, 295, 297, 299, 300, and 302 of this Code, when the property taken is mail matter or large cattle, the offender shall suffer the penalties next higher in degree than those provided in said articles.

Art. 303. Robbery of cereals, fruits, or firewood in an uninhabited place or private building. —In the cases enumerated in Articles 299 and 302, when the robbery consists in the taking of cereals, fruits, or firewood, the culprit shall suffer the penalty next lower in degree than that prescribed in said articles.

Art. 304. Possession of picklocks or similar tools. —Any person who shall without lawful cause have in his possession picklocks or similar tools especially adopted to the commission of the crime of robbery, shall be punished by arresto mayor in its maximum period to prision correccional in its minimum period.

The same penalty shall be imposed upon any person who shall make such tools. If the offender be a locksmith, he shall suffer the penalty of prision correccional in its medium and maximum periods.

Art. 305. False keys. —The term "*false keys*" shall be deemed to include:

1. The tools mentioned in the next preceding articles.

2. Genuine keys stolen from the owner.

3. Any keys other than those intended by the owner for use in the lock forcibly opened by the offender.

Chapter Two
BRIGANDAGE

Art. 306. Who are brigands; Penalty. —When more than three armed persons form a band of robbers for the purpose of committing robbery in the highway, or kidnapping persons for the purpose of extortion or to obtain ransom or for any other purpose to be attained by means of force and violence, they shall be deemed highway robbers or brigands.

Persons found guilty of this offense shall be punished by prision mayor in its medium period to reclusion temporal in its minimum period if the act or acts committed by them are not punishable by higher penalties, in which case, they shall suffer such high penalties.

If any of the arms carried by any of said persons be an unlicensed firearms, it shall be presumed that said persons are highway robbers or brigands, and in case of convictions the penalty shall be imposed in the maximum period.

Art. 307. Aiding and abetting a band of brigands. —Any person knowingly and in any manner aiding, abetting or protecting a band of brigands as described in the next preceding article, or giving them information of the movements of the police or other peace officers of the Government (or of the forces of the United States Army), when the latter are acting in aid of the Government, or acquiring or receiving the property taken by such brigands shall be punished by prision correccional in its medium period to prision mayor in its minimum period.

It shall be presumed that the person performing any of the acts provided in this article has performed them knowingly, unless the contrary is proven.

Chapter Three
THEFT

Art. 308. Who are liable for theft. —Theft is committed by any person who, with intent to gain but without violence against or intimidation of persons nor force upon things, shall take personal property of another without the latter's consent.

Theft is likewise committed by:

1. Any person who, having found lost property, shall fail to deliver the same to the local authorities or to its owner;

2. Any person who, after having maliciously damaged the property of another, shall remove or make use of the fruits or object of the damage caused by him; and

3. Any person who shall enter an inclosed estate or a field where trespass is forbidden or which belongs to another and without the consent of its owner, shall hunt or fish upon the same or shall gather cereals, or other forest or farm products.

Art. 309. Penalties. —Any person guilty of theft shall be punished by:

1. The penalty of prision mayor in its minimum and medium periods, if the value of the thing stolen is more than 12,000 pesos but does not exceed 22,000 pesos, but if the value of the thing stolen exceeds the latter amount the penalty shall be the maximum period of the one prescribed in this paragraph, and one year for each additional ten thousand pesos, but the total of the penalty which may be imposed shall not exceed twenty years. In such cases, and in connection with the accessory penalties which may be imposed and for the purpose of the other provisions of this Code, the penalty shall be termed prision mayor or reclusion temporal, as the case may be.

2. The penalty of prision correccional in its medium and maximum periods, if the value of the thing stolen is more than 6,000 pesos but does not exceed 12,000 pesos.

3. The penalty of prision correccional in its minimum and medium periods, if the value of the property stolen is more than 200 pesos but does not exceed 6,000 pesos.

4. Arresto mayor in its medium period to prision correccional in its minimum period, if the value of the property stolen is over 50 pesos but does not exceed 200 pesos.

5. Arresto mayor to its full extent, if such value is over 5 pesos but does not exceed 50 pesos.

6. Arresto mayor in its minimum and medium periods, if such value does not exceed 5 pesos.

7. Arresto menor or a fine not exceeding 200 pesos, if the theft is committed under the circumstances enumerated in paragraph 3 of the next preceding article and the value of the thing stolen does not exceed 5 pesos. If such value exceeds said amount, the provision of any of the five preceding subdivisions shall be made applicable.

8. Arresto menor in its minimum period or a fine not exceeding 50 pesos, when the value of the thing stolen is not over 5 pesos, and the offender shall have acted under the impulse of hunger, poverty, or the difficulty of earning a livelihood for the support of himself or his family.

Art. 310. Qualified theft. —The crime of theft shall be punished by the penalties next higher by two degrees than those respectively specified in the next preceding article, if committed by a domestic servant, or with grave abuse of confidence, or if the property stolen is motor vehicle, mail matter or large cattle or consists of coconuts taken from the premises of the plantation or fish taken from a fishpond or fishery, or if property is taken on the occasion of fire, earthquake, typhoon, volcanic erruption, or any other calamity, vehicular accident or civil disturbance. (As amended by R. A. 120 and B. P. Blg. 71. May 1, 1980)

Art. 311. Theft of the property of the National Library and National Museum. —If the property stolen be any property of the National Library or the

National Museum, the penalty shall be arresto mayor or a fine ranging from 200 to 500 pesos, or both, unless a higher penalty should be provided under other provisions of this Code, in which case, the offender shall be punished by such higher penalty.

Chapter Four
USURPATION

Art. 312. Occupation of real property or usurpation of real rights in property. —Any person who, by means of violence against or intimidation of persons, shall take possession of any real property or shall usurp any real rights in property belonging to another, in addition to the penalty incurred for the acts of violence executed by him, shall be punished by a fine from 50 to 100 per centum of the gain which he shall have obtained, but not less than 75 pesos.

If the value of the gain cannot be ascertained, a fine of from 200 to 500 pesos shall be imposed.

Art. 313. Altering boundaries or landmarks. —Any person who shall alter the boundary marks or monuments of towns, provinces, or estates, or any other marks intended to designate the boundaries of the same, shall be punished by arresto menor or a fine not exceeding 100 pesos, or both.

Chapter Five
CULPABLE INSOLVENCY

Art. 314. Fraudulent insolvency. —Any person who shall abscond with his property to the prejudice of his creditors, shall suffer the penalty of prision mayor, if he be a merchant and the penalty of prision correccional in its maximum period to prision mayor in its medium period, if he be not a merchant.

Chapter Six
SWINDLING AND OTHER DECEITS

Art. 315. Swindling (estafa). —Any person who shall defraud another by any of the means mentioned hereinbelow shall be punished by:

1*st.* The penalty of prision correccional in its maximum period to prision mayor in its minimum period, if the amount of the fraud is over 12,000 pesos

but does not exceed 22,000 pesos, and if such amount exceeds the latter sum, the penalty provided in this paragraph shall be imposed in its maximum period, adding one year for each additional 10,000 pesos; but the total penalty which may be imposed shall not exceed twenty years. In such cases, and in connection with the accessory penalties which may be imposed under the provisions of this Code, the penalty shall be termed prision mayor or reclusion temporal, as the case may be;

2nd. The penalty of prision correccional in its minimum and medium periods, if the amount of the fraud is over 6,000 pesos but does not exceed 12,000 pesos;

3rd. The penalty of arresto mayor in its maximum period to prision correccional in its minimum period if such amount is over 200 pesos but does not exceed 6,000 pesos; and

4th. By arresto mayor in its maximum period, if such amount does not exceed 200 pesos, provided that in the four cases mentioned, the fraud be committed by any of the following means:

1. With unfaithfulness or abuse of confidence, namely:

(a) By altering the substance, quantity, or quality or anything of value which the offender shall deliver by virtue of an obligation to do so, even though such obligation be based on an immoral or illegal consideration.

(b) By misappropriating or converting, to the prejudice of another, money, goods, or any other personal property received by the offender in trust or on commission, or for administration, or under any other obligation involving the duty to make delivery of or to return the same, even though such obligation be totally or partially guaranteed by a bond; or by denying having received such money, goods, or other property.

(c) By taking undue advantage of the signature of the offended party in blank, and by writing any document above such signature in blank, to the prejudice of the offended party or of any third person.

2. By means of any of the following false pretenses or fraudulent acts executed prior to or simultaneously with the commission of the fraud:

(a) By using fictitious name, or falsely pretending to possess power, influence, qualifications, property, credit, agency, business or imaginary transactions, or by means of other similar deceits.

(b) By altering the quality, fineness or weight of anything pertaining to his art or business.

(c) By pretending to have bribed any Government employee, without prejudice to the action for calumny which the offended party may deem proper to bring against the offender. In this case, the offender shall be punished by the maximum period of the penalty.

(d) By post-dating a check, or issuing a check in payment of an obligation when the offender therein were not sufficient to cover the amount of the check. The failure of the drawer of the check to deposit the amount necessary to cover his check within three (3) days from receipt of notice from the bank and/or the payee or holder that said check has been dishonored for lack of insufficiency of funds shall be prima facie evidence of deceit constituting false pretense or fraudulent act. (As amended by R. A. 4885, approved June 17, 1967.)

(e) By obtaining any food, refreshment or accommodation at a hotel, inn, restaurant, boarding house, lodging house, or apartment house and the like without paying therefor, with intent to defraud the proprietor or manager thereof, or by obtaining credit at hotel, inn, restaurant, boarding house, lodging house, or apartment house by the use of any false pretense, or by abandoning or surreptitiously removing any part of his baggage from a hotel, inn, restaurant, boarding house, lodging house or apartment house after obtaining credit, food, refreshment or accommodation therein without paying for his food, refreshment or accommodation.

3. Through any of the following fraudulent means:

(a) By inducing another, by means of deceit, to sign any document.

(b) By resorting to some fraudulent practice to insure success in a gambling game.

(c) By removing, concealing or destroying, in whole or in part, any court record, office files, document or any other papers.

Art. 316. Other forms of swindling. —The penalty of arresto mayor in its minimum and medium period and a fine of not less than the value of the damage caused and not more than three times such value, shall be imposed upon:

1. Any person who, pretending to be owner of any real property, shall con-

vey, sell, encumber or mortgage the same.

2. Any person, who, knowing that real property is encumbered, shall dispose of the same, although such encumbrance be not recorded.

3. The owner of any personal property who shall wrongfully take it from its lawful possessor, to the prejudice of the latter or any third person.

4. Any person who, to the prejudice of another, shall execute any fictitious contract.

5. Any person who shall accept any compensation given him under the belief that it was in payment of services rendered or labor performed by him, when in fact he did not actually perform such services or labor.

6. Any person who, while being a surety in a bond given in a criminal or civil action, without express authority from the court or before the cancellation of his bond or before being relieved from the obligation contracted by him, shall sell, mortgage, or, in any other manner, encumber the real property or properties with which he guaranteed the fulfillment of such obligation.

Art. 317. Swindling a minor.—Any person who taking advantage of the inexperience or emotions or feelings of a minor, to his detriment, shall induce him to assume any obligation or to give any release or execute a transfer of any property right in consideration of some loan of money, credit or other personal property, whether the loan clearly appears in the document or is shown in any other form, shall suffer the penalty of arresto mayor and a fine of a sum ranging from 10 to 50 per cent of the value of the obligation contracted by the minor.

Art. 318. Other deceits.—The penalty of arresto mayor and a fine of not less than the amount of the damage caused and not more than twice such amount shall be imposed upon any person who shall defraud or damage another by any other deceit not mentioned in the preceding articles of this chapter.

Any person who, for profit or gain, shall interpret dreams, make forecasts, tell fortunes, or take advantage of the credulity of the public in any other similar manner, shall suffer the penalty of arresto mayor or a fine not exceeding 200 pesos.

Chapter Seven
CHATTEL MORTGAGE

Art. 319. Removal, sale or pledge of mortgaged property. —The penalty or arresto mayor or a fine amounting to twice the value of the property shall be imposed upon:

1. Any person who shall knowingly remove any personal property mortgaged under the Chattel Mortgage Law to any province or city other than the one in which it was located at the time of the execution of the mortgage, without the written consent of the mortgagee, or his executors, administrators or assigns.

2. Any mortgagor who shall sell or pledge personal property already pledged, or any part thereof, under the terms of the Chattel Mortgage Law, without the consent of the mortgagee written on the back of the mortgage and noted on the record hereof in the office of the Register of Deeds of the province where such property is located.

Chapter Eight
ARSON AND OTHER CRIMES INVOLVING DESTRUCTIONS

Art. 320. Destructive arson. —The penalty of reclusion temporal in its maximum period to reclusion perpetua shall be imposed upon any person who shall burn:

1. Any arsenal, shipyard, storehouse or military powder or fireworks factory, ordinance, storehouse, archives or general museum of the Government.

2. Any passenger train or motor vehicle in motion or vessel out of port.

3. In an inhabited place, any storehouse or factory of inflammable or explosive materials.

Art. 321. Other forms of arson. —When the arson consists in the burning of other property and under the circumstances given hereunder, the offender shall be punishable:

1. By reclusion temporal or reclusion perpetua:

(a) if the offender shall set fire to any building, farmhouse, warehouse, hut, shelter, or vessel in port, knowing it to be occupied at the time by one or

more persons;

(b) If the building burned is a public building and value of the damage caused exceeds 6,000 pesos;

(c) If the building burned is a public building and the purpose is to destroy evidence kept therein to be used in instituting prosecution for the punishment of violators of the law, irrespective of the amount of the damage;

(d) If the building burned is a public building and the purpose is to destroy evidence kept therein to be used in legislative, judicial or administrative proceedings, irrespective of the amount of the damage; Provided, however, That if the evidence destroyed is to be used against the defendant for the prosecution of any crime punishable under existing laws, the penalty shall be reclusion perpetua;

(e) If the arson shall have been committed with the intention of collecting under an insurance policy against loss or damage by fire.

2. By reclusion temporal:

(a) If an inhabited house or any other building in which people are accustomed to meet is set on fire, and the culprit did not know that such house or building was occupied at the time, or if he shall set fire to a moving freight train or motor vehicle, and the value of the damage caused exceeds 6,000 pesos;

(b) If the value of the damage caused in paragraph (b) of the preceding subdivision does not exceed 6,000 pesos;

(c) If a farm, sugar mill, cane mill, mill central, bamboo groves or any similar plantation is set on fire and the damage caused exceeds 6,000 pesos; and

(d) If grain fields, pasture lands, or forests, or plantings are set on fire, and the damage caused exceeds 6,000 pesos.

3. By prision mayor:

(a) If the value of the damage caused in the case mentioned in paragraphs (a), (c), and (d) in the next preceding subdivision does not exceed 6,000 pesos;

(b) If a building not used as a dwelling or place of assembly, located in a populated place, is set on fire, and the damage caused exceeds 6,000 pesos;

4. By prision correccional in its maximum period to prision mayor in its medium period:

(a) If a building used as dwelling located in an uninhabited place is set on fire and the damage caused exceeds 1,000 pesos;

(b) If the value or the damage caused in the case mentioned in paragraphs (c) and (d) of subdivision 2 of this article does not exceed 200 pesos.

5. By prision correccional in its medium period to prision mayor in its minimum period, when the damage caused is over 200 pesos but does not exceed 1,000 pesos, and the property referred to in paragraph (a) of the preceding subdivision is set on fire; but when the value of such property does not exceed 200 pesos, the penalty next lower in degree than that prescribed in this subdivision shall be imposed.

6. The penalty of prision correccional in its medium and maximum periods, if the damage caused in the case mentioned in paragraph (b) of subdivision 3 of this article does not exceed 6,000 pesos but is over 200 pesos.

7. The penalty of prision correccional in its minimum and medium periods, if the damage caused in the case mentioned paragraph (b) subdivision 3 of this article does not exceed 200 pesos.

8. The penalty of arresto mayor and a fine ranging from fifty to one hundred per centum if the damage caused shall be imposed, when the property burned consists of grain fields, pasture lands, forests, or plantations when the value of such property does not exceed 200 pesos. (As amended by R. A. 5467, approved May 12, 1969)

Art. 322. Cases of arson not included in the preceding articles.—Cases of arson not included in the next preceding articles shall be punished:

1. By arresto mayor in its medium and maximum periods, when the damage caused does not exceed 50 pesos;

2. By arresto mayor in its maximum period to prision correccional in its minimum period, when the damage caused is over 50 pesos but does not exceed 200 pesos;

3. By prision correccional in its minimum and medium periods, if the damage caused is over 200 pesos but does not exceed 1,000 pesos; and

4. By prision correccional in its medium and maximum periods, if it is over 1,000 pesos.

Art. 323. Arson of property of small value.—The arson of any uninhabited hut, storehouse, barn, shed, or any other property the value of which does not exceed 25 pesos, committed at a time or under circumstances which clearly exclude all danger of the fire spreading, shall not be punished by the penalties respectively prescribed in this chapter, but in accordance with the damage caused and under the provisions of the following chapter.

Art. 324. Crimes involving destruction. —Any person who shall cause destruction by means of explosion, discharge of electric current, inundation, sinking or stranding of a vessel, intentional damaging of the engine of said vessel, taking up the rails from a railway track, maliciously changing railway signals for the safety of moving trains, destroying telegraph wires and telegraph posts, or those of any other system, and, in general, by using any other agency or means of destruction as effective as those above enumerated, shall be punished by reclusion temporal if the commission has endangered the safety of any person, otherwise, the penalty of prision mayor shall be imposed.

Art. 325. Burning one's own property as means to commit arson. — Any person guilty of arson or causing great destruction of the property belonging to another shall suffer the penalties prescribed in this chapter, even though he shall have set fire to or destroyed his own property for the purposes of committing the crime.

Art. 326. Setting fire to property exclusively owned by the offender. — If the property burned shall be the exclusive property of the offender, he shall be punished by arresto mayor in its maximum period to prision correccional in its minimum period, if the arson shall have been committed for the purpose of defrauding or causing damage to another, or prejudice shall actually have been caused, or if the thing burned shall have been a building in an inhabited place.

Art. 326-A. In cases where death resulted as a consequence of arson. —If death resulted as a consequence of arson committed on any of the properties and under any of the circumstances mentioned in the preceding articles, the court shall impose the death penalty.

Art. 326-B. Prima facie evidence of arson. —Any of the following circumstances shall constitute prima facie evidence of arson:

1. If after the fire, are found materials or substances soaked in gasoline, kerosene, petroleum, or other inflammables, or any mechanical, electrical

chemical or traces or any of the foregoing.

2. That substantial amount of inflammable substance or materials were stored within the building not necessary in the course of the defendant's business; and

3. That the fire started simultaneously in more than one part of the building or locale under circumstances that cannot normally be due to accidental or unintentional causes: Provided, however, That at least one of the following is present in any of the three above-mentioned circumstances:

(a) That the total insurance carried on the building and/or goods is more than 80 per cent of the value of such building and/or goods at the time of the fire;

(b) That the defendant after the fire has presented a fraudulent claim for loss.

The penalty of prision correccional shall be imposed on one who plants the articles above-mentioned, in order to secure a conviction, or as a means of extortion or coercion. (As amended by R. A. 5467, approved May 12, 1969).

Chapter Nine
MALICIOUS MISCHIEF

Art. 327. Who are liable for malicious mischief. —Any person who shall deliberately cause the property of another any damage not falling within the terms of the next preceding chapter shall be guilty of malicious mischief.

Art. 328. Special cases of malicious mischief. —Any person who shall cause damage to obstruct the performance of public functions, or using any poisonous or corrosive substance; or spreading any infection or contagion among cattle; or who cause damage to the property of the National Museum or National Library, or to any archive or registry, waterworks, road, promenade, or any other thing used in common by the public, shall be punished:

1. By prision correccional in its minimum and medium periods, if the value of the damage caused exceeds 1,000 pesos;

2. By arresto mayor, if such value does not exceed the abovementioned amount but it is over 200 pesos; and

3. By arresto menor, in such value does not exceed 200 pesos.

Art. 329. Other mischiefs. —The mischiefs not included in the next preceding article shall be punished:

1. By arresto mayor in its medium and maximum periods, if the value of the damage caused exceeds 1,000 pesos;

2. By arresto mayor in its minimum and medium periods, if such value is over 200 pesos but does not exceed 1,000 pesos; and

3. By arresto menor or fine of not less than the value of the damage caused and not more than 200 pesos, if the amount involved does not exceed 200 pesos or cannot be estimated.

Art. 330. Damage and obstruction to means of communication. —The penalty of prision correccional in its medium and maximum periods shall be imposed upon any person who shall damage any railway, telegraph or telephone lines.

If the damage shall result in any derailment of cars, collision or other accident, the penalty of prision mayor shall be imposed, without prejudice to the criminal liability of the offender for the other consequences of his criminal act.

For the purpose of the provisions of the article, the electric wires, traction cables, signal system and other things pertaining to railways, shall be deemed to constitute an integral part of a railway system.

Art. 331. Destroying or damaging statues, public monuments or paintings. —Any person who shall destroy or damage statues or any other useful or ornamental public monument shall suffer the penalty of arresto mayor in its medium period to prision correccional in its minimum period.

Any person who shall destroy or damage any useful or ornamental painting of a public nature shall suffer the penalty of arresto menor or a fine not exceeding 200 pesos, or both such fine and imprisonment, in the discretion of the court.

Chapter Ten
EXEMPTION FROM CRIMINAL LIABILITY IN CRIMES AGAINST PROPERTY

Art. 332. Persons exempt from criminal liability. —No criminal, but only civil liability, shall result from the commission of the crime of theft, swindling or malicious mischief committed or caused mutually by the following persons:

1. Spouses, ascendants and descendants, or relatives by affinity in the same line.

2. The widowed spouse with respect to the property which belonged to the deceased spouse before the same shall have passed into the possession of another; and

3. Brothers and sisters and brothers-in-law and sisters-in-law, if living together.

The exemption established by this article shall not be applicable to strangers participating in the commission of the crime.

Title Eleven
CRIMES AGAINST CHASTITY

Chapter One
ADULTERY AND CONCUBINAGE

Art. 333. Who are guilty of adultery. —Adultery is committed by any married woman who shall have sexual intercourse with a man not her husband and by the man who has carnal knowledge of her knowing her to be married, even if the marriage be subsequently declared void.

Adultery shall be punished by prision correccional in its medium and maximum periods.

If the person guilty of adultery committed this offense while being abandoned without justification by the offended spouse, the penalty next lower in degree than that provided in the next preceding paragraph shall be imposed.

Art. 334. Concubinage. —Any husband who shall keep a mistress in the conjugal dwelling, or shall have sexual intercourse, under scandalous circumstances, with a woman who is not his wife, or shall cohabit with her in any other place, shall be punished by prision correccional in its minimum and medium periods.

The concubine shall suffer the penalty of destierro.

Chapter Two
RAPE AND ACTS OF LASCIVIOUSNESS

Art. 335. When and how rape is committed. —Rape is committed by having carnal knowledge of a woman under any of the following circumstances:

1. By using force or intimidation;
2. When the woman is deprived of reason or otherwise unconscious; and
3. When the woman is under twelve years of age, even though neither of the circumstances mentioned in the two next preceding paragraphs shall be present.

The crime of rape shall be punished by reclusion perpetua.

Whenever the crime of rape is committed with the use of a deadly weapon or by two or more persons, the penalty shall be reclusion perpetua to death.

When by reason or on the occasion of the rape, the victim has become insane, the penalty shall be death.

When rape is attempted or frustrated and a homicide is committed by reason or on the occasion thereof, the penalty shall be likewise death.

When by reason or on the occasion of the rape, a homicide is committed, the penalty shall be death. (As amended by R. A. 2632, approved June 18, 1960, and R. A. 4111, approved June 20, 1964)

Art. 336. Acts of lasciviousness. —Any person who shall commit any act of lasciviousness upon other persons of either sex, under any of the circumstances mentioned in the preceding article, shall be punished by prision correccional.

Chapter Three
SEDUCTION, CORRUPTION OF MINORS AND WHITE SLAVE TRADE

Art. 337. Qualified seduction. —The seduction of a virgin over twelve years and under eighteen years of age, committed by any person in public authority, priest, home-servant, domestic, guardian, teacher, or any person who, in any capacity, shall be entrusted with the education or custody of the woman seduced, shall be punished by prision correccional in its minimum and medium periods.

The penalty next higher in degree shall be imposed upon any person who shall seduce his sister or descendant, whether or not she be a virgin or over eighteen years of age.

Under the provisions of this Chapter, seduction is committed when the offender has carnal knowledge of any of the persons and under the circumstances described herein.

Art. 338. Simple seduction. —The seduction of a woman who is single or a widow of good reputation, over twelve but under eighteen years of age, committed by means of deceit, shall be punished by arresto mayor.

Art. 339. Acts of lasciviousness with the consent of the offended party. —The penalty of arresto mayor shall be imposed to punish any other acts of lasciviousness committed by the same persons and the same circumstances as those provided in Articles 337 and 338.

Art. 340. Corruption of minors. —Any person who shall promote or facilitate the prostitution or corruption of persons underage to satisfy the lust of another, shall be punished by prision mayor, and if the culprit is a pubic officer or employee, including those in government-owned or controlled corporations, he shall also suffer the penalty of temporary absolute disqualification. (As amended by Batas Pambansa Blg. 92)

Art. 341. White slave trade. —The penalty of prision mayor in its medium and maximum period shall be imposed upon any person who, in any manner, or under any pretext, shall engage in the business or shall profit by prostitution or shall enlist the services of any other for the purpose of prostitution. (As amended by Batas Pambansa Blg. 186.)

Chapter Four
ABDUCTION

Art. 342. Forcible abduction. —The abduction of any woman against her will and with lewd designs shall be punished by reclusion temporal.

The same penalty shall be imposed in every case, if the female abducted be under twelve years of age.

Art. 343. Consented abduction. —The abduction of a virgin over twelve years and under eighteen years of age, carried out with her consent and with lewd designs, shall be punished by the penalty of prision correccional in its minimum and medium periods.

Chapter Five
PROVISIONS RELATIVE TO THE PRECEDING CHAPTERS OF TITLE ELEVEN

Art. 344. Prosecution of the crimes of adultery, concubinage, seduction, abduction, rape and acts of lasciviousness. —The crimes of adultery and concubinage shall not be prosecuted except upon a complaint filed by the offended spouse.

The offended party cannot institute criminal prosecution without including both the guilty parties, if they are both alive, nor, in any case, if he shall have consented or pardoned the offenders.

The offenses of seduction, abduction, rape or acts of lasciviousness, shall not be prosecuted except upon a complaint filed by the offended party or her parents, grandparents, or guardian, nor, in any case, if the offender has been expressly pardoned by the above named persons, as the case may be.

In cases of seduction, abduction, acts of lasciviousness and rape, the marriage of the offender with the offended party shall extinguish the criminal action or remit the penalty already imposed upon him. The provisions of this paragraph shall also be applicable to the co-principals, accomplices and accessories after the fact of the above-mentioned crimes.

Art. 345. Civil liability of persons guilty of crimes against chastity. — Person guilty of rape, seduction or abduction, shall also be sentenced:

1. To indemnify the offended woman.
2. To acknowledge the offspring, unless the law should prevent him from so doing.
3. In every case to support the offspring.

The adulterer and the concubine in the case provided for in Articles 333 and 334 may also be sentenced, in the same proceeding or in a separate civil proceeding, to indemnify for damages caused to the offended spouse.

Art. 346. Liability of ascendants, guardians, teachers, or other persons entrusted with the custody of the offended party. —The ascendants, guardians, curators, teachers and any person who, by abuse of authority or confidential relationships, shall cooperate as accomplices in the perpetration of the crimes embraced in chapters, second, third and fourth, of this title, shall be punished as principals.

Teachers or other persons in any other capacity entrusted with the education and guidance of youth, shall also suffer the penalty of temporary special disqualification in its maximum period to perpetual special disqualification.

Any person falling within the terms of this article, and any other person guilty of corruption of minors for the benefit of another, shall be punished by special disqualification from filling the office of guardian.

Title Twelve

CRIMES AGAINST THE CIVIL STATUS OF PERSONS

Chapter One

SIMULATION OF BIRTHS AND USURPATION OF CIVIL STATUS

Art. 347. Simulation of births, substitution of one child for another and concealment or abandonment of a legitimate child. —The simulation of births and the substitution of one child for another shall be punished by prision mayor and a fine of not exceeding 1,000 pesos.

The same penalties shall be imposed upon any person who shall conceal or abandon any legitimate child with intent to cause such child to lose its civil status.

Any physician or surgeon or public officer who, in violation of the duties of his profession or office, shall cooperate in the execution of any of the crimes mentioned in the two next preceding paragraphs, shall suffer the penalties therein prescribed and also the penalty of temporary special disqualification.

Art. 348. Usurpation of civil status. —The penalty of prision mayor shall be imposed upon any person who shall usurp the civil status of another, should he do so for the purpose of defrauding the offended part or his heirs; otherwise, the penalty of prision correccional in its medium and maximum periods shall be imposed.

Chapter Two
ILLEGAL MARRIAGES

Art. 349. Bigamy.—The penalty of prision mayor shall be imposed upon any person who shall contract a second or subsequent marriage before the former marriage has been legally dissolved, or before the absent spouse has been declared presumptively dead by means of a judgment rendered in the proper proceedings.

Art. 350. Marriage contracted against provisions of laws.—The penalty of prision correccional in its medium and maximum periods shall be imposed upon any person who, without being included in the provisions of the next proceeding article, shall have not been complied with or that the marriage is in disregard of a legal impediment.

If either of the contracting parties shall obtain the consent of the other by means of violence, intimidation or fraud, he shall be punished by the maximum period of the penalty provided in the next preceding paragraph.

Art. 351. Premature marriages.—Any widow who shall marry within three hundred and one day from the date of the death of her husband, or before having delivered if she shall have been pregnant at the time of his death, shall be punished by arresto mayor and a fine not exceeding 500 pesos.

The same penalties shall be imposed upon any woman whose marriage shall have been annulled or dissolved, if she shall marry before her delivery or before the expiration of the period of three hundred and one day after the legal separation.

Art. 352. Performance of illegal marriage ceremony.—Priests or ministers of any religious denomination or sect, or civil authorities who shall perform or authorize any illegal marriage ceremony shall be punished in accordance with the provisions of the Marriage Law.

Title Thirteen
CRIMES AGAINST HONOR

Chapter One
LIBEL

Section One Definitions, forms, and punishment of this crime

Art. 353. Definition of libel. —A libel is public and malicious imputation of a crime, or of a vice or defect, real or imaginary, or any act, omission, condition, status, or circumstance tending to cause the dishonor, discredit, or contempt of a natural or juridical person, or to blacken the memory of one who is dead.

Art. 354. Requirement for publicity. —Every defamatory imputation is presumed to be malicious, even if it be true, if no good intention and justifiable motive for making it is shown, except in the following cases:

1. A private communication made by any person to another in the performance of any legal, moral or social duty; and
2. A fair and true report, made in good faith, without any comments or remarks, of any judicial, legislative or other official proceedings which are not of confidential nature, or of any statement, report or speech delivered in said proceedings, or of any other act performed by public officers in the exercise of their functions.

Art. 355. Libel means by writings or similar means. —A libel committed by means of writing, printing, lithography, engraving, radio, phonograph, painting, theatrical exhibition, cinematographic exhibition, or any similar means, shall be punished by prision correccional in its minimum and medium periods or a fine ranging from 200 to 6,000 pesos, or both, in addition to the civil action which may be brought by the offended party.

Art. 356. Threatening to publish and offer to present such publication for a compensation. —The penalty of arresto mayor or a fine from 200 to 2,000 pesos, or both, shall be imposed upon any person who threatens another to publish a libel concerning him or the parents, spouse, child, or other members of the family of the latter or upon anyone who shall offer to prevent the publication of such libel for a compensation or money consideration.

Art. 357. Prohibited publication of acts referred to in the course of official proceedings. —The penalty of arresto mayor or a fine of from 20 to 2,000 pesos, or both, shall be imposed upon any reporter, editor or manager or a newspaper, daily or magazine, who shall publish facts connected with the private life of another and offensive to the honor, virtue and reputation of said person, even though said publication be made in connection with or under the pretext that it is necessary in the narration of any judicial or administrative proceedings wherein such facts have been mentioned.

Art. 358. Slander. —Oral defamation shall be punished by arresto mayor in its maximum period to prision correccional in its minimum period if it is of a serious and insulting nature; otherwise the penalty shall be arresto menor or a fine not exceeding 200 pesos.

Art. 359. Slander by deed. —The penalty of arresto mayor in its maximum period to prision correccional in its minimum period or a fine ranging from 200 to 1,000 pesos shall be imposed upon any person who shall perform any act not included and punished in this title, which shall cast dishonor, discredit or contempt upon another person. If said act is not of a serious nature, the penalty shall be arresto menor or a fine not exceeding 200 pesos.

Section Two General provisions

Art. 360. Persons responsible. —Any person who shall publish, exhibit, or cause the publication or exhibition of any defamation in writing or by similar means, shall be responsible for the same.

The author or editor of a book or pamphlet, or the editor or business manager of a daily newspaper, magazine or serial publication, shall be responsible for the defamations contained therein to the same extent as if he were the author thereof.

The criminal and civil action for damages in cases of written defamations as provided for in this chapter, shall be filed simultaneously or separately with the court of first instance of the province or city where the libelous article is printed and first published or where any of the offended parties actually resides at the time of the commission of the offense: *Provided*, *however*, That where one of the offended parties is a public officer whose office is in the City of Manila at the time of the commission of the offense, the action shall be filed in the Court of First Instance of the City of Manila, or of the city or province where the libelous article is printed and first published, and in case such public officer does not hold office in the City of Manila, the action shall be filed in the Court of First Instance of the province or city where he held office at the time of the commission of the offense or where the libelous article is printed and first published and in case one of the offended parties is a private individual, the action shall be filed in the Court of First Instance of the province or city where he actually resides at the time of the commission of the offense or where the libelous matter is printed and first published: *Provided*, *further*, That the civil action shall be filed in the same court where the criminal action is filed and vice versa: *Provided*, *furthermore*, That the court where the criminal action or civil action for damages is first filed, shall acquire jurisdiction to the exclusion of other courts: And, provided, finally, That this amendment shall not apply to cases of written defamations, the civil and/or criminal actions which have been filed in court at the time of the effectivity of this law.

Preliminary investigation of criminal action for written defamations as provided for in the chapter shall be conducted by the provincial or city fiscal of the province or city, or by the municipal court of the city or capital of the province where such action may be instituted in accordance with the provisions of this article.

No criminal action for defamation which consists in the imputation of a crime which cannot be prosecuted de oficio shall be brought except at the instance of and upon complaint expressly filed by the offended party. (As amended by R. A. 1289, approved June 15, 1955, R. A. 4363, approved June 19, 1965)

Art. 361. Proof of the truth. —In every criminal prosecution for libel, the truth may be given in evidence to the court and if it appears that the matter charged as libelous is true, and, moreover, that it was published with good motives and for justifiable ends, the defendants shall be acquitted.

Proof of the truth of an imputation of an act or omission not constituting a crime shall not be admitted, unless the imputation shall have been made against Government employees with respect to facts related to the discharge of their official duties.

In such cases if the defendant proves the truth of the imputation made by him, he shall be acquitted.

Art. 362. Libelous remarks.—Libelous remarks or comments connected with the matter privileged under the provisions of Article 354, if made with malice, shall not exempt the author thereof nor the editor or managing editor of a newspaper from criminal liability.

Chapter Two
INCRIMINATORY MACHINATIONS

Art. 363. Incriminating innocent person.—Any person who, by any act not constituting perjury, shall directly incriminate or impute to an innocent person the commission of a crime, shall be punished by arresto menor.

Art. 364. Intriguing against honor.—The penalty of arresto menor or fine not exceeding 200 pesos shall be imposed for any intrigue which has for its principal purpose to blemish the honor or reputation of a person.

Title Fourteen
QUASI-OFFENSES

Sole Chapter
CRIMINAL NEGLIGENCE

Art. 365. Imprudence and negligence.—Any person who, by reckless imprudence, shall commit any act which, had it been intentional, would constitute a grave felony, shall suffer the penalty of arresto mayor in its maximum period to prision correccional in its medium period; if it would have constituted a less grave felony, the penalty of arresto mayor in its minimum and medium periods shall be imposed; if it would have constituted a light felony, the penalty of arresto menor in its maximum period shall be imposed.

Any person who, by simple imprudence or negligence, shall commit an act which would otherwise constitute a grave felony, shall suffer the penalty of arresto mayor in its medium and maximum periods; if it would have constituted a less serious felony, the penalty of arresto mayor in its minimum period shall be imposed.

When the execution of the act covered by this article shall have only resulted in damage to the property of another, the offender shall be punished by a fine ranging from an amount equal to the value of said damages to three times such value, but which shall in no case be less than twenty-five pesos.

A fine not exceeding two hundred pesos and censure shall be imposed upon any person who, by simple imprudence or negligence, shall cause some wrong which, if done maliciously, would have constituted a light felony.

In the imposition of these penalties, the court shall exercise their sound discretion, without regard to the rules prescribed in Article sixty-four.

The provisions contained in this article shall not be applicable:

1. When the penalty provided for the offense is equal to or lower than those provided in the first two paragraphs of this article, in which case the court shall impose the penalty next lower in degree than that which should be imposed in the period which they may deem proper to apply.

2. When, by imprudence or negligence and with violation of the Automobile Law, to death of a person shall be caused, in which case the defendant shall be punished by prision correccional in its medium and maximum periods.

Reckless imprudence consists in voluntary, but without malice, doing or falling to do an act from which material damage results by reason of inexcusable lack of precaution on the part of the person performing of failing to perform such act, taking into consideration his employment or occupation, degree of intelligence, physical condition and other circumstances regarding persons, time and place.

Simple imprudence consists in the lack of precaution displayed in those cases in which the damage impending to be caused is not immediate nor the danger clearly manifest.

The penalty next higher in degree to those provided for in this article shall be imposed upon the offender who fails to lend on the spot to the injured parties such help as may be in this hand to give. (As amended by R. A. 1790, approved June 21, 1957).

FINAL PROVISIONS

Art. 366. Application of laws enacted prior to this Code.—Without prejudice to the provisions contained in Article 22 of this Code, felonies and misdemeanors, committed prior to the date of effectiveness of this Code shall be punished in accordance with the Code or Acts in force at the time of their commission.

Art. 367. Repealing Clause.—Except as is provided in the next preceding article, the present Penal Code, the Provisional Law for the application of its provisions, and Acts Nos. 277, 282, 480, 518, 519, 899, 1121, 1438, 1523, 1559, 1692, 1754, 1955, 1773, 2020, 2036, 2071, 2142, 2212, 2293, 2298, 2300, 2364, 2549, 2557, 2595, 2609, 2718, 3103, 3195, 3244, 3298, 3309, 3313, 3397, 3559, and 3586, are hereby repealed.

The provisions of the Acts which are mentioned hereunder are also repealed, namely:

Act 666, Sections 6 and 18.

Act 1508, Sections 9, 10, 11, and 12.

Act 1524, Sections 1, 2, and 6.

Act 1697, Sections 3 and 4.

Act 1757, Sections 1, 2, 3, 4, 5, 6, 7, (first clause), 11, and 12.

Act 2381, Sections 2, 3, 4, 6, 8, and 9.

Act 2711, Sections 102, 2670, 2671, and 2672.

Act 3247, Sections 1, 2, 3, and 5; and General Order, No. 58, series of 1900, Section 106.

And all laws and parts of laws which are contrary to the provisions of this Code are hereby repealed.

Approved: December 8, 1930

TITLE OF ACTS REPEALED BY THE REVISED PENAL CODE ARE

1. Act No. 277. Law on Libel and threats to publish libel, etc., now provided for in Arts. 353, 362.

2. Act No. 282, amended by Act No. 1692. Law defining and penalizing the crimes of treason, insurrection, sedition, etc., now provided for in Arts. 114—116 and Arts 134—142.

3. Act No. 480. Law governing cockfighting and cockpits, now governed by Art. 199 and special laws.

4. Act No. 518, amended by Act Nos. 1121 and 2036. Law defining and penalizing highway robbery or brigandage, now covered by Arts. 306—307.

5. Act No. 519. Law on vagrancy now penalized by Art. 202.

6. Act No. 666, Secs. and 6 and 18. Law on trade-marks and trade-names now provided for in Arts. 188—189.

7. Act No. 899, Law regarding suspension on sentence, etc., upon U. S. citizens.

8. Act No. 1438, amended by Act Nos. 3203, 3309, and 3559, provisions governing juvenile offenders and delinquent children, their care and custody, now governed by Art. 80.

9. Act No. 1508, Secs. 9, 10, 11, and 12. The Chattel Mortgage Law, now penalized in Art. 319.

10. Act No. 1523. Law prohibiting importation, sale etc., of lottery tickets and lottery, now penalized in Arts. 195—196.

11. Act No. 1524. Sec. 4. Law governing discretion of Governor-General in granting conditional pardons, now covered by Art. 159.

12. Act No. 15533, Secs. 1, 2, and 6 amended by Act No. 1559. Law providing for diminution of sentences by reason of good conduct and diligence, now governed by Art. 97.

13. Act No. 1697, Secs. 3 and 4. Act for the punishment of perjury in official investigations, now provided for in Arts. 180—183.

14. Act No. 1754. Law on counterfeiting and forgery, now defined and penalized in Arts. 160—169.

15. Act No. 1775. Act penalizing crimes against legislative bodies, now provided for in Arts. 143—145.

16. Act No. 1757. Secs. 1, 2, 3, 4, 5, 6, 7, (first clause), 11 and 12 amended by Act No. 3242. Act prohibiting gambling, now provided for in Arts. 195—199.

17. Act No. 1173. Law on the crime of adulterio, estupro, rapto, violacion, calumnia, injuria, etc., now governed by Arts. 333—346.

18. Act Nos. 2071 and 2300. Act governing slavery, involuntary servitude, peonage, and the sale or purchase of human beings, now penalized in Arts. 272—274.

19. Act No. 2212. Act providing for the confiscation and disposition of money, articles, instruments, appliances and devices in gambling, now provided for in Art. 45.

20. Act No. 293. Act penalizing willful destruction, injury, or taking or carrying away any property of the Philippine Library, now provided for in Art. 311.

21. Act No. 2364. Act penalizing infidelity in the custody of prisoners detained for or a convicted of a crime, now governed by Arts. 223—225.

22. Act No. 2381. Secs. 2, 3, 4, 5, 6, 8, and 9. Act restricting the use of opium, etc., now provided for in Arts. 190—194.

23. Act No. 2549. Act prohibiting the forcing, compelling, or obliging of any laborer or other employee to purchase merchandise, commodities, or personal property under certain conditions, and the payment of wages of a laborer or employee by means of tokens or objects other than legal tender currency, now

penalized by Art. 288, and also governed by Com. Act No. 303 and the Minimum Wage Law, Rep. Act No. 602, as amended by Rep. Act. No. 812.

24. Act No. 2557. Act providing for the allowance to persons convicted of preventive imprisonment, etc., now embodied in Art. 29.

25. Act No. 2595. Law fixing prescription of the crime of libel and of a civil action arising therefrom, now provided in Art. 90.

26. Act No. 2711, Secs. 102, 2670, 2671, and 2672. Act amending the Revised Administrative Code.

27. Act No. 3104 amending Acts 2726. Law governing manner in which the death penalty shall be executed, now embodied in Arts. 18—85.

28. Act No. 3586 and 3397. Law governing habitual delinquency, now provided in Art. 62, par. 5.

29. General Orders No. 58, series of 1900, Sec. 106. Code of Criminal Procedure.

30. Other laws repealed by the Revised Penal Code are Acts Nos. 2030, 2142, 2298, 2712, 3195, 3244, 3298, and 3313, which are merely amendatory laws on the old Penal Code.

OTHER PENAL LAWS

PRESIDENTIAL DECREE NO. 1602

SIMPLIFYING AND PROVIDING STIFFER PENALTIES FOR VIOLATIONS OF PHILIPPINE GAMBLING LAWS

WHEREAS, Philippine Gambling Laws particularly Articles 195—199, the Revised Penal Code, Republic Act No. 3063 (Horse Racing Bookies), Presidential Decree No. 499 (Cockfighting), Presidential Decree No. 483, (Game Fixing), Presidential Decree No., 519 (Slot Machines) and Presidential Decree No. 1036 (Jai-alai Bookies) and other City and Municipal Ordinances gambling all over the country have become ineffective and easily circumvented in view of the confusing and inappropriate system of penalties imposed on violations thereof.

WHEREAS, there is an urgent need to update these gambling laws for simplicity and clearer understanding and to standardize and provide stiffer penalties for their violations to make them more effective and responsive to the present norms of conduct and behavior of the people.

NOW, THEREFORE, I, FERDINAND E. MARCOS, President of the Philippines, by virtue of the powers vested in me by the Constitution and in order to effect the desired and necessary changes and reforms in the social and economic structure of our society, do hereby order and declare to be part of the laws of the land, the following:

Sec. 1. Violations and Penalties. —The penalty of prision mayor in its medium degree or a fine ranging from Five Hundred Pesos to Two Thousand Pesos and in case of recidivism the penalty of prision correccional in its medium degree or a fine of ranging from One Thousand Pesos to Six Thousand Pesos shall be imposed upon:

(a) Any person other than those referred to in the succeeding subsection who in any manner, shall directly or indirectly take part in any game of cockfighting, jueteng, bookies (jai-alai or horse racing to include game fixing) and other lotteries, cara y cruz or pompiang and the like, black jack, lucky nine, "pusoy" or Russian Poker, monte, baccarat and other card games, palk que, domino, mahjong, high and low, slot machines, roullette, pinball and other mechanical inventories or devices, dog racing, boat racing, car raising and other races, basketball, volleyball, boxing, seven-eleven dice games and the like and other contests to include game fixing, point shaving and other machinations banking or percentage game, or any other game or scheme, whether upon chance or skill, which do not have a franchise from the national government, wherein wagers consisting of money, articles of value of representative of value are made;

(b) Any person who shall knowingly permit any form of gambling referred to in the preceding subdivision to be carried on in inhabited or uninhabited places or any building, vessel or other means of transportation owned or controlled by him. If the place where gambling is carried on has a reputation of a gambling place or that prohibited gambling is frequently carried on therein or the place is a public or government building or barangay hall, the culprit shall be punished by the penalty provided for in its maximum period and a fine of Six Thousand Pesos.

The penalty of prision correccional in its maximum degree and a fine of Six Thousand Pesos shall be imposed upon the maintainer, conductor of the above gambling schemes.

The penalty of prision mayor in its medium degree and temporary absolute disqualification and a fine of Six Thousand Pesos shall be imposed if the maintainer, conductor or banker is a government official, or if a player, promoter, referee, umpire, judge or coach in cases of game-fixing, point-shaving and other game machination.

The penalty of prision correccional in its medium degree and a fine ranging from Five Hundred pesos to Two Thousand Pesos shall be imposed upon any person who shall knowingly and without lawful purpose in any hour of any day shall have in his possession any lottery list, paper, or other matter containing letter, figures, signs or symbols which pertain to or in any manner used in the game of jueteng, jai-alai or horse racing bookies and similar game or lottery which has taken place or about to take place.

Sec. 2. Barangay Official.—Any barangay official in whose jurisdiction such gambling house is found and which house has the reputation of a gambling place shall suffer the penalty of prision correccional in its medium period and a fine ranging from Five Hundred to Two Thousand Pesos and temporary absolute disqualifications.

Sec. 3. Informer's Reward.—Any person who shall give the information that will lead to the arrest and final conviction of the offender shall be rewarded an amount equivalent to Twenty Per Centum (20%) of the cash money confiscated form the offender.

Sec. 4. Repealing Clause.—The provisions of Articles 196, 197, 198 and 199 of the Revised Penal Code, as amended, Republic Act No. 3063, Presidential Decree Nos. 483, 499, 510, 1306, Letter of Instructions, laws, executive orders, rules and regulations, City and Municipal Ordinances which are inconsistent with this Decree are hereby repealed or accordingly modified.

Sec. 5. Effectivity.—This Decree shall take effect immediately upon publication thereof by the Minister of the Ministry of Public Information at least once in a newspaper of general circulation.

DONE in the City of Manila, this 11th day of June in the year of Our Lord, nineteen hundred and seventy-eight.

PRESIDENTIAL DECREE NO. 1613

AMENDING THE LAW ON ARSON

WHEREAS, findings of the police and intelligence agencies of the government reveal that fires and other crimes involving destruction in Metro Manila and other urban centers in the country are being perpetuated by criminal syndicates, some of which have foreign connections;

WHEREAS, the current law on arson suffer from certain inadequacies that impede the successful enforcement and prosecution of arsonists;

WHEREAS, it is imperative that the high incidence of fires and other crimes involving destruction be prevented to protect the national economy and preserve the social economic and political stability of the country;

NOW, THEREFORE, I, FERDINAND E. MARCOS, President of the Philippines, by virtue of the powers vested in me by the Constitution do hereby order and decree as part of the law of the land, the following:

Sec. 1. Arson. —Any person who burns or sets fire to the property of another shall be punished by Prision mayor.

The same penalty shall be imposed when a person sets fire to his own property under circumstances which expose to danger the life or property of another.

Sec. 2. Destructive Arson. —The penalty of Reclusion temporal in its maximum period to Reclusion perpetua shall be imposed if the property burned is any of the following:

1. Any ammunition factory and other establishment where explosives, inflammable or combustible materials are stored;

2. Any archive, museum, whether public or private or any edifice devoted to culture, education or social services;

3. Any church or place or worship or other building where people usually assemble;

4. Any train, airplane or any aircraft, vessel or watercraft, or conveyance for transportation of persons or property;

5. Any building where evidence is kept for use in any legislative, judicial,

administrative or other official proceedings;

6. Any hospital, hotel, dormitory, lodging house, housing tenement, shopping center, public or private market, theater or movie house or any similar place or building;

7. Any building, whether used as dwelling or not, situated in a populated or congested area.

Sec. 3. Other Cases of Arson. —The penalty of Reclusion temporal to Reclusion perpetua shall be imposed if the property burned is any of the following:

1. Any building used as offices of the government or any of its agencies;
2. Any uninhabited house or dwelling;
3. Any industrial establishment, shipyard, oil well or mine shaft, platform or tunnel;
4. Any plantation, farm, pastureland, growing crop, grain filed, orchard, bamboo grove or forest;
5. Any rice mill, cane mill or mill central; and
6. Any railway or bus station, airport, wharf or warehouse.

Sec. 4. Special Aggravating Circumstances in Arson. —The penalty in any case of arson shall be imposed in its maximum period:

1. If committed with intent to gain;
2. If committed for the benefit of another;
3. If the offender is motivated by spite or hatred towards the owner or occupant of the property burned;
4. If committed by a syndicate.

The offense is committed by a syndicate if it is planned or carried out by a group of three (3) or more persons.

Sec. 5. Where Death Results From Arson. —If by reason of or on the occasion of arson death results, the penalty of Reclusion perpetua to death shall be imposed.

Sec. 6. Prima Facie Evidence of Arson. —Any of the following circumstances shall constitute prima facie evidence of arson:

1. If the fire started simultaneously in more than one part of the building or establishment;
2. If substantial amount of flammable substances or materials are stored

within the building not necessary in the business of the offender nor for household use;

3. Gasoline, kerosene, petroleum or other flammable or combustible substances or materials soaked therewith or containers, thereof, or any mechanical, electrical, chemical, or electronic contrivance designed to start a fire, or ashes or traces of any of the foregoing are found in the ruins or premises of the burned building or property;

4. If the building or property is insured for substantially more than its actual value at the time of the issuance of the policy;

5. If during the lifetime of the corresponding fire insurance policy more than two fires have occurred in the same or other premises owned or under the control of the offender and/or insured;

6. If shortly before the fire a substantial portion of the effects insured and stored in building or property had been withdrawn from the premises except in the ordinary course of business;

7. If a demand for money or other valuable consideration was made before the fire in exchange for the desistance of the offender or for the safety of other person or property of the victim.

Sec. 7. Conspiracy to Commit Arson. —Conspiracy to commit arson shall be punished by prision mayor in its minimum period.

Sec. 8. Confiscation of Object of Arson. —The building which is the object of arson including the land on which it is situated shall be confiscated and escheated to the State, unless the owner thereof can prove that he has no participation in nor knowledge of such arson despite the exercise of due diligence on his Art.

Sec. 9. Repealing Clause. —The provisions of Articles 320 to 326-B of the Revised Penal Code and all laws, executive orders, rules and regulations, or parts thereof, inconsistent with the provisions of this Decree are hereby repealed or amended accordingly.

Sec. 10. Effectivity. —This Decree shall take effect immediately upon publication thereof at least once in a newspaper of general circulation.

Done in the City of Manila, this 7th day of March nineteen hundred and seventy nine.

PRESIDENTIAL DECREE NO. 1744

AMENDING ARTICLE THREE HUNDRED AND TWENTY OF THE REVISED PENAL CODE PROVISIONS ON ARSON

WHEREAS, there have been rampant and wanton burnings of residential houses, public buildings, markets, hotels and other commercial establishments;

WHEREAS, to effectively discourage and deter the commission of arson, and to prevent destruction of properties and protect the lives of innocent people, it is necessary that the capital punishment be imposed upon arsonists;

NOW, THEREFORE, I, FERDINAND E. MARCOS, President of the Philippines by virtue of the power vested in me by the Constitution, do hereby order and decree that Article 320, Revised Penal Code be amended:

Sec. 1. Article 320 of the Revised Penal Code shall read as follows:

"Art. 320. Destructive Arson.—The penalty of reclusion temporal in its maximum period to death shall be imposed upon any person who shall burn:

1. One (1) or more buildings or edifices, consequent to one single act of burning or as a result of simultaneous burnings, or committed on several or different occasions;

2. Any building of public or private ownership, devoted to the public in general or where people usually gather or congregate for a definite purpose such as but not limited to official governmental function or business, private transaction, commerce, trade workshop, meetings and conferences, or merely incidental to a definite purpose such as but not limited to hotels, motels, transient dwellings, public conveyance or stops or terminals, regardless of whether the offender had knowledge that there are persons in said building or edifice at the time it is set on fire and regardless also of whether the building is actually inhabited or not.

3. Any train or locomotive, ship or vessel, airship or airplane, devoted to transportation or conveyance, or for public use, entertainment or leisure.

4. Any building, factory, warehouse installation and any appurtenances

thereto, which are devoted to the service of public utilities.

5. Any building the burning of which is for the purpose of concealing or destroying evidence of another violation of law, or for the purpose of concealing bankruptcy or defrauding creditors or to collect from insurance.

Irrespective of the application of the above enumerated qualifying circumstances, the penalty of death shall likewise be imposed when the arson is perpetrated or committed by two (2) or more persons or by a group of persons, regardless of whether their purpose is merely to burn or destroy the building or the burning merely constitutes an overt act in the commission or another violation of law.

The penalty of reclusion temporal in its maximum period to death shall also be imposed upon any person who shall burn:

1. Any arsenal, shipyard, storehouse or military powder or fireworks factory, ordinance, storehouse, archives or general museum of the government.

2. In an inhabited place, any storehouse or factory of inflammable or explosive materials.

If as a consequence of his commission of any of the acts penalized under this Article, death or injury results, or any valuable documents, equipment, machineries, apparatus, or other valuable properties were burned or destroyed, the mandatory penalty of death shall be imposed."

Sec. 2. Provisions of Articles 320, 321 and 322 of the Revised Penal Code which are or may be inconsistent herewith are hereby repealed.

Sec. 3. Effectivity. —This Decree shall take effect immediately.

Done in the City of Manila, this 11th day of November, in the year of Our Lord, nineteen hundred and eighty.

Republic Act No. 3019

ANTI-GRAFT AND CORRUPT PRACTICES ACT

Be it enacted by the Senate and House of Representatives of the Philippines in Congress assembled:

Section 1. Statement of policy. —It is the policy of the Philippine Government, in line with the principle that a public office is a public trust, to repress certain acts of public officers and private persons alike which constitute graft or corrupt practices or which may lead thereto.

Sec. 2. Definition of Terms. —As used in this Act, the term

(a) "Government" includes the national government, the local governments, the government-owned and government-controlled corporations, and all other instrumentalities or agencies of the Republic of the Philippines and their branches.

(b) "Public officer" includes elective and appointive officials and employees, permanent or temporary, whether in the classified or unclassified or exempt service receiving compensation, even nominal, from the government as defined in the preceding subparagraph.

(c) "Receiving any gift" includes the act of accepting directly or indirectly a gift from a person other than a member of the public officer's immediate family, in behalf of himself or of any member of his family or relative within the fourth civil degree, either by consanguinity or affinity, even on the occasion of a family celebration or national festivity like Christmas, if the value of the gift is under the circumstances manifestly excessive.

(d) "Person" includes natural and juridical persons, unless the context indicates otherwise.

Sec. 3. Corrupt practices of public officers. —In addition to acts or omissions of public officers already penalized by existing law, the following shall constitute corrupt practices of any public officer and are hereby declared to be unlawful:

(a) Persuading, inducing or influencing another public officer to perform an act constituting a violation of rules and regulations duly promulgated by competent authority or an offense in connection with the official duties of the latter, or allowing himself to be persuaded, induced, or influenced to commit such violation or offense.

(b) Directly or indirectly requesting or receiving any gift, present, share, percentage, or benefit, for himself or for any other person, in connection with any contract or transaction between the Government and any other party, wherein the public officer in his official capacity has to intervene under the law.

(c) Directly or indirectly requesting or receiving any gift, present, or other pecuniary or material benefit, for himself or for another, from any person for whom the public officer, in any manner or capacity, has secured or obtained, or will secure or obtain, any Government permit or license, in consideration for the help given or to be given, without prejudice to Section thirteen of this Act.

(d) Accepting or having any member of his family accept employment in a private enterprise which has pending official business with him during the pendency thereof or within one year after its termination.

(e) Causing any undue injury to any part, including the Government, or giving any private party any unwarranted benefits, advantage or preference in the discharge of his official administrative or judicial functions through manifest partiality, evident bad faith or gross inexcusable negligence. This provision shall apply to officers and employees of offices or government corporations charged with the grant of licenses or permits or other concessions.

(f) Neglecting or refusing, after due demand or request, without sufficient justification, to act within a reasonable time on any matter pending before him for the purpose of obtaining, directly or indirectly, from any person interested in the matter some pecuniary or material benefit or advantage, or for the purpose of favoring his own interest or giving undue advantage in favor of or discriminating against any other interested party.

(g) Entering, on behalf of the Government, into any contract or transaction manifestly and grossly disadvantageous to the same, whether or not the public officer profited or will profit thereby.

(h) Directly or indirectly having financial or pecuniary interest in any business, contract or transaction in connection with which he intervenes or takes part in his official capacity, or in which he is prohibited by the Constitution or by any law from having any interest.

(i) Directly or indirectly becoming interested, for personal gain, or having a material interest in any transaction or act requiring the approval of a board, panel or group of which he is a member, and which exercises discretion in such approval, even if he votes against the same or does not participate I the action of the board, committee, panel or group.

Interest for personal gain shall be presumed against those public officers responsible for the approval of manifestly unlawful, inequitable, or irregular transactions or acts by the board, panel or group to which they belong.

(j) Knowingly approving or granting any license, permit, privilege or benefit in favor of any person not qualified for or not legally entitled to such license, permit, privilege or advantage, or of a mere representative or dummy of one who is not so qualified or entitled.

(k) Divulging valuable information of a confidential character, acquired by his office or by him on account of his official position to unauthorized persons, or releasing such information in advance of its authorized release date.

The person giving the gift, present, share, percentage or benefit referred to in subparagraphs (b) and (c); or offering or giving to the public officer the employment mentioned in subparagraph (d); or urging the divulging or untimely release of the confidential information referred to in subparagraph (k) of this section shall, together with the offending public officer, be punished under Section nine of this Act and shall be permanently or temporarily disqualified in the discretion of the Court, from transacting business in any form with the Government.

Sec. 4. Prohibition on private individuals.

(a) It shall be unlawful for any person having family or close personal relation with any public official to capitalize or exploit or take advantage of such family or close personal relation by directly or indirectly requesting or receiving any present, gift or material or pecuniary advantage from any other person having some business, transaction, application, request or contract with the government, in which such public official has to intervene. Family relation shall include the spouse or relatives by consanguinity or affinity in the third civil degree. The word "close personal relation" shall include close personal friendship, social and fraternal connections, and professional employment all giving rise to intimacy which assures free access to such public officer.

(b) It shall be unlawful for any person knowingly to induce or cause any public official to commit any of the offenses defined in Section 3 hereof.

Sec. 5. Prohibition on certain relatives. —It shall be unlawful for the spouse or for any relative, by consanguinity or affinity within the third civil degree, of the President of the Philippines, the Vice-President of the Philippines, the President of the Senate, or the Speaker of the House of Representatives, to intervene, directly or indirectly, in any business, transaction, contract or application with the Government: Provided, That this section shall not apply to any person who, prior to the assumption of office of any of the above officials to whom he is related, has been already dealing with the Government along the same line of business, nor to any transaction, contract or application already existing or pending at the time of such assumption of public office, nor to any application filed by him the approval of which is not discretionary on the part of the official or officials concerned but depends upon compliance with requisites provided by law, or rules or regulations issued pursuant to law, nor to any act lawfully performed in an official capacity or in the exercise of a profession.

Sec. 6. Prohibition on Members of Congress. —It shall be unlawful hereafter for any Member of the Congress during the term for which he has been elected, to acquire or receive any personal pecuniary interest in any specific business enterprise which will be directly and particularly favored or benefited by any law or resolution authored by him previously approved or adopted by the Congress during the same term.

The provision of this section shall apply to any other public officer who recommended the initiation in Congress of the enactment or adoption of any law or resolution, and acquires or receives any such interest during his incumbency.

It shall likewise be unlawful for such member of Congress or other public officer, who, having such interest prior to the approval of such law or resolution authored or recommended by him, continues for thirty days after such approval to retain such interest.

Sec. 7. Statement of assets and liabilities. —Every public officer, within thirty days after the approval of this Act or after assuming office, and within the month of January of every other year thereafter, as well as upon the expiration of his term of office, shall prepare and file with the office of the corresponding Department Head, or in the case of Head of Department or chief of an independent office, with the Office of the President, or in the case of members of the Congress and the officials and employees thereof, with the Office of the Secretary of the corresponding House, a true detailed and sworn statement of assets and liabilities, including a statement of the amounts and sources of his income, the amounts of his personal and family expenses and the amount of income taxes paid for the next preceding calendar year: Provided, That public officers assuming office less than two months before the end of the calendar year, mat file their first statements in the following months of January.

Sec. 8. Dismissal due to unexplained wealth. —If in accordance with the provisions of Republic Act Numbered One thousand three hundred seventy-nine, a public official has been found to have acquired during his incumbency, whether in his name or in the name of other persons, an amount of property and/or money manifestly out of proportion to his salary and to his other lawful income, that fact shall be a ground for dismissal or removal. Properties in the name of the spouse and unmarried children of such public official may be taken into consideration, when their acquisition through legitimate means cannot be satisfactorily shown. Bank deposits shall be taken into consideration in the enforcement of this section, notwithstanding any provision of law to the contrary.

Sec. 9. Penalties for violations.

(a) Any public officer or private person committing any of the unlawful acts or omissions enumerated in Sections 3, 4, 5 and 6 of this Act shall be punished with imprisonment for not less than one year nor more than ten years, perpetual disqualification from public office, and confiscation or forfeiture in favor of the Government of any prohibited interest and unexplained wealth manifestly out of proportion to his salary and other lawful income.

(b) Any complaining party at whose complaint the criminal prosecution was initiated shall, in case of conviction of the accused, be entitled to recover in the criminal action with priority over the forfeiture in favor of the Government, the amount of money or the thing he may have given to the accused, or the fair value of such thing. Any public officer violating any of the provisions of Section 7 of this Act shall be punished by a fine of not less than one hundred pesos nor more than one thousand pesos, or by imprisonment not exceeding one year, or by both such fine and imprisonment, at the discretion of the Court.

The violation of said section proven in a proper administrative proceeding shall be sufficient cause for removal or dismissal of a public officer, even if no criminal prosecution is instituted against him.

Sec. 10. Competent court. —Until otherwise provided by law, all prosecutions under this Act shall be within the original jurisdiction of the proper Court of First Instance.

Sec. 11. Prescription of offenses. —All offenses punishable under this Act shall prescribe in ten years.

Sec. 12. Termination of office. —No public officer shall be allowed to resign or retire pending an investigation, criminal or administrative, or pending a prosecution against him, for any offense under this Act or under the provisions of the Revised Penal Code on bribery.

Sec. 13. Suspension and loss of benefits. —Any public officer against whom any criminal prosecution under a valid information under this Act or under the provisions of the Revised Penal Code on bribery is pending in court, shall be suspended from office. Should he be convicted by final judgment, he shall lose all retirement or gratuity benefits under any law, but if he is acquitted, he shall be entitled to reinstatement and to the salaries and benefits which he failed to receive during suspension, unless in the meantime administrative proceedings have been filed against him.

Sec. 14. Exception. —Unsolicited gifts or presents of small or insignificant value offered or given as a mere ordinary token of gratitude or friendship according to local customs or usage, shall be excepted from the provisions of this Act. Nothing in this Act shall be interpreted to prejudice or prohibit the practice of any profession, lawful trade or occupation by any private person or by any public officer who under the law may legitimately practice his profession, trade or occupation, during his incumbency, except where the practice of such profession, trade or occupation involves conspiracy with any other person or public official to

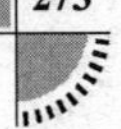

commit any of the violations penalized in this

Sec. 15. Separability clause.—If any provision of this Act or the application of such provision to any person or circumstances shall not be affected by such declaration.

Sec. 16. Effectivity.—This Act shall take effect on its approval, but for the purpose of determining unexplained wealth, all property acquired by a public officer since he assumed office shall be taken into consideration.

Approved, August 17, 1960.

Presidential Decree No. 749

GRANTING IMMUNITY FROM PROSECUTION TO GIVERS OF BRIBES AND OTHER GIFTS AND TO THEIR ACCOMPLICES IN BRIBERY AND OTHER GRAFT CASES AGAINST PUBLIC OFFICERS

Whereas, public office is a public trust: public officers are but servants of the people, whom they must serve with utmost fidelity and integrity;

Whereas, it has heretofore been virtually impossible to secure the conviction and removal of dishonest public servants owing to the lack of witnesses: bribe or gift givers being always reluctant to testify against the corrupt for fear of being indicted and convicted themselves of bribery and corruption;

Whereas, it is better by far and more socially desirable, as well as just, that the bribe or gift giver be granted immunity from prosecution so that he may freely testify as to the official corruption, than that the official who receives the bribe or gift should be allowed to go free, insolently remaining in public office, and continuing with his nefarious and corrupt practices, to the great detriment of the public service and the public interest.

Now, therefore, I, Ferdinand E. Marcos, President of the Philippines, by virtue of the powers in me vested by the Constitution, do hereby decree and order that:

Section 1. Any person who voluntarily gives information about any violation of Articles 210, 211, and 212 of the Revised Penal Code; Republic Act Numbered Three Thousand Nineteen, as amended; Section 345 of the Internal Revenue Code and Section 3604 of the Tariff and Customs Code and other provisions of the said Codes penalizing abuse or dishonesty on the part of the public officials concerned; and other laws, rules and regulations punishing acts of graft, corruption and other forms of official abuse; and who willingly testifies against any public official or employee for such violation shall be exempt from prosecution or punishment for the offense with reference to which his information and testimony were given, and may plead or prove the giving of such prosecution: Provided, that this immunity may be enjoyed even in cases where the information and testimony are given against a person who is not a public official but who is a principal, or accomplice, or accessory in the commission of any of the above-mentioned violations; Provided, further, that this immunity may be enjoyed by such informant or witness notwithstanding that he offered or gave the bribe or gift to the public official or his accomplice for such gift or bribe-giving; and Provided, finally, that the following conditions concur:

1. The information must refer to consummated violations of any of the above-mentioned provisions of law, rules and regulation;

2. The information and testimony are necessary for the conviction of the accused public officer.

3. Such information and testimony are not yet in the possession of the State;

4. Such information and testimony can be corroborated on its material points; and

5. The informant or witness has not been previously convicted of a crime involving moral turpitude,

Sec. 2. The immunity granted hereunder shall not attach should it turn out subsequently that the information and/or testimony is false and malicious or made only for the purpose of harassing, molesting or in any way prejudicing the public officer so denounced shall be entitled to any action, civil or criminal, against said informant or witness.

Sec. 3. All preliminary investigations conducted by a prosecuting fiscal, judge or committee, and all proceedings undertaken in connection therewith, shall be strictly confidential or private in order to protect the reputation of the official under investigation in the event that the report proves to be unfounded or no prima facie case is established.

Sec. 4. All acts, decrees and rules and regulations inconsistent with the provisions of this Decree are hereby repealed or modified accordingly.

Sec. 5. This Decree shall take effect immediately.

Done in the City of Manila, this 18th day of July, in the year of Our Lord, nineteen hundred and seventy-five.

REPUBLIC ACT NO. 8353

AN ACT EXPANDING THE DEFINITION OF THE CRIME OF RAPE, RECLASSIFYING THE SAME AS A CRIME AGAINST PERSONS, AMENDING FOR THE PURPOSE ACT NO. 3815, AS AMENDED, OTHERWISE KNOWN AS THE REVISED PENAL CODE, AND FOR OTHER PURPOSES

Be it enacted by the Senate and House of Representatives of the Philippines in Congress assembled:

SECTION 1. Short Title.—This Act shall be known as "*The Anti-Rape Law of* 1997."

SECTION 2. Rape as a Crime Against Persons.—The crime of rape shall hereafter be classified as a Crime Against Persons under Title Eight of Act No. 3815, as amended, otherwise known as the Revised Penal Code. Accordingly, there shall be incorporated into Title Eight of the same Code a new chapter to be known as Chapter Three on Rape, to read as follows:

"Chapter Three Rape

"**Article 266-A. Rape: When And How Committed.**—Rape is committed:

"1) By a man who shall have carnal knowledge of a woman under any of the following circumstances:

"a) Through force, threat, or intimidation;

"b) When the offended party is deprived of reason or otherwise unconscious;

"c) By means of fraudulent machination or grave abuse of authority; and

"d) When the offended party is under twelve (12) years of age or is demented, even though none of the circumstances mentioned above be present.

"2) By any person who, under any of the circumstances mentioned in paragraph 1 hereof, shall commit an act of sexual assault by inserting his penis into another person's mouth or anal orifice, or any instrument or object, into the genital or anal orifice of another person.

"**Article 266-B. Penalty.** —Rape under paragraph 1 of the next preceding article shall be punished by reclusion perpetua.

"Whenever the rape is committed with the use of a deadly weapon or by two or more persons, the penalty shall be reclusion perpetua to death.

"When by reason or on the occasion of the rape, the victim has become insane, the penalty shall become reclusion perpetua to death.

"When the rape is attempted and a homicide is committed by reason or on the occasion thereof, the penalty shall be reclusion perpetua to death.

"When by reason or on the occasion ofthe rape, homicide is committed, the penalty shall be death.

"The death penalty shall also be imposed if the crime of rape is committed with any of the following aggravating/qualifying circumstances:

"1) When the victim is under eighteen (18) years of age and the offender is a parent, ascendant, step-parent, guardian, relative by consanguinity or affinity within the third civil degree, or the common-law spouse of the parent of the victim;

"2) When the victim is under the custody of the police or military authorities or any law enforcement or penal institution;

"3) When the rape is committed in full view of the spouse, parent, any of the children or other relatives within the third civil degree of consanguinity;

"4) When the victim is a religious engaged in legitimate religious vocation or calling and is personally known to be such by the offender before or at the time of the commission of the crime;

"5) When the victim is a child below seven (7) years old;

"6) When the offender knows that he is afflicted with the Human Immuno-Deficiency Virus (HIV)/Acquired Immune Deficiency Syndrome (AIDS) or any other sexually transmissible disease and the virus or disease is transmitted to the victim;

"7) When committed by any member of the Armed Forces of the Philippines or para-military units thereof or the Philippine National Police or any law enforcement agency or penal institution, when the offender took advantage of his position to facilitate the commission of the crime;

"8) When by reason or on the occasion of the rape, the victim has suffered permanent physical mutilation or disability;

"9) When the offender knew of the pregnancy of the offended party at the time of the commission of the crime; and

"10) When the offender knew of the mental disability, emotional disorder and/or physical handicap of the offended party at the time of the commission of the crime.

"Article 266-C. Effect of Pardon.—The subsequent valid marriage between the offended party shall extinguish the criminal action or the penalty imposed.

"In case it is the legal husband who is the offender, the subsequent forgiveness by the wife as the offended party shall extinguish the criminal action or the penalty: Provided, That the crime shall not be extinguished or the penalty shall not be abated if the marriage is void *ab initio*.

"Article 266-D. Presumptions.—Any physical overt act manifesting resistance against the act of rape in any degree from the offended party, or where the offended party is so situated as to render her/him incapable of giving valid consent, may be accepted as evidence in the prosecution of the acts punished under Article 266-A."

SECTION 3. Separability Clause.—If any part, section, or provision of this Act is declared invalid or unconstitutional, the other parts thereof not affected thereby shall remain valid.

SECTION 4. Repealing Clause.—Article 336 of Act No. 3815, as amended, and all laws, acts, presidential decrees, executive orders, administrative orders, rules and regulations inconsistent with or contrary to the provisions of this Act are deemed amended, modified or repealed accordingly.

SECTION 5. Effectivity.—This Act shall take effect fifteen (15) days after completion of its publication in two (2) newspapers of general circulation.

Approved:

(SGD.) JOSE DE VENECIA, JR.

Speaker of the House of Representatives

(SGD.) ERNESTO M. MACEDA

President of the Senate

This Act, which is a consolidation of Senate Bill No. 950 and House Bill No. 6265, was finally passed by the Senate and the House of Representatives on June 5, 1997 and September 3, 1997, respectively.

(SGD.) ROBERTO P. NAZARENO

Secretary General

House of Representatives

(SGD.) LORENZO E. LEYNES, JR.

Secretary of the Senate

Approved: September 30, 1997

(SGD.) FIDEL V. RAMOS

President of the Philippines

REPUBLIC ACT NO. 8177

AN ACT DESIGNATING DEATH BY LETHAL INJECTION AS THE METHOD OF CARRYING OUT CAPITAL PUNISHMENT, AMENDING FOR THE PURPOSE ARTICLE 81 OF THE REVISED PENAL CODE, AS AMENDED BY SECTION 24 OF REPUBLIC ACT NO. 7659

Sec. 1. Article 81 of the Revised Penal Code, as amended by Section 24 of Republic Act No. 7659 is hereby further amended to read as follows:

"Art. 81. *When and how the death penalty is to be executed.* —The death sentence shall be executed with preference to any other penalty and shall consist in putting the person under the sentence to death by lethal injection. The death sentence shall be executed under the authority of the Director of the Bureau of Corrections, endeavoring so far as possible to mitigate the sufferings of the person under the sentence during the lethal injection as well as during the proceedings prior to the execution.

"The Director of the Bureau of Corrections shall take steps to ensure that the lethal injection to be administered is sufficient to cause the instantaneous death of the convict.

"Pursuant to this, all personnel involved in the administration of lethal injection shall be trained prior to the performance of such task.

"The authorized physician of the Bureau of Corrections, after thorough examination, shall officially make a pronouncement of the convict's death and shall certify thereto in the records of the Bureau of Corrections.

The death sentence shall be carried out not earlier than one (1) year nor later than eighteen (18) months after the judgment has become final and executory without prejudice to the exercise by the President of his executive clemency powers at all times."

Sec. 2. Persons already sentenced by judgment, which has become final and executory, who are waiting to undergo the death penalty by electrocution or gas poisoning shall be under the coverage of the provisions of this Act upon its effectivity. Their sentences shall be automatically modified for this purpose.

Sec. 3. Implementing Rules. —The Secretary of Justice in coordination with the Secretary of Health and the Bureau of Corrections shall, within thirty (30) days from the effectivity of this Act, promulgate the rules to implement its provisions.

Sec. 4. Repealing Clause. —All laws, presidential decrees and issuances, executive orders, rules and regulations or parts thereof inconsistent with the provisions of this Act are hereby repealed or modified accordingly.

Sec. 5. Effectivity. —This Act shall take effect fifteen (15) days after its publication in the Official Gazette or in at least two (2) national newspapers of general circulation, whichever comes earlier. Publication shall not be later than ten (10) days after the approval thereof.

Approved: March 20, 1996

REPUBLIC ACT NO. 9262

AN ACT DEFINING VIOLENCE AGAINST WOMEN AND THEIR CHILDREN, PROVIDING FOR PROTECTIVE MEASURES FOR VICTIMS, PRESCRIBING PENALTIES THEREFORE, AND FOR OTHER PURPOSES

Be it enacted by the Senate and House of Representatives of the Philippines in Congress assembled:

SECTION 1. Short Title.—This Act shall be known as the "Anti-Violence Against Women and Their Children Act of 2004".

SEC. 2. Declaration of Policy.—It is hereby declared that the State values the dignity of women and children and guarantees full respect for human rights. The State also recognizes the need to protect the family and its members particularly women and children, from violence and threats to their personal safety and security.

Towards this end, the State shall exert efforts to address violence committed against women and children in keeping with the fundamental freedoms guaranteed under the Constitution and the Provisions of the Universal Declaration of Human Rights, the convention on the Elimination of all forms of discrimination Against Women, Convention on the Rights of the Child and other international human rights instruments of which the Philippines is a party.

SEC. 3. Definition of Terms.—As used in this Act, (a) "Violence against women and their children" refers to any act or a series of acts committed by any person against a woman who is his wife, former wife, or against a woman with whom the person has or had a sexual or dating relationship, or with whom he has a common child, or against her child whether legitimate or illegitimate, within or without the family abode, which result in or is likely to result in physical, sexual, psychological harm or suffering, or economic abuse including threats of such acts, battery, assault, coercion, harrasment or arbitrary deprivation of liberty. It includes, but is not limited to, the following acts:

A. "Physical Violence" refers to acts that include bodily or physical harm;

B. "Sexual violence" refers to an act which is sexual in nature, committed against a woman or her child. It includes, but is not limited to:

a. rap, sexual harassment, acts of lasciviousness, treating a woman or her child as a sex object, making demeaning and sexually suggestive remarks, physically attacking the sexual parts of the victim's body, forcing her/him to watch obscene publications and indecent shows or forcing the woman or her child to do indecent acts and/or make films thereof, forcing the wife and mistress/lover to live in the conjugal home or sleep together in the same room with the abuser;

b. acts causing or attempting to cause the victim to engage in any sexual activity by force, threat of force, physical or other harm or threat of physical or other harm or coercion;

c. Prostituting the woman or child.

C. "Psychological violence" refers to acts or omissions causing or likely to cause mental or emotional suffering of the victim such as but not limited to intimidation, harassment, stalking, damage to property, public ridicule or humiliation, repeated verbal abuse and mental infidelity. It includes causing or allowing the victim to witness the physical, sexual or psychological abuse of a member of the family to which the victim belongs, or to witness pornography in any form or to witness abusive injury to pets or to unlawful or unwanted deprivation of the right to custody and/or visitation of common children.

D. "Economic abuse" refers to acts that make or attempt to make a woman financially dependent which includes, but is not limited to the following:

1. withdrawal of financial support or preventing the victim from engaging in any legitimate profession, occupation, business or activity, except in cases wherein the other spouse/partner objects on valid, serious and moral grounds as defined in Article 73 of the Family Code;

2. deprivation or threat of deprivation of financial resources and the right to the use and enjoyment of the conjugal, community or property owned in common;

3. destroying household property;

4. controlling the victims' own money or properties or solely controlling the

conjugal money or properties.

(b) "Battery" refers to an act of inflicting physical harm upon the woman or her child resulting to the physical and psychological or emotional distress.

(c) "Battered Woman Syndrome" refers to a scientifically defined pattern of psychological and behavioral symptoms found in women living in battering relationships as a result of cumulative abuse.

(d) "Stalking" refers to an intentional act committed by a person who, knowingly and without lawful justification follows the woman or her child or places the woman or her child under surveillance directly or indirectly or a combination thereof.

(e) "Dating relationship" refers to a situation wherein the parties live as husband and wife without the benefit of marriage or are romantically involved over time and on a continuing basis during the course of the relationship. A casual acquaintance or ordinary socialization between two individuals in a business or social context is not a dating relationship.

(f) "Sexual relations" refers to a single sexual act which may or may not result in the bearing of a common child.

(g) "Safe place or shelter" refers to any home or institution maintained or managed by the Department of Social Welfare and Development (DSWD) or by any other agency or voluntary organization accredited by the DSWD for the purposes of this Act or any other suitable place the resident of which is willing temporarily to receive the victim.

(h) "Children" refers to those below eighteen (18) years of age or older but are incapable of taking care of themselves as defined under Republic Act No. 7610. As used in this Act, it includes the biological children of the victim and other children under her care.

SEC. 4. Construction. —This Act shall be liberally construed to promote the protection and safety of victims of violence against women and their children.

SEC. 5. Acts of Violence Against Women and Their Children. —The crime of violence against women and their children is committed through any of the following acts:

a. Causing physical harm to the woman or her child;

b. Threatening to cause the woman or her child physical harm;

c. Attempting to cause the woman or her child physical harm;

d. Placing the woman or her child in fear of imminent physical harm;

e. Attempting to compel or compelling the woman or her child to engage in conduct which the woman or her child has the right to desist from or desist from conduct which the woman or her child has the right to engage in, or attempting to restrict or restricting the woman's or her child's freedom of movement or conduct by force or threat of force, physical or other harm or threat of physical or other harm, or intimidation directed against the woman or child. This shall include, but not limited to, the following acts committed with the purpose or effect of controlling or restricting the woman's or her child's movement or conduct:

1. Threatening to deprive or actually depriving the woman or her child of custody to her/his family;

2. Depriving or threatening to deprive the woman or her children of financial support legally due her or her family, or deliberately providing the woman's children insufficient financial support;

3. Depriving or threatening to deprive the woman or her child of a legal right;

4. Preventing the woman in engaging in any legitimate profession, occupation, business or activity or controlling the victim's own mon4ey or properties, or solely controlling the conjugal or common money, or properties;

f. Inflicting or threatening to inflict physical harm on oneself for the purpose of controlling her actions or decisions;

g. Causing or attempting to cause the woman or her child to engage in any sexual activity which does not constitute rape, by force or threat of force, physical harm, or through intimidation directed against the woman or her child or her/his immediate family;

h. Engaging in purposeful, knowing, or reckless conduct, personally or through another, that alarms or causes substantial emotional or psychological distress to the woman or her child. This shall include, but not be limited to, the following acts:

1. Stalking or following the woman or her child in public or private places;

2. Peering in the window or lingering outside the residence of the woman or

her child;

3. Entering or remaining in the dwelling or on the property of the woman or her child against her/his will;

4. Destroying the property and personal belongingness or inflicting harm to animals or pets of the woman or her child; and

5. Engaging in any form of harassment or violence;

i. Causing mental or emotional anguish, public ridicule or humiliation to the woman or her child, including, but not limited to, repeated verbal and emotional abuse, and denial of financial support or custody of minor children of access to the woman's child/children.

SEC. 6. Penalties. —The crime of violence against women and their children, under Section 5 hereof shall be punished according to the following rules:

a. Acts falling under Section 5 (a) constituting attempted, frustrated or consummated parricide or murder or homicide shall be punished in accordance with the provisions of the Revised Penal Code.

If these acts resulted in mutilation, it shall be punishable in accordance with the Revised Penal Code; those constituting serious physical injuries shall have the penalty of prison mayor; those constituting less serious physical injuries shall be punished by prision correccional; and those constituting slight physical injuries shall be punished by arresto mayor.

Acts falling under Section 5(b) shall be punished by imprisonment of two degrees lower than the prescribed penalty for the consummated crime as specified in the preceding paragraph but shall in no case be lower than arresto mayor.

b. Acts falling under Section 5(c) and 5(d) shall be punished by arresto mayor;

c. Acts falling under Section 5(e) shall be punished by prision correccional;

d. Acts falling under Section 5(f) shall be punished by arresto mayor;

e. Acts falling under Section 5(g) shall be punished by prision mayor;

f. Acts falling under Section 5(h) and Section 5(i) shall be punished by prision mayor.

If the acts are committed while the woman or child is pregnant or committed in the presence of her child, the penalty to be applied shall be the maximum pe-

riod of penalty prescribed in the section.

In addition to imprisonment, the perpetrator shall (a) pay a fine in the amount of not less than One hundred thousand pesos (P100,000.00) but not more than three hundred thousand pesos (300,000.00); (b) undergo mandatory psychological counseling or psychiatric treatment and shall report compliance to the court.

SEC. 7. Venue. —The Regional Trial Court designated as a Family Court shall have original and exclusive jurisdiction over cases of violence against women and their children under this law. In the absence of such court in the place where the offense was committed, the case shall be filed in the Regional Trial Court where the crime or any of its elements was committed at the option of the compliant.

SEC. 8. Protection Orders. —A protection order is an order issued under this act for the purpose of preventing further acts of violence against a woman or her child specified in Section 5 of this Act and granting other necessary relief. The relief granted under a protection order serve the purpose of safeguarding the victim from further harm, minimizing any disruption in the victim's daily life, and facilitating the opportunity and ability of the victim to independently regain control over her life. The provisions of the protection order shall be enforced by law enforcement agencies. The protection orders that may be issued under this Act are the barangay protection order (BPO), temporary protection order (TPO) and permanent protection order (PPO). The protection orders that may be issued under this Act shall include any, some or all of the following reliefs:

a. Prohibition of the respondent from threatening to commit or committing, personally or through another, any of the acts mentioned in Section 5 of this Act;

b. Prohibition of the respondent from harassing, annoying, telephoning, contacting or otherwise communicating with the petitioner, directly or indirectly;

c. Removal and exclusion of the respondent from the residence of the petitioner, regardless of ownership of the residence, either temporarily for the purpose of protecting the petitioner, or permanently where no property rights are violated, and if respondent must remove personal effects from the residence, the court shall direct a law enforcement agent to accompany the respondent has gathered his things and escort respondent from the residence;

d. Directing the respondent to stay away from petitioner and designated family or household member at a distance specified by the court, and to stay away from the residence, school, place of employment, or any specified place frequented by the petitioner and any designated family or household member;

e. Directing lawful possession and use by petitioner of an automobile and other essential personal effects, regardless of ownership, and directing the appropriate law enforcement officer to accompany the petitioner to the residence of the parties to ensure that the petitioner is safely restored to the possession of the automobile and other essential personal effects, or to supervise the petitioner's or respondent's removal of personal belongingness;

f. Granting a temporary or permanent custody of a child/children to the petitioner;

g. Directing the respondent to provide support to the woman and/or her child if entitled to legal support. Notwithstanding other laws to the contrary, the court shall order an appropriate percentage of the income or salary of the respondent to be withheld regularly by the respondent's employer for the same to be automatically remitted directly to the woman. Failure to remit and/or withhold or any delay in the remittance of support to the woman and/or her child without justifiable cause shall render the respondent or his employer liable for indirect contempt of court;

h. Prohibition of the respondent from any use or possession of any firearm or deadly weapon and order him to surrender the same to the court for appropriate disposition by the court, including revocation of license and disqualification to apply for any license to use or possess a firearm. If the offender is a law enforcement agent, the court shall order the offender to surrender his firearm and shall direct the appropriate authority to investigate on the offender and take appropriate action on matter;

i. Restitution for actual damages caused by the violence inflicted, including, but not limited to, property damage, medical expenses, childcare expenses and loss of income;

j. Directing the DSWD or any appropriate agency to provide petitioner may need; and

k. Provision of such other forms of relief as the court deems necessary to protect and provide for the safety of the petitioner and any designated family or household member, provided petitioner and any designated family or household member consents to such relief.

Any of the reliefs provided under this section shall be granted even in the absence of a decree of legal separation or annulment or declaration of absolute nullity of marriage.

The issuance of a BPO or the pendency of an application for BPO shall not preclude a petitioner from applying for, or the court from granting a TPO or PPO.

SEC. 9. Who may file Petition for Protection Orders. —A petition for protection order may be filed by any of the following:

a. the offended party;

b. parents or guardians of the offended party;

c. ascendants, descendants or collateral relatives within the fourth civil degree of consanguinity or affinity;

d. officers or social workers of the DSWD or social workers of local government units (LGUs);

e. police officers, preferably those in charge of women and children's desks;

f. Punong Barangay or Barangay Kagawad;

g. lawyer, counselor, therapist or healthcare provider of the petitioner;

h. At least two (2) concerned responsible citizens of the city or municipality where the violence against women and their children occurred and who has personal knowledge of the offense committed.

SEC. 10. Where to Apply for a Protection Order. —Applications for BPOs shall follow the rules on venue under Section 409 of the Local Government Code of 1991 and its implementing rules and regulations. An application for a TPO or PPO may be filed in the regional trial court, metropolitan trial court, municipal trial court, municipal circuit trial court with territorial jurisdiction over the place of residence of the petitioner: Provided, however, That if a family court exists in the place of residence of the petitioner, the application shall be filed with that court.

SEC. 11. How to Apply for a Protection Order. —The application for a protection order must be in writing, signed and verified under oath by the applicant. It may be filed as an independent action or as incidental relief in any civil or criminal case the subject matter or issues thereof partakes of a violence as described in this Act. A standard protection order application form, written in English with translation to the major local languages, shall be made available to facilitate applications for protections order, and shall contain, among other, the following information:

a. names and addresses of petitioner and respondent;

b. description of relationships between petitioner and respondent;

c. a statement of the circumstances of the abuse;

d. description of the reliefs requested by petitioner as specified in Section 8 herein;

e. request for counsel and reasons for such;

f. request for waiver of application fees until hearing; and

g. an attestation that there is no pending application for a protection order in another court.

If the applicants is not the victim, the application must be accompanied by an affidavit of the applicant attesting to (a) the circumstances of the abuse suffered by the victim and (b) the circumstances of consent given by the victim for the filling of the application. When disclosure of the address of the victim will pose danger to her life, it shall be so stated in the application. In such a case, the applicant shall attest that the victim is residing in the municipality or city over which court has territorial jurisdiction, and shall provide a mailing address for purpose of service processing.

An application for protection order filed with a court shall be considered an application for both a TPO and PPO.

Barangay officials and court personnel shall assist applicants in the preparation of the application. Law enforcement agents shall also extend assistance in the application for protection orders in cases brought to their attention.

SEC. 12. Enforceability of Protection Orders. —All TPOs and PPOs issued under this Act shall be enforceable anywhere in the Philippines and a violation thereof shall be punishable with a fine ranging from Five Thousand Pesos

(P5,000.00) to Fifty Thousand Pesos (P50,000.00) and/or imprisonment of six (6) months.

SEC. 13. Legal Representation of Petitioners for Protection Order. — If the woman or her child requests in the applications for a protection order for the appointment of counsel because of lack of economic means to hire a counsel de parte, the court shall immediately direct the Public Attorney's Office (PAO) to represent the petitioner in the hearing on the application. If the PAO determines that the applicant can afford to hire the services of a counsel de parte, it shall facilitate the legal representation of the petitioner by a counsel de parte. The lack of access to family or conjugal resources by the applicant, such as when the same are controlled by the perpetrator, shall qualify the petitioner to legal representation by the PAO.

However, a private counsel offering free legal service is not barred from representing the petitioner.

SEC. 14. Barangay Protection Orders (BPOs); Who May Issue and How. —Barangay Protection Orders (BPOs) refer to the protection order issued by the *Punong Barangay* ordering the perpetrator to desist from committing acts under Section 5 (a) and (b) of this Act. A *Punong Barangay* who receives applications for a BPO shall issue the protection order to the applicant on the date of filing after *ex parte* determination of the basis of the application. If the *Punong Barangay* is unavailable to act on the application for a BPO, the application shall be acted upon by any available *Barangay Kagawad.* If the BPO is issued by a *Barangay Kagawad* the order must be accompanied by an attestation by the *Barangay Kagawad* that the *Punong Barangay* was unavailable at the time for the issuance of the BPO. BPOs shall be effective for fifteen (15) days. Immediately after the issuance of an *ex parte* BPO, the Punong Barangay or Barangay Kagawad shall personally serve a copy of the same on the respondent, or direct any barangay official to effect is personal service.

The parties may be accompanied by a non-lawyer advocate in any proceeding before the *Punong Barangay.*

SEC. 15. Temporary Protection Orders. —Temporary Protection Orders (TPOs) refers to the protection order issued by the court on the date of filing of the application after *ex parte* determination that such order should be issued. A court may grant in a TPO any, some or all of the reliefs mentioned in this Act and shall be effective for thirty (30) days. The court shall schedule a hearing on the issuance of a PPO prior to or on the date of the expiration of the TPO. The court shall order the immediate personal service of the TPO on the respondent by the court sheriff who may obtain the assistance of law enforcement agents for the service. The TPO shall include notice of the date of the hearing on the merits of the issuance of a PPO.

SEC. 16. Permanent Protection Orders. —Permanent Protection Order (PPO) refers to protection order issued by the court after notice and hearing.

Respondents non-appearance despite proper notice, or his lack of a lawyer, or the non-availability of his lawyer shall not be a ground for rescheduling or postponing the hearing on the merits of the issuance of a PPO. If the respondents appears without counsel on the date of the hearing on the PPO, the court shall appoint a lawyer for the respondent and immediately proceed with the hearing. In case the respondent fails to appear despite proper notice, the court shall allow ex parte presentation of the evidence by the applicant and render judgment on the basis of the evidence presented. The court shall allow the introduction of any history of abusive conduct of a respondent even if the same was not directed against the applicant or the person for whom the applicant is made.

The court shall, to the extent possible, conduct the hearing on the merits of the issuance of a PPO in one (1) day. Where the court is unable to conduct the hearing within one (1) day and the TPO issued is due to expire, the court shall continuously extend or renew the TPO for a period of thirty (30) days at each particular time until final judgment is issued. The extended or renewed TPO may be modified by the court as may be necessary or applicable to address the needs of the applicant.

The court may grant any, some or all of the reliefs specified in Section 8 hereof in a PPO. A PPO shall be effective until revoked by a court upon application of the person in whose favor the order was issued. The court shall ensure immediate personal service of the PPO on respondent.

The court shall not deny the issuance of protection order on the basis of the lapse of time between the act of violence and the filing of the application.

Regardless of the conviction or acquittal of the respondent, the Court must determine whether or not the PPO shall become final. Even in a dismissal, a PPO shall be granted as long as there is no clear showing that the act from which the order might arise did not exist.

Sec. 17. Notice of Sanction in Protection Orders. —The following statement must be printed in bold-faced type or in capital letters on the protection order issued by the *Punong Barangay* or court:

"Violation of this order is punishable by law."

Sec. 18. Mandatory Period For Acting on Applications For Protection Orders—Failure to act on an application for a protection order within the reglementary period specified in the previous section without justifiable cause shall render the official or judge administratively liable.

Sec 19. Legal Separation Cases. —In cases of legal separation, where violence as specified in this Act is alleged, Article 58 of the Family Code shall not apply. The court shall proceed on the main case and other incidents of the case as soon as possible. The hearing on any application for a protection order filed by the petitioner must be conducted within the mandatory period specified in this Act.

Sec. 20. Priority of Application for a Protection Order. —Ex parte and adversarial hearings to determine the basis of applications for a protection order under this Act shall have priority over all other proceedings. Barangay officials and the courts shall schedule and conduct hearings on applications for a protection order under this Act above all other business and, if necessary, suspend other proceedings in order to hear applications for a protection order.

Sec. 21. Violation of Protection Orders. —A complaint for a violation of a BPO issued under this Act must be filed directly with any municipal trial court, metropolitan trial court, or municipal circuit trial court that has territorial jurisdiction over the barangay that issued the BPO. Violation of a BPO shall be punishable by imprisonment of thirty (30) days without prejudice to any other criminal or civil action that the offended party may file for any of the acts committed.

A judgement of violation of a BPO ma be appealed according to the Rules of Court. During trial and upon judgment, the trial court may motu proprio issue a protection order as it deems necessary without need of an application.

Violation of any provision of a TPO or PPO issued under this Act shall constitute contempt of court punishable under Rule 71 of the Rules of Court, without prejudice to any other criminal or civil action that the offended party may file for any of the acts committed.

Sec. 22. Applicability of Protection Orders to Criminal Cases. —The foregoing provisions on protection orders shall be applicable in impliedly instituted with the criminal actions involving violence against women and their children.

Sec. 23. Bond to Keep the Peace. —The Court may order any person against whom a protection order is issued to give a bond to keep the peace, to present two sufficient sureties who shall undertake that such person will not commit the violence sought to be prevented.

Should the respondent fail to give the bond as required, he shall be detained for a period which shall in no case exceed six (6) months, if he shall have been prosecuted for acts punishable under Section 5(a) to 5(f) and not exceeding thirty (30) days, if for acts punishable under Section 5(g) to 5(I).

The protection orders referred to in this section are the TPOs and the PPOs issued only by the courts.

Sect. 24. Prescription Period. —Acts falling under Sections 5(a) to 5(f) shall prescribe in twenty (20) years. Acts falling under Sections 5(g) to 5(I) shall prescribe in ten (10) years.

Sec. 25. Public Crime. —Violence against women and their children shall be considered a public offense which may be prosecuted upon the filing of a complaint by any citizen having personal knowledge of the circumstances involving the commission of the crime.

Sec. 26. Battered Woman Syndrome as a Defense. —Victim-survivors who are found by the courts to be suffering from battered woman syndrome do not incure any criminal and civil liability notwithstanding the absence of any of the elements for justifying circumstances of self-defense under the Revised Penal Code.

In the determination of the state of mind of the woman who was suffering from battered woman syndrome at the time of the commission of the crime, the courts shall be assisted by expert psychiatrists/ psychologists.

Sec. 27. Prohibited Defense.—Being under the influence of alcohol, any illicit drug, or any other mind-altering substance shall not be a defense under this Act.

Sec. 28. Custody of children.—The woman victim of violence shall be entitled to the custody and support of her child/children. Children below seven (7) years old older but with mental or physical disabilities shall automatically be given to the mother, with right to support, unless the court finds compelling reasons to order otherwise.

A victim who is suffering from battered woman syndrome shall not be disqualified from having custody of her children. In no case shall custody of minor children be given to the perpetrator of a woman who is suffering from Battered woman syndrome.

Sec. 29. Duties of Prosecutors/Court Personnel.—Prosecutors and court personnel should observe the following duties when dealing with victims under this Act:

a. communicate with the victim in a language understood by the woman or her child; and

b. inform the victim of her/his rights including legal remedies available and procedure, and privileges for indigent litigants.

Sec. 30. Duties of Barangay Officials and Law Enforcers.—Barangay officials and law enforcers shall have the following duties:

a. respond immediately to a call for help or request for assistance or protection of the victim by entering the necessary whether or not a protection order has been issued and ensure the safety of the victim/s;

b. confiscate any deadly weapon in the possession of the perpetrator or within plain view;

c. transport or escort the victim/s to a safe place of their choice or to a clinic or hospital;

d. assist the victim in removing personal belongs from the house;

e. assist the barangay officials and other government officers and employees who respond to a call for help;

f. ensure the enforcement of the Protection Orders issued by the *Punong Barangy* or the courts;

g. arrest the suspected perpetrator wiithout a warrant when any of the acts of violence defined by this Act is occurring, or when he/she has personal knowledge that any act of abuse has just been committed, and there is imminent danger to the life or limb of the victim as defined in this Act; and

h. immediately report the call for assessment or assistance of the DSWD, social Welfare Department of LGUs or accredited non-government organizations (NGOs).

Any barangay official or law enforcer who fails to report the incident shall be liable for a fine not exceeding Ten Thousand Pesos (P10,000.00) or whenever applicable criminal, civil or administrative liability.

Sec. 31. Healthcare Provider Response to Abuse—Any healthcare provider, including, but not limited to, an attending physician, nurse, clinician, barangay health worker, therapist or counselor who suspects abuse or has been informed by the victim of violence shall:

a. properly document any of the victim's physical, emotional or psychological injuries;

b. properly record any of victim's suspicions, observations and circumstances of the examination or visit;

c. automatically provide the victim free of charge a medical certificate concerning the examination or visit;

d. safeguard the records and make them available to the victim upon request at actual cost; and

e. provide the victim immediate and adequate notice of rights and remedies provided under this Act, and services available to them.

Sec. 32. Duties of Other Government Agencies and LGUs—Other government agencies and LGUs shall establish programs such as, but not limited to, education and information campaign and seminars or symposia on the nature, causes, incidence and consequences of such violence particularly towards educating the public on its social impacts.

It shall be the duty of the concerned government agencies and LGU's to ensure the sustained education and training of their officers and personnel on the prevention of violence against women and their children under the Act.

SEC. 33. Prohibited Acts. —A *Punong Barangay*, *Barangay Kagawad* or the court hearing an application for a protection order shall not order, direct, force or in any way unduly influence he applicant for a protection order to compromise or abandon any of the reliefs sought in the application for protection under this Act. Section 7 of the Family Courts Act of 1997 and Sections 410, 411, 412 and 413 of the Local Government Code of 1991 shall not apply in proceedings where relief is sought under this Act.

Failure to comply with this Section shall render the official or judge administratively liable.

SEC 34. Persons Intervening Exempt from Liability. —In every case of violence against women and their children as herein defined, any person, private individual or police authority or barangay official who, acting in accordance with law, responds or intervenes without using violence or restraint greater than necessary to ensure the safety of the victim, shall not be liable for any criminal, civil or administrative liability resulting therefrom.

SEC. 35. Rights of Victims. —In addition to their rights under existing laws, victims of violence against women and their children shall have the following rights:

a. to be treated with respect and dignity;

b. to avail of legal assistance form the PAO of the Department of Justice (DOJ) or any public legal assistance office;

c. To be entitled to support services form the DSWD and LGUs'

d. To be entitled to all legal remedies and support as provided for under the Family Code; and

e. To be informed of their rights and the services available to them including their right to apply for a protection order.

SEC. 36. Damages. —Any victim of violence under this Act shall be entitled to actual, compensatory, moral and exemplary damages.

SEC. 37. Hold Departure Order. —The court shall expedite the process of issuance of a hold departure order in cases prosecuted under this Act.

SEC. 38. Exemption from Payment of Docket Fee and Other Expenses. —If the victim is an indigent or there is an immediate necessity due to imminent danger or threat of danger to act on an application for a protection order, the court shall accept the application without payment of the filing fee and other fees and of transcript of stenographic notes.

SEC. 39. Inter-Agency Council on Violence Against Women and Their Children (IAC-VAWC). In pursuance of the abovementioned policy, there is hereby established an Inter-Agency Council on Violence Against Women and their children, hereinafter known as the Council, which shall be composed of the following agencies:

a. Department of Social Welfare and Development (DSWD);
b. National Commission on the Role of Filipino Women (NCRFW);
c. Civil Service Commission (CSC);
d. Council for the Welfare of Children (CWC);
e. Department of Justice (DOJ);
f. Department of the Interior and Local Government (DILG);
g. Philippine National Police (PNP);
h. Department of Health (DOH);
i. Department of Education (DepEd);
j. Department of Labor and Employment (DOLE); and
k. National Bureau of Investigation (NBI).

These agencies are tasked to formulate programs and projects to eliminate VAW based on their mandates as well as develop capability programs for their employees to become more sensitive to the needs of their clients. The Council will also serve as the monitoring body as regards to VAW initiatives.

The Council members may designate their duly authorized representative who shall have a rank not lower than an assistant secretary or its equivalent. These representatives shall attend Council meetings in their behalf, and shall receive emoluments as may be determined by the Council in accordance with existing budget and accounting rules and regulations.

SEC. 40. Mandatory Programs and Services for Victims.—The DSWD, and LGU's shall provide the victims temporary shelters, provide counseling, psycho-social services and /or, recovery, rehabilitation programs and livelihood assistance.

The DOH shall provide medical assistance to victims.

SEC. 41. Counseling and Treatment of Offenders.—The DSWD shall provide rehabilitative counseling and treatment to perpetrators towards learning constructive ways of coping with anger and emotional outbursts and reforming their ways. When necessary, the offender shall be ordered by the Court to submit to psychiatric treatment or confinement.

SEC. 42. Training of Persons Involved in Responding to Violence Against Women and their Children Cases. —All agencies involved in responding to violence against women and their children cases shall be required to undergo education and training to acquaint them with:

a. the nature, extend and causes of violence against women and their children;

b. the legal rights of, and remedies available to, victims of violence against women and their children;

c. the services and facilities available to victims or survivors;

d. the legal duties imposed on police officers to make arrest and to offer protection and assistance; and

e. techniques for handling incidents of violence against women and their children that minimize the likelihood of injury to the officer and promote the safety of the victim or survivor.

The PNP, in coordination with LGU's shall establish an education and training program for police officers and barangay officials to enable them to properly handle cases of violence against women and their children.

SEC. 43. Entitled to Leave. —Victims under this Act shall be entitled to take a paid leave of absence up to ten (10) days in addition to other paid leaves under the Labor Code and Civil Service Rules and Regulations, extendible when the necessity arises as specified in the protection order.

Any employer who shall prejudice the right of the person under this section shall be penalized in accordance with the provisions of the Labor Code and Civil Service Rules and Regulations. Likewise, an employer who shall prejudice any person for assisting a co-employee who is a victim under this Act shall likewise be liable for discrimination.

SEC. 44. Confidentiality. —All records pertaining to cases of violence against women and their children including those in the barangay shall be confidential and all public officers and employees and public or private clinics to hospitals shall respect the right to privacy of the victim. Whoever publishes or causes to be published, in any format, the name, address, telephone number, school, business address, employer, or other identifying information of a victim or an immediate family member, without the latter's consent, shall be liable to the contempt power of the court.

Any person who violates this provision shall suffer the penalty of one (1) year imprisonment and a fine of not more than Five Hundred Thousand pesos (P500,000.00).

SEC. 45. —Funding—The amount necessary to implement the provisions of this Act shall be included in the annual General Appropriations Act (GAA).

The Gender and Development (GAD) Budget of the mandated agencies and LGU's shall be used to implement services for victim of violence against women and their children.

SEC. 46. Implementing Rules and Regulations. —Within six (6) months from the approval of this Act, the DOJ, the NCRFW, the DSWD, the DILG, the DOH, and the PNP, and three (3) representatives from NGOs to be identified by the NCRFW, shall promulgate the Implementing Rules and Regulations (IRR) of this Act.

SEC. 47. Suppletory Application—For purposes of this Act, the Revised Penal Code and other applicable laws, shall have suppletory application.

SEC. 48. Separability Clause. —If any section or provision of this Act is held unconstitutional or invalid, the other sections or provisions shall not be affected.

SEC. 49. Repealing Clause—All laws, Presidential decrees, executive orders and rules and regulations, or parts thereof, inconsistent with the provisions of this Act are hereby repealed or modified accordingly.

SEC. 50. Effectivity—This Act shall take effect fifteen (15) days from the date of its complete publication in at least two (2) newspapers of general circulation.

JOSE DE VENECIA, JR. FRANKLIN DRILON

Speaker of the House Of the Representatives President of the Senate

This Act, which is a consolidation of Senate Bill No. 2723 and House Bill

Nos. 5516 and 6054, was finally passed by the Senate and the House of Representatives on January 29, 2004 and February 2, 2004, respectively.

ROBERTO P. NAZARENO OSCAR YABES

Secretary General of the House of Representatives

Secretary of the Senate

Approved: MARCH 08, 2004

GLORIA MACAPAGAL-ARROYO

President of the Philippines

Philippines Anti-Terrorism Bill

25/05/2005

In response to the terrorist attacks in February, the draft bill on terrorism has been introduced in May 2005.

This bill consolidates all the draft bills that were submitted in response to those attacks.

This bill and its sister proposal, the ID card bill have been marked as "urgent" by the President and is not set to undergo much parliamentary scrutiny since it is already approved by the President.

Draft as of May 4, 2005

Republic of the Philippines

HOUSE OF REPRESENTATIVES

Quezon City, Metro Manila

THIRTEENTH CONGRESS

First Regular Session Bill No.

Introduced by the Committee on Justice

and the Committee on Foreign Affairs

AN ACT DEFINING TERRORISM, ESTABLISHING INSTITUTIONAL MECHANISMS TO PREVENT AND SUPPRESS ITS COMMISSION, PROVIDING PENALTIES THEREFORE AND FOR OTHER PURPOSES

Be it enacted in the Senate and House of Representatives of the Philippines in Congress assembled:

SECTION 1. Short Title. —*This Act shall be known as the "Anti-Terrorism Act of* 2005:"

SEC. 2. Declaration of Policy. —*It is hereby declared the policy of the State to safeguard and protect the lives/properties and environment, promote the dignity of the people, and to strongly condemn terrorism as a crime against the law of nations and humanity. The State shall take all the necessary measures to* *prevent, suppress, and penalize terrorism in all its forms. It shall continue to respect and promote the values, rights and freedom enshrined in the Philippine Constitution. Consistent with its foreign policy, the State shall extend cooperation and undertake mutual assistance with oilier States and international organizations in the investigation, apprehension and prosecution of persons involved in terrorism.*

SEC. 3. Terrorism. —*Terrorism is the premeditated, threatened, actual Use of violence, force, or by any other means of destruction perpetrated against person/s, property/ies, or the environment, with the intention of creating or sowing a slate of danger, panic, fear, or chaos to the general public, group of persons or particular person, or of coercing or intimidating the government to do or abstain from doing an act.*

SEC. 4. Terrorism; How Committed. —Terrorism is committed by any person or group of persons, whether natural or juridical, who, with intent to create or sow danger, panic, fear or chaos to the general public or a group of persons or particular person, or to cocrcc or intimidatc the government to do or to abstain from doing an act through the premeditated, threatened, or actual use of force, violence or oilier means of destruction, commits any of the following acts:

(1) Threatening or causing death or serious bodily harm (on person or persons),

(2) Threatening or causing serious risk to health or safely of (the public or any segment of the public;

(3) Threatening or causing substantial damage or wanton destruction or resorting to arson on critical infrastructure or property, public or private;

(4) Threatening or causing serious interference with or serious disruption of an essential service, facility or system, whether public or private, other than a result of lawful advocacy, protest, dissent or stoppage of work;

(5) Hijacking or threatening to hijack any kind of aircraft, electric or railroad train, locomotive, passenger bus or oilier means of mass transportation, or public conveyance, or piracy of ship or sea vessel;

(6) Taking or threatening to kidnap or deprive any person of his/her liberty;

(7) Assassinating or threatening to assassinate, or kidnapping or threatening to kidnap the President or the Vice President of (lie Philippines, the Presi-

dent of the Senate, the Speaker of the Mouse of Representatives or the Chief Justice of the Supreme Court)

(8) Killing or violently attacking an internationally protected person or depriving the liberty of such person in violation of the Convention on the Protection and Punishment of Crimes Against Internationally Protected Persons, including Diplomatic Agents, and oilier international agreements;

(9) Attacking or threatening to attack the cyberspace, by destroying the actual machinery of the information and communication infrastructure, disrupting the information technology underlying the internet, government or private networks or systems, or committing any unlawful act against networks, servers, computers or other information and communication systems;

(10) Willfully destroying the natural resources in land, water and air, such as forests or marine and mineral resources, or intentionally causing oil or toxic spillages, or other similar acts of destruction against the environment that threatens ecological security;

(11) Unlawfully manufacturing, processing, selling, acquiring, possessing, using, diverting, supplying or transporting chemical, biological, radiological or nuclear agents, or equipment and instruments used in their production, distribution, release or spread that would endanger directly or indirectly the safety of one or more individuals, or to cause mass destruction or great damage to property; or

(12) Unlawfully manufacturing, selling, acquiring, supplying, disposing, using or possessing explosives, bombs, grenades, projectiles, devices or other lethal weapons, or substances or machinery used or intended to be used for the manufacture of explosives in furtherance of, or incident to, or in—connection with, an act of terrorism defined herein.

Any person who commits any act of terrorism shall suffer the penalty of life imprisonment and a fine of Ten Million Pesos (Flip 10,000,000.00): Provided, That, if an act of terrorism should result in the death of a person, or if committed with the use of uniform, paraphernalia, communication equipment, or other implements peculiar to the armed-forces or other-law enforcement agencies, or if the offender is a government official or-employee or has retired, resigned, dismissed or otherwise separated from the government service, the penalty of death shall be

imposed.

SEC. 5. Conspiracy or Proposal to Commit Terrorism. —*There is a conspiracy to commit terrorism when two or more persons come to an agreement to commit any act of terrorism as defined herein and decide to commit it.*

There is proposal to commit terrorism when any person who has decided to commit any act of terrorism as defined herein proposes its execution to some other person or persons.

The conspiracy or proposal to commit any act of terrorism shall be punished by imprisonment of not less than six (6) years and one (1) day but not more than twelve (12) years and a fine of Five Million Pesos (Php 5,000,000.00); *Provided*, That if the person is a government official or employee or has retired, resigned, dismissed or otherwise separated from the government service, the maximum penalty and (lie accessory penalty of perpetual disqualification to hold public office shall be imposed.

SEC. 6. Inciting to Terrorism. —*It shall be unlawful for any person or group of persons, natural or juridical, to incite others to the execution of any of the acts specified in Section 4 of this Act by means of speeches, proclamations, writings, emblems, banners or other representations tending to incite others to terrorism.*

Any person who incites others to commit terrorism shall suffer the penalty of not less than six (6) years and one (1) day but not more than twelve (12) years and a fine of Five Million Pesos (Php 5,000,000.00): *Provided*, That, if the person is a government official or employee or has retired resigned, dismissed or otherwise separated from the government service, the maximum penalty and the accessory penalty of perpetual disqualification to hold public office shall be imposed.

SEC. 7. Acts that Facilitate, Contribute to or Promote Terrorism. —*It shall be unlawful for any person or group of persons, whether natural or juridical, to knowingly, willfully and voluntarily facilitate, contribute to or promote terrorism through any of the following acts:*

(1) Establishing, maintaining or serving as contact or link with any person or group of persons or organization/s who have pursued or are pursuing terrorism;

(2) Arranging or assisting in the conduct of meeting of two (2) or more

persons, knowing that the meeting is to support or is in furtherance of terrorism;

(3) Participating in training and providing training facilities to any person or group of persons, organizations to carry out terrorism;

(4) Providing or offering to provide training, skill or expertise in furtherance of terrorism;

(5) Recruiting in order to facilitate or commit terrorism;

(6) Facilitating the entry or stay in the Philippines of aliens, knowing that the aliens have pursued or are pursuing terrorism;

(7) Facilitating, providing, soliciting or encouraging financial or material support for the commission of terrorism; or

(8) Harboring or concealing any person whom one knows or has reasonable ground to believe, to be the person who carried out any act slated in this Section or who committed or is likely to commit any act of terrorism.

Any person who commits any of the acts stared in this Section shall suffer the penalty of life imprisonment and a fine of Ten Million Pesos (P100,000,000.00); *Provided*, That, if the act should result in the death of a person, or if such act was committed with the use of firearms or ammunition, or uniform, paraphernalia, communication equipment, or other implements peculiar to the armed forces or other law enforcement agencies, or if the offender is a public officer or employee, the death penalty shall be imposed.

SEC. 8. Proscription of Organization. —*For the purpose of tins Act, an organization may be proscribed as terrorist organization by the Secretary of Justice upon the recommendation of the Anti-Terrorism Council created by this Act if such organization is characterized by any of the following*:

(1) Any member or members thereof openly and publicly declares, admits, acknowledges, to have committed any of the acts punishable under this Act;

(2) Any member or members thereof have committed an act or acts of terrorism as defined and described in Sections 4, 5, 6 and 7 of tins Act;

(3) It is proscribed by the United Nations or other international organizations.

Proscriptions shall be published in the government gazette and major newspapers. Any proscribed organization or member thereof may move for de-proscription or de-listing before the Department of Justice (DOJ), whose decision is appeal able to the Court of Appeals.

SEC. 9. Membership in a Terrorist Organization. —Where an organization has been proscribed as a terrorist organization, it shall be unlawful for any person who knowingly, willfully, and by overt acts, affiliates himself, becomes, or remains a member of such organization unless he can prove a lack of personal knowledge of the organization's activities; or that he has not taken any part in the activities of the organization at anytime while it was proscribed; or that lie took immediate steps to terminate his membership there from as soon as practicable after it was proscribed; or that the organization was not declared a terrorist organization at the lime one became a member or begun to profess to be a member.

Any person convicted under this section shall suffer the penalty of imprisonment from not less than six (6) years and one (1) day to not more than twelve (12)'years: *Provided* that, if the offender is a a government official or employee, or has retired, resigned, dismissed or otherwise separated from the government service, the maximum penalty and the accessory penalty of perpetual disqualification to hold public office shall be imposed.

SEC. 10. Making False Threats of Acts of Terrorism. —*It shall be unlawful for any person to*:

(1) Communicate or make available by any means, any information which he knows or believes to be false to another person with (he intention of inducing him or any other person a false belief that a terrorist act has been, is being or will be carried out; or,

(2) Place any article or substance in any place, or dispatch any article or substance by mail or by any other means of sending things from one place to another with the intention of inducing in another person a false belief that —

(i) the article or substance is likely to explode or ignite and thereby cause personal injury or damage to properly; or

(ii) the article contains or the substance consists of any dangerous, hazardous, radioactive or harmful substance; any toxic chemical; or any microbial or other biological agent, or toxin, that is likely to cause death, disease or personal injury or damage to property.

For purposes of subsections (1) and (2), a reference to a person inducing in another person a false belief does not require the first-mentioned person to have any particular person in mind as the person in whom lie intends to induce the false belief. The penalty of imprisonment for a period of not less than six (6) years and one (1) day to not more than twelve years and a fine of Fifty Thousand Pesos (Php 50,000.00) to One Hundred Thousand Pesos (Php 100,000.00) shall be imposed upon any person convicted under this Section. Provided that, if the offender is a government official or employee, or has retired resigned, dismissed or otherwise separated from the government service, the maximum penalty and the accessory penalty of perpetual disqualification to hold public office shall be imposed.

SEC. 11. Failure to Disclose Acts of Terrorism. —*Any person, who, having personal knowledge or information of any acts punished under this Act, conceals or docs not disclose and makes known the same, as soon as possible to the government or any of its authorized agencies, shall suffer the penalty of imprisonment of not less than six (6) years and one (1) but not more than twelve (12) years and a fine of Fifty Thousand Pesos (Php 50,000.00) to One Hundred Thousand Pesos (Php 100,000.00): Provide, if the offender is a government official or employee, or has retired, resigned, dismissed or otherwise separated from the government service, the maximum penalty and the accessory penalty of perpetual disqualification to hold public office shall be imposed.*

SEC. 12. Infidelity in the Custody of Prisoner. —*Any public officer who, during his tour of duty, deliberately allows or connives in the escape of a prisoner under his custody or charge, who is accused of, or sentenced by final judgment for committing any of the acts punishable under this Act, shall suffer the penalty of imprisonment of not less than ten (10) years and one (1) day to not more than twelve (12) years. Furthermore, the accessory penalty of perpetual absolute disqualification to hold public office shall be imposed on the said public officer.*

If the escape or evasion by such prisoner shall have taken place through the negligence of the public officer charged with the conveyance and custody of (lie said prisoner as the case may be, during his tour of duty, said public officer shall suffer the penalty of imprisonment of not less than eight (8) years and one (1) day to not more than eight (10) years, and the accessory penalty of perpetual absolute disqualification to hold public office.

SEC. 13. Criminal Liability of Officers of Partnership, Corporation, Association and other Juridical Person. —*In case of any violation of this Act committed by a partnership, corporation, association, foundation or any juridical person, a partner, president, director, or manager who consents to or knowingly tolerates such violation shall be held criminally liable as co-principal. Provided that, the offending partnership, corporation, association, foundation or any juridical person shall either be penalized with a fine of not less than One Hundred Thousand (Php 100,000.00) Pesos to not more than Five Hundred Thousand Pesos (Php 500,000.00), or be dissolved or both, at the discretion of the Court.*

SEC. 14. Arrest and Detention. —*Any peace officer or a private person may, without warrant, arrest a person: (a) when, in his presence, the person to be arrested has committed, is actually committing, or attempting to commit any of the offense under this Act; or (b) when any of said offense has in fact been committed and lie has reasonable ground to believe that the person to be arrested has committed the same.*

Any person arrested under this Section may be detained for a period of not more than fifteen (15) days following his arrest.

The period of detention may be extended beyond fifteen (15) days if the person arrested without a warrant demands for a preliminary investigation and consents to it in writing and in the presence of his or her counsel. He shall be entitled to all other rights under Republic Act No. 7438, otherwise known as "An Act Defining Certain Rights of Persons Arrested, Detained, or Under Custodial Investigation."

The Commissioner of Immigration may detain without bail any alien charged with any act of terrorism penalized under this Act.

SEC. 15. Additional Penalty if Offender is an Alien. —*In addition to the penalties herein prescribed, any alien who violates any of the provisions of tin's Act shall be deported without further proceedings immediately after service of sentence.*

SEC. 16. Immunity from Prosecution. —*Any person who serves as a witness for the government or provides evidence in a criminal case involving any violation of this Act, or who voluntarily or by virtue of a* subpoena ad testificandum *or* subpoena duces tecum, *produces, identifies or gives testimony on, but not limited to books, papers, documents, tapes containing words, sounds, pictures or images,* *photos, maps, diagrams, sketches, recordings, disc or any other form of written, recorded, or real evidence; shall be immune from any criminal prosecution, subject to the compliance with the provisions of Presidential Decree No. 1732, otherwise known as "Decree Providing Immunity from Criminal Prosecution to Government Witnesses" and the pertinent provisions of the Rules of Court.*

SEC. 17. Witness Protection; Reporting Leading to Arrest and Conviction of Terrorists. —Any person who provides material information, whether testimonial or documentary, necessary for the investigation or prosecution of individual or group of organization of individuals accused of committing any of the offenses under this Act shall be entitled to the protection and subject to the obligation imposed under the Witness Protection Program pursuant to Republic Act No. 6981.

SEC. 18. Applicability of Republic Act No. 9160, as amended by Republic Act No. 9194. —Terrorism and other violations of this Act shall be considered unlawful activities under RA 9160, otherwise known as the "Anti-Money Laundering Act of 2001," as amended.

Upon determination that a reasonable ground to suspect exists dial any monetary instrument or property is in any way related to terrorism and other violations under this Act, the Anti-Money Laundering Council (AMLC) may issue a freeze order, which shall be effective immediately, on the said monetary instrument/s and/or properties fur a period not exceeding ninety (90) days unless extended by the Court of Appeals. Notice to the purported owner/s that his/their monetary instrument/s and/or properly has/have been frozen shall be issued simultaneously with the issuance of the freeze order. The purported owner/s of the monetary instrument/s and/or property shall have three (3) working days upon receipt of the notice to explain why the free order should be lifted. The AMLC has three (3) working days to resolve the freeze order case from receipt of the purported owner/s' explanation. If the AMLC fails to act within three (3) working days from the receipt of the said purported owner's explanation, the freeze order shall automatically be dissolved.

A freeze order 'shall stop all movements or transactions of or involving the monetary instrument/s and properly. In cases where checks drawn against a

bank account subject of a freeze order were issued within fifteen (15) days prior to the issuance of the freeze order, the freeze order shall likewise result in the automatic cancellation and stop payment thereof. All movements or transactions, irrespective of the amount involved, occurring within the same period shall be reported to the AMLC.

Provided, that deposits or investments with any banking institutions or non-bank financial institutions may be inquired into or examined without prior court order pursuant to RA 9160, as amended: Provided, further, That any person of covered institution knowing that any money, instrument, or property or its proceeds, represents, involves, or relates to terrorism or the furtherance thereof and fails to report the same as suspicious transaction to the AMLC shall be criminally liable pursuant to Section 13 of this Act.

SEC. 19. Communication Assistance/or Law Enforcement Agencies. —

(a) The provisions of Republic Act No. 4200, otherwise known as the "Anti-Wire Tapping Act" to the contrary notwithstanding, any peace officer may apply *ex parte* before the executive judge of any Regional Trial Court for an order, or extension of such an order, requiring a provider of wire or electronic communication service to provide intercepted communication and call identifying information to law enforcement agencies, or authorizing or approving the installation, use and/or retrieval of surveillance device, in connection with an investigation for any offense punishable under this Act.

(b) For purposes of this Act, a surveillance device shall include but not limited to the following:

1) Data surveillance device or program capable of being used to record or monitor the input of information into, or the output of information from, the computer;

2) Listening device capable of being used to overhear, record, monitor or listen to a conversation or words spoken to or by any person in conversation, but does not include a hearing aid or similar device used by a person with impaired hearing to overcome the impairment and permit that person to hear only sounds ordinarily audible to the human ear;

3) Optical surveillance device capable of being used to record visually or

observe an activity, but does not include spectacles, contact lenses, or similar device used by a person with impaired eyesight to overcome that impairment;

4) Electronic tracking device capable of being used to determine or monitor the location of a person or an object or the status of an object;

5) Pen register capable of recording or decoding electronic or other impulses which identified the numbers dialed or otherwise transmitted on the telephone line to which such device is attached, but such term does not include any device used by a provider or customer of a wire or electronic communication service for billing, or recording as an incident to billing, for communication services provided by such provider or any device used by a provider or customer of a wire communication service for cost accounting or other like purposes in the ordinary course of its business;

6) Trap and trace device capable of capturing the incoming electronic or other impulses which identify the originating number of an instrument or device from which a wire or electronic communication was transmitted; or

7) A device that is a combination of any two or more of the devices referred to in paragraphs (1) to (6) of this Section.

(c) When peace officer has certified that the information likely to be obtained by such interception, installation or use is relevant to an ongoing investigation for any offense punishable under this Act, the court shall issue an *ex parte* order requiring a provider of wire or electronic communication service or authorizing the installation, use and/or retrieval of the devices applied for, for a period not to exceed sixty (60) days. An extension of such an order may be granted, provided that such extension shall not exceed sixty (60) days.

Such order shall state one or more of the following —

(1) the premises to be subjected to surveillance;

(2) the use of surveillance device in or on a specified object or class of object;

(3) the use of surveillance device with respect to the conversations, activities/or location of a specified person or a person whose identity is unknown;

(4) the order be sealed until otherwise ordered by the court;

(5) the person using the line to which the device is to be attached, or the company who has been ordered by the court to provide assistance to the "appli-

cant, -not to disclose the existence of the device or the existence of the investigation to the listed subscriber, or to any other person, unless or until otherwise ordered by the court."

(6) the provider of wire or electronic communication service to provide intercepted communication and call identifying information to the peace officer; or

(7) the entry into the premises, and into oilier specified premises adjoining or providing access to the premises, in order to install or retrieve the surveillance device.

(d) A provider of wire or electronic communication service, landlord, custodian, or other person shall install or assist in the installation of such device forthwith on the appropriate line and furnish such peace officer forthwith all information, facilities, and technical assistance necessary to accomplish the installation, use and/or retrieval of the device unobtrusively and with a minimum of interference with the services that the person so ordered by the court, accord the party will respect to whom the installation, use and/or retrieval is to take place, if such assistance is directed by a court order.

(e) Unless otherwise ordered by the court, the information obtained by the device shall be furnished to the peace officer designated in the court order, at reasonable intervals during regular business hours for the duration of the order.

(f) Any person who discloses information obtained, gathered or acquired pursuant to this Section, for the purpose other than that for which it was authorized, shall suffer the penalty of imprisonment of not less than six (6) months and one (1) day to not more than six (6) years: *Provided*, That, if the offender is a government official or employee or has retired, resigned, dismissed or otherwise separated from the government service, the maximum penalty and the accessory penalty of perpetual disqualification to hold public office shall be imposed.

(g) A court order shall not be required to authorize the installation, use or retrieval of surveillance device in any case where a peace officer, in connection with an investigation for any offense punishable under this Act, obtains the written consent of a party to the communication to be monitored or recorded in connection with any offense punishable under this Act.

(h) No cause of action shall lie in any court against any provider of a wire or electronic communication service, its officers, employees, agents, or oilier specified persons for providing information, facilities, or assistance in accordance with the terms of a court order under this Act. A good faith reliance on a court older under this Act, is a complete defense against any civil or criminal action brought under this Act or any oilier law;

(h) Any communication, written or spoken word, conversation, discussion, information, photos, or data taken, obtained or acquired in violation of this Section shall not be admissible as evidence in any judicial, quasi-judicial, legislative or administrative hearing or investigation.

(i) Any person who hinders, obstructs or otherwise prevents the peace officer from performing his duties stated in Section 21 of this Act shall suffer the penalty of imprisonment of not less than six (6) months and one (1) day to not more than six (6) years: *Provided*, That, if the offender is a government official or employee or has retired, resigned, dismissed or otherwise separated from the government service, the maximum penalty and the accessory penalty of perpetual disqualification to hold public office shall be imposed.

SEC. 20. Seizure of Vehicle, Vessel, Aircraft, Equipment, or Other Property or Instrument. —*Any vehicle, vessel, aircraft, equipment, or oilier property or instrument used in furtherance of, or incident to, or in connection with any act of terrorism as defined in this Act shall be presumed prima facie evidence to have been unlawfully used n furtherance of or incident to or in connection with any act of terrorism as defined in this Act, and shall carry with it the confiscation and forfeiture thereof, in favor of the government, including but not limited to all the proceeds of the crime, such as money and other assets obtained thereby and instruments or tools with which it was committed unless they are property of third person not liable for the offense and who docs not knowingly authorize, tolerate or consent the use of the same.*

SEC. 21. Prosecution of and jurisdiction Over Cases Involving Terrorism and Terrorist Activities. —*The Regional Trial Court shall have jurisdiction to try all offenses punishable under this Act.*

Any person may be charged with or convicted of any offense punishable under "Sections 4, 5, 6 and 7 of this Act without prejudice to the prosecution of any act or acts penalized under the Revised Penal Code or oilier special laws provided that such act or acts are not absorbed in the offense charged."

When there is a variance between the offense charged in the complaint or information, and that proved or established by the evidence, the accused shall be convicted of the offense proved included in the charge if the intent to create or sow a state of danger, panic or chaos to the general public or group of persons or particular persons was not proven during the trial. No person, however, shall be twice put in jeopardy of punishment for the same offense.

SEC. 22. Non-Applicability of Probation and Plea-Bargaining;.—*The provisions of the Probation Law or Presidential Decree No. 908, as amended, shall not be applicable for offenses punishable under this Act. Neither hall the provisions on pica bargaining provided for in the Rules of Court be made applicable to offenses punishable by this Act.*

SEC. 23. Mutual Assistance and Cooperation Between the Philippines and Other States or International Organizations.—When a foreign State or International Organization makes a request for assistance concerning any matter related to any act of terrorism, the Council as created under Section 24 of this Act shall take the appropriate action on the matter, provided that such request of the Philippine Government to a foreign State or International Organization shall be coursed through the Council.

SEC. 24. Anti-Terrorism Council.—*There is hereby created an Anti-Terrorism Council under the Office of the President, which shall serve as the central policy-making, coordinating, supervising and monitoring body of the government on all matters of domestic and international terrorism. It shall be composed of the Executive Secretary as Chairperson and the National Security Adviser (NSA) as Vice Chairperson, with the following as members:*

a. Secretary of Foreign Affairs;

b. Secretary of Justice;

c. Secretary of National Defense;

d. Secretary of the Interior and Local Government;

e. Presidential Adviser on the Peace Process;

f. Director General, National Intelligence Coordinating Agency; and

g. Others as may be designated by the President

The Council shall organize an Anti-Terrorism Command Center which shall direct, coordinate, supervise and monitor the implementation of various measures against terrorism. It shall be headed by the National Security Adviser as the National Coordinator and shall be staffed, among others, by personnel coming from various agencies of the government.

In addition to their regular functions, the following agencies shall provide technical and other necessary support to the Council: the Armed Forces of the Philippines (AFP); Philippine National Police (PNP); National Bureau of Investigation (N131); Philippine Drug Enforcement Agency (PDEA); Bureau of Immigration (BI); Office of the Civil Defense (OCD); Philippine Center on Transnational Clime (PCTC); Anti-Money Laundering Council (AMLC); Consular Office of the Department of Foreign Affairs; Office of Transport Security (OTS); Health Emergency Management Services (HEMS); Philippine Nuclear Research Institute (PNR1); Environmental Management Bureau (EMB); Security and Exchange Commission (SEC); Bureau of Customs (BOC); National Prosecution Service (NAPROSS); National Telecommunication Commission (NTC); Board of Investments (B01), Commission on Information and Communication Technology (CICT), Bureau of Trade Regulation (BTR), Office of the Muslim Affairs (OMA), National Commission on Indigenous Peoples (NCIP); and oilier agencies as maybe deemed necessary by the Council.

SEC. 25. Functions of the Council. —*In pursuit of its mandate under the preceding section, the Council shall have the following functions*:

a. Formulate a comprehensive program and establish institutional mechanisms, when necessary, to deter and prevent acts of terrorism to include, programs to prepare the government and the country to cope with nil forms of terrorist attacks and their consequences, such as, but not limited to, the use of chemical, biological, radiological or nuclear weapons, or oilier weapons of catastrophic effect;

b. Supervise and coordinate the implementation of government policies, plans and measures to prevent and suppress acts of terrorism;

c. Conduct policy researches and studies in addressing terrorism;

d. Direct and monitor the conduct of anti-terrorism and counter-terrorism measures and post-conflict actions to address the effects of terrorism;

e. Direct and monitor the immediate investigation and speedy prosecution of cases involving acts of terrorism and monitor the progress of such cases;

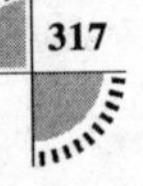

f. Transfer the-conduct of investigation of specific . cases from one law enforcement agency to another;

g. Establish a comprehensive data-base information systems and linkages on anti-terrorism and counter-terrorism operations and post-conflict actions;

h. Approve the grant of monetary rewards and incentives to informants who are willing to give vital information for the arrest of those who committed the acts of terrorism;

i. Recommend the inclusion of vital witnesses under the Witness Protection, Security and Benefits Program;

j. Keep records of its proceedings and decisions, and such records shall be subject to such security classifications as the Council may, in its sound discretion, direct to safeguard the national interest;

k. Recommend to the Department of Justice the proscription and de-proscription of terrorist organizations.

l. Call upon any department, bureau, office or oilier executive agency for assistance; and

m. Exercise such oilier functions as may be assigned by the President.

SEC. 26. Suppletory Application of the Revised Penal Code and Other Generator Special Laws. —*The provisions of the Revised Penal Code and other general or special laws have a suppletory application to the provisions of this Act.*

SEC. 27. Implementing Rules and Regulations. —*Within sixty (60) days from the effectivity of this Act, the Anti-Terrorism Council shall promulgate the Implementing Rules and Regulations as may be necessary to ensure the efficient and effective implementation of the provisions of this Act.*

SEC. 28. Extra-Territorial Application of this Act. —*The provision of Article 2(5) of the Revised Penal Code is hereby amended to include the crimes penalized under Sections 4, 5, 6 and 7 of this Act.*

SEC. 29. Separability Clause. —*If any provision or portion of this Act or the application thereof to any person or circumstances is declared to be unconstitutional or invalid, the other provisions or portions of this Act, and the application of such provision or section to other persons or circumstances, shall not be affected thereby.*

SEC. 30. Amendatory Clause. —*Republic Act No. 9160, as amended by*

Republic Act No. 9194, Republic Act No. 4200, Commonwealth Act No. 613, as amended, and P. D. 968 are hereby amended or modified accordingly.

SEC. 31. Repealing Clause. —*All laws, decrees, executive orders, rules or regulations or parts thereof, inconsistent with (lie provisions of tin's Act arc hereby repealed, amended or modified accordingly.*

SEC. 32. Effectivity. —*This Act shall take effect fifteen (15) days after its publication in the Official Gazette or two (2) newspapers of general circulation.*

后　记

如果说翻译是一件枯燥而痛苦的事情的话,那么翻译法典是一件更枯燥、更痛苦的事情。自从导师谢望原教授将此菲律宾刑法的英文稿交给我后,我就提心吊胆、如牛负重,然而,当我把翻译的中文稿之最后一字符敲入电脑时,又有种如释重负之感,但欣喜之余难免惶恐不安,怕翻译出来的菲律宾刑法颠三倒四、语无伦次、不知所云,可能与英文大相径庭。

开始翻译时,天气燥热,俯仰之间,宿舍里已开始供暖,译稿也已完成。将近 5 个月的闭门翻译确实让我欢喜让我忧,有时因为一句话甚至是一个单词而令我焦头烂额,好在高等学府的博士楼人才济济,我可以不耻下问,当某个法条或者某个单词的翻译找到正解后,就如获大宝、乐不可支。

翻译首先要了解这个国家的历史、政治、文化背景,要不翻译工作就很难进行,但是,我没有去过菲律宾(为了我翻译的菲律宾刑法,今后一定会创造条件去),所以只能是“纸上谈兵”。目前,我国翻译过来的有关菲律宾的著述凤毛麟角,关于法律方面的著述也屈指可数,最早翻译过来的菲律宾法典应该是《菲律宾宪法》,虽然也有研究亚洲法律的,但是对菲律宾刑法没人提及,加之法典中还夹杂着西班牙语和菲律宾语,对我的翻译工作若如雪上加霜。

翻译工作既要英文功底好也要中文功底扎实,中文要求意简言赅,既要简练,又要精确,但是很多英文却只可领会,不可言传,英文虽然看懂了,但是用中文就不知道如何表达,有一种欲达而不能、可望而不可即的感觉。在翻译过程中,我在很多措辞上面已尽力而为,但是如果拐弯抹角仍然词不达意、不知所云的话,也只好作罢,不求完美无缺,只求大醇小疵、希望各位同仁谅解,不吝指教。我的邮箱是 a81447060@126.com,如果您在阅读时发现有错误请及时告诉我,以免误导读者诸君。

本书之所以能得以出版,首先感谢北京大学出版社为我提供了难得的机会!感谢各位同窗、各位师兄师姐、师弟师妹以及我的学生和各位帮助过我的好友!

感谢长沙市人民检察院的各位领导、同事，是他们的关心、支持和鼓励，使我终于获得到中国人民大学来攻读博士学位的机会，正因为有此读书机会才有本书的出版！

感谢我的爱妻饶珊晖女士，感谢岳父母和父母，是他们为我腾出大量的时间使我完成此法典的翻译！

感谢我的硕士研究生导师孙昌军教授，是他将我领入刑法这一神圣而瑰丽的殿堂，且一如既往地关心、支持我。

特别感谢我的博士生导师谢望原教授，他对学生耳提面命、诲人不倦，在百忙中抽出时间对译稿认真审校，一丝不苟，其渊博的学识、严谨的学风、诚挚的为人，令弟子钦佩，受益无穷。